WHERE WISDOM MAY BE FOUND

Where Wisdom May Be Found

*The Eternal Purpose
of Christian Higher Education*

EDITED BY EDWARD P. MEADORS

PICKWICK *Publications* · Eugene, Oregon

WHERE WISDOM MAY BE FOUND
The Eternal Purpose of Christian Higher Education

Copyright © 2019 Wipf and Stock. All rights reserved. Except for brief quotations in critical publications or reviews, no part of this book may be reproduced in any manner without prior written permission from the publisher. Write: Permissions, Wipf and Stock Publishers, 199 W. 8th Ave., Suite 3, Eugene, OR 97401.

Pickwick Publications
An Imprint of Wipf and Stock Publishers
199 W. 8th Ave., Suite 3
Eugene, OR 97401

www.wipfandstock.com

PAPERBACK ISBN: 978-1-4982-9610-6
HARDCOVER ISBN: 978-1-4982-9612-0
EBOOK ISBN: 978-1-4982-9611-3

Cataloguing-in-Publication data:

Names: Meadors, Edward P., editor.

Title: Where wisdom may be found : the eternal purpose of Christian higher education / edited by Edward P. Meadors.

Description: Eugene, OR : Pickwick Publications, 2019 | Includes bibliographical references.

Identifiers: ISBN 978-1-4982-9610-6 (paperback) | ISBN 978-1-4982-9612-0 (hardcover) | ISBN 978-1-4982-9611-3 (ebook)

Subjects: LCSH: Education (Christian theology). | Universities and colleges—Religion | Learning and scholarship—Religious aspects—Christianity.

Classification: BT738.17 .W54 2019 (print) | BT738.17 .W54 (ebook)

Manufactured in the U.S.A.   AUGUST 27, 2019

Contents

List of Contributors | vii
Preface | xiii

1. The Liberating Yoke | 1
   Edward P. Meadors
2. The Role of Biblical Exegesis within the Christian College Curriculum | 28
   Clinton E. Arnold
3. The Theology of Wisdom: Creation as Context; Christ as Content; Canon as Curriculum | 43
   Kevin J. Vanhoozer
4. Philosophy as the Love of Wisdom | 56
   James S. Spiegel
5. Wise Politics: Classical Philosophy, Medieval Christianity, and the Contemporary World | 67
   Paul R. DeHart
6. Finding Wisdom in Literature | 81
   Leland Ryken
7. The Feminine Quality of History | 92
   Rick Kennedy
8. Word Made Flesh: The Transformational Power of Theatre | 98
   Angela Konrad
9. Becoming a Soulful Wordsmith | 111
   Jeffry C. Davis
10. The Wisdom of Art | 122
    Cameron Anderson

11 The Wisdom of Music | 136
     Tony Payne

12 The Joy of Mathematics | 146
     Jim Bradley and Russ Howell

13 The Biological Sciences: Living Testimony to the Wisdom of God | 159
     Dorothy F. Chappell

14 The Wisdom Required for Global Health | 173
     Nathan Thielman

15 Chemistry, Christianity, and Wisdom | 187
     Stephen Contakes

16 Wisdom in Physics | 202
     Arnold E. Sikkema

17 Seeking Wisdom in Engineering and Computer Science | 214
     Derek C. Schuurman

18 Geology: Wise Stewardship of the Earth | 227
     Michael Guebert

19 The Wisdom of Ethical Sustainability | 238
     Brian R. Brock

20 Psychology and Christian Wisdom | 249
     David N. Entwistle

21 Sociology for People of Faith … and Anyone | 259
     James M. Ault Jr.

22 Anthropology's Contribution to Integrated Christian Wisdom | 276
     Kersten Bayt Priest

23 To Us and Through Us: A Theology of Business | 291
     Kenman L. Wong

24 Finding Wisdom in Economics | 302
     Hadley T. Mitchell

25 Transformation and Restoration through Athletics and Kinesiology | 312
     Dave Wolf

26 Concluding Sapiential Postscript: "Get Wisdom" | 323
     Jeffrey P. Greenman

List of Contributors

Cameron Anderson (MFA, Cranbrook Academy of Art) is an artist and the former Executive Director of Christians in the Visual Arts (CIVA). Anderson lectures frequently on the arts, media, advertising, and contemporary culture. His books include *The Faithful Artist: A Vision for Evangelicalism and the Arts* and *Faith and Vision: Twenty-five Years of Christians in the Visual Arts.*

Clinton E. Arnold (PhD, University of Aberdeen) is the Dean of Talbot School of Theology. Dr. Arnold is the editor of the four-volume *Zondervan Illustrated Bible Backgrounds Commentary*, the general editor of the *Zondervan Exegetical Commentary on the New Testament,* and author of numerous scholarly articles and books including *Ephesians: Power and Magic, Powers of Darkness: Principalities and Powers in Paul's Letters,* and *The Colossian Syncretism.*

James M. Ault Jr. (PhD, Brandeis) is an award winning documentary film maker educated in sociology at Harvard and Brandeis. Dr. Ault has produced and directed documentaries for PBS, the Lilly Endowment, and the Pew Charitable Trust. His book, *Spirit and Flesh* was named one of the five best non-fiction books of 2005 by the Christian Science Monitor. Select documentaries include: *Born Again: Life in a Fundamentalist Baptist Church, Africa Christianity Rising, The Asheville Poverty Initiative,* and *Mechanic Manyeruke: Zimbabwe's Gospel Music Legend.*

Jim Bradley (PhD, University of Rochester) is Professor of Mathematics emeritus at Calvin College. Having received his bachelor of science in mathematics from MIT, Dr. Bradley's mathematical specialty is game theory and operations research. He is co-editor with Dr. Russell Howell of *Mathematics in a Postmodern Age: A Christian Perspective* and *Mathematics through the Eyes of Faith.* He has served as editor of the *Journal of the Association of*

Christians in the Mathematical Sciences and has published several articles on mathematics and Christian belief.

Brian R. Brock (D.Phil, University of London) is Professor of Moral and Practical Theology at the University of Aberdeen, where he also writes and teaches on Christian ethics. Dr. Brock is author of *Singing the Ethos of God: On the Place of Christian Ethics in Scripture, Christian Ethics in a Technological Age, Wondrously Wounded: Theology, Disability, and the Body of Christ*, and *Captive to Christ, Open to the World: On Doing Christian Ethics in Public*. He is also managing editor of the *Journal of Disability and Religion*.

Dorothy F. Chappell (PhD, Miami University of Ohio) is Dean of Natural and Social Sciences and Professor of Biology at Wheaton College (IL). Dr. Chappell has served as the President of the American Scientific Affiliation, Academic Dean at Gordon College, and on several boards including the Board of Trustees of the Phycological Society of America, the Board of Advisors of the John Templeton Foundation, the Board of Trustees of Wheaton College, and the Board of Trustees at Gordon College. She is co-author of *Not Just Science: Questions Where Christian Faith and Natural Science Intersect*, which was recognized as a "2006 Book of Distinction" by the John Templeton Press.

Stephen Contakes (PhD, University of Illinois) is professor of chemistry at Westmont College (CA). Building on graduate and postdoctoral research in bioinorganic and biophysical chemistry at Caltech, Dr. Contakes teaches courses in inorganic, analytical, physical chemistry, and chemistry within the liberal arts. His research, published in more than a dozen scientific journals, involves the synthesis of molecular assemblies and light-driven electron transfer catalysts for water remediation applications.

Jeffry C. Davis (PhD, University of Illinois) is Dean of Humanities at Wheaton College, where he was formerly Chair and Professor of English and Director of Interdisiplinary Studies. Dr. Davis is the author of *Interdisciplinary Inclinations: Introductory Reflections for Students Integrating Liberal Arts and Christian Faith* and co-editor of *Liberal Arts for the Christian Faith*. He serves on the editorial board of the *Journal of Interdisciplinary Studies*.

Paul R. DeHart (PhD, University of Texas at Austin) is Associate Professor of Political Science at Texas State University, where he specializes in natural law, social contract theory, the grounds of political authority and obligation, and the relationship between religion and political order. He is author of *Uncovering the Constitution's Moral Design* (University of Missouri Press) and editor (with Carson Holloway) of *Reason, Revelation, and the Civic Order: Political Philosophy and the Claims of Faith* (Northern Illinois University Press).

David N. Entwistle (PsyD, Biola University) is Professor of Psychology at Malone University (OH). Dr. Entwistle has worked as a clinical psychologist in residential, inpatient, and outpatient settings. He is the author of numerous scholarly articles and author or co-author of chapters in several edited books. He is the author of *Integrative Approaches to Psychology and Christianity: An Introduction to Worldview Issues, Philosophical Foundations, and Models of Integration* (now in its third edition) and the workbook *The Service Learning Book: Getting Ready, Serving Well, and Coming Back Transformed*.

Jeffrey P. Greenman (PhD, University of Virginia) is President and Professor of Theology and Ethics at Regent College (Vancouver, BC). Formerly, Dr. Greenman served as Associate Dean of Biblical & Theological Studies and Professor of Christian Ethics at Wheaton College. Dr. Greenman is the author or editor of eleven books including *The Pedagogy of Praise*, *Understanding Jacques Ellul* (co-author), and *Unwearied Praises: Exploring Christian Faith through Classic Hymns*.

Michael Guebert (PhD, Pennsylvania State University) is professor of Earth and Environmental Sciences at Taylor University (IN). His teaching and specialty areas are geology and hydrology. Dr. Guebert received the Hiltunen Faculty Award in 2011 and the Teaching Excellence and Campus Leadership Award in 2007 at Taylor. He has received many grants in correlation with domestic and international environmental service projects.

Russ Howell (PhD, Ohio State University), Professor of Mathematics at Westmont College (CA), has held appointments at U. C. Berkeley, Calvin College, the University of Maryland, Oxford University, and the U.S. Air Force Academy. A prolific author, Dr. Howell's major book publications include *Mathematics through the Eyes of Faith* (co-edited with James Bradley), *Complex Analysis for Mathematics and Engineering* (co-authored with John Mathews), and *Mathematics in a Postmodern Age* (co-edited with James Bradley).

Rick Kennedy (PhD, University of California at Santa Barbara) is Professor of History at Point Loma Nazarene University (CA). An intellectual/cultural historian, Dr. Kennedy has authored books and articles on the history of logic, mathematics, architecture, astronomy, education, historiography, and

Christian thought. His recent books include *The First American Evangelical: A Short Life of Cotton Mather* and *Jesus, History, and Mount Darwin: An Academic Excursion*.

Angela Konrad (MFA, University of Victoria) is Professor of Theatre at Trinity Western University (Langley, BC), where she teaches acting and directing. She is Artistic Director of Dark Glass Theatre, a company founded to foster empathy through story. She has received multiple Jessie Richardson Theatre Award nominations, winning once for Outstanding Direction (*Grace*) and three times for Outstanding Production (*Grace, Jesus Hopped the 'A' Train,* and *Outside Mullingar*).

Edward P. Meadors (PhD, University of Aberdeen) is Professor of Biblical Studies at Taylor University (IN), where he has taught since 1995. Dr. Meadors's expertise is in the Synoptic Gospels, Apocalyptic Literature, Global Theology, and the Roman background of the New Testament. His books include *Jesus, the Messianic Herald of Salvation, Idolatry and the Hardening of the Heart,* and *Creation, Sin, Covenant, and Salvation*.

Hadley T. Mitchell (PhD, University of Tennessee) is Professor of Economics at Taylor University. In addition to his Ph.D. in Economics, Dr. Mitchell has Masters Degrees in Finance, Systematic Theology, and Philosophy. Throughout his career, his professional scholarship has focused on the integration of faith, ethics, and economics.

Tony Payne (D.M.A., Northwestern University) in his 35 years at Wheaton College has served as Professor of Music, General Manager of the 70-year-old Wheaton College Artist Series, Director of the Conservatory of Music, and Director of Special Programs. His interests include global and experiential learning, pedagogy of technology, and international church music. Having composed dozens of works in a variety of genres, including over 100 hymns and songs for Christian worship, he remains active as author, composer and editor of hymnals.

Kersten Bayt Priest (PhD, Loyola University), Assistant Professor in the Department of Behavioral Sciences at Indiana Wesleyan University, is a sociologist of culture with advanced degrees in Cultural Anthropology and Sociology. Dr. Priest's scholarly research and writing has focused on qualitative ethnography in South Carolina, urban and suburban Chicago, Peru, South Africa, the Dominican Republic, and India.

Leland Ryken (PhD, University of Oregon) is professor of English emeritus at Wheaton College (IL). A prolific author of many books, Dr. Ryken's scholarship explores classic literature from the Christian perspective. Representative books include *The Liberated Imagination: Thinking Christianly about the Arts*, *The Christian Imagination: The Practice of Faith in Literature*, *How to Read the Bible as Literature*, and *Words of Delight: A Literary Introduction to the Bible*.

Derek C. Schuurman (PhD, McMaster University, ON) is Professor of Computer Science at Calvin University (MI). Dr. Schuurman worked as an electrical engineer before completing a PhD in robotics and computer vision. His recent writings have focused on topics relating faith and technology, including the book *Shaping a Digital World: Faith, Culture and Computer Technology*, and the chapter "Responsible Automation: Faith and Work in an Age of Intelligent Machines" in *The Wonder and Fear of Technology* (D.H. Kim ed.).

Arnold E. Sikkema (PhD, University of British Columbia) is Professor of Physics at Trinity Western University (Langley, BC). Dr. Sikkema is the Executive Director of the *Canadian Scientific & Christian Affiliation*. His research interests include Reformational philosophy of biophysics and emergence theory, the character of physical law, and reductionism & emergence. Representative book chapters include "Quantum Theory" (*A Science and Religion Primer*), "Death of the Watchmaker: Modern Science and the Providence of God (*Living in the LambLight*), and "Nuancing Emergentist Claims: Lessons from Physics" (*The Future of Creation Order*).

James S. Spiegel (PhD, Michigan State University) is Professor of Philosophy at Taylor University (IN). Dr. Spiegel has authored numerous books on issues in ethics, aesthetics, philosophy of religion, and popular culture—including the award-winning *How to Be Good in a World Gone Bad*. Other select books include *Faithful Learning in Philosophy*, *The Making of an Atheist*, *Hypocrisy: Moral Fraud and Other Vices*, and *Hell and Divine Goodness: A Philosophical-Theological Inquiry*.

Nathan Thielman (MPH, University of North Carolina; MD, Duke University) is an infectious diseases physician and Professor of Medicine and Global Health at Duke University School of Medicine. Dr. Thielman's research focuses on clinical and social issues that affect persons living with or at risk for HIV in low-resource settings, specifically the Kilimanjaro Region of Tanzania. At Duke he is Director of the Global Health Pathway for Residents and Fellows, Director for the Master of Science in Global Heath

Program, and member of the Center for Health Policy and Inequalities Research.

Kevin J. Vanhoozer (PhD, Cambridge University) is Research Professor of Systematic Theology at Trinity Evangelical Divinity School (Deerfield, IL). Dr. Vanhoozer has written books on hermeneutics, culture, and theology – including the award-winning *Biblical Authority after Babel: Retrieving the Solas in the Spirit of Mere Protestant Christianity*. Other recent books include *Faith Speaking Understanding: Performing the Drama of Doctrine*, *Pictures at a Theological Exhibition: Scenes of the Church's Worship, Witness, and Wisdom* and the forthcoming *Hearers and Doers: A Pastor's Guide to Making Disciples through Scripture and Doctrine*.

Dave Wolf (M.A. Azusa Pacific University) is Associate Professor of Kinesiology and Head Men's Soccer Coach at Westmont College (CA), where he has also served as Athletic Director. Coach Wolf is a former professional soccer player (MISL and NPSL) and First Team All American at Wheaton College (IL), where he secured the midfield of Wheaton's 1984 National Championship Team (NCAA Div III). In 25 years at Westmont, Wolf has produced a record of 297-143-47 (.658) and multiple coaching awards.

Kenman L. Wong (PhD, University of Southern California) is Professor of Business Ethics at Seattle Pacific University (WA). Dr. Wong teaches and researches in the areas of Business Ethics and Market based methods to alleviate Global Poverty. His articles have been published in the *Journal of Business Ethics, Journal of Markets & Morality,* and *Christian Scholars Review.* His books include *Beyond Integrity: A Judeo-Christian Approach to Business Ethics* (co-author); *Business for the Common Good* (co-author); and *Medicine and the Marketplace: The Moral Dimensions of Managed Care.*

Preface

*"Great are the works of the Lord;
They are studied by all who delight in them."*

(PS 111:2)

IN THE FIRST CHAPTER of Romans the apostle Paul appeals to creation as evidence of divine revelation: "since the creation of the world his invisible attributes, his eternal power and divine nature, have been clearly seen, being understood through that which has been made" (Rom 1:20). It is upon divine revelation both in Scripture and in creation that this collection of essays comes forth; namely, that God himself was the first cause of humanity, nature, and the physical universe, so that all creation retains inherent evidence, however faint, of its origin in the creative design of God. There is therefore no arena of legitimate scholarship that is of disinterest to the people of God.

The authors of this volume share a common faith in Jesus Christ complemented by a shared calling to commend wisdom and truth through the dynamic revelations of our respective disciplines. Each author is wary of disciplinary malpractice, perhaps especially of superficial "cookie-cutter" christianizations of our fields that reduce discipline-specific complexities to evangelistic oversimplifications. At the same time, we clearly do not apologize for promoting as the highest form of education a vision that entails the interrelatedness and compatibility of all arenas of research and expression, including theology and contemplation of the supernatural. Our conversations are cross-disciplinary for the purpose of mutual edification, corporate enlightenment, the advancement of comprehensive truth, the acquisition of wisdom, and the celebration of God's glory revealed in all of creation.

Humbly, we look through a glass dimly and the creation that we each explore suffers fracture from the human history we've inherited. Yet, we have a triumphant hope, as the apostle Paul commends later in Romans, for "the sufferings of this present time are not worthy to be compared with the glory that is to be revealed to us" (Rom 8:18). As ones who share this hope, we pass on these insights from the disciplines we love to affirm their inherent value and to commend their study for the discovery of truth, beauty, wisdom, and hope.

Finally, we commend these essays as a challenge to this generation of students. A constant refrain in Scripture is the reminder that God does not desire for his people to be lazy, indifferent, ignorant, or aesthetically obtuse. The holiness of God involves inner integrity wherein all components of reality find their meaning, purpose, and function. Our calling to be "holy as God is holy" presupposes appreciation for all dimensions of God's reality, along with the awareness that our maturation individually and corporately depends on our advancement in understanding all reality for our comprehensive benefit and for our increased appreciation of God's comprehensive glory. Rigorous scholarship motivated by fascination and altruistic purpose is thus an act of worship optimal for every human being and essential to every generation. For as we draw nearer to comprehensive truth, we draw nearer to God.

The editor would like to extend special thanks to Ashley Miley (student proofreader), Caleb Shupe (copy editor), George Callihan (typesetter), and the entire team at Wipf and Stock publishers. Publishing a volume such as this is a journey whose success depends on the quality of professional relationships made along the way. The grace, flexibility, and patience of each author combined with the relaxed efficiency of Wipf and Stock has exemplified the ethos for which this volume aspires.

1

The Liberating Yoke

Edward P. Meadors

תְּחִלַּת חָכְמָה יִרְאַת יְהוָה

ἀρχὴ σοφίας φόβος κυρίου

Initium Sapientiae Timor Domini

The Fear of the Lord *is the Beginning of Wisdom*

(PROV 9:10)

The Prayer of this Volume

Dear Heavenly Father,

Your word promises that you give wisdom generously to those who ask (Jas 1:5). We ask for wisdom for ourselves, our families, our students, our churches, our colleges, our leaders, our communities, our nations, and our world. And we pray for faith and courage to live according to the wisdom you give as we worship you by the grace of your atoning love.

Amen.

Thesis

Where can wisdom be found? And where is the place of understanding?

... God understands its way; and He knows its place. (Job 28:12, 23)

> Who is wise? Let him give heed to these things and consider the lovingkindness of the Lord. (Ps 107:43)

Wisdom is to think and live God's way. Wisdom is essential for a successful life in a broken world. Who are the wise? The wise are those whose God is the Lord and whose ambition is to please him. Where is wisdom to be found? In the Lord himself of course. For God is omnipresent and his eternal power and divine nature are still evident in the things he has made (Rom 1:20). For those with eyes to see, ears to hear, and minds to comprehend, wisdom is all around us. As Clement of Alexandria surmised, "For God is the cause of all good things. . . . The way of truth is therefore one. But into it, as a perennial river, streams flow from all sides" (Clement, *Misc.* 1.5).

The thesis of this volume is simple: the purpose of education is to cultivate eternal wisdom. Wisdom reveals eternal truth through all the disciplines with the goal of restoring the *imago Dei* in God's people. The disciplines, inclusive of the humanities and physical sciences, play essential roles in evangelism and discipleship because they establish valid global connections with humankind and the created world. Wisdom equips students to translate knowledge from their chosen majors into logical preparation for the gospel of Jesus Christ. And wisdom uniquely enables students to build characters of integrity based on the integration of truth synthesized from all the disciplines as they network in wisdom-driven dialogue. Guided by wisdom, students can experientially realize the truth of the testimony they first professed in baptism. They can die to vanity and metamorphose new lives of integrity as members of the body of Christ (2 Cor 5:17–19). In eternity by the grace of God, they can confidently anticipate full restoration to the image of God (2 Cor 3:18; Phil 3:20; Rom 12:2). For atonement with God is the alpha and omega of Christian higher education: "We proclaim him, admonishing everyone and teaching everyone with all wisdom, that we may present everyone complete in Christ" (Col 1:28). Wisdom tutors throughout Christian education as she moves the people of God toward the goal of completion in Christ, where the *imago Dei* is be restored, citizenship in the kingdom of God inherited, and eternal worship orchestrated in spirit and absolute truth.

Part A: The Theology of Christian Education

1. The Sermonic Charge
2. Conversion and Repentance
3. Wisdom as the Fear of the Lord

Part B: The Application of Christian Education

4. The Christian College and Human Sexuality
5. The Price of Christian Higher Education and Philanthropic Discipleship
6. Christian Higher Education and the Family
7. Christian Higher Education and the Church
8. The Apprentice Model
9. Connecting the Dots
10. The College Curriculum as *Preparatio Evangelica*

Part A: *The Theology of Christian Education*

1. The Sermonic Charge

Wisdom is the goal of education. The discovery and cultivation of what eternally matters is the purpose of life. And the goal of life is eternal relationship with God, his covenant people, and the heavenly hosts. There is only one way to enter and sustain this eternal intimacy and that is through the way of wisdom consummated in the gospel of Jesus Christ. With the higher calling of God crying out, the apostle Paul therefore admonished Timothy, "continue in the things you have learned and become convinced of, knowing from whom you have learned them; and that from childhood you have known the sacred writings which are able to give you the wisdom that leads to salvation through faith which is in Christ Jesus" (2 Tim 3:14–16).

God, the beginning and the end, is eternal wise love (1 John 4:8). His divine law is holy and righteous and good (Rom 7:12). His law, the benevolent tutor (Gal 3:24), is wisdom motivated by love for the sake of *shalom* (Matt 22:35–40; Prov 31:26).[1] "Love therefore is the fulfillment of the law" (Rom 13:10) and the treasured prize of wise pedagogy: "The goal of our instruction is love from a pure heart, and a good conscience, and a sincere faith" (1 Tim 1:5). Wisdom's love is true, pure, responsible, just, holy, and eternal. Anything less is not love.

Wisdom and love are one in the character of God, the exemplary life of Christ, and the ethic engendered by the indwelling of the Holy Spirit. Never pitted one against the other, the attributes of God harmoniously synthesize

---

1. *Shalom* is a Hebrew word meaning comprehensive eternal peace with God, self, humankind, and creation.

the integrity of the divine nature. Wisdom acts to motivate ceaseless pursuit of the *imago Dei*. Seeking the face of God (Ps 27:8), the wise desire transformation "by the renewing of the mind to prove what the will of God is, that which is good, excellent, and perfect" (*teleios*; Rom 12:1–2). This pursuit, Paul says, is our logical (*logikos*) service of worship. Because of their eternal essence, these attributes of God transcend in value all human objects of desire.

Even the abstract components which appropriate salvation fall short of the perfection God calls us to in holy love, "Now abide faith, hope, and love, but the greatest of these is love" (1 Cor 13:13). Love preexisted, is constant, infinite, and eternal—thus the treasure of the truly wise. In all things relationships matter most. And so it is that the people of God gladly forsake the folly of pride for the blessedness of *shalom*.

And so it was that when Jesus' wisdom was put to the test, he identified the love of God and the love of neighbor as the two greatest commandments (Matt 22:37–40). Why? Because the end of all things is eternal atonement with God, the people of God, creation, and the heavenly hosts. That this *shalom* can be restored through the cross of Christ is the true gospel (Rev 4–5).

It is evident, then, that the end of education is character realization as envisioned in the maturation of the love, wisdom, and holiness ordained by Jesus in the Sermon on the Mount (Matt 5:48). This "perfection" or educational maturation begins now (2 Cor 3:18) and will be consummated in the future (Phil 3:21). "We shall be changed" (1 Cor 15:51). Education fits us out for eternity as it facilitates and accelerates the incarnation of wisdom within.

Wisdom energizes education with the vigor of the Holy Spirit and controls education with the counsel of truth. Wisdom is original, the only one of its kind, by comparison to which all else is common. Wisdom's genesis transcends time. Pretentious "ground breakings," if detached from eternal wisdom, wear out and nauseate before proving false. True wisdom entered human history at creation and exploded from the cross, resurrection, and ascension of Christ before radiating from Jerusalem. The resurrection and the life, wisdom greets every generation with the invitation for understanding, purpose, integrity, and *shalom*—education whose reward is intimacy with God.

Holiness, the divine integrity, the oneness of God devoid of internal contradiction, is the divine standard God has resolutely established for his people: "you are to be holy, as I am holy" (Lev 19:2; 1 Pet 1:16; Matt 5:48). Dedication to this end is what distinguishes the true covenant people of God from all counterfeits, "You shall consecrate yourselves therefore and be holy, for I am the Lord your God" (Lev 20:7). Aware of this, the truly wise recognize the wisdom of delighting in the law of the Lord (Ps 1:2) not for the law's merit but for the abundant life that is shared by those who live God's way. The Creator gives, breathes, sustains, invigorates, and resurrects life for eternal communion. By contrast *unwise* teaching rationalizes self-worship and its symptoms—vanity, overindulgence, sensory dysfunction, death of character and the deterioration of the *imago Dei*. Alert to this eternal truth, loving wisdom confronts vanity aware that tutorial indifference to fallacious living is itself a vice, which, when practiced, makes the educator complicit in their pupils' demise.

The call of wisdom is offensive to the contemporary secular mind only because it is untried and misunderstood. The call to holy integrity in atonement with God through faith in Jesus Christ is a call to the invigoration, adventure, and unimagined flourishing that contemporaries yearn for but cannot attain in secular humanism. The way of God's wisdom is not legalistic, unreasonable, naively idealistic, destructively intense, oppressive, or antiquated. To the contrary, wisdom brings solace, enabling, energy, faith, confidence, hope, perseverance, identity, freedom, understanding, liberation, invigoration, and lifelong pursuits that gratify in ever-increasing proportions. Wisdom advances what eternally matters. Indeed, wisdom is an evangelical foundation of rock able to repel the storms of life (Matt 7:24–27). While iterations of secular humanism run their courses and fade, wisdom endures from generation to generation.

Jesus' sapiential teaching aspires, above all else, for *shalom*: "Come to me, all who are weary and heavy-laden, and I will give you rest. Take my yoke upon you, and *learn* from me, for I am gentle and humble in heart; and you shall find rest for your souls. For my yoke is easy, and my load is light" (Matt 11:28–30).[2] This *shalom*, of course, is to be found exclusively in reconciliation with God in his kingdom (Matt 6:33), as Jesus emphasized throughout his earthly ministry.

In the same spirit, Paul's famous admonition in 2 Timothy 3:14–17 envisions education that is sapientially based upon a Christological soteriology.[3] Consider his word choice: "continue," "learned," "convinced of," "knowing," "writings," "wisdom," "salvation," "faith," "in Christ Jesus," "inspiration," "profitable," "teaching," "reproof," "correction," "training in righteousness," "adequate," "equipped for every good work." These are the goals of Christian education.

Where can wisdom of this kind be found?

---

2. Sapiential is an adjective derived from Latin that describes objects as wise or coming from wisdom.

3. Christology derives from Greek and refers to the study of Christ, his identity, nature, and functions. Soteriology derives from Greek and refers to the study of salvation (from what, to what, by whom, and how).

Christian education builds upon the foundation of the reality of God. And it is here where Christian higher education and secular education diverge. Christian institutions of higher education have remained true to their callings and missions, when other historic institutions have *exchanged* their foundational missions for what they have perceived to be truer, more enlightened alternatives. For this reason, while secular institutions have had to reinvent their identities and reformulate their missions to accommodate secular orthodoxies, truly Christian institutions have remained secure in purpose and calling, competently contextualizing their inherited wisdom in fresh expressions of love and truth.

Students seek out Christian colleges and universities[4] because they have shared Christian convictions. In most cases, these students have had what they believe to have been authentic encounters with the living God, who inspired them to enter a covenant relationship with him through union with his Son Jesus Christ. This mysterious union, according to Christian consensus, was made possible through Jesus' death and resurrection, and is made effective by God's grace and appropriated through faith in Jesus as LORD (Rom 10:9–10). The newfound faith of the aspiring college student makes incumbent upon them the offering of their lives in service and stewardship for the advancement of God's work on earth. The sacrifice of their lives to God brings a sense of calling and mission and an aspiration to be productive for God in meaningful ways with eternal significance. With these convictions comes a refreshing sense of identity and purpose and a deep longing for discerning God's will.

This hunger for wisdom leads to the recognition of college as an optimal environment for intellectual growth. Colleges offer library resources, expert personnel, diverse disciplines, irenic community dialogue, and aesthetic beauty. The legitimacy of Christianity's presence here starts with the valid premise of God as the primary agent of all creation including humankind and the natural world. The liberal arts comprised of the classical *trivium* (grammar, logic, and rhetoric) and *quadrivium* (arithmetic, geometry, astronomy, and music) complemented by the humanities (ancient and modern languages, anthropology, archaeology, art, communications, history, literature, physical education, political science, psychology, sociology, religious studies) and the physical sciences (astronomy, chemistry, geology, physics, atmospheric science, and oceanography) constitute channels of wisdom and dimensions of reality that together share origin in God and are thus fully compatible with the special revelation of Scripture and the

---

4. The word college derives from Latin and refers generally to "educational institutions." The term university also derives from Latin and refers to an institution of higher education and research that grants undergraduate and graduate degrees.

anointing of the Holy Spirit. All departments interrelate and none are autonomous. Hence every corner of thought is important theologically as it traces back to God's first cause and as it relates to God's providential end purpose.[5]

Wisdom is Evangelical

Why do we need Christian colleges? Because eternal truth is inherently evangelical.

The term *evangelical* shares the same Greek etymology as the biblical words evangelize (*euangelizein*), gospel (*euangelion*), and evangelist (*euangelistes*). This semantic family combines the prefix *eu*, "good," and the root *angelion*, "report," in the Septuagint Greek translation of the Old Testament, where *euangelizein* translates the Hebrew verb *basar* (Isaiah 61:1). For Christians the term is self-defining because the LORD Jesus revealed himself as "the anointed one" (Isa 61:1), whose mission was to preach the good news (*euangelizein*) in fulfillment of Isaiah, by the Holy Spirit, to the poor, in the face of persecution (Luke 4:14–21). Jesus' synthesis of proclamation and visitation affirms that the "gospel truth" is both liberating and pacifying with respect to the real life fears of our world.

Romans 1:16–17 is paradigmatic for all Christian educators: "For I am not ashamed of the gospel (*euangelion*), for it is the power of God for salvation to everyone who believes, to the Jew first and also to the Greek. For in it the righteousness of God is revealed from faith to faith; as it is written, "But the righteous man shall live by faith." Christian conversion thus appropriates salvation both through intellectual faith *and* through behavioral faith. "The righteous shall *live* by faith" (Hab 2:4; Rom 1:17; Gal 3:11; Heb 10:38). Christian colleges are about the business of helping us understand what living by faith looks like, both intellectually and behaviorally.

2. Conversion and Repentance

Authentic Christianity involves comprehensive conversion, which steadily matures as the Christian's integrity strengthens and as their atonement with Christ and his kingdom intensifies. Christian discipleship is taught and learned as Matthew 28:18–20 confirms.

---

5. The term providence comes from Latin and refers to God's continual action to move history toward his consummate purpose. The rationale undergirding confidence in divine providence is divine omnipotence: If God is all-powerful, then nothing is able to prevent him from accomplishing his purposes throughout history.

First, the disciple of Christ has an authentic encounter with God in space and time and in truth. This encounter is the intellectual foundation for conversion and Christian reorientation. Previous pursuits gain accurate reappraisal on the basis of their juxtaposition to divine reality, and subsequent pursuits emerge strategically on the basis of their continuity with divine purpose and meaning. Pursuits that do not have eternal value are forsaken and those that do are rigorously pursued with the confidence of God's blessing. This experience, appropriately described as "mystical" due to God's spiritual and invisible nature, is an individual experience, but it is also a corporate one shared by all people of God, including the archetypal figures in the Bible: Abraham, Moses, the prophets, the disciples of Jesus, and the apostle Paul, all of whose lives began anew after encounters with God. In turn, their witness defines Christian orthodoxy.

Second, encounter with God compels the inevitable decision of whether or not to enter covenant relationship with God. Authentic Christians make the conscious decision to profess publicly their belief in God and their decided commitment to live with him as their God, their exclusive object of worship. This decision necessitates an *intellectual* conversion that does not conclude with conviction of God's existence and Jesus' resurrection. Covenant relationship with God calls for a deep conversion of the will and a commitment of abiding trust in the optimal goodness of God's design for humanity throughout time and into eternity. Confidence in this truth compels Christians to submit their lives to God for the purpose of productive service and responsible stewardship. The pursuit of these goals together with the abiding presence of the Holy Spirit gives meaning and purpose to the Christian's daily life.

This second step is what the Bible calls *repentance*—a turning away from self-worship and fallacious ideologies to live in the light of the reality of God and life eternal. One's encounter with God changes everything, beginning with the mind of the believer. That, in fact, is what repentance is—*a change of mind* about God followed by expanding realization of God and committed partnership in his work.

Preeminent categories of thought thereafter find new purpose and meaning: literature, history, economics, science, social relationships, the physical body, sex, art, language, politics, family, community, music, psychology, communication, philosophy, ethics, and religion. These domains and all their sub specialties escalate in importance as dimensions of life that the Christian believes were originally conceived in the mind of God. And each has a part to play in God's redemptive plan.

The kind of repentance we describe originates biblically in the Old Testament prophetic oracles and transmits successively through the ministries of John the Baptist, Jesus, and the apostles. The Greek terms *epistrepho* ("turning from" false worship), *metamellomai* ("remorse" for sin), and *metanoia* ("change of mind") each trace their Greek lineage to the dynamic Hebrew term *shuv*, which envisions a "complete turning from sin and self to God."

Commensurate with the biblical call to repentance is the awakening of the human intellect. Such was the case for the apostle Paul, whose categories of thinking—history, law, Israel, Scripture, Gentiles, the future, religious rituals, ethics, Judaism, messiahship, covenant, sacrifice, divine justice, atonement, circumcision, food, justification—all radically changed following his encounter with the risen Christ. Personal achievement became garbage (Phil 3:8) and human wisdom nonsense (1 Cor 1:20), while Jesus' self-sacrifice, the crucifixion, became Paul's boast—God's means of salvation, his true revelation of wisdom and power (1 Cor 1:21–31).

Authentic repentance involves not just a change of mind but also an *expansion* of mind. Growth through continued repentance invigorates with continued encounters with previously unrecognized truths. Having faith in the eternal value of education, Christian debutants, fresh off their conversion experiences, pursue education at Christian institutions where tested Christian scholars capably guide them to higher peaks and deeper valleys of truth, toughened by the turbulent waters and thorny thickets in between.

Repentance requires humility because encounter with God confirms the reality that the repentant one is not God. The repentant are not worthy of worship, while God is—both because God is God and because God's gracious love compels worship from his covenant people, who know their rescue is an unmerited gift.

Astonished by his grace, the Christian's response is to express their love for God by seeking God's will and pursuing God's call. The Christian's abiding presupposition is that God has created them for a purpose, and God will enable them to accomplish that purpose through his Holy Spirit and with the guidance of his inspired word. Their prize, God's presence with them, secures an inner peace that puts life's exploits in proper perspective (Rom 5:1).

The Christian is equally aware that God calls them to steward their life wisely, productively, and with perseverance. The grace of God of which they are now beneficiaries has come at the cost of Jesus' sacrificial death and has been transmitted throughout history through the sacrifices of prophets, apostles, and Christian martyrs whose models of authenticity constitute the Christian standard (Mark 8:34–38).

The calling of the Christian is thus to be the very best person that one can be and to produce the best work that one can produce. Christians are called to produce fruits in keeping with repentance (Matt 3:8)—that is, to be their best and to do their best. In day to day life, this looks like walking through each day, from waking to sleeping, aspiring to make the wisest possible decisions in every decision that is made and expressing the greatest love possible to each person encountered, one person at a time. Maturing in wisdom from one conversation to the next, each day should end with the student wiser than they were at sunrise. This maturation requires balance, conscientious integrity, and vigilant dedication.

God's calling thus aims to cultivate good judgment through the rigors and relationships of life. To love God with all of one's heart, soul, mind, and strength and to love one's neighbor as oneself is a volitional covenant responsibility.

The Security of Wisdom's Children

God does not send forth his newly adopted children intellectually naive. Wisdom is a source of confident security that is intellectually within the grasp of all: "For this commandment which I command you today is not too difficult for you, nor is it out of reach. It is not in heaven, that you should say, 'Who will go up to heaven for us to get it for us and make us hear it, that we may observe it?' Nor is it beyond the sea, that you should say, 'Who will cross the sea for us to get it for us and make us hear it, that we may observe it?' But the word is very near you, in your mouth and in your heart, that you may observe it" (Deut 30:1014; Rom 10:6–8). Wisdom's children go forth with hearts grounded in the good sense ability to recognize wisdom when they hear it.

What is the character of wisdom?

- Wisdom has eternal perspective.
- Wisdom aspires for what is best, never settling for less than holy atonement with Yahweh.
- Wisdom worships God exclusively (Exod 20:3; Mark 12:29–30).
- Wisdom honors all human beings as created in the image of God (Jas 3:9).
- Wisdom advances reconciliation and peace.
- Wisdom cultivates intellectual, physical, emotional, psychological, and relational health.
- Wisdom speaks openly and welcomes public scrutiny.

- Wisdom does not coerce, intimidate, flatter, indoctrinate, or seduce.
- Wisdom transcends bias toward culture, wealth, degree, honors, name, race, gender, nationality, reputation, pedigree, social agenda, and power (Prov 24:23).
- Wisdom discourages laziness and rewards productivity (Matt 25:14–30).
- Wisdom appraises all truth proposals, disqualifying the fallacious for lack of merit and honoring the true for its virtue.
- Wisdom does not reward mediocrity or fanciful speculation.
- Wisdom studies comprehensively, listens alertly, sees with focus, and walks soberly.
- Wisdom is not jealous or self-seeking.
- Wisdom does not honor the immoral, the amoral, the cynic, the obstinate, the indifferent, or the brazenly indulgent. Knowing the destructive consequences of vice, wisdom encourages submission to divine and natural law (Rom 1:18–32).
- Wisdom is circumspect regarding the destructive ends of hedonism: "He who loves pleasure will become a poor man" (Prov 21:17).
- Wisdom rests intentionally for divine re-creation (Exod 20:8–11; Mark 2:27–28).
- The wise live in habitual repentance, turning from evil to embrace God as the sustainer of abundant life and peace.
- Wisdom affirms Plato's quotation of Socrates, "the unexamined life isn't worth living," as fully in accord with biblical commendation (Ps 26:2; Prov 23:7; 1 Cor 1:28; 2 Cor 13:5).
- The wise construct their own characters as offerings of worship to God: "so teach us to number our days, that we may present to you a heart of wisdom" (Ps 90:12).

All of this the still small voice confirms in the minds and hearts of Christian young people. These things are true. And wisdom is always within reach. And wisdom always engenders humankind's most noble potential: "the wisdom from above is first pure, then peaceable, gentle, reasonable, full of mercy and good fruits, unwavering, without hypocrisy" (Jas 3:17).

Where Can Wisdom Be Found?

Wisdom is to be had in all the disciplines and through mentors of varying personalities, backgrounds, generations, and perspectives. The integration of wisdom from all arenas takes place through cross-disciplinary discussion, interdisciplinary teaching, and integrative scholarship and exposition. That the disciple makes decisions based upon the combined wisdom gleaned in each discipline evidences their maturation into persons of intellectual integrity—integrity in the etymological sense of their being fully *integrated*. That they execute decisions that are the wisest of all options available evidences their moral integrity—that their wills are disciplined by their wisdom educated minds. They not only are able to discern what is best but to do what is best to the extent that they have the power to do so. Their will is to do God's will. Their work evidences their faith.

3. Wisdom as the Fear of the Lord

"The fear of the Lord is the beginning of wisdom" (Prov 9:10). What, then, is the fear of the Lord?

Fear, like so many biblical words, is a dynamic term pregnant with theological meaning. The fear of the Lord is neither anxious nor despairing, but alert to the deserving destruction of the insolent and the fortunate prosperity of the faithful. Those who fear the Lord relate to God in an intimate relationship that is true to reality. Their God *is* God and they order their lives and their thought worlds accordingly.

Satiated with love, the fear of the Lord we commend is not crippled by a phobia of God's being capricious or cruel. To the contrary, the fear of the Lord is the intellectual awareness that sadistic cruelty is an inevitable darkness from which only God can deliver his people (Col 1:13). The fear of the Lord is not fear of life with God but fear of life without God.

Soteriologically, the fear of the Lord characterizes a Christian's countenance upon conversion. Christians repent from fallacious ideologies to embrace the eternal truth of wisdom. Salvation thus involves the metamorphosis of the mind crucified with Christ, buried with Christ, and raised with Christ into the body of Christ (Gal 2:19–20; Rom 6:1–13; 12:1–2). For the Christ with whom Christians atone is himself the embodiment of wisdom: "Then a shoot will spring from the stem of Jesse, and a branch from his roots will bear fruit. The Spirit of the Lord will rest on him, the spirit of wisdom and understanding, the spirit of counsel and strength, the spirit of knowledge and the fear of the Lord. And he will delight in the fear of the Lord"

(Isa 11:1–3a). Atonement is the eternally wise plan of God carried out with the full knowledge of the Son: "*By his* knowledge the Righteous One, My servant, will justify the many, as he will bear their iniquities" (Isa 53:11b). Jesus perfected this saving wisdom upon the cross in obedience to the foreordained plan of God. For this reason, Christianity preaches Jesus' death as the manifestation of the power and *wisdom* of God: "we preach Christ crucified, to Jews a stumbling block and to Gentiles foolishness, but to those who are the called, both Jews and Greeks, *Christ the power of God and the wisdom of God*" (1 Cor 1:23–24). This gospel saves because it is sovereignly intelligent; it is the genius of the eternal *logos* who created everything that human beings investigate (John 1:1–4). The representation and distribution of this divine intelligence is the call of the people of God, who have taken on "the *mind* of Christ" (1 Cor 2:16; Phil 2:5).

Pedagogically, the fear of the Lord is the beginning and end of true Christian teaching. The goal is not prestigious exclusivity but humble repentance and reconciliation. The fear of the Lord is the intellectual place where wise professors of all disciplines desire their students to focus habitually. God is the creator of life, the sustainer of life, the restorer of life, the giver of meaning and purpose, the agent of absolute truth, the eternal artist, scientist, storyteller, architect, judge, philosopher, and political scientist. He is the wonderful counselor, eternal father, prince of peace, and only sure refuge for souls seeking *shalom* in a world of anxiety. As creator, he is the ultimate anthropologist, sociologist, and psychiatrist and thus finds pleasure in his peoples' engagement in these disciplines.

This is the vision of Christian education and the goal of Christian discipleship. It is the teleological direction that divine providence moves us toward through the Holy Spirit. And it is the achievement that God by his grace has made possible through the death, resurrection, and exaltation of Jesus Christ our Lord. Looking toward the day of our resurrection, we engage rigorously in education that fosters wisdom's advance in us, through us, and throughout the world that God so loves. Education in wisdom fits students out for eternity, where the fear of the Lord and the love of the Lord embrace.

Part B: The Application of Christian Education

While wisdom calls her followers to fear the Lord, secular orthodoxy worships self and affirms unconditional tolerance of many acts that biblical wisdom discourages. While biblical wisdom depicts two ways, the way of the wise and the way of the fool, the house built on rock and the house built on sand, secular orthodoxy conceives fifty shades of grey, situational ethics, moral relativity, pluralism, and relative truth. Those on the pilgrimage toward wisdom therefore inevitably face conscientious objection to secular orthodoxy. Anointed by the Holy Spirit, their affinity is for truth and their aversion against falsehood.

Real orthodoxy, as opposed to counterfeit, is inherited not contrived. Orthodoxy reflects the character of God: it is the same yesterday, today, and forever. It transcends the foul winds of generational distortions to transmit immutable truth to those who truly seek the face of God. To those who pray for wisdom, God gives the intellectual self-control to interpret Scripture reasonably according to its God-breathed original intent. Respecting Scripture as God's authoritative disclosure of the true wisdom that leads to salvation through faith in Christ, the child of God indwelled by the Holy Spirit is wary of the human compulsion to rationalize Scripture in order to accommodate selfish desires. The wise acknowledge Scripture's prerogative to speak authoritatively for itself without human emendation. Allowance is given for clear passages to set the parameters for interpreting less clear passages and for all passages to be interpreted in continuity with the whole counsel of God. Wise to the human proclivity for rationalization and self-worship, orthodoxy encourages common sense counsel from orthodox precedents, "Do not speculate beyond the text. Do not require of it something more than what it simply says" (John Chrysostom, *The Gospel of Matthew*, Homily 4.3). Honest hermeneutics are prerequisite to integrity in Christ.

In the midst of this cognitive dissonance, it is critical for students to understand the reasons why contemporary culture is the way that it is. There are practical reasons for understanding Darwin, Rousseau, Kant, Hume, Heidegger, Marx, Camus, Sartre, Nietzsche, Freud, Carl Rogers, and other major ideological contributors to postmodernism, including the most influential pop culture celebrities. Amidst the culture wars, the Christian informed by Scripture is aware that their battle is not against flesh and blood. It is against fallacious ideologies that perpetuate antagonism to truth and thereby put humanity at risk of further separation from God and the wisdom inherent within natural law. For those in Christian education the battle is therefore against *isms* that have become idols and *ologies* that substitute for the cross. Evangelism to postmoderns necessitates critical understanding of today's intellectual counterfeits—today's false wisdoms—before meaningful dialogue can unfold. The call is not to berate contemporary society but to collaborate with God in the covenantal task of lovingly persuading society toward repentance. Postmodern culture, the *world* of fallen humanity, is not beyond the reach of God's love (John 3:16). The humanities figure strategically as essential means toward that end.

4. The Christian College and Human Sexuality

Upon confrontation with fallacious ideologies, the most promising and biblical strategy for evangelism and discipleship is one prefaced by evangelistic prayer, one filled with comprehensive liberal arts education, and one directed by gracious critical thinking.

For the Christian, critical thinking, like everything else, should be regulated by love and valid presuppositions. For the eternal well-being of all people, logical inquiry evaluates truth propositions with objective scrutiny to test for validity. When propositions prove false, honorable thinkers reject them as such for the advancement of truth and the common good of humankind—"common good" being an outcome known to be optimal to human health, productivity, and the wellbeing of future generations. As wisdom discriminates truth from falsehood, so the Christian college community is called to educate students how to address claims prefaced by "studies have been done." Well, the student is taught to ask, "let me see these studies and evaluate their presuppositions, premises, and conclusions" to see if they are true. Circumspection has to mark the Christian in the modern world where contradictory schools of thought compete for the prize of cultural orthodoxy.

Those who reject absolute truth may not acquiesce, but, sadly, that is their responsibility and their conscience will have to bear the weight of moral injustice and its long-term consequences. True love does not affirm falsehood. Postmodernism will run its course and history, in time, will pronounce the final verdict on the side of truth. Advocates of truth will then receive vindication.

Evangelical points of contact with postmodern culture, *preparatio evangelica*, are as close as the English language. The premiere entry point for dialogue is the word *love*.

Where does love fit in contemporary worldviews that attempt to supplant classic Christianity? How does love emerge from an identity that begins with self? Can love really cultivate within redefined "open" marriages that sanction promiscuity? What does love look like in social Darwinism? Is eternal love compatible with unconditional toleration of self-destructive behavior and narcissistic unconditional self-approval? Does love trump moral corruption—so that we are obliged to give an A when a lazy F has been turned in?

Popularly described as "making love," sex is God's design for human procreation and human flourishing. It cries out for evaluation by scholars of integrity and unbiased wisdom.

What is the biblical theology of sexual intercourse? What is the biblical theology of marriage? What are the long-term benefits of faithful, monogamous, heterosexual marriage? What are the disadvantages, if any, of homosexual behavior? What are the critical strengths and weaknesses of competing arguments?

What does human anatomy have to say? What do medical studies show? What are the statistics for fidelity within homosexual relationships as compared with heterosexual? Are the statistics valid? How do we know? What are the arguments for and against homosexuals adopting children? Shouldn't it be an inalienable human right for children to be adopted by parents who share the sexual orientation of their birth parents? Why not?

What are we to make of the American Psychological Association? Are the APA's statistics generated by critical integrity? How are we to evaluate the conflicting claims of geneticists, social scientists, politicians, psychologists, physicians, and the Supreme Court justices?

Globally, what are the perspectives of different nations and people groups? How are their positions on sexuality informed by their histories, religions, and political ideologies? How do we know that their perspectives on sexuality are inferior to ours?

How do we know that postmodernism should establish the world's standard? What are we to make of revisionist hermeneutics that biblically exonerate homosexual behavior? Is there an approach to human sexuality that is optimally wise and optimally satisfying? Who is the authority on this issue and why? Who, *de facto,* is God?

Clearly, students aspiring for wisdom who have thought through these issues carefully in the context of the disciplines will be better able to engage in the conversations required for evangelism and discipleship in the contemporary world. Eternal love requires rigorous education to prevent dogmatism on the one hand and scandalous affirmation of human corruption on the other. The issue is front and center, especially for students trying to make sense of their own erotic desires while remaining faithful to the moral teachings of Jesus (Matt 5:18–48).

This is a strategic time for the global church to clarify God's design for sex and marriage. To not do so is to fail this generation—especially college students whose minds and bodies ache for directive answers. The church councils of Nicaea, Constantinople, Chalcedon, and Ephesus met the christological heresies of their day with concentration, clarity, and corporate conviction. The theological challenges of our day necessitate no less. And it is the Christian college's responsibility to take the lead.

5. The Price of Christian Higher Education and Philanthropic Discipleship

The investor in Christian higher education believes investment in the acquisition of wisdom is worth the escalating costs. Why? Because wise philanthropy invests in the apprenticing of tomorrow's philanthropists.[6] Philanthropy is about discipleship, not once and done handouts.

Wisdom is essential to success in every field, as Solomon discerned with respect to politics and government (1 Kgs 3:9–15). Visionary philanthropists realize that the acquisition of wisdom is every generation's greatest need, its value being greater than gold (Prov 8:11; 16:16).

Are we waxing eloquent or is this really the case? This is indeed the literal truth, because human flourishing and global peace require wisdom. Money cannot end corruption. Wisdom can. Marriage cannot be sustained without wisdom. Parenting requires wisdom. The earth cannot be stewarded with long-term maximum benefits without wisdom. Business cannot maximize profits legally without wisdom. Economies cannot grow without wise investments and regulations. Civilizations cannot live in peace without wise leaders capable of wise diplomacy. We cannot steward the earth for future generations without wisdom.

Wisdom comes through meditation over the full spectrum of the disciplines, which in synthesis can capably understand the reality we live in. Unlike gold, wisdom cannot be bought or sold; it must be taught, learned, and courageously put into practice.

Genuine philanthropists yearn for wisdom's promotion through education, because the children and grandchildren philanthropists love will someday face life in societies spawned by today's ideologies. Fallacious ideologies will multiply disillusionment, folly, and in extreme cases, terrorism, by contrast to wise teaching, which will secure justice, peace, and prosperity—*shalom*.

Sharing this burden, the Christian college has the goal of commending the goal of wise investing for maximum philanthropic potential over the course of a lifetime. The goal, as Jesus himself taught, is to produce thirty, sixty, and a hundredfold from the talents God has given (Matt 25:14–29; Luke 19:12–27) for the eternal welfare of humankind. Wisdom therefore smiles upon business and economics as sacred and honorable professions that express authentic worship of God, when investment and innovative entrepreneurship are motivated by the loving desire to improve life for others and give back to God with increased returns.

---

6. Philanthropy derives from Greek and means "the love of humankind." The term conventionally refers to the act of charitable giving.

Wisdom affirms that pure religion is active faith rooted in cognitive truth: "Pure and undefiled religion in the sight of our God and Father is to visit orphans and widows in their distress, and to keep oneself unstained by the world" (Jas 1:27). James represents a New Testament consensus in this respect (Matt 7:21; 12:33–37; 16:27; 25:31–46; Luke 3:8; John 3:21; 5:29; Rom 2:6; 2 Cor 5:10; 1 Pet 1:14–17; Rev 20:12; 22:12). Why? Because wisdom understands that God's goal for history is human reconciliation and divine atonement in eternal covenant relationship. Philanthropy, the love of neighbor, is the second greatest commandment taught in Scripture (Lev 19:18; Matt 22:39).

A Superior Fun

Ratcheting down in intensity for the moment, we move to the other side of the college ethos. Wisdom wears a smile. And comic relief is requisite fresh air for the academic life.

College is also about fun. And that's good. The freshman year is a rite of passage from childhood to adulthood when kids should indulge in sheer ridiculousness. Hilarity brings together personalities of humor, adventure, and satirical awareness. Controlled by healthy boundaries, this brief chapter of life ignites a love expressive of the joy of the Lord. Unmerited fraternal laughter is realized eschatology, a foresight into the joyous exhilaration to be had by the people of God eternally—*we shall laugh* (Luke 6:21). The healthy Christian college community thus laughs together with purpose, meaning, and thanksgiving.

The Christian college community knows, however, that while the wise know when to laugh and why to laugh, this world of mortality is one fraught with suffering, deceptions, and injustices that frequently make lament appropriate and laughter a delayed longing. Life is not Disneyworld. Pollyanna is a delusion. Hence, Jesus' real(ized) eschatology: "Blessed are you who weep now, for you shall laugh" (Luke 6:21); "Woe to you who laugh now, for you shall mourn and weep" (Luke 6:25).

The goal of the Christian college education is to move students from freshmen hilarity to a sustainable joy found exclusively in faithful, meaningful work and fellowship with God and his people. Grounded in wisdom, the stabilized student thinks through the consequences of get rich schemes economically and health and wealth gospels theologically to invest their faith in honest business and orthodox theology—each for the greatest long-term gains. Wisdom is the active decision to obey God's will continually with the awareness that oneness with God and his people surpasses all ephemeral highs that life has to offer. The exhilaration, adventure, and wonder of life exists in its fullness only in harmony with God's creative design. The student cultivates the understanding that the choice of paths is not a dilemma between Epicurean moderation and Stoic submission but between the diminishing returns of the ephemeral and the compounding joy of the eternal.

6. Christian Higher Education and the Family

Christian higher education advances wisdom in the hearts and minds of students with a depth and breadth that parents alone cannot administer. Hearing the call of God toward further growth in wisdom, the Christian family understands the priceless value of their investment in institutions that further the Kingdom of God through discipleship in rigorous curricula. Christian parents do not have children purely for the sake of having cute cuddly bundles of joy. That is a temporary pleasure, and if self-contained, a selfish motive. The eternal joy of family, by contrast, deepens through responsible commitment that graduates into corporate participation in God's plan for humankind. In this respect, the family shares its identity with the church and the Christian college. The parents' desire is not to freeze their children into childhood but to see them grow and mature into productive disciples of Christ, who will be productive, persevering, strong, and wise—capable parents themselves one day, who will then invest their resources generously into ventures of eternal significance (Prov 23:15–16). The vision of Christian education begins with the family:

> Hear, O sons, the instruction of a father,
> And give attention that you may gain understanding,
> For I give you sound teaching;
> Do not abandon my instruction.
> When I was a son to my father,
> Tender and the only son in the sight of my mother,
> Then he taught me and said to me,
> "Let your heart hold fast my words;
> Keep my commandments and live;
> Acquire wisdom! Acquire understanding!
> Do not forget nor turn away from the words of my mouth.
> Do not forsake her, and she will guard you;
> Love her, and she will watch over you.
> The beginning of wisdom is: Acquire wisdom;

> And with all your acquiring, get understanding.
> Prize her, and she will exalt you;
> She will honor you if you embrace her.
> "She will place on your head a garland of grace;
> She will present you with a crown of beauty."
> Hear, my son, and accept my sayings
> And the years of your life will be many.
> I have directed you in the way of wisdom;
> I have led you in upright paths.
> When you walk, your steps will not be impeded;
> And if you run, you will not stumble.
> Take hold of instruction; do not let go.
> Guard her, for she is your life. (Prov 4:1–13)

Wisdom, not merit, not upward social mobility, not prestige, name, reputation, legacy or even employment is the wise Christian parents' ultimate desire for their children. Wise parents desire the very best for their children. And wisdom is the very best.

7. Christian Higher Education and the Church

The Christian student, indwelled by the Holy Spirit and moved toward maturity in Christ, is hungry for edifying relationship within Christian community. This dynamic relationship begins in the final stages of conversion when the believer becomes a member of the new covenant people of God. They acquire in the body of Christ a personal, social, and community identity that defines them for eternity. Their character is now in Christ personally, in the body of Christ corporately, and guided by the holy will of Christ ethically. The character of God is now their benchmark for lifestyle. God has poured his love within their hearts (Rom 5:5), where his law is forever inscribed (Jer 31:33; 2 Cor 3:3). The covenant formula is now their dynamic identity—God is their God and they are a member of his people (e.g., Jer 31:33; Rev 21:3). Hence, upon conversion, the young Christian, having professed their death, burial, and resurrection with Christ, emerges with newness of life into an eternity within the corporate body of Christ, the church (Gal 2:19–20; Rom 6:1–13).

College is a time for deepening students' devotional relationship with Jesus. Anxious overstimulation mitigates within communities that cultivate ears to hear in solitary prayer and meditation. Learning to hear

Christ's voice in silence cultivates a discipline that keeps under control the tyranny of college chaos. This devotion is what the author of Hebrews calls the disciplined entrance into God's rest (Heb 4:3–11). Devotional living, the student discovers, is a priceless dimension of salvation—a balm for the duration of one's life. With daily time spent with the Wonderful Counselor, followed by comprehensive exposure to the liberal arts, students' admiration for their risen LORD can and should intelligently heighten, even upon encounter with counter-Christian ideologies. This, Isaiah 26:3 reminds us, is one dimension of *shalom*. The purpose of daily devotions is not a routine of self-indoctrination but intelligent growth in wisdom.

Ekklesia, the Greek New Testament term translated "church" means "assembly." For this reason, Martin Luther chose to translate *ekklesia* with the German term *"Gemeinde,"* the German dynamic equivalent of "community." Germans still use the term almost synonymously with *Kirche*. This range of ideas is appropriate when we recall that the earliest churches were Jewish synagogues (*sunagogai* = "gathering together places"), which incorporated faith in Jesus into existing traditional Jewish liturgies. James, perhaps the earliest book of the New Testament, thus refers to the Christian assembly not as *ekklesia* but as *sunagoge* (Jas 2:2).

Later in history, the term "church" originated from the Greek word *kuriakos*, "belonging to the LORD." Taken together, *ekklesia* and *kuriakos* envision the church as the LORD's covenant people, the human institution conceived by God at creation and reestablished again and again throughout Scripture. Its continuing growth is evidence of God's grace and his continuing work of corporate salvation.

In college, community becomes transformative in the healing that follows conflict resolutions between roommates, temporarily traumatic changes of majors, recovery from sports injuries, the frustration of a low grade, restoration following the moral failure of cheating, emotional healing upon a relational breakup, the death of grandparents, siblings or classmates, the divorce of parents, bouts with anxiety and depression, and bewildering encounters with doubt. It is here, amidst the realities of life, that Christian community becomes salt and light, where course content speaks, where those who mourn find sympathy and comfort, and where permanent impact happens. It is also here where the ministry of the body of Christ proves most meaningful. For lasting impressions from wise corporate community ministry can mark students' characters permanently as they proceed on their continued paths toward wisdom.

The Christian college is for "projects in process." Indeed, the "rock" upon which Christ built his church was a person, Peter, whose faith, impulsiveness, hypocrisy, reconciliation, repentance, theological growth, and inspiration (as seen in 1 and 2 Peter) is exemplary for constructive discipleship today. Christian students, today's "living stones," do not enter Christian colleges perfect, but like Peter, having encountered the Lord, aspire to be faithful and complete in Christ, and to become "living stones" in the eternal temple of God (1 Pet 2:5). The mission of the Christian college is to participate in God's work of turning the hardened rocks of Mark 8 into the living stones of 1 Peter 2:3. The metaphor is apt.

About this vocation, Christian colleges are a strategic part of the global church—the *ekklesia* universal. Both the Christian college and the global church belong to the Lord in the sense of *kuriakos*—both ministries belong to the Lord and are of the Lord. As the Apostolic Father Ignatius put it in his letter to the Smyrnaens, "wherever Jesus Christ is, there is the catholic church" (Ign. *Smyrn.* 8:2). And so it is that pastors and teachers alike receive their marching orders from the same Lord, whose objective is the united perfection of all in holy integrity: "And he gave some as apostles, and some as prophets, and some as evangelists, and some as pastors and teachers, for the equipping of the saints for the work of service, to the building up of the body of Christ; until we all attain to the unity of the faith, and of the knowledge of the Son of God, to a mature man, to the measure of the stature which belongs to the fullness of Christ" (Eph 4:11–13).

And it is here where the Christian university is uniquely enabled by its shared identity with the church. For amidst the challenges of real life, the Christian community marches on with a confident stability not had by "those who have no hope" (1 Thess 4:13). In the face of real life, "weeping with those who weep," the Christian university finds strength in Scripture, prayer, supportive fellowship, accountability partnerships, sacred music, corporate worship, the abiding presence of the Holy Spirit, and the promise of the resurrection of the dead. Surviving the tests of life and the acids of criticism, cohesive community education equips students to start families, plant churches, direct businesses, and administrate organizations with the virtues of grace, forgiveness, reconciliation, perseverance, and eternal perspective learned from real Christians through real life situations in college. The investment proves priceless when students encounter "real life" upon graduation. For their foundation is established in real life on the bedrock of eternal wisdom.

8. The Apprentice Model:

"The tongue of the wise makes knowledge acceptable" (Prov 15:2).

The apprentice model for teaching is the Christian professor's inheritance from Christ. The calling to make Christian disciples involves replicating the passions and abilities that God has inspired through the disciplines, where joyful stimulation more than repays the intellectual rigors and the economic sacrifices of the profession. The apprentice model envisions the discipleship of inspired, committed students who will in turn apprentice others. The end is historic impact on successive generations with the good news of God's abundant life revealed truthfully in every dimension of life and through every aspect of human discovery and creative expression.

The apprentice model carries over into extracurricular activities where discipleship is the ultimate goal of music, theatre, and athletics. Conductors, directors, and coaches have opportunities to cultivate wisdom through the rigors of honing skills, learning new material, developing group chemistry, and performing intelligently with passion and self-control. Measurable success in terms of rave reviews and winning records is obviously front and center, but the seminal goal is discipleship—the apprenticing of future conductors, directors, and coaches who will be able to cultivate wisdom in future generations courageously and confidently in a manner worthy of the gospel (Phil 1:27).

The Place of Prayer in Christian Higher Education

Prayer is seminal to the long-term goals of the discipleship model, because, if Christianity is true, one's chosen discipline finds its purpose and meaning in God's economy where communication vitalizes all relationships. Every credible field of learning informs meaningful prayers of adoration, confession, thanksgiving, and supplication. This is true because every field endeavors for increased understanding:

> For if you cry for discernment,
> Lift your voice for understanding;
> If you seek her as silver
> And search for her as for hidden treasures;
> Then you will discern the fear of the Lord
> And discover the knowledge of God.
> For the Lord gives wisdom;
> From his mouth come knowledge and understanding.
> He stores up sound wisdom for the upright;
> He is a shield to those who walk in integrity,

> Guarding the paths of justice,
> And he preserves the way of his godly ones.
> Then you will discern righteousness and justice
> And equity and every good course.
> For wisdom will enter your heart
> And knowledge will be pleasant to your soul. (Prov 2:3–10)

The Christian college has the calling of equipping students to pray *strategically* for the carrying out of Jesus' mission on earth. This plays out in strategic prayer for the world, students' home countries, government officials, local communities, friends, families, and churches, with hearts tuned to current events. The student learns compassion and love as their heart empathizes with those for whom they pray. Indispensable to the success of a Christian college, prayer is a strategic educational mission directed by wisdom. Prayer is responsible imitation of Christ's ministry intelligently worked out in believing conversation with God. The Lord's Prayer exemplifies this vision (Matt 6:9–13) in the context of educational engagement (Luke 11:1).

Educational Purpose

Christians should never lose sight of the fact that the purpose of learning is not learning, nor is the purpose of critical thinking critical thinking. Noble critical thinking aims for decisions that act for the best of possible outcomes in arenas where optimal decisions result in the betterment of human lives, while indifference, by contrast, could result in human suffering and intellectual disillusionment, cynicism, and despair. The apprenticing of students with this vision has the potential of perpetuating a genealogy of disciples who impact history for good. The goal is not a diploma, a job, a resume, professional achievement, promotion, recognition, consumption, materialistic acquisition, or upward social mobility. The goal is wisdom that facilitates enduring relationships that deepen and intensify for eternity. Without wisdom, beautiful campuses and prestigious degrees are white washed walls.

The world needs wise graduates. Students are entering a complex world of competition, media spin, greed, infidelity, corruption, war, civil war, epidemic infectious diseases, pornography, sex trafficking, genocide, racism, poverty, declining educational standards, deforestation, drug trafficking, family breakdown, domestic violence, gambling, psychological despair, moral indifference, national debt, eroding social security, inefficient health care, judicial corruption, culturally induced narcissism, and terrorism. In the midst of the mess humanity has made, the call of Christian education is to love this fractured world with the spirit and truth of God's wisdom inherent in the gospel. The call is not to the naïve blindness of Disney Pollyanna but to the sight and vision of divine wisdom.

Therefore essential to the success of Christian higher education is its relevance to contemporary culture and current events. Students snore at irrelevant minutia but find fascination in material that connects with the real world. Contact points open students' eyes to the big questions that remain the same from generation to generation: truth, time, identity, doubt, tragedy, comedy, death, human sexuality, the human conscience, divine supremacy and free will, evil, gender, beauty, marriage, friendship, the environment, eternity, the human conscience, and God. When academic fads fade, classic themes roll on unimpeded because they innately reside in the hearts, souls, and minds of humans everywhere from one generation to the next. The liberal arts deal with truths that people want and need to understand. Conserving this focus, Christian education has self-generating teleological inertia. Understanding the location of one's discipline within God's providential design is the calling and responsibility of the Christian professor in every discipline.

9. Connecting the Dots

The educational end we are seeking, wisdom integrated across the curriculum, requires more than accumulated knowledge, the memorization, retention, and regurgitation of information. We aspire for the ability to "connect the dots" among truths verified in all disciplines. Then, with an integrated education of connected dots, we seek the construction of a work ethic, a liturgy, and a corporate life established upon integrated truth. A lifestyle so directed constitutes a life of wisdom, a life of integrity, and a life of holiness free of inner contradictions. Such a lifestyle, stabilized by a humble self-awareness before God and humanity, walks a path toward the restoration of the *imago Dei*.

The responsibility of a college curriculum is to assemble the essential dots in all disciplines that constitute comprehensive wisdom. These dots include absolute truths, absolute falsehoods, complexities that require suspended judgement, and outright mysteries. Some dots are essential for students to endorse, others essential to reject, others essential for continued contemplation, and others require the humble concession that the student is not able on this side of eternity to connect all the dots of comprehensive reality—"we look in a mirror dimly" (1 Cor 13:12). The student wills to live according to this accumulating wisdom in a manner that defines their characters as citizens of the kingdom of God, who forthrightly forsake vanity for truth and integrity. Faith is not a cause for intellectual shame, because the way of wisdom is not intellectual suicide but intellectual liberation and confirmation.

10. The College Curriculum as Preparatio Evangelica

How does wisdom direct the disciplines and the thesis that the academic disciplines are essential for Christian evangelism and discipleship? The rationale is simple. Just as Scripture gives the wisdom that leads to salvation through faith in Jesus Christ, so too do the disciplines inform us of innumerable eternal truths. Wisdom and folly tell their contrasting stories in sociology, political science, economics, art, music, history, psychology, physics, engineering, journalism, language, communications, technology, business, religious studies, anthropology, and indeed every legitimate arena of inquiry. The wages of truth and falsehood are universally evident. Every discipline has a benchmark that distinguishes an A from an F. The truly educated, those with ears to hear and eyes to see, know the difference.

Today, when engaging with secular culture, the disciplines are invaluable as *preparatio evangelica*, both because they establish lines of intelligent conversation and because expertise in one's chosen field wins respectful conversation with secular listeners. Knowledge of the cultural dimensions of a domestic or foreign land heightens potential for meaningful dialogue. Familiarity with that culture's history, politics, economic structure, government, social dynamics, language, literature, music, and art provide invaluable preparation for global friendships.

Most importantly, people must have cultural reference points in order to understand the gospel. Many such reference points exist in the academic disciplines. Dismissal of the wisdom resident within the disciplines can only result in a falling short of the global church's evangelistic potential, if evangelism's goal is to inspire disciples who themselves join the pilgrimage toward comprehensive eternal wisdom. Curricular wisdom is foundational *preparatio evangelica*.

Wisdom is about the construction of persons, not the accumulation of merit. This looks like the cultivation of women and men of integrity, who think like Christ, speak the truth like Christ, love sacrificially like Christ, and act in all contexts for the establishment of eternal *shalom*: "we proclaim him, admonishing every man and teaching every man with all wisdom, that we may present every man complete in Christ" (Col 1:28).

The end is *Soli Deo Gloria*, as the Book of Revelation discloses: the dead in Christ are raised, evil comes to its end in the lake of fire, cosmic peace ensues, a new heavens and a new earth emerge, and reconciled people from every nation, tribe, and people contribute to supernatural cosmic worship sounded in spirit and absolute truth. Comprehensive Christian education endeavors toward this end.

Closing Prayer

Heavenly Father,

May discipleship within the global body of Christ flourish in accord with your will as your Spirit has breathed wisdom into holy Scripture and as you have consummated wisdom in the person of Jesus Christ our Lord. May your people live intelligently in love for you and in love for one another and the whole world with eternal fellowship with you our treasured end. May we discard vanity and sin to steward wisely your gifts, and may we exercise them in humility for the benefit of humankind and for your glory. To the only wise God, the beginning and end of truth, be glory, honor, and praise, now and forevermore.

Amen.

2

The Role of Biblical Exegesis within the Christian College Curriculum

CLINTON E. ARNOLD

Do your best to present yourself to God as one approved, a worker who has no need to be ashamed, rightly handling the word of truth.

(2 TIM 2:15)

FOR CHRISTIANS, THE STARTING point for acquiring wisdom is the Bible. This is because God has chosen to reveal himself authoritatively in his written word as demonstrated by the life and ministry of our LORD. Jesus himself modeled *biblical* wisdom through fidelity to the holy Scriptures in his messianic call as the Son of God. After his baptism, three times Jesus rebuffed Satan's temptations with the preface, "it is written" (Matt 4:4, 7, 10). Indeed, Jesus was resolute in his mission to fulfill Scripture faithfully and obediently. He viewed the Torah, the Writings, and the Prophets as revelation directly from God that spoke to all of life, and especially Jesus' own mission and work. From his baptism at the beginning of his ministry, where God defined his ministry in terms of Psalm 2:7 and Isaiah 42:1 (Matt 3:17), to the very end of his earthly ministry, where he quoted Psalm 22 from the cross and explained his identity as risen LORD to the disciples on the road to Emmaus (Luke 24:27), Jesus knowingly acted to both explain and fulfill Scripture. Therefore God calls Christians today, those who are "in Christ" and "in union with Christ," to follow Jesus' example by devoting themselves to Scripture-directed lives regardless of vocation and calling.

The New Testament authors followed the example of Jesus in regarding the books that we know as the Old Testament as written divine revelation designed by God to give us the wisdom that leads to salvation through faith in Christ Jesus (2 Tim 3:16). The Bible is therefore our canon, our orthodox measure for authentic Christian faith and practice. For all of us, the Bible is our point of departure for growth in wisdom and love for God and humankind.

A uniquely Christian education is thus profoundly informed by all that we can learn from the Bible. It provides the essential framework for understanding God's creational design, our place in creation, the phenomenon of evil and its corruption of the world, God's merciful and benevolent response, how we are to live in a way that is pleasing to God, and God's plans for the future.

But the Bible is a long and in many ways complex composition that includes sixty-six books written by believing authors from the Ancient Near East, who wrote in Hebrew, Aramaic, and Greek. Sound understanding of the Bible therefore requires diligent study. And this is where exegesis enters the picture.

What Is Exegesis?

"Exegesis" denotes careful and critical study of a text of literature. Christian exegesis goes beyond surface-level readings to unearth God's intended message through his inspired prophets and apostles. This involves proven methods of interpretation in the fields of history, linguistics, archaeology, biblical sociology, ancient Near Eastern religion, literary analysis, and biblical theology (understanding a text in light of its context among the macro-themes of the whole Bible). Along the way, exegesis partners closely with its disciplinary cousin, hermeneutics—the science of how to interpret texts of literature. It might be said that hermeneutics is the study of interpretive methods, while exegesis is the actual practice.

The term "exegesis" is derived from the Greek term *exēgeomai*, which means "to interpret," "to set forth in detail," or "to explain."[1] In contemporary biblical studies, it is most commonly used to take into account the analysis of the biblical languages as part of the process of interpreting the text. In essence, exegesis refers to a careful and thorough study that utilizes every method relevant for achieving the most objective interpretation

---

1. See Bauer et al., *Greek-English Lexicon*; Liddell and Scott, *Greek-English Lexicon*.

possible—taking into account genre, literary features, cultural elements, historical context, literary context, biblical theology, and systematic theology. Working with the precise wording and word usage of any given passage in Hebrew, Aramaic, or Greek is part of the process.

Consequently, "exegetical commentaries" employ each of these methods in their attempts to explain the Bible's original meaning. These endeavors are essential for all of us as we discern our vocations from a biblical perspective in imitation of Christ our Lord.

The Place of the Heart and the Role of the Holy Spirit

The biblical character Ezra exuded a posture toward the Bible that should also be reflected in every believer who seeks wisdom and truth. Ezra "set his heart to study the Law of the Lord" (Ezra 7:10). As the Babylonian exile was coming to an end and many of the people of God had returned to the land of Israel to rebuild and prepare for the future, Ezra sought to help ground the people in God's revelation. Consequently, he also committed himself to practice God's word and to teach it throughout Israel.

Anyone who is serious about the task of integrating faith and learning will want to follow Ezra's example. We should construct comprehensive education with the best bricks and mortar of our respective disciplines. While we may do that independently, we understand corporately that our separate disciplinary buildings share the same theological foundation of wisdom as revealed in Scripture, which informs all of our work.

To be sure, there is a heart element involved in the exegetical process. The Psalmist exclaims, "I have stored your word in my heart" (Ps 119:11) and the writer of Proverbs advises, "Let your heart hold fast my words" (Prov 4:4). There is a deep resolve in the soul of the Christian educator to drink deeply from the word of God. This applies not just to the devotional life of the professor, but also extends to the academic discipline. It involves the patient and long-term investigation of Scripture to mine its eternal truth. Their lives are like the good soil Jesus spoke of, "who, hearing the word, hold it fast in an honest and good heart, and bear fruit with patience" (Luke 8:15).

We invite the Holy Spirit to guide us in this process. The Holy Spirit is the "Spirit of wisdom." As such, the Spirit can impart wisdom to us, not only to inform decisions in our personal lives, but also to help us understand creation in the way that God has designed it. The prophet Isaiah declared, "the Spirit of the Lord shall rest upon him, the Spirit of wisdom and understanding, the Spirit of counsel and might, the Spirit of knowledge and the fear of the LORD" (Isa 11:2). The LORD Jesus, of whom this prophecy speaks, models for us a perfect dependence upon the Holy Spirit.

The same Spirit who filled Jesus with wisdom offers to impart wisdom to the people of God today. With this in mind, the apostle Paul prays regularly for the Ephesian believers "that the God of our LORD Jesus Christ, the Father of glory, may give you the Spirit of wisdom and of revelation in the knowledge of him" (Eph 1:17). John's Gospel reveals that the Spirit comes upon believers to function as a *paraklētos*, which the RSV, NIV (1984), and HCSB translate as "counselor" (John 14:26; 15:26; 16:7). Part of the function of the indwelling Spirit in the lives of believers is to give help and understanding in how to live as representatives of Christ in the world. The Holy Spirit is God's agent of divine counsel and instruction: "If any of you lacks wisdom, you should ask God, who gives generously to all without finding fault, and it will be given to you" (Jas 1:5).

What form might this prayer take in our respective disciplines? Here is one suggestion:

> Father, as I begin this time of study of your word, I pray that you would grant me wisdom from the Spirit whom you have given to me. I pray that you would illuminate the eyes of my heart so that I can see the relevance of the truth of Scripture for my discipline. Enable me to understand my discipline from your perspective. I ask that you would help me to discern truth from error, the good from the bad, and the helpful from the unhelpful. Please help me to know how to honor Christ as LORD of my discipline.

The Goal of Biblical Exegesis for the Christian Educator

First, the goal of exegesis is to attain as objective and accurate an interpretation of the biblical text as possible. This contributes to discovering God's mind on all matters of life—including our disciplines.

We must start with discerning the relevance of the biblical text for our personal lives. The Bible is one of the principal means that God uses for shaping character and bringing our lives into alignment with his design and purpose. I have been a Christian educator for over thirty years. Yet, I grew up in a non-Christian home with a different set of values and various forms of dysfunction. From the point I became a Christian in my teen years, God has used the in-depth study of his word to reshape me as a person. I discovered God's design for community, relationships, sexuality, money, vocation, and so much more. I found that God is working to accomplish a mission through his people prior to the time that Jesus returns in consummation of his purposes. This growing understanding has provided me with a strong sense of purpose and vocation throughout my life. I believe this is what God wants every Christian educator to experience and model for students.

It seems that, more than ever, college students are drifting, lacking purpose, and depressed. A recent CIRP Freshman survey revealed that 84 percent of college freshmen felt anxious, 51 percent felt depressed, and 47 percent anticipate seeking personal counseling.[2] While professional therapy may be necessary for many, there is a strong possibility that a great number could be helped by personal spiritual formation. Christian educators—in every discipline—play an important role in this process.

For too long and for too many people, personal devotion was seen as the extent of the relevance of the study of the Bible for Christians. There is often a bifurcation between one's faith and one's vocation or discipline. Yet the Bible has much to say about all of life. As Chalres Colson notes, "True Christianity goes beyond John 3:16—beyond private faith and personal salvation."[3] The Christian educator should be uniquely motivated not simply to learn about one's discipline, but to explore God's design, to marvel in its intricacies, and to worship him as a result of academic discovery.

God lays claim to every discipline and his word speaks truth that is relevant to every discipline. As Christian educators, we engage in biblical exegesis to mine the truths that provide framework, perspective, and corrective guidance within our respective disciplines. The intent of this volume is to point the way forward and illustrate what this integrative task may look like.

The "How" of Biblical Exegesis for Integration

As a composition of historical and literary documents, the Bible requires an interpretive approach appropriate to the complexities of ancient literature. Thus, it is crucial to give full and appropriate attention to the various elements that comprise the interpretive process as I introduce them below. For deeper inquiry, there are a host of excellent books on hermeneutics and exegesis.[4]

---

2. "2016 The Freshman Survey (TFS) Infographic Codebook," 2.

3. Dockery, "Introduction," 12.

4. See, for example, DeRouchie, *How to Understand and Apply the Old Testament*; Naselli, *How to Understand and Apply the New Testament*; Blomberg, *Handbook of New Testament Exegesis*; Fee and Stuart, *How to Read the Bible for All Its Worth*; Duvall and Hays, *Grasping God's Word*; Bartholomew, *Introducing Biblical Hermeneutics*; Osborne, *The Hermeneutical Spiral*.

Genre:

The Bible consists of a wide variety of literary genres that include historical narrative, poetry, wisdom literature, proverbs, prophetic texts, law, letters, parables, and beatitudes. Each of these categories have a set of unique features that educate the interpreter in understanding the author's intended meaning.

Literary Techniques:

Within each genre, there are sections of discourse that may reflect unique literary devices that were common in the ancient world. These would include parallelism, repetition, chiastic structures, rhetorical devices, assonance, apocalyptic symbolism, and a variety of others. Familiarity with these different literary forms is essential to accurate interpretation.

Historical and Cultural Setting:

As with any piece of literature, biblical documents must be read as part of their time and culture. A knowledge of Jewish and Ancient Near Eastern history is foundational for understanding the Old Testament. Likewise, familiarity with first-century Judaism, Hellenism, and the Roman Empire helps in understanding the New Testament. The discovery of the Dead Sea Scrolls has also helped in illuminating many facets of a first-century Jewish culture that was contemporary with Jesus, Paul, and the early church.

Literary Context:

There is a tendency in the church to think of the Bible as a collection of verses. The danger in this approach is that it can easily disconnect a verse from its immediate context resulting in a faulty interpretation. In reading the Bible, it is crucial for interpreters to locate a particular sentence or saying in the context of the larger discourse and to discern the flow of thought within that discourse.

Precise Wording and Details of Grammar:

Exegesis involves the use of the original languages for interpreting the meaning of words, clauses, sentences, internal sections, and entire compositions.

Interpreting accurately the use of adverbial participles, genitive cases, and other grammatical forms relates directly to how a passage translates, is interpreted, and is then applied in the life and professional context of the believer. For this reason, careful exegesis is foundational to spiritual formation and Christian intellectual maturation.

Gifted translators have already done much of this work for us. We are blessed to live in a time when we have more than one English version to choose from. As part of the interpretive process, it is often good to begin by reading the passage in a handful of English versions. I find it helpful to read three versions that represent different translation philosophies. At one end of the spectrum are formal equivalent translations that try to approximate "word-for-word" precision. These are often referred to as "literal" translations. They include the KJV, ESV, RSV, NRSV, and the NASB. At the other end of the spectrum are dynamic equivalent translations that strive for a "thought-for-thought" rendering. These require far more interpretation to achieve their goal. They would include the NLT, REB, NEB, CEV, and *The Message*. In the middle of this range are translations that try to find an optimal blend of both approaches. These include the NIV and HCSB. Of course all English versions must interpret, so the differences lie in the degree of interpretation. Disagreement among the versions indicates an underlying passage whose grammar permits a range of possible translations. In these cases, the reader is wise to allow the context to establish the range of legitimate meanings. If the proposed interpretation is foreign to the context, it should be rejected.

All of the interpretive work I have described sounds like a daunting task. And, indeed, it is time consuming. But an abundance of substantive commentaries on the Bible by outstanding scholars accelerates the interpretive process. Exegetical commentaries discuss the text in detail drawing on all of the key interpretive elements. Some of these commentaries can be a challenge to read for those who have not been trained in Greek and Hebrew, but others are designed to be read by those who have not learned these languages but desire to have insights from what the languages reveal. To assist in the process of deciding on which to choose, annotated bibliographies are available to point you in the right direction.[5]

---

5. See especially Evans, *Guide to Biblical Commentaries*. See also Longman, *Old Testament Commentary Survey*; Carson, *New Testament Commentary Survey*; Denver Seminary regularly publishes a guide to Old Testament and New Testament commentaries in their free online journal: see http://www.denverseminary.edu/the-denver-journal/2017/.

Doing Exegesis in Community

What I have portrayed so far about the task of exegesis represents an individual process of investigation, albeit in consultation with good written resources. But exegesis can and should also be conceived as a project that is done in community. The Christian college or university setting is the ideal place for this to happen. In the body of Christ, we share a rich heritage of community exegesis and theological dialog going all the way back to the Jerusalem Council in Acts 15 and the early councils that codified and closed the canon, and then the Seven Ecumenical Councils that refined our understanding of Jesus in the face of early heresies.

Today, the natural place to begin in our university contexts is through engagement with one or more members of the biblical and theological studies faculty, especially ones with an interest in your particular discipline. This form of dialogue is mutually beneficial in that the discipline expert gains greater insight into interpreting the relevant biblical texts and tracing the relevant biblical-theological themes. At the same time, the biblical and theological studies faculty gains insight into the language, the questions, the methodologies, and the concerns of the other person's discipline. This intellectual fellowship is a rich opportunity waiting to be tapped with greater and greater rewards as fresh insights accumulate. Hence, the commendation of Christian intellectual fellowship across the disciplines is part of the mission of this volume. Exegesis is vital to this end as consensus on exegetical methodology is the primary point of departure for mutually edifying dialog.

Along the way, it is important for all to keep in mind that biblical and theological studies faculty do not function as a new priestly caste that God has given to the church to mediate the Scripture to others in a way that stands above questioning. The Protestant Reformation taught us to recognize the priesthood of all believers and the perspicuity of the Scripture—that all have equal interpretive access to the Bible and that it is sufficiently clear for people to understand. Nevertheless, Scripture reveals that God has gifted some with the gift of teaching (see Rom 12:7; 1 Cor 12:28–29; Eph 4:11). These members of the faculty have a responsibility to serve other members by functioning as dialogue partners in the process of integrating faith and learning. This happens best in a relational context where there is trust, mutual respect, and a humble desire to learn from one another.

Biblical and theological studies faculty need to remember that they, too, are fallible and vulnerable to unhealthy pressures and trends within their guild. Consequently, biblical research must survive the acids of peer review prior to serious consideration. History has shown that Bible scholars sometimes utilize flawed methods that consequently produce invalid conclusions. These trends in biblical scholarship are why many no longer revere seminaries and universities that strike them as Christian in name and history only.

For these reasons, Christian institutions should feel a renewed sense of responsibility to the church in rehabilitating the nobility of Christian scholarship. Jesus came to establish the church, not the university. We exist alongside the church to serve it and strengthen it as a significant part of our mission. Churches entrust their young people to Christian colleges and universities not only to provide them with a broad education and training in vocation, but also to help shape them in faith and character. In his magisterial work on the drift of Christian colleges and universities from their Christian roots, James Tunstead Burtchaell details the steps by which many institutions compromised their Christian convictions by conforming to secular orthodoxies. His thesis is that this digression in almost all cases took place as a result of severed ties with the church. Hence, the subtitle of his monograph is *The Disengagement of Colleges & Universities from their Christian Churches*.[6]

To be sure, there were valid reasons for universities to separate from their ecclesiastical governing bodies. Adopting principles of the Enlightenment, universities discarded traditions that were proven to be more cultural than biblical. Such reforms were commendable. The actual degeneration of universities began not with application of rational and empirical methods but with premature intellectual skepticism that resulted in dogmatic rejection of the supernatural, including the authoritative truth of sacred Scripture. Such universities simply replaced old extra-biblical traditions with new extra-biblical ideologies with the result that they ceased to be Christian in any meaningful sense.

Exegesis in Partnership with Other University Disciplines

Moving to a more positive subject, in my thirty years of teaching in a Christian university context, my most rewarding classroom experience was a class I taught with two professors from psychology and anthropology. We shared a rich diversity of students who engaged with us on the topic, "Issues in Spiritual Warfare," which explored the phenomenon of demonic influence from a biblical-theological perspective, a psychological perspective, and an anthropological and missiological perspective. Each week of the three-hour class, one of us made a presentation for the first half of the class (with each

---

6. Burtchaell, *Dying of the Light*.

of us presenting every third week) and the second half of the class we engaged in open dialogue.

The three of us started meeting and dialoguing two years before we thought of offering the class. It soon became a rich discussion that connected to real-life phenomena and even life and death situations. Then, when we created the class, we merely extended the discussion. We each had something to say to the students, but we also found our thinking and practice greatly enriched by our colleagues' expertise and the insights of our students, many of whom were internationals with fresh perspectives.[7] The dividends of this team-teaching experience eventually took the form of an integrative book I authored on the topic.[8] So, for me at least, community intellectual fellowship has proven advantageous to my individual scholarship.

Interpretive Problems and Issues

Of course, controversy regarding how to interpret crux texts in the Bible is inevitable. When this happens, we need to reexamine our methods of interpretation—our exegesis. Have we assumed a particular interpretation after a superficial reading of the text without doing the hard work of exegesis? Is our interpretation artificially predisposed toward subjective results because of an inherited tradition, a popular ideology, a social conviction, a political bias, or the psychological influences of the spirit of our age? In the face of these influences, valid exegesis is a trustworthy accountability partner—all that Paul professes in 2 Timothy 3:16, "All Scripture is inspired by God and profitable for teaching, for reproof, for correction, for training in righteousness."

We also need to be aware of possible (often unintentional) fallacious reasoning on the part of those we are reading or with whom we are dialoguing about a tough passage. Over the years, I have heard various forms of the following arguments that have had the result of rendering a passage irrelevant or hopelessly obscure.

---

7. The class and some of our findings were featured in a cover story article in *Christianity Today*: see Tennant, "Possessed or Obsessed," 46–63.

8. Arnold, *3 Crucial Questions*.

There Are So Many Views on This Issue, No One Can Ever Really Know the Answer

While there are a variety of views expressed on most interpretive issues, this does not mean that every view is equally valid or that the issue is insoluble. Careful exegesis is a refining fire, often separating the spurious from the true. Therefore, wise exegesis has to be patient. It will not settle for premature conclusions.

There Are Respectable Scholars on Both Sides of This Issue (So We Cannot Know for Sure)

Another form of exegetical malpractice takes the form of simplistic appeal to the reputations of the scholars involved in the discussion. One cannot presuppose the accuracy of respected scholars' exegesis, simply because all scholars sometimes get it wrong. Augustine, Luther, Calvin, Wesley, Edwards, as great as they were, all made miscalculations on occasion—a humanness shared by celebrity Christian scholars today. Good scholars can make errors of judgment. Perhaps the exegetical issue falls outside their area of expertise or their conclusion has failed to take into account all the evidence. Or, perhaps they have been unduly influenced by cultural pressures, social pressures, or traditions within their guild. Simplistic appeals to authority, especially when they align with our personal biases, can condition us to forego the hard work of exegesis to settle for comfortable but unsubstantiated conclusions.

It Is a Cultural Matter (So the Passage Is Irrelevant to Us)

Sometimes people appeal to the unique cultural setting of a passage and then contend that its teaching is irrelevant to us because we do not share the precise setting as the original hearers of the biblical text. This approach is highly problematic because there is usually a deeper theological conviction that is informing a contingent application of that truth in a particular context. It is important for us to remember that all of Scripture is wrapped in specific cultural settings because this is how God has chosen to reveal himself.

I remember hearing a well-respected scholar declare that when he was preaching through the text of 1 Peter, he would skip the slavery passages because we no longer have this immoral institution in our society. Yet this way of approaching the text fails to take into account that there is much we can learn from these passages that inform how we respond in different kinds of authority structures that may be part of our culture, such as employer-employee relationships. It also fails to take into account the suffering of others in our world today who do suffer literal slavery or a form of enslavement related to sex trafficking. Finally, the dismissal of a text because of its historical distance overlooks the fact that understanding contemporary culture is impossible without understanding the historical factors that produced contemporary culture. The global problem of racism, for example, ties directly to social dynamics of previous centuries.

This New Understanding Is the Best
(So Your View Is Outdated and Unacceptable)

Beware of the urge to favor new views on interpretive issues. Because they are untested, they may have flaws yet to be discovered. As you engage with competing views on a particular interpretation, try to discern when the alternative view was first expressed and if it has been thoroughly substantiated with sound exegesis. If not, it is wise to suspend judgement on the new perspective until conclusive exegesis warrants a final judgement. Remember that the Bible has been studied, taught, and preached for over two thousand years. A radically new, accurate interpretation is unlikely. Professional exegetes will be quick to tell you that avant-garde proposals often stem from the inventiveness of a scholar seeking an "original" publication (a measurable achievement that secular scholarship prizes). Unfortunately, the result in these cases is not true exegesis, the extracting of the intended meaning from the text, but eisegesis, the reading of foreign ideas into the text. Exegesis, it must be remembered, is not revision, rewriting, or embellishing, but accurate interpretation and explanation of the author's original intent.

That Passage Is in the Old Testament
(So the Passage Is Irrelevant to Us)

Sometimes in popular debate, people assume that the Old Testament is "old" because it is outdated. The Torah, the prophetic texts, and the historical writings are regarded as more artifactual than relevant. While it is true that Paul describes Christ as the "goal" of the Law (Rom 10:4), this does not mean the Torah is obsolete. We need a much more nuanced approach to the Law that recognizes that it not only anticipates the coming of the Messiah, but it also reveals the holiness and righteousness of God. It provides us with a framework that informs the New Testament writers on how we can walk and please God and thereby fulfill the command, "You shall be holy, for I the LORD your God am holy" (Lev 19:2; 1 Pet 1:16).

Prioritizing Defining Passages to the Detriment of the Comprehensive Revelation of Scripture

There is a human tendency to absolutize select passages of Scripture while muting or explaining away other passages in order to accommodate a desired theological perspective. In extreme cases this maneuver practices theology on the construct of a humanly constructed "canon within the canon." The danger with this approach is that it can lead to misinterpretation of both sets of passages. Martin Luther fell prey to this by stressing grace to such an extent that he could no longer accommodate the canonical book of James. James's emphasis that "faith apart from works is useless" (Jas 2:20; see also 2:26) offended Luther, so he dismissed James as "a right strawy epistle." Hasty simplifications of this kind preempt discovery of the internal integrity and theological coherence of the entire Bible and the inspirational power of the rejected parts of the Bible. We would be the poorer without the wisdom book of James. In addition, that "faith without works is dead" is a truth that both Jesus and Paul support elsewhere in Scripture (Matt 25:14–46; Rom 2:6–10). Such is not evidence for a "works based salvation" but the truth that authentic faith in Christ manifests itself in loving acts that evidence the presence of Christ in the life of the believer. To be a follower of Christ is to participate actively in his ministry.

We have to resist the urge to reconfigure Scripture so that it conforms to our preferred theological constructs. Evangelical Christians should be vigilant to resist theological idolatry by devoting ourselves to sound, objective exegesis.

Conclusion

In his presidential address to the International Society for New Testament Studies, Martin Hengel chided the guild for becoming too specialized. He quipped, "A New Testament scholar who understands the New Testament alone *cannot* rightly understand it at all."[9] He argued for a new horizon in which NT scholars would be proficient in OT studies and the ancient Near

---

9. Hengel, "Tasks of New Testament Scholarship," 67–86.

East, early Judaism, the Greco-Roman world, the biblical languages, and early patristics.

As intimidating and demanding as this challenge may be, Hengel was right. While New Testament scholars are wise to build upon an area of in-depth expertise, we, too, share the responsibility of understanding our expertise within the broader contexts of history and indeed all the legitimate arenas of academic inquiry. Friendship across the curriculum is to our advantage.

For faculty in a Christian university setting, this is an expansive vision. How can one be an expert in their own discipline while being conversant in biblical exegesis and other related fields? The answer is not a second or third PhD, but honest, patient engagement in sound exegesis that speaks to the issues of our day. Sound exegesis is a prerequisite of disciplinary integration of faith and learning.

Prefaced by prayer and enabled by the Holy Spirit, exegesis is sheer joy, the delights myriad. As Leonard Goppelt put it, "The representation of the theology of the New Testament is the summit, as it were, to which the arduous mountain paths of New Testament exegesis lead."[10] Sustained exegesis is like walking a path on the way to the summit of a mountain. As we traverse the trail, we find beautiful lakes, springs and waterfalls, wildflowers, meadows, and rock formations at every turn. Then, at the arduous journey's end, we discover a breathtaking panorama that makes the journey's labor eternally satisfying. For the end of biblical exegesis is the acquisition of eyes to see, ears to hear, hearts to love, and minds to acknowledge the awesome creativity and infinite wisdom of our God.

Bibliography

"2016 The Freshman Survey (TFS) Infographic Codebook." https://www.heri.ucla.edu/infographics/TFS-2016-Infographic-Codebook.pdf.
Arnold, Clinton E. *3 Crucial Questions about Spiritual Warfare*. Grand Rapids: Baker, 1997.
Bartholomew, Craig G. *Introducing Biblical Hermeneutics*. Grand Rapids: Baker, 2015.
Bauer, Walter, et al., eds. *A Greek-English Lexicon of the New Testament and Other Early Christian Literature*. 3rd ed. Chicago: University of Chicago Press, 2001.
Blomberg, Craig L. *A Handbook of New Testament Exegesis*. Grand Rapids: Baker, 2010.
Burtchaell, James T. *The Dying of the Light: The Disengagement of Colleges & Universities from their Christian Churches*. Grand Rapids: Eerdmans, 1998.

---

10. This analogy was inspired by Leonhard Goppelt, who wrote, "the representation of the theology of the New Testament is the summit, as it were, to which the arduous mountain paths of New Testament exegesis lead, and the vantage point from which one can look back upon them" (*Ministry of Jesus*, xxv).

Carson, Don A. *New Testament Commentary Survey*. 7th ed. Grand Rapids: Baker, 2013.

DeRouchie, Jason S. *How to Understand and Apply the Old Testament*. Phillipsburg: P&R Publishing, 2017.

Dockery, David S. "Introduction: Shaping a Worldview." In *Shaping a Christian Worldview: The Foundation of Christian Higher Education*, edited by David S. Dockery and Gregory Alan Thornbury, 1–15. Nashville: B&H Academic, 2002.

Duvall, J. Scott, and J. Daniel Hays. *Grasping God's Word*. Grand Rapids: Zondervan, 2012.

Evans, John F. *A Guide to Biblical Commentaries and Reference Works*. 10th ed. Grand Rapids: Zondervan, 2016.

Fee, Gordon D., and Douglas Stuart. *How to Read the Bible for All Its Worth*. 4th ed. Grand Rapids: Zondervan, 2014.

Goppelt, Leonhard. *The Ministry of Jesus in Its Theological Significance*. Vol. 1 of *Theology of the New Testament*. Translated by John Alsup. Grand Rapids: Eerdmans, 1981.

Hengel, Martin. "Tasks of New Testament Scholarship." *Bulletin for Biblical Research* 6 (1996) 67–86.

Liddell, Henry George, and Robert Scott. *A Greek-English Lexicon*. 9th ed. Oxford: Oxford University Press, 1996.

Longman, Tremper, III. *Old Testament Commentary Survey*. Grand Rapids: Baker, 2013.

Naselli, Andrew D. *How to Understand and Apply the New Testament*. Phillipsburg: P&R Publishing, 2017.

Osborne, Grant R. *The Hermeneutical Spiral*. Downers Grove: InterVarsity, 2007.

Tennant, Agnieszka. "Possessed or Obsessed." *Christianity Today* 45.11 (September 2001) 46–63.

3

The Theology of Wisdom

Creation as Context;
Christ as Content;
Canon as Curriculum

KEVIN J. VANHOOZER

THE OPENING LINE OF John Calvin's great work, *Institutes of the Christian Religion*, serves as the perfect introduction to the present chapter: "Nearly all the wisdom we possess ... consists of two parts: the knowledge of God and of ourselves."[1] Calvin then ups the ante by claiming the two parts of knowledge are inseparably related: "Without knowledge of self, there is no knowledge of God ... and without knowledge of God there is no knowledge of self." Socrates got it wrong: we cannot "know ourselves" by introspection only. We are a puzzle to ourselves unless we look beyond ourselves, up unto the heavens, where dwells our creator and whence comes our help. In the words of Augustine: "You have made us for yourself, and our heart is restless until it rests in you."[2]

Introduction: What Is Theology?

Theology is the study of God. If Calvin and Augustine are right, theology also answers the riddle of human existence. First and foremost, however,

---

1. Calvin, *Institutes* 1.1.1.
2. Augustine, *Confessions*, 1.1.

theology is the quest to know and speak well of God. As an academic field, the terrain is both difficult and dangerous. Difficult, because God is not like other objects that we can examine or experiment on; dangerous, because to make a mistake in this field is to lapse into either blasphemy or idolatry, two kinds of mortal foolishness that fail to ascribe appropriate worthiness to God and thus lead to false worship, devotion to what is not God.

The right way to do theology is to learn *from* God how to think and speak *about* God. The medieval adage remains helpful: "Theology is taught by God, teaches of God, and leads to God."[3] The starting point lies with God making himself known: "revelation." God reveals himself in deed and word: in the history of Israel, Jesus Christ, the church, and in the Old and New Testament Scripture that records and interprets this unified history. Christian theologians accept the Bible as God's Word, God's own interpretation of his mighty acts. The whole of the Bible recounts the true story of the world from beginning (the creation) to end (new creation), the center of which is the story of Christ and his cross.

Though some things can in principle be known about God through "general" revelation simply by observing the natural order (Ps 19:1; Rom 1:19–20), this "natural" theology ultimately falls short. It falls short in the first place because self-interested sinners distort the data (Rom 1:21–25), but also because it leaves out the truths of "special" revelation, namely, all the things God has freely said and done that show him to be not simply the creator but the LORD of the covenant who made a promise to Abraham to bless all the families of the earth through his family. The gospel of Jesus Christ is the fulfillment of this promise, God's word made man, and therefore God's most eloquent and definitive revelation. "Gospel" means good news; the subject matter of Christian theology, the goodness and the grace of God poured out in Jesus Christ, is not only good news but the best news we can hear. Theology is therefore "that delightful activity in which the church praises God by ordering its thinking towards the gospel of Christ."[4] There is joy in doing theology because the object of theology is joyful news: "God is with us; God is for us!"

Christian theology does not begin empty-handed, then, but with gratitude for the prophetic and apostolic testimony to God's loving purpose in history. To speak well of and know the God of Abraham, Isaac, Jacob, and Jesus Christ requires trust in the reliability of the Scriptures, what the apostle Paul calls the "good deposit" (1 Tim 6:20; 2 Tim 1:14). It is precisely

---

3. Sometimes (mistakenly) attributed to Thomas Aquinas, as in Turretin, *Institutes*, 2.

4. Webster, *Holiness*, 8.

this good deposit of which theologians are called to be guardians and stewards. Augustine may have got there via a mistranslation of Isaiah 7:9, but his principle was nevertheless sound: "If you will not believe, you will not understand." Perhaps the most cited definition of theology is Anselm's "faith seeking understanding" (*fides quaerens intellectum*). Theology begins in faith, accepting the truth of Scripture's testimony about what God is like and what God has done. Reason plays a vital role, however, in making sense of what Scripture says: its presuppositions, entailments, and implications, making explicit what is often only implicit. Theology is thus the science of what faith knows from special revelation.

Theology is essentially the attempt to think biblically about God, the world, and ourselves. The overlap with biblical studies is undeniable, yet there are two important differences. Whereas the focus of biblical studies is largely historical and descriptive (i.e., determining what happened and what the biblical authors meant), theology is the normative attempt to say what the church today is to believe about God on the basis of the Scriptures. In particular, theology wants to hear what God is saying to the church today and to discern how his word relates to all areas of contemporary life in order to respond rightly to God's living address. In sum: theology is the study of God and all things in relation to God insofar as God has revealed these things in Scripture.

Theology differs from biblical studies, secondly, in its fundamental practical orientation: glorifying God and cultivating godliness. This may come as a surprise to many who associate theology with abstract theorizing about matters on which we can only speculate. This is indeed a danger: not idolatry but *idle knowledge*. It is not enough to believe or know the truth: "even the demons believe" (Jas 2:19). Christian believers must act on what they know; otherwise, their knowledge is fruitless—stillborn. The truth of the gospel must be done. Faith demonstrates knowledge by *obeying* the truth (Rom 2:8), *walking in step with* the truth (Gal 2:14), and *practicing* the truth (1 John 1:6). The Puritan theologian William Ames puts it well: "Theology is the doctrine or teaching of living to God."[5] Doctrine that remains only in theology textbooks is like prescription medicine that is never taken.

Theology also differs from philosophy. Both involve wisdom—not simply theoretical knowledge (*scientia*) but the practical knowledge of what is useful for human flourishing (*sapientia*)—yet the end of philosophy is the good life, whereas theology aims for the godly life, and right relationship to God. Theology, then, is the search for a very particular kind of knowledge:

---

5. Ames, *Marrow of Theology*, 77.

the knowledge of how to live well, with others, in the world to the glory of God.

In what follows I shall expound on this insight in a number of theses that explore creation as the context of godly wisdom, the person and work of Jesus Christ as the content of godly wisdom, and canonical Scripture as the pedagogical means of coming to learn this godly wisdom. However, if we are to understand theology as a kind of wisdom, it will be helpful first to review the story of theology's on-off relationship with the university.

Theology in the Academy: A Brief History

It is surely significant that the university had its origins in Medieval Christianity. Higher education took place in monastic or cathedral schools until the eleventh century, and these also became the first universities of Bologna (1088), Paris (ca. 1150), and Oxford (1167). Theology occupied pride of place, the so-called "queen of the sciences." The various disciplines of the uni-versity were indeed uni-fied in an integral framework. C. S. Lewis refers to this Medieval synthesis as "the whole organisation of their theology, science, and history into a single, complex, harmonious mental Model of the Universe."[6]

The universe was one because everything could be referred back to God. Saint Bonaventure begins his 13th-century treatise, *On the Reduction of the Arts to Theology*, by citing James 1:17: "Every good and perfect gift is from above, coming down from the Father of lights." Bonaventure believed that all forms of human knowing ultimately serve one chief purpose: to lead us back to God, their source and goal.

Bonaventure's "reduction"—from the Latin *re* + *ducere*, a "leading back" (to God)—has nothing to do with the reductionism that too often characterizes modern sciences that betray an overconfidence in reason and claim too much for their own discipline, as if reality were "nothing but" matter, or love "nothing but" behavior aimed at propagating our genes to the next generation, or religion "nothing but" wish fulfillment. Now, physics, sociobiology, and psychology all have important contributions to make towards knowledge, but when they seek to be autonomous, and reject a theological framework, these forms of reductionism more easily become seductive idols and ideologies. Charles Taylor has documented the way secularization has taken root in the modern university.[7] When everything is viewed in this-worldly terms only, reality is naturalized and there is no

---

6. Lewis, *Discarded Image*, 11.

7. Taylor, *Secular Age*.

room for the supernatural in the university inn. One way of describing the history of the Western university is to chart the path from theism to deism and finally atheism (i.e., metaphysical and methodological naturalism). Theology is no longer queen of the sciences in the modern university ("Off with her head!"), but in exile, her place usurped by autonomous reason and religious studies (i.e., the study of human religious behavior). The modern secular university has, for all intents and purposes, become a theology-free zone.

John Henry Newman saw the secular handwriting on the wall of the ivory tower in the middle of the nineteenth century, when he addressed a series of nine discourses on *The Idea of a University* to the University of Dublin. Newman argued that theology deserved to stay in the university for, without it, the web that connects the various disciplines would unravel. This unraveling of the sense of a coherent whole would also exacerbate the tendency to adhere to one's own discipline's way of looking at things. Newman rightly saw that reductionism – the tendency to generalize about everything on the basis of the truths of one's own specialization—could be held in check only by theology. Theology is the index of each discipline's incompleteness, not because theologians know more (they don't) but because the object of theology, God the creator, exceeds the limits of the created order, and thus of the reach of any science, *including* theology itself.

Theses on Theological Wisdom

Unlike most academic specializations, theology does not deal with problems that can be solved and then forgotten, but with mysteries to be entered into, explored, and inhabited. Doctrines are conceptual summaries of the story of Scripture: the nature of its protagonists, the meaning of the events, and the coherence of its plot. The Bible tells the true story of God, the world, and ourselves. It is a mystery story, or rather, a revelation of the mystery story, the mystery being: how can ungodly and unholy creatures enter into a right and righteous relationship with an infinitely holy God? Christian doctrine is an aid to reading this story rightly for the sake of a right relationship with God. The doctrine of the Trinity, that God is one being in three persons, is theology's deepest mystery. Yet it is also the answer to the revelation of the mystery at the heart of the story of the Bible: ungodly sinners enter into right relationship with God the Father thanks to their union with God the Son effected through God the Holy Spirit.

Theology's proper aim, in addition to deepening our relationship to God, is the cultivation of godly wisdom. The purpose of doctrine is not simply to state truths but to make disciples, people who have the mind of Christ. In particular, *doctrine helps disciples by fostering the ability to understand, discern, and then do what is required to embody the mind of Christ in specific situations.* Let me now explain how theology fosters Christian wisdom in nine theses under three headings: creation, Christ, and canon. Taken together, these nine theses provide a model of best theological practice, a practice that begins in faith, continues in hope and joy, and ends in greater love for God and neighbor.

Creation as Context for Theological Wisdom (The Teleological Principle): Knowing God the Father

1. *The theological wisdom that leads to human flourishing depends on understanding the whole created order in which we live, move towards our end, and have our being.*

In order to live well we must know our proper end or purpose. Things work best when they are used for the purpose for which they were made. I learned this the hard way as a ten-year-old when I substituted a paper clip for a lost screw in my skateboard. The paper clip broke within seconds, the front wheels fell off, and I went sprawling and broke my arm. What I had thought was cleverness proved me a fool instead. I now know what screws, and paper clips, are for. What are humans for?

The doctrine of creation teaches us that humans exist with a specific nature designed for a specific purpose: we are creatures in God's image, appointed stewards of his creation. This is our design plan, our proper function. Everything that exists, as created by God, has a nature and a purpose, an ontology and a teleology. While other creatures fulfill their nature simply by existing (a rose by any other name would smell as sweet), humans have the terrifying ability to deny their true natures, to choose to malfunction, and thereby fail to image God.

God's laws are not arbitrary impositions that constrain human freedom but rather laws for the right use of human freedom, enabling conditions of human flourishing. For example, the command to have no other gods before Yahweh (Exod 20:3) is not an oppressive gesture of religious ideology but a way of preventing human beings from devoting their lives to something unworthy or illusory. There is no flourishing in the service of an idol.

Theological wisdom involves living in harmony with the real world, which is not a spontaneous combustion but an intelligent creation. To know ourselves as being in the world is thus to know ourselves as having a nature (ontology) and purpose (teleology) determined by God the Creator. Wisdom involves understanding, the capacity to perceive patterns and to grasp the whole created order of which the human creature is but a part. To understand who we are as humans is to know how to fit in to the rest of the created order.

2. *Theological wisdom requires attention not only to the big picture (the created order) but also to the particulars of our created context in order to discern what is fitting to say and do in a given situation.*

The wise person discerns how to participate fittingly in the created order. Thomas Aquinas defines practical wisdom or prudence as knowing the right thing to do and the right way to do it.[8] Yet creation is complex, and often different situations call for different types of response. Practical wisdom thus needs to attend closely to the particulars of our immediate context in order to determine a fitting course of action. For example, is it fitting to our human creatureliness and glorifying to our Creator to conceive babies in test tubes, or to genetically modify embryos in order to prevent a disabling condition, or to assist a terminally ill person to end her life? Such bioethical issues require not only understanding of our origins and destiny, but knowledge of concrete particulars.[9]

Theologians need the insights of the other academic disciplines in order to come to an adequate knowledge of particular problems and situations. Yet this knowledge alone is often not enough to help us discern what to do. If we are to give theologically thick descriptions of the particular situations in which we find ourselves, we need to relate the findings of other academic disciplines to the bigger story of which we are a part: the story of the creation, fall, and redemptions of creatures in the image of God. Wisdom is the ability to discern what creatures in God's image should do in particular situations given the larger story in which they are caught up, namely, the story of God's creation of and love for the world.

3. *Theological wisdom is a quality of persons who give practical demonstrations of their understanding, doing everything to the glory of God by participating rightly in the created order.*

The kind of wisdom theology seeks goes beyond information or head knowledge. It cannot be reduced to the terabytes of information stored in computer memories. Nor is it simply theoretical, a matter of *knowing that*. It is one thing to know how to fly a plane in theory, quite another to pilot a jet safely to the ground. Wisdom is intelligence that knows the big picture, is aware of its particular situation, and has learned from experience. The wise

8. Thomas Aquinas, *Summa Theologica* I-II.A.57.5.
9. See further Kilner, *Why the Church Needs Bioethics*.

person not only knows what is fitting to do in particular situations, but goes on to do it. The process of becoming wise is short-circuited when we do not *live* what we know.

Knowledge alone cannot help us. We have to know what to do with our knowledge if we wish to pursue the end for which we were created, namely, to flourish in creation, live well with others, and glorify God. Theological wisdom is a form of responsibility to God. Just as it is impossible to please God without faith (Heb 11:6), so it is impossible to be truly wise without acknowledging God as God, author of the created order and the original of which we are pale images. Henri Blocher writes: "man can know reality in truth, and thus steer his course in life, only if he proceeds in the knowledge of God, and acknowledges his absolute LORDship."[10]

The "the fear of the LORD" is the font of all wisdom (Ps 111:10; Prov 9:10). We see that wisdom is a matter not only of discerning what is right but also the willingness to do what is right, and in the right way. Theological wisdom is thus an intellectual awareness of how to act in God-honoring ways in particular situations, a moral disposition to do so, and the form the ensuing action takes. In sum: Christian wisdom is the ability to see, judge, and act in the world in ways that correspond to the created order.

Christ as Content of Theological Wisdom (The Material Principle): Knowing God the Son

4. *The sum of all wisdom is comprehended in Christ.*

The New Testament identifies Jesus Christ as the wisdom of God (1 Cor 1:24). This does not contradict what we said earlier about wisdom as conformity to the created order, however, for "by him all things were created, in heaven and on earth, visible and invisible . . . all things were created through him and for him" (Col 1:16). The apostle Paul goes on to say that in Christ are hidden "all the treasures of wisdom and knowledge" (Col 2:3). How can we make sense of that?

Jesus is the paradigm of Christian wisdom not simply because he was a teacher of wisdom (there have been others) but because in a unique way he revealed and embodied God's own wisdom. Jesus is the definitive revelation of God, the fulfillment of the law, the key to the meaning of the whole created order. More than that: Jesus is the prudence of God insofar as it is in him that God acts righteously to bring all things into right relationship with him. Christ is the wisdom of God and it is "in Christ" that we find both the knowledge of God and of ourselves.

10. Blocher, "Fear of the LORD," 17.

Elsewhere I have described the task of theology as saying *what is* "in Christ."[11] In Christ, there is "the fullness of God" (Col 1:19) and Jesus is "the radiance of the glory of God and the exact imprint of his nature" (Heb 1:3). Yet in Christ there is also the fullness of humanity, the true "image of God" (2 Cor 4:4).[12] Most importantly, in Christ there is right-relatedness – reconciliation—with God. Christ marks the place where God works out the salvation of the world. Therefore, if we want to know where the story of human being begins and ends, we had best look to Christ.

5. *The summit of all wisdom is concentrated in the cross of Christ.*

We have seen that wisdom involves knowing how fittingly to participate in the created order. However, the created order has fallen into disorder, an evil that is frequently the topic of biblical wisdom literature: why do the righteous suffer and the wicked prosper? The problem of evil throws an ugly wrench into the homespun wisdom of Proverbs.

The whole that Christian wisdom strives to understand is not simply the created order as fallen but the created order as it is being renewed in Jesus Christ. The ultimate framework of Christian understanding is not a theory about the cosmos but a story about the Christ. This is the difference between the wisdom of Socrates and the wisdom of Jesus. Socrates thought that reason could reach eternal truth, yet eternal truth is instead revealed where the world least expected it: in the story of a Galilean carpenter.

What is in Christ is reconciliation with God, yet we only come to understand this by following the whole biblical story. Yet even those following the story of God's choice of Abraham's seed to be a holy nation through which all nations would be blessed would be confounded by the way God accomplished his purpose. The cross marks the spot where God justifies the ungodly in a way that does not diminish his godliness. The crucifixion of Jesus, what from the world's eyes was a tragic, horrendous, and shameful event, in God's good plan becomes the right way to make all things right. Stated differently: Jesus' atoning death on the cross was the enacted wisdom of God, the wisdom of God made broken flesh.[13] Theological wisdom is a matter of cruciform fittingness, of bringing our thoughts about God, the world, and ourselves into line with the story of the gospel.

6. *Disciples aim to embody and enact the cruciform, counter-cultural wisdom of the way of Jesus Christ.*

---

11. Vanhoozer, *Faith Speaking Understanding*, 231.

12. For more on how Christology is essential to theological anthropology, see Cortez, *ReSourcing Theological Anthropology*.

13. See Johnson, *Reconciling Wisdom of God*.

It is not enough to admire Jesus Christ: disciples must take up their own crosses and follow him (Mark 8:34). Disciples do not need to suffer in order to bring about reconciliation with God; only Christ's suffering does that. Rather, the cruciform way of discipleship is the form witness to God's wisdom takes. The challenge of discipleship is to live out the new reality that has come to be in Christ.

Disciples follow Jesus by acting out his life in them in their own particular circumstances and situations. The way of the cross may look like weakness or folly to a world that tends to equate human flourishing with the headlong selfish pursuit of this-worldly wealth, fame, and glory (1 Cor 1:18). Theological wisdom takes the long view, putting the things of this world into the perspective of eternity. Viewed against the backdrop of heaven, short-term earthly gains appear as the puny things they are: "For what will it profit a man if he gains the whole world and forfeits his soul?" (Matt 16:26).

The acid test of Christian discipleship is fitting participation in the story of what God the Father is doing in God the Son through God the Holy Spirit to make all things new. Doctrine helps the church to make disciples by deepening their understanding of who God is, what God is doing in Christ, and to what end. Instructed by Christian doctrine, disciples grow in wisdom as they see, judge, and act their way through ordinary life by saying and doing what corresponds to the gospel of Jesus Christ.

Canon as Curriculum of Theological Wisdom (The Formal Principle): Knowing God the Holy Spirit

7. The Scriptures provide both the spectacles of faith (Calvin) and the framework of understanding that coordinates these two lenses (OT and NT) and focuses them on Christ.

Can wisdom be taught? Paul says that the sacred writings, the canonical Scriptures of the Old and New Testaments, are "able to make you wise for salvation through faith in Christ Jesus" (2 Tim 3:15). The evangelical theologian Bernard Ramm develops an analogy where Scripture is the textbook, the Holy Spirit the teacher of truth (cf. John 14:26), the church a schoolroom, and disciples the pupils.[14] The Bible is a crucial element in the divine pedagogy—a canonical curriculum. Calvin likens the Scriptures to eyeglasses that enable us to see the world as a theater of God's glory.[15] The Bible (the book of special revelation) allows us to read the book of nature

---

14. Ramm, *Witness of the Spirit*, 57.
15. Calvin, *Institutes* 1.6.1.

(general revelation) more clearly and distinctly. Just as importantly: the Bible allows us to see the history of Israel, Jesus, and the church as a theater of the gospel. Of course, the spectacles work only when the Holy Spirit enlightens darkened understanding, illumining readers so that they can see and hear what God is saying.

Wisdom involves understanding how things fit together in God's created order, and the biblical narrative is an indispensable cognitive instrument for helping people to see the whole. The whole in question is the story of its creation, fall, and redemption that centers on Christ. The Bible teaches wisdom by recounting the story that puts everything in its proper place. Imagination is an essential ingredient in wisdom inasmuch as it is the imagination that enables us to view the biblical story as a unified whole rather than as an assemblage of unrelated parts. The first essential imaginative move is seeing how the story of Jesus is the continuation and fulfillment of the history of Israel. It takes theological imagination to see that the God who brought Israel out of Egypt is also the Father who brought Jesus out of the grave.

8. *Imagining our place and time in history—the "real" world—as part of and in terms of the story of the Bible is the continuation of wisdom.*

Wisdom is the ability to see, judge, and do the right thing in a particular situation. The Bible makes us wise unto salvation, but not by serving as a moral calculus. It takes wisdom to know which biblical principles to apply, and where, when, and how to do so. Yet wisdom involves more than the application of principles. It also has to do with learning to locate oneself in the biblical story. Theological understanding of the Bible involves learning to think not simply about but *along* the biblical texts, the story-shaped framework for understanding God and ourselves. Scripture makes us wise unto salvation not simply by giving us information or principles but by transforming our imaginations so that we begin to participate fittingly in the story it tells. This is one of the principal means the Spirit uses to guide the church into all the truth (John 16:13).

All too often we get our moral bearings from social conventions or from stories drawn from elsewhere than Scripture. Other pictures of the "real" world—for example, the story Darwin tells about the propagation of genes from one generation to the next—hold the world's imagination captive. The books of the Bible teach us wisdom, first, by debugging the programs that have captured our imaginations and, second, by reorienting them to the way things truly are and are coming to be in Jesus Christ. The Spirit uses the Bible to train our imaginations to discern the way all things hold together in Christ (Col 1:17). In this way, the various books of the Old and New Testaments minister reality by narrating what is really happening in human history.[16]

9. *We learn how to discern what is fitting to say and do as disciples, and how to make right theological judgments, by becoming apprentices to the unity-in-diversity of the whole Christ-centered canon.*

The fact of the matter is that Christians today are in the same redemptive-historical situation as that of the authors and readers of the New Testament: between the first and second comings of Jesus Christ. Though our cultural and social context may be different, we are part of the same drama of redemption. In this sense, then, we are their apprentices, "learning from them how to understand Christ (and all things) in the light of Scripture and Scripture (and all things) in the light of Christ."[17]

What disciples learn from their apprenticeship to the biblical authors is biblical wisdom: an understanding of how Old and New Testaments—and, indeed, all things—fit together in the story of Jesus Christ.[18] Yet this understanding too must be demonstrated in practice. Readers of the Bible display wisdom when they are able to embody the mind of Christ in their own particular circumstances, acting out the part of faithful disciples in new cultural scenes and historical contexts. Scripture makes readers wise unto salvation by training them how to speak and act in ways that live out the life of Christ in them. In Calvin's words: "Nothing shall ever hinder me from openly avowing what I have learned from the word of God; for nothing but what is useful is taught in the school of this master. It is my only guide, and to acquiesce in its plain doctrines shall be my constant rule of wisdom."[19]

As a form of wisdom, theology as I have presented it here is not simply an academic subject but a way of life. Indeed: living to God is the ultimate theological project. Doctrine directs disciples to do whatever they do, in word of deed, to the glory of God, embodying the mind of Christ in the power of the Spirit. Theology may today be marginalized in the halls of academe, but the church must consider it as of first importance, for nothing is as important as learning Christ (cf. Eph 4:20), the wisdom of God (1 Cor 1:24).

---

16. For more on the relation of imagination, Scripture, and wisdom, see Vanhoozer, *Pictures at a Theological Exhibition*, esp. 17–46.

17. Starling, *Hermeneutics as Apprenticeship*, 19.

18. See further Vanhoozer, "Love's Wisdom."

19. Calvin, *Letters of John Calvin*, 330.

Bibliography

Ames, William. *The Marrow of Theology*. Translated by J. D. Eusden. Grand Rapids: Baker, 1968.

Aquinas, Thomas. *Summa Theologica*. 5 vols. Notre Dame: Christian Classics, 1981.

Augustine. *Confessions*. Translated by Henry Chadwick. Oxford: Oxford University Press, 1991.

Blocher, Henri. "The Fear of the Lord as the 'Principle' of Wisdom." *Tyndale Bulletin* 28 (1977) 3–28.

Calvin, John. *Institutes of the Christian Religion*. Edited by John T. McNeil. Library of Christian Classics 20. Philadelphia: Westminster, 1960.

———. *Letters of John Calvin*. Eugene, OR: Wipf & Stock, 2007.

Cortez, Marc. *ReSourcing Theological Anthropology: A Constructive Account of Humanity in Light of Christ*. Grand Rapids: Zondervan, 2018.

Johnson, Adam J. *The Reconciling Wisdom of God: Reframing the Doctrine of the Atonement*. Bellingham: Lexham, 2016.

Kilner, John F., ed. *Why the Church Needs Bioethics: A Guide to Wise Engagement with Life's Challenges*. Grand Rapids: Zondervan, 2011.

Lewis, C. S. *The Discarded Image: An Introduction to Medieval and Renaissance Literature*. Cambridge: Cambridge University Press, 1964.

Ramm, Bernard. *The Witness of the Spirit: An Essay on the Contemporary Relevance of the Internal Witness of the Holy Spirit*. Grand Rapids: Eerdmans, 1959.

Starling, David I. *Hermeneutics as Apprenticeship: How the Bible Shapes our Interpretive Habits and Practices*. Grand Rapids: Baker Academic, 2016.

Taylor, Charles. *A Secular Age*. Cambridge: Harvard University Press, 2007.

Turretin, Francis. *Institutes of Elenctic Theology*, Vol. 1. Translated by George Musgrave Giger. Phillipsburg: P&R Publishing, 1992.

Vanhoozer, Kevin J. *Faith Speaking Understanding: Performing the Drama of Doctrine*. Louisville: Westminster John Knox, 2014.

———. "Love's Wisdom: The Authority of Scripture's Form and Content for Faith's Understanding and Theological Judgment." *Journal of Reformed Theology* 5.3 (2011) 247–75.

———. *Pictures at a Theological Exhibition: Scenes of the Church's Worship, Witness, and Wisdom*. Downers Grove: InterVarsity, 2016.

Webster, John. *Holiness*. Grand Rapids: Eerdmans, 2003.

4

Philosophy as the Love of Wisdom
James S. Spiegel

When I came to Belhaven College as a freshman in the early 1980s, I had no idea what major to choose, let alone what career to pursue. So I consulted my youth minister, Tony, for advice. I was disappointed when he was unable to peg me for a particular career and even more so when he left me with this counsel: "One day, Jim, you'll meet someone and think, 'I want to be just like that person,' and that's how you'll know what career to pursue.'" Uh huh. Right. Thanks, Tony. I walked away thinking this was the lamest advice I'd ever heard.

From there I proceeded to major in Biology, figuring I might go into medicine. I did well in my coursework, but my science classes never inspired me. The only classes that managed to scratch where my soul really itched were in the humanities—literature, the arts, and especially philosophy, where we discussed human nature, goodness, beauty, and the meaning of life and wrestled with big issues like free will and the problem of evil. We also delved into the nature of knowledge itself, even probing the foundations of science, asking questions about my major field that no other Biology majors seemed to care much about. As my scientific interests faded, my philosophical curiosity grew.

All of this philosophical inquiry at Belhaven was guided by a single individual—Dr. Wynn Kenyon, a one man Philosophy department. Kenyon was as unique an individual as I've ever known. A sturdy figure, both physically and intellectually, he possessed a rare combination of analytical skills and "big picture" understanding. One moment he would be explaining a subtle point on the doctrine of essences, and the next he would show the implications of that point for the entire history of modern philosophy and theology. Despite his intellectual prowess, Kenyon was humble and even boyishly playful. He was a practical jokester and seemed to appreciate being the butt of jokes as much as playing jokes on others. On top of this, he was a wonderful family man—a loving husband and tender, dedicated father. Kenyon was the whole package. A wise Christian man, completely committed to helping others grow in wisdom.

So I took as many classes as I could manage from this man, while also fulfilling all of the requirements for the Biology major. But midway through my senior year, I still had no idea what to do with my life. So one evening during Christmas break, I prayed for guidance, some sort of leading as to the direction God would have me go. As I prayed, Dr. Kenyon came to mind. And then it occurred to me that *I wanted to be just like him*. Not only that, *I wanted to do what he does*—devote my entire life to the pursuit of wisdom and help other people do the same. Tony's counsel wasn't lame after all, I smilingly realized. In fact, my life trajectory actually pivoted on that advice, and for the last quarter century I've been teaching Philosophy at a Christian liberal arts college much like Belhaven, striving to emulate my wise mentor, Dr. Kenyon.

The Meaning of Philosophy

The word "philosophy" literally means "love of wisdom," which should make the subject an easy sell in a book like this, focusing as it does on gleaning wisdom from the academic disciplines. But this is misleading, for a couple of reasons. For one thing, it appears that most contemporary philosophers don't conceive of their work as essentially involving the pursuit of wisdom. In a recent compendium of definitions of "philosophy" from noted Western philosophers, only a small fraction of the respondents even mentioned wisdom as a goal or main concern of philosophy.[1] If this is reflective of the academic philosophy guild generally, then it seems that somewhere along the line my discipline abandoned its original purpose. More on that shortly.

Secondly, the Greek root for "wisdom" in the word "philosophy" is not exactly what is intended in the title and focus of this book. The term is derived from *philo* (love) and *sophia* (wisdom), hence philosophy as "the love of wisdom." But *sophia* denotes *theoretical* wisdom, which is significantly distinct from the sense of wisdom suggested by the other Greek term *phronesis*, which refers to *practical* wisdom. A person may excel in the area of theoretical wisdom yet fail miserably as a moral specimen. In fact,

---

1. Edmonds and Walburton, *Philosophy Bites*.

some of the most brilliant philosophers in Western history have been moral wretches.[2]

In philosophy, to possess *sophia* is to have theoretical understanding of issues in logic, metaphysics, science, and so on. Such insights, however, do not essentially involve human conduct, what it means to be good or to live well. *Phronesis*, in contrast, is all about practical moral insight. To unpack this concept, it is helpful to consult Aristotle, who defined *phronesis* as "a reasoned and true state of capacity to act with regard to human goods."[3] In other words, it is a kind of discernment regarding the best courses of action in various life situations. So while it is an intellectual virtue, *phronesis* is necessary for moral excellence. Without it, Aristotle maintained, a person can't be morally virtuous. We find the same idea in Thomas Aquinas's account of *prudentia*, which he understood as "good counsel about matters regarding man's entire life and the end of human life."[4] In agreement with Aristotle, Aquinas claimed, "There can be no moral virtue without prudence."[5]

So for Aristotle, the common core of *sophia* and *phronesis* is insight. Both traits are intellectual virtues, cognitive skills which enable a person to gain understanding, though their objects differ somewhat (theoretical truths in the case of *sophia* and practical moral truths in the case of *phronesis*). From a Christian perspective, both forms of wisdom are of crucial importance. All Christians are called to *phronesis*, as is evident in the fact that moral insight is necessary for living the life of virtue to which the Scriptures call us. On a daily basis the Christian life calls for moral judgments regarding all sorts of issues, from situations in our personal lives to matters of national public policy. And the pursuit of *sophia* is no less important for Christians, as our call to engage culture (as Paul models for us in Acts 17) and to "demolish arguments" opposing the Gospel (2 Cor 10:5) requires a high level of theoretical understanding. We may assume the same regarding Peter's exhortation to "always be prepared to give an answer to everyone who asks you to give the reason for the hope that you have" (1 Pet 3:15). Adequate preparation for this naturally presupposes a theoretical foundation, and to excel in this apologetic task requires a strong knowledge base in a number of areas, given relevant issues in cosmology, origins, the metaphysics of divine personhood, biblical manuscript historicity, and Jesus studies, to name just a few major subject areas.

---

2. For some disturbing but enlightening exposes of numerous instances of morally corrupt scholars in the canon of Western minds, see Johnson, *Intellectuals* and Jones, *Degenerate Moderns*.

3. Aristotle, *Nicomachean Ethics*, 1140:20–21.

4. Thomas Aquinas, *Summa Theologica* I-II.57.4.

5. Thomas Aquinas, *Summa Theologica* I-II.58.4.

So both theoretical and practical wisdom are important intellectual virtues. Now how does the study of philosophy aid the Christian in her pursuit of them? I was fortunate enough to cut my philosophical teeth under a professor who was committed to both *sophia* and *phronesis*. You might say that Dr. Kenyon was essentially a latter-day American edition of Socrates, whose undying (and dying) devotion to both forms of wisdom profoundly influenced his immediate philosophical descendants, Plato and Aristotle, and through them set the intellectual agenda for Western civilization for the next two and half millennia. Their approach still constitutes the methodological core of what it means to do philosophy. And as we will see, both this method and some of their central doctrines are highly relevant to the Christian pursuit of wisdom.

Socratic Philosophy

It all began in the 5th century BC when the Oracle at Delphi—a priestess who reputedly spoke for the god Apollo—declared that Socrates was the wisest man in Athens. When word of this got back to Socrates, he was incredulous and decided to refute this claim by finding someone wiser than himself. Here commenced his notorious street interviews, as Socrates began to accost people with reputations for wisdom to find one person with knowledge about matters regarding which Socrates took himself to be ignorant. He inquired about basic concepts, such as goodness, knowledge, beauty, and justice. But he discovered that those who were most widely regarded as wise actually had fewer reasons for their beliefs and were less patient than the so-called ignorant.

Eventually, after each interview Socrates found himself concluding, "He thinks that he knows something which he does not know, whereas I am quite conscious of my ignorance. At any rate it seems that I am wiser than he is to this small extent, that I do not think that I know what I do not know."[6] In this fashion, the Oracle's declaration was confirmed. But along the way, Socrates's street interviews put him at odds with Athenian leaders and eventually led to his indictment for impiety. More specifically, the charges were religious heresy (failure to worship the state gods) and corrupting the youth (undermining trust in the Athenian leaders). Socrates defended himself in court and lost, resulting in his receiving the death penalty, via hemlock.

It was not long before even the Athenian leaders realized their tragic mistake, as a bronze statue honoring Socrates was erected soon after his execution. It became clear to nearly everyone that the snub-nosed gadfly

6. Plato, *Apology*, 21d.

really was a virtuous teacher and had the best interest of Athens at heart. So the man has since been honored in the West, but more than this, his unique method became definitive for doing philosophy. A major aspect of Socrates's approach is *elenchus*—systemic logical scrutiny through critical cross-examination. It involves dialogue, conversation between two or more people, whether or not this culminates in agreement on the issue discussed. The essential features of *elenchus* are:

1. *Asking questions*—whether sincere or ironic, a carefully posed question is the most important tool for the serious seeker of truth;

2. *Defining terms*—clarifying the meaning of key concepts in order to prepare the way for sound argumentation and to avoid vagueness, ambiguity, and other roadblocks of inquiry;

3. *Exposing ignorance and hidden assumptions*—the posing of questions invariably reveals the limits of one's understanding and generates awareness of important presuppositions;

4. *Using arguments*—it is not enough to appeal to authority, emotion, or popular opinion to back up one's views; truth claims must be tethered with good reasons which provide evidential warrant for one's beliefs.

For Socrates, *elenchus* was the active pursuit of virtue both for the individual and the community. It was for this that Socrates toiled and gave his life as a moral prophet for the sake of his fellow Athenians. This pursuit of virtue, being an essentially moral endeavor, distinguishes the Socratic approach as a quest for *phronesis* rather than mere *sophia*. For Socrates, practical and intellectual pursuits were inseparable. And when it came to ethics, he insisted, to know the good is to do it. Genuine moral knowledge entails a lifestyle consistent with the virtues about which one has insights. But more than this, Socrates held that virtue has a divine source, claiming that "real wisdom is the property of God."[7] Today this dimension of the Socratic moral quest is rejected by most of the Western philosophical community.

Socrates's student Plato and his student Aristotle fully embraced Socrates's approach to philosophical inquiry, both methodologically and, in many respects, doctrinally. So convinced was Plato of the importance of precisely defining terms that he devoted entire dialogues to this task, including temperance (*Charmides*), courage (*Laches*), goodness (*Euthyphro*), love (*Symposium*), knowledge (*Theaetetus*), and justice, (*Republic*). Aristotle, likewise, placed a primacy on carefully defining terms, and he formalized both this and the use of Socratic questioning with a rigorous application of

---

7. Plato, *Apology*, 23a.

conceptual categories.[8] Plato and Aristotle also heavily stressed the importance of virtue and developed elaborate analyses of essential moral traits.[9] Both recognized that a civil society cannot flourish without a citizenry that is morally virtuous.[10] As regards moral development, they agreed that virtue is not teachable (in the way that one would teach math or history, for example). Plato concluded from this that virtue must come by divine dispensation. Aristotle, however, maintained that virtue can only be acquired through intentional practice and habit formation. But Plato and Aristotle were both strong believers in teleology—the notion that there are ends or purposes in nature, including all aspects of human life and human nature itself. Aristotle even incorporated teleology into his causal theory of change.[11] Finally, both Plato and Aristotle defended the theistic convictions of Socrates, each advancing causal arguments for the existence of God and bringing this reality to bear on a variety of philosophical inquiries, including ethics, aesthetics, physics, and metaphysics.

So there were many shared methodological and doctrinal convictions among Socrates, Plato, and Aristotle. I will refer to these collectively as "Socratic philosophy." As I noted, it is a tradition which deeply influenced Western cultural history and, at least methodologically, remains largely intact in the Western academy today, though it is somewhat truncated, as key doctrinal elements, specifically related to views on human nature, the centrality of virtue, and the reality of God, are subtracted in many quarters.

This presents a challenge, then, as we proceed to consider how the field of philosophy is critical for Christian higher education. For one may ask whether we mean philosophy as practiced today or as originally conceived and practiced by the ancient Athenian patriarchs of the discipline. Depending on how we answer this question, some key moral and anthropological elements of Socratic philosophy will either be included or ignored. So, for the sake of clarity, I will distinguish between the *formal* aspects of Socratic

---

8. All of Aristotle's works feature extensive discussion of conceptual categories used to analyze the topics he discusses, but his numerous logical treatises, including *Categories*, *Topics*, *On Interpretation*, *Prior Analytics*, and *Posterior Analytics*, dwell almost entirely on conceptual categories and definitions.

9. Plato discusses virtue in numerous dialogues, but nowhere as extensively as in his *Republic*. And Aristotle wrote two ethical treatises: *Eudemian Ethics* and *Nicomachean Ethics*.

10. One of Plato's primary claims in the *Republic* is that a just society is one where each major domain of the state (workers, soldiers and rulers) fulfills its function, and specific virtues are necessary for the fulfillment of those functions (temperate workers, courageous soldiers, and wise rulers). Similarly, for Aristotle the virtue of the citizens is essential for a just state. See his *Politics*, book 3.

11. See especially Aristotle's *Physics*, book 2, chapters 3–8.

philosophy (i.e., *elenchus*: asking questions, defining terms, identifying presuppositions, and using arguments) and its *moral-anthropological* aspects, specifically human teleology (the idea that human beings have a fixed nature or essence) and aspects of the doctrine of virtue. It is clear that philosophical studies, as practiced in the mainstream academy today, substantially provide formal *elenchus* training that is crucial for all students in higher education, whatever their field of study. And, from a Christian perspective, it is also clear that the moral-anthropological elements of Socratic philosophy, while not always affirmed in the mainstream philosophical guild, are nonetheless valuable aspects of this tradition that may also benefit students in Christian higher education. In what follows I will unpack some benefits of both when it comes to the Christian's wisdom quest.

Formal Aspects of Socratic Philosophy

Elenchus is valuable for Christian higher education because it is valuable for *all* education. In every academic discipline, truth is pursued, whether that is truth about history, science, mathematics, the arts, or anything else. And wherever truth is pursued, there will be dialectical inquiry—the use of reasoning and argumentation to defend truth claims. What was Robespierre's role in the French Revolution? How old is the Earth? Can the Riemann hypothesis in mathematics be proven? Is *One Flew Over the Cuckoo's Nest* best classified as a comedy or a tragedy? Our answers to such questions (even if one's answer is that they are *un*answerable) must be defended, and this can be done adequately only if we carefully define our terms, ask probing questions related to the subject matter, and identify and assess the presuppositions we bring to the issues. That is to say, the Socratic method of *elenchus* is critical to our quest for truth regarding these and all other instances of rational inquiry.

Now suppose someone challenges this point, claiming that we don't need to use this method. One may insist, instead, that we may proceed via intuition or simple common sense to just as effectively access truth. Or suppose someone scuttles the whole notion of truth, as Pontius Pilate seemed to do in the face of Jesus, sardonically asking, "What is truth?" Along these lines, one might side with the pragmatists and insist that all that matters is what works in practice, or with the postmodern perspectivalists and say that there is no "truth" but only local points of view. Whatever skeptical attitude one might bring against the Socratic approach, notice that their skeptical posture may be undermined with the simple question: Why believe *that*? Why believe that *intuition* is more reliable than evidence gathering and argumentation as a path to truth? Why believe that what is *practical* is all that matters (or that, sans truth, practical outcomes are even possible)? And why believe that there are only *local perspectives* and no universal truths? Answers to these questions return us to the process of *elenchus*, prompting all sorts of further questions and arguments in defense of the alternative views proposed. So these aspects of the Socratic method are actually unavoidable. We all depend upon these formal processes for the acquisition of truth. The only question is whether we do so in a careful and disciplined way.[12] It is the aim of philosophical training to ensure that we develop and sharpen these formal skills so we can be the most effective learners possible, whatever we happen to be studying.[13]

Socratic Philosophy and the Acquisition of Virtue

As noted earlier, contemporary Western philosophers are generally on board with the formal aspects of Socratic philosophy but not as much so with the moral-anthropological aspects. In part, this is a reflection of the academy's drift away from theistic assumptions which prevailed in the West throughout most of history. Socrates, Plato, and Aristotle were all theists of a sort, not only affirming the existence of God but, in the case of the latter two, also offering extensive arguments in defense of theism. With this theistic foundation the notion of an abiding human *telos* and a thick concept of virtue are coherent, reasonable ideas, whereas outside of a theistic conceptual framework, they are difficult to sustain. But, to whatever degree they can be incorporated into higher education in the mainstream academy, they are crucial for *Christian* higher education and the pursuit of wisdom.

Throughout Scripture we are called to embody the moral virtues or, as the apostle Paul refers to them, the "fruit of the Spirit," which include love, joy, peace, patience, kindness, goodness, faithfulness, gentleness and self-control (Gal 5:22). But *how* are we to heed this call? How do we *become* morally virtuous in these ways? There are different theological schools of thought on this question, which vitally concerns the relationship between knowledge and virtue. It is interesting to note that Socratic philosophy

12. That philosophical knowledge is a prerequisite for expertise in *every* academic discipline is signified by the fact that experts in various fields have an earned PhD—a doctorate of Philosophy.

13. It is noteworthy that Jesus Christ's teaching method featured many aspects of *elenchus*, especially the use of rhetorical questions and appeals to evidential justification. In terms of argument forms, Jesus was particularly fond of the use of *a fortiori* and *reductio ad absurdum* arguments. For more on Jesus' logical techniques, as well as other aspects of his philosophical orientation, see Groothuis, *On Jesus*.

provides helpful resources for understanding and reinforcing two major, but apparently conflicting, perspectives on the issue. Plato endorsed the "divine dispensation" view, which says that we grow in virtue by divine fiat, as God spiritually endows us with these traits, whereas the Aristotelian "habituation" view says moral virtue is attainable only through active training.

Beginning with the divine dispensation thesis, Plato was convinced that this follows from the fact that (1) people are not virtuous by nature and (2) virtue cannot be taught, so it must be acquired somehow. But if it is not acquired through other people, then it must have a supernatural source, namely God. As Plato puts it, "Virtue will be acquired neither by nature nor by teaching. Whoever has it gets it by divine dispensation without taking thought."[14] Plato's claim here seems to be corroborated by Scripture in such passages as James 1:17: "Every good and perfect gift is from above, coming down from the Father of the heavenly lights, who does not change like shifting shadows," and 2 Peter 1:3: "His divine power has given us everything we need for a godly life through our knowledge of him who called us by his own glory and goodness." As for the virtue of wisdom in particular, there is biblical evidence that this is acquired by prayer. Solomon asked the LORD for wisdom, and he granted this request (1 Kgs 3:1–15). And James says, "If any of you lacks wisdom, you should ask God, who gives generously to all without finding fault, and it will be given to you" (Jas 1:5). It would appear, then, that Plato is correct in claiming that moral virtue, including wisdom, comes by divine dispensation.

Aristotle readily granted that moral virtue is not teachable. Intellectual virtues can be taught, he maintained, but not such moral traits as courage, temperance, wisdom, and justice. However, he rejected Plato's notion that this implies that moral virtues come by divine dispensation. Rather, he claimed that such traits are the product of doing virtuous acts, which settle into habits and eventually harden into a stable character. The courageous person became that way because he or she repeatedly did courageous things. Similarly, on the negative side, for the cowardly person. As Aristotle puts it, "States of character arise out of like activities. This is why the activities we exhibit correspond to the differences between these. It makes no small difference, then, whether we form habits of one kind or another from our very youth; it makes a very great difference, or rather *all* the difference."[15] There is strong biblical support for this habituation view of virtue. Paul writes,

> Do you not know that in a race all the runners run, but only one gets the prize? Run in such a way as to get the prize. Everyone

14. Plato, *Meno* 99e–100a.
15. Aristotle, *Nicomachean Ethics*, 1103:21–25.

> who competes in the games goes into strict training. They do it to get a crown that will not last, but we do it to get a crown that will last forever. Therefore I do not run like someone running aimlessly; I do not fight like a boxer beating the air. No, I strike a blow to my body and make it my slave so that after I have preached to others, I myself will not be disqualified for the prize. (1 Cor 9:24–27)

And elsewhere he tells us, "train yourself to be godly. For physical training is of some value, but godliness has value for all things, holding promise for both the present life and the life to come" (1 Tim 4:7–8).

So who is right here? Which view should we endorse—Plato's divine dispensation view or Aristotle's habituation view? Since Scripture seems to affirm the insights of both sides, perhaps we would be wise to consider the possibility that both views provide genuine insights into the matter. Some further biblical clues would encourage such a balanced approach. Numerous passages essentially command us to have faith (e.g., Prov 3:5–6; Mark 1:15; John 14:1; Acts 16:31; Heb 11:6; 1 John 3:23), but we are also told that "it is by grace you have been saved, through faith—and this is not from yourselves, it is the gift of God" (Eph 2:8–9). So when it comes to the virtue of faith, could it be that it is both a gift *and* a work that we do? Or better, perhaps the work of faith that we engage in is *itself* a divine gift. In that case, it would appear that faith comes both by divine dispensation *and* by personal choice and habituation. In other words, both views are correct. And if we extend this insight about faith to all moral virtues, then we might say that both Plato and Aristotle are correct, though each seized on a particular facet of a broader truth.

What I have tried to illustrate in this section is that Socratic philosophy provides helpful resources for thinking about the acquisition of virtue—resources which enhance our ability to be morally discerning and to make good choices in life. And, of course, this is the stuff of *phronesis*.

Conclusion

In highlighting and applying the Socratic philosophical tradition, I have tried to show how (1) the universal methodological "core" of the discipline is beneficial for all human learning and (2) some distinctive themes within this tradition are especially valuable for nurturing Christian wisdom. Regarding this latter endeavor, if space allowed we could see how other philosophers and schools of thought from ancient to contemporary times provide insights about issues in ethics, theology, psychology, aesthetics, metaphysics, epistemology, cognitive science, linguistics and many other areas of thought, the advancement of which nourishes the Christian mind, expanding our understanding of God, his world, and our place in it. There is a vast sea of literature on all of these topics, though not without its Scylla and Charybdis. Many hazards lurk in the writings of the Humes, Marxes, and Nietzsches, and even some Christian allies, but there are precious gems as well. If we proceed with caution and care, the potential benefits for growing in wisdom are myriad.

It has been said that if you do what you love, you'll never have to work a day in your life. This is how I feel about my work as a philosophy professor. I am being paid to pursue wisdom and to share the joy of this endeavor with young people. As a profession it could not dovetail more perfectly with my calling as a Christian. I follow in the footsteps of fellow lovers of wisdom, from Socrates to my mentor Wynn Kenyon. And like them I proceed on the conviction that all wisdom is a gift from God.

Bibliography

Aquinas, Thomas. *Summa Theologica*. 5 vols. Notre Dame: Christian Classics, 1981.
Aristotle. *Nicomachean Ethics*. Translated by W. D. Ross. *The Basic Works of Aristotle*. New York: Random House, 1941.
———. *Physics*. Translated by Robin Waterfield. Oxford: Oxford University Press, 2008.
———. *The Politics*. Translated by T. A. Sinclair. London: Penguin, 1981.
Edmonds, David, and Nigel Walburton. *Philosophy Bites*. Oxford: Oxford University Press, 2010.
Groothuis, Douglas. *On Jesus*. Belmont, CA: Wadsworth, 2003.
Johnson, Paul. *Intellectuals*. New York: Harper Collins, 1989.
Jones, E. Michael. *Degenerate Moderns*. San Francisco: Ignatius, 1993.
Plato. *Apology*. In *The Collected Dialogues of Plato*, translated by Hugh Tredennick and edited by Edith Hamilton and Huntington Cairns, 3–26. Bollingen Series 71. Princeton: Princeton University Press, 1961.
———. *Meno*. In *The Collected Dialogues of Plato*, translated by Hugh Tredennick and edited by Edith Hamilton and Huntington Cairns, 353–84. Bollingen Series 71. Princeton: Princeton University Press, 1961.

5

Wise Politics

Classical Philosophy, Medieval Christianity, and the Contemporary World

Paul R. DeHart

Introduction

THE THEORETICAL STUDY OF politics originated in ancient Greece with the work of Plato and Aristotle.[1] Great thinkers of ancient and medieval Christianity, such as Saint Augustine of Hippo and Thomas Aquinas, also engaged the central questions of political order. The advent of Christianity, however, dramatically altered the social, moral, and political topography of antiquity, introducing new ideas and possibilities for the analysis and construction of political order. Christian political thought often borrowed from (and transformed) classical philosophers like Plato and Aristotle. But there are fundamental discontinuities as well.[2]

The architects of modernity rejected the medieval synthesis. Theorists, such as Thomas Hobbes, emphasized power, materialistic determinism (matter in motion determined by prior matter in motion), universal causal laws governing material motion, and the manipulation of nature in light of

---

1. This book's bibliography references the translations of primary sources I cite. I cite the book and line number for Plato and the book, chapter, and line for Aristotle.
2. See Gilson's *Spirit of Medieval Philosophy* and Oakley's *Empty Bottles of Gentilism*.

our knowledge of the laws by which nature is governed.³ Hobbes, among others, held that such laws apply also to human behavior. Contemporary political science has endorsed the modernist idea that political behavior can and should be explained by deterministic causal laws. In this regard, contemporary political science has perhaps been too wed to fallacious philosophies of science. From a Christian perspective, human behavior (political behavior included) is intelligible because it is part of a divinely created universe rationally ordered by eternal law. But human behavior is not fully predictable or determined because human beings possess free will and because human life is subject to contingency. Political life is therefore neither fully determined by causal laws, nor is it random and inexplicable.⁴

The Development of Political Thought from Antiquity to Modernity

Ancient Monarchy

According to historian Francis Oakley, kingship has been the most pervasive political organization in human history.⁵ Monarchy's origins reach into the deep recesses of the Neolithic period. It remained the dominant political order up to the Industrial Revolution in the late 18th century. Ancient kingship (whether in China, Africa, Mesopotamia, or the ancient Near East) was more than just a mode of political organization; it was, according to Henri Frankfort, "anchored in the cosmos."⁶ The purpose of the king was to perform services (or rites) to god (or the gods) in order to maintain cosmic harmony. The king was a god, the son of a god, the special creation of a god, or the unique representative of the god(s). His person was therefore sacred. The entire purpose of human society, with the king at its summit, was religious. Deep in the recesses of time, before written history, political order and religion were not only intertwined, they were inseparable. What we call political order performed a religious function.

Amidst the sea of sacral monarchy occurred something scholars denominate the "republican parenthesis": a period in which a new political order emerged among the Greek *poleis* (plural for the Greek polis, which has been rendered *city* or *city state*).⁷ It was in one such polis (or city) that

---

3. See Hobbes's *Leviathan or the Matter*.

4. See MacIntyre, *After Virtue*, 88–108.

5. This paragraph draws heavily upon the account of ancient monarchy described in Oakley, *Empty Bottles of Gentilism*, especially 18–39.

6. Frankfort, *Kingship and the Gods*, 344, cited in Oakley, *Empty Bottles of Gentilism*, 19.

7. Oakley, *Empty Bottles of Gentilism*, 32.

political philosophy was born. And at the zenith of Greek political reflection stand Socrates, Plato, and Aristotle, who developed their arguments in ethics and politics in response to a group of teachers that had descended on Athens called Sophists.

The Sophists

The Sophists were itinerant teachers who offered to teach the sons of Athenians how to succeed in Athenian life by means of making persuasive arguments. Sophists deemed the task of persuading others more important than truth itself. At the fountainhead of Greek Sophism stands Protagoras who taught that "man is the measure of all things, of those that are that they are, of those that are not that they are not."[8] For Protagoras, human perception determines reality. He concluded that justice is nothing more than a convention or creation of human communities—justice is whatever a particular polity decides it is. Thus, justice is relative, varying from one community to another.

Another Sophist, Thrasymachus, famously defined justice as "nothing but the advantage of the stronger party."[9] By this he meant that in any polis there is a contest for power. When one party (perhaps the property-less or the wealthy few) acquires political power, they lay down laws that serve their advantage, and they call anyone who fails to follow these self-serving laws a lawbreaker and unjust. Justice is just a label that refers to obeying whatever those with the most power command.

Still other Sophists offered different accounts of justice. Common to all of them is the notion that justice is neither universal nor objective but constructed by each community for itself. Political order is therefore nothing more than power relations. Some Sophists (like Protagoras) counseled obeying the law (following conventional justice) because no society's code of law is truer than any other's; there is therefore no basis for setting one's own judgment against the judgment of the community enshrined in law.[10] Others (like Antiphon) advised obeying the law when necessary to avoid punishment and disobeying whenever breaking the law is advantageous and one can get away with it.[11] For the Sophists, whether or not to follow the requirements of justice was merely a matter of prudential calculation and self-interest.

8. Cited in Copleston, *History of Philosophy*, 87.
9. See Plato's *Republic*, 1.338b–39a.
10. Copleston, *History of Philosophy*, 90.
11. See the excerpt from Antiphon included in Steinberger, *Readings in Classical Political Thought*, 26.

Socrates, Plato, and Aristotle

Socrates, Plato, and Aristotle rejected the ethical relativism advanced by the Sophists (the view that right and wrong vary across time and place or even from individual to individual) and their related claim that justice is entirely a matter of a particular community's laws and conventions. While Socrates never addressed the classical question concerning the best kind of political order or regime, he held that the true political art is concerned with virtue and the best possible condition of the soul.[12] He claimed that it is never just to commit injustice—never right to do wrong.[13] In other words, Socrates rejected relativism and consequentialism (the view that right and wrong depend on what actions produce the best consequences). Socrates also held that the true political art is not primarily public; indeed, he considered it dangerous to practice the art publicly.[14] Socrates's student Plato, however, was very much concerned with public political order and its relation to the soul.

In *The Republic*, Plato examined the nature of justice and whether or not anyone has good reason to be just. In the first book Plato has the protagonist of the dialogue, Socrates, address Thrasymachus's contention that justice is really just the interest of the stronger party. Socrates argues that political power is only rightly exercised when it is exercised for the good of those who are ruled rather than for the benefit of those who rule (I.342e and 347b–e). Plato's brothers Glaucon and Adeimantus then pose a more difficult challenge (II.358e–67e). They want Socrates to show that justice is both good in itself and beneficial. In response, Socrates argues that the virtue of justice pertains both to the rightly ordered self and to the rightly ordered political community. In both the just (or health) soul and the just political community each part occupies its proper place and performs its proper function (IV.433a–34a, 435b–c, 441d–e, 443c–e). In the polis this means philosopher kings should rule auxiliaries who both defend the republic and govern workers (artisans or craftsmen) (V.473d). In the individual, justice pertains to the rightly ordered soul in which reason rules the spirited part (or *thumos*: the seat of anger, shame, fear, courage, honor), which in turn rules the appetites (hunger, thirst, bodily pleasure, the desire for wealth) (IV.441e–42a). In both the just city and the just person, that which exercises rule takes its bearings from an objective and transcendent good (VII.518c–19c).

---

12. Plato, *Apology*, lines 30a–c.

13. Plato, *Apology*, lines 28b–c, 31a, 32b–e; *Crito* in *The Trial and Death of Socrates*, 49a–b.

14. Plato, *Apology*, lines 31d–32e.

In his last great work, *The Laws*, Plato's protagonist, the Athenian Stranger, argues that "laws which are not established for the good of the whole [polis] are bogus . . . and people who say those laws have a claim to be obeyed are wasting their breath." That is, in order for law to be law it must be for the common good and not merely an enactment for the benefit of a part of the community. As well, the Athenian Stranger insists that in a successful polis "law is the master of the government and the government is its slave," and those who are usually called "rulers" should instead be considered "servants of the laws" (IV.vi.715–16). A polis where the rule of law is absent is, he says, on the verge of collapse.

While Aristotle's political science is more directed to empirical analysis than Plato's, it also takes its bearings from the objectivity of the good. In his *Politics*, Aristotle claimed that every association exists for some good purpose. In all their actions, after all, human beings aim at some good (whether real or apparent). And the human association that aims at the highest and most authoritative good is the most authoritative association. The political association—or polis—is just such an association (I.i.1252a1). Aristotle grounds this claim in the further claim that the polis is self-sufficient (I.ii.1252b27).

We can see what Aristotle means by considering his view that the polis is an association of associations (I.ii.1252b27). The household (which includes husband and wife, children, and servants) is comprised of individuals. Individuals form households because they cannot live—and certainly cannot live well—on their own (I.ii.1252a34–b9). But it turns out that households are not capable of adequately providing the goods of human life by themselves. So households associate into villages. Villages allow for greater provision of the basic goods of human life (I.ii.1252b15). But they cannot defend themselves against invasion. Villages therefore associate together to form a polis.

The polis came into existence for the sake of living, says Aristotle. It continues to exist, however, for the sake of wellbeing: "The [polis] is an association intended to enable its members, in their households and kinships, to live *well*. Its purpose is a perfect and self-sufficient life" (III.ix.1280b29). Consequently, the polis exists "to provide something more than a military pact of protection against injustice or to facilitate mutual acquaintance and exchange of goods" in which "neither side is concerned with the [virtue or vice] of the other, or with preventing the behavior of any person covered by the agreements from being unjust or wicked, but only with the prevention of injustice as between each other." Rather, "all who are anxious to ensure government under good laws make it their business to have an eye to the virtue and vice of the citizens" (III.ix.1280a34). That which is truly called a polis "must concern itself with virtue. Otherwise the association is a mere alliance differing only in location and restricted territorial extent from an alliance whose parties are at a distance from each other; and under such conditions law becomes a mere agreement, or, as Lycophron the sophist put it, 'a mutual guarantor of justice', but quite unable to make citizens good and just" (III.ix.1280a34).

While government and law in a stable polis concern themselves with the formation of good and just citizens, virtuous citizens prioritize the good of the polis above the advantage of the individual, household, or village. Though the polis is comprised of these various parts, the polis is a whole greater than the sum of its parts. Thus, whenever there is a conflict between the good of the whole and the advantage of a part, the good of the whole—the common good—ought to prevail. Aristotle famously compares the polis to a body and the parts to limbs. A limb like the hand only has its particular function—and so is only properly a hand—in light of its relation to the whole. He takes this to illustrate the priority of the whole to any part (I.ii.1253a18).

Aristotle's Regime Classification

Political theorist George Klosko notes that Aristotle and his students at the Lyceum catalogued and analyzed the constitutions of 158 Greek *poleis* (city-states).[15] Aristotle classified them along two dimensions: the number of rulers (the one, the few, and the many) and the orientation of rule (whether toward the good of the whole or the selfish advantage of the ruler[s]). In just regimes political rule is exercised for the common good; in corrupt regimes power is exercised for the benefit of those who rule. Aristotle identified six regime types. Three orient toward the common good: kingship (rule by the one best person for the good of the whole), aristocracy (rule by the few with the most wisdom and virtue), and polity (a regime in which both the few and the many have a role in political rule). And three orient toward the selfish advantage of those who rule: tyranny (rule by the one for his own gain), oligarchy (rule by the very wealthy, who are usually few, at the expense of the many), and democracy (rule by those with little property, who are usually many, for their individual benefit) (III.vii.1297a32–b4).

Aristotle proceeds to rank these different regimes from best to worst. Kingship is the best because kingship is rule by one outstanding person who significantly outstrips everyone else in the wisdom to discern and virtue to pursue the common good (III.xvii.1288a8–a15). Tyranny is corruption of or deviation from kingship, and "[D]eviation from the first and most divine must be the worst." Consequently, tyranny is the worst. Aristocracy is the

---

15. Klosko, *History of Political Theory*, 117.

second best and oligarchy the second worst. Polity is the least good (but still just) and democracy the least bad (IV.ii.1289a38). Aristotle's polity is a mixed regime in which the demos (the property-less) and the oligarchs (the very rich) hold each other in check, while true aristocrats (individuals of wisdom and virtue) or the middle class (which, though just as self-interested as oligarchs or the demos, behaves as if it is virtuous *when following its own interest*) can throw their weight behind whichever side (oligarchs or demos) is promoting law or policy most in keeping with the common good (IV.ix).

While Aristotle holds kingship to be the absolutely best regime, he does not take it to be the best for most people in most times and places. Most societies lack a citizenry possessed of sufficient virtue to sustain kingship or aristocracy. Polity is the best regime for most societies given the virtue of the people. Thus, Aristotle's political science takes its bearing from the absolute best, but focuses on the sort of regime most appropriate for a people *given their character or virtue* (IV.xi.1295a25).

The Christian Revolution

The Christian revolution radically reshaped the moral, social, and political topography of the ancient Greco-Roman world. Where the ancient pagan world neither separated nor distinguished civil government from worship of the gods, early Christians (perhaps drawing on the rejection of kings performing religious rites in Hebrew Scripture evident in Samuel's criticism of Saul in 1 Samuel 13:8–14 and certainly on Jesus' teaching regarding the lawfulness of paying taxes to Caesar [Mark 12:13–17]) posited distinct jurisdictions for civil government and administration of the church. What we call the separation of church and state was not a modern innovation or an Enlightenment idea, it was the outworking of Christian revelation. The same is true of religious liberty.

In a letter to the Roman proconsul Scapula written in response to the persecution of Christians in Carthage, Tertullian (AD 160–220) claimed, "It is also a person's human right (*humani iuris*) and inborn capacity (*naturalis potestatis*) to worship whatever he intends; the religious practice of one person neither harms nor helps another. It is no part of religion to coerce religious practice, for it is by free choice not coercion that we should be led to religion."[16] Tertullian thus conjoined a natural right to worship as one sees fit with the idea that religious practice must be voluntary and not compelled. The notion that religious observance must be freely chosen entails the idea that the church is a voluntary society. Moreover, this voluntary society is distinct from the political and social order of any particular place.

16. Tertullian, *Ad Scapulam*; cited in Wilken, "Christian Roots of Religious Freedom," 64.

The church represents a cross-cutting allegiance: It draws members from various societies but is coterminous with none of them. Consequently, allegiance to this new society—which Saint Paul calls the polis of heaven and the assembly of God—could come into conflict with the demands of one's temporal polis or assembly.[17]

Early Christians proclaimed that Jesus of Nazareth was the Messiah for whom Israel had been waiting *and* that he was Lord. In the Roman empire, however, Lord was a title that belonged to Caesar. Moreover, upon his consolidation of rule over the empire, Caesar Augustus announced his gospel of Roman peace and justice. In his letter to Roman Christians, Saint Paul announced the gospel of Lord Jesus, the Messiah. In so doing the apostle took the language Roman emperors used to describe their rule and authority and applied it to one crucified on a Roman cross—the ultimate symbol of imperial might. On Saint Paul's view, Caesar claimed allegiance and authority that belonged to Jesus of Nazareth.[18]

At the same time, in Romans 13 Paul maintains that political authority is established by God. Paul's ascription of Lord—an official title of Roman emperors—to Jesus and his claim that human government is established by God together entail that Jesus is Lord *over* Caesar *and* that Caesar (or human government) has been delegated a limited realm of responsibility *under* the Messiah. This vision of political order animates the early Christian martyr Polycarp's exchange with the Roman proconsul Stadius Quadratus, who ultimately sentenced Polycarp to death. When told to revile Christ, denounce his followers, and swear by Caesar's guardian spirit, Polycarp replied, "For eighty and six years I have been his servant, and he has done me no wrong; how can I blaspheme my King [*basileus*] who has saved me?" Polycarp invoked Jesus' kingship as the basis for refusing to obey the command of those administering the civil government. He also held that civil rulers are "appointed by God."[19] Such authorities deserve our respect. But when the commands of civil government conflict with the law of Christ, then those commands must be disobeyed in light of the Messiah's kingship over all kings.

Church and State: Augustine, Gelasius I, and Aquinas

The Christian reframing of the relation between political order and the divine radically desacralized human politics. Augustine's *City of God* rejected

---

17. The Greek word *ecclesia* commonly translated as *church* in the New Testament was the word for an *assembly* of citizens in a Greek *polis*.

18. On Paul's appropriation of Roman imperial language, see Wright, *Pauline Perspectives* and Wright, *Simply Good News*.

19. Polycarp cited in Nicholas Wolterstorff, *The Mighty and the Almighty*, 13.

the pervasive idea that political order exists to perform sacred rites.[20] Augustine viewed the purpose of political order as the maintenance of peace and justice in this life.[21] Political order was *not* responsible for maintaining cosmic harmony or providing the highest good—eternal life. Political order, in other words, was not sacred (V.17, 217). Because political order does not aim at the highest good, Augustine was unconcerned with the type of regime (whether monarchy, republic, etc.) under which Christians live (V.17, 217).

In a letter to the Roman emperor Anastasius written in 494 AD, Pope Gelasius I maintained that God established two distinct jurisdictions and authorities to rule the world—temporal jurisdiction entrusted to secular rulers and spiritual jurisdiction entrusted to the church. Two years later, in the fourth tract of the Bond of Anathema against the Emperor, Gelasius held that emperors (and temporal rulers more generally) had no competence and no jurisdiction in matters entrusted to the church. He also held that priests and bishops ought to obey secular rulers in the realm entrusted to them.[22] This doctrine came to be known as the two-swords doctrine. Gelasius declared that these two swords are to be exercised by different hands and that those who administer temporal government are to stay out of the administration of the church. This is the clearest early Christian articulation of distinct jurisdictions. This distinction notwithstanding, civil authorities continued to appoint bishops and priests until the resolution of the lay investiture controversy in the 12th century.[23] In sum, early Christianity posited a society distinct from polis or empire and a jurisdiction beyond the reach of public authority.

In the high middle ages, Saint Thomas Aquinas synthesized the best of pagan political philosophy with the Christian political vision. For instance, Aquinas defines law as an ordinance of reason for the common good made by the person(s) entrusted with the care of the community and promulgated (that is, made known).[24] Each part of this definition supplies a necessary condition in order for law to bind—for law to impose an obligation on those under it to obey. Thus, a command contrary to the common good, even if

20. On the desacralization of political order in Augustine, see Oakley, *Empty Bottles of Gentilism*, 117–37.

21. This is the implication of Augustine's distinction between the city of God and the city of man (XIV.4, 587–88; XIV.28, 632–33), his claim that the earthly city aims at earthly peace (XIX.14, 940), and his claim that the final good cannot be attained in this life (XIX.4, 918–19). See Augustine, *City of God against the Pagans*. I have cited Augustine by book, chapter, and page number.

22. See "Letter Twelve to Emperor Anastasius" and "The Fourth Tract on the Bond of Anathema" in Rahner, *Church and State in Early Christianity*, 173–78.

23. Oakley, *Mortgage of the Past*, 33–41.

24. *Summa Theologiae* I-II.90.1–4.

made by duly appointed authority, fails to bind in conscience. For Aquinas, as for Plato and Aristotle, law and political order takes its bearing from an objective common good.

With this definition of law in hand, Aquinas analyzes different kinds of law and their relation. Aquinas held that all human beings are under a natural moral law that, in its basic requirements (do good and avoid evil, refrain from theft, preserve human life . . .), binds all persons at all times and in all places. Its basic precepts are universal. They are also known to all persons insofar as they exercise reason (though this knowledge may be latent and inchoate).[25] Human law—the law a community posits for itself—depends on natural law for its power to bind.[26] Human law contrary to natural law fails to impose an obligation to obey. Indeed, human law contrary to natural law is an act of force or violence rather than law in the true sense. Such laws fail to bind. Whether one should disobey depends on the effects of disobedience on the common good. It may be that disobedience would cause a scandal or subvert habits of obedience to good laws. In such cases, obedience may be the best response (not because the law demands it but because of the impact on the common good). But a human law may also contradict the requirements of divine law contained in special revelation. In all such cases one *must* disobey the human law in question.[27] And, importantly, the most basic requirements of the moral law are also requirements of the divine law (for instance, the Ten Commandments). In all cases of conflict between human law and divine law, human law is trumped by the law of Christ.

The architecture of Aquinas's theory of law distinguishes between human law derived from natural law and divine law grounded upon special revelation. And these two distinct laws have different ends that they pursue by different means.[28] Divine law aims at the highest good of eternal happiness. The "purpose" of human law "is the temporal tranquility of the state."[29] Though in his work *On Kingship* Aquinas says that Kings should promote the wellbeing of their subjects in a way that comports with their ultimate end—eternal happiness—he also distinguishes between the governance institutions, constitution, law, and jurisdiction of civil government and that of the church. Human government, for him, seeks the provision of our temporal and natural good in a way compatible with our eternal good

25. *Summa Theologiae* I-II.94, esp. arts. 2, 4.
26. *Summa Theologiae* I-II.95.2.
27. *Summa Theologiae* I-II.96.4.
28. "The form of the community [modus communitatis] to which human law is directed [ordinatur] is different from the form of community to which divine law is directed" (*Summa Theologiae* I-II.100.2, cited in Finnis, *Aquinas*, 224).
29. *Summa Theologiae* I-II.98.1, cited in Finnis, *Aquinas*, 224.

while leaving the administration of spiritual affairs and the performance of religious rites entirely to the church.[30] Moreover, the obligation to obey the commands of secular authority is conditional upon those commands not violating divine law. Aquinas's account of law thus preserves the Western Christian desacralization of ancient political order.[31]

Finally, drawing on the Hebraic idea that human beings are created in the image of God, early Christian thinkers affirmed the natural, moral equality of all human beings. According to the fourth-century Christian writer Lactantius, God "endow[s] us all with moral equality. With him there is no slave or master. Since we all have the same father, so we are all alike his freeborn children."[32] Denouncing the "mad acquisitiveness" of the rich, Ambrose of Milan thundered "Nature knows no rich men; she makes us all poor at birth.... Nature makes no distinctions, either when we are born or when we die. It creates us all equals, as equals it enfolds us all in the grave's embrace."[33] Similarly, Pope Gregory I averred, "[I]t is clear that nature produced all men equal ... Hence all who are over others ought to consider in themselves not the authority of their rank, but the equality of their condition, and rejoice not to be over men, but to do them good. For indeed our ancient fathers are said to have been not kings of men, but shepherds of flocks." He concludes that "man is by nature preferred to brute beasts, but not to other men: and therefore it is said to him that he should be feared by the beasts but not by men; since to wish to be feared by one's equal is to be proud against nature."[34]

The political implications of natural equality remained to be drawn out by later Christian thinkers steeped in ancient and medieval theology. According to Francisco Suarez, a seventeenth-century Thomist, "in the nature of things all men are born free; so that, consequently, no person has political jurisdiction over another person, even as no person has dominion over another; nor is there any reason why such power should, [simply] in the nature of things, be attributed to certain persons over certain other persons, rather than *vice versa*."[35] The sixteenth-century Anglican divine Richard Hooker similarly held that "all" human beings are "equals in nature." He also held that "without consent" there is "no reason that one man should take upon

---

30. See Finnis, *Aquinas*, 322: "[T]he Church has its own governing arrangements, its own constitution and law ... and its own mission and jurisdiction."
31. Oakley, *Mortgage of the Past*, 102–18.
32. Lactantius, *Divine Institutes*, 52.
33. Ambrose, "Story of Naboth," 76.
34. Gregory I, "Pastoral Rule, Part 2," 197.
35. Suarez, *Treatise on Laws*, Book III, Chapter II, 430.

him to be LORD or judge over another" because "the assent of them who are to be governed seemeth necessary."[36]

Conclusion

The Christian revolution shattered the unity of ancient political order, whether monarchy, republic, or empire, and rearranged the pieces. Where ancient political order fused politics and religious observance, Christianity distinguished man's highest good and its provision from his natural, temporal good and its provision. Christianity then assigned the concern for the highest good to divine law and the church rather than to civil government. Thus, the Christian revolution lowered the horizon of civil government. Christianity also introduced the natural equality of individuals and the notion that human persons possess free will. Indeed, it was Christianity that gave birth to the idea that each person has a natural right to religious liberty, because one's religious practice should be a matter of free choice rather than coercion.

In addition to discontinuities with ancient political practice, ancient and medieval Christian political thought also appropriated Plato's and Aristotle's commitment to the rule of law rather than men. The medieval British cleric and jurist Henry de Bracton aptly summed up the view of law and political authority in the Christian middle ages: "The King is under the Law for it is Law that maketh him a King."[37] According to C. S. Lewis, for Bracton, as for Aquinas, "political power (whether assigned to king barons, or the people) is never free and never originates. Its business is to enforce something that is already there, something given in the divine reason or in the existing custom."[38] Put another way, political power is not power over the community but a power that derives from it. Consequently, political power is considerably limited by custom and by natural and divine law. Those in authority (whether king, nobles, or the people) are not free to govern arbitrarily or to dictate however they see fit. Rather, such persons should be controlled by law.

At the dawn of modernity in the 16th century a new conception of law and political authority took hold. Originally called the Divine Right of Kings, the 17th-century British philosopher Thomas Hobbes understood

---

36. Hooker, *Of the Laws of Ecclesiastical Polity*. The first passage is from 1.8.7; the second from 1.10.4.

37. Bracton, *De Legibus* 1.8, cited in Lewis, *Poetry and Prose*, 48.

38. Lewis, *Poetry and Prose*, 48.

that the central idea bore no essential relation to monarchy.[39] Hobbes instead spoke of the *sovereign* state—whether monarchical, aristocratic, or democratic. For Hobbes, sovereign power is both absolute and indivisible. Thus, Hobbes, and modern theorists more generally, claimed that law is nothing but the command of the sovereign. The sovereign is therefore *not* under or constrained by law.[40] Modern proponents of the sovereign state also rejected the notion of any jurisdiction outside that of the civil sovereign or temporal governments. Thus, the modern doctrine of the sovereign state rejected both the rule of law and the Gelasian notion of separate jurisdictions of church and civil government. What Christianity sundered, early modernity sought to reunite.

Early Christian thinkers had to work out the Lordship of Christ over Caesar while acknowledging God had granted Caesar authority within a limited scope. Likewise Christians thinking about politics today must acquire the habit of seeing Christ as Lord over the modern state while acknowledging that government is ordained by God insofar as it acts within its proper sphere—though we must add, not when it acts outside that sphere. And, importantly, civil government exceeds its jurisdiction whenever it contradicts the law of Christ. Finally, Christians thinking about politics today must forge again the old alliance with Plato and Aristotle concerning the rule of law. As Johannes Althusius reminds us, "an absolute and supreme power standing above all laws is called tyrannical" (*Politica* IX, p. 71). And tyranny is incompatible with Scripture's teaching that political authority is established for human good (Rom 13:4).

Bibliography

Ambrose. "The Story of Naboth." In *From Irenaeus to Grotius: A Sourcebook in Christian Political Thought*, edited by Oliver O'Donovan and Joan Lockwood O'Donovan, 74–79. Grand Rapids: Eerdmans, 1999.
Aquinas, Thomas. *Summa Theologica*. 5 vols. Notre Dame: Christian Classics, 1981.
Augustine. *The City of God against the Pagans*. Translated by W. W. Dyson. Cambridge: Cambridge University Press, 1998.
Copleston, Frederick. *A History of Philosophy, Volume I: Greece and Rome: From the Pre-Socratics to Plotinus*. New York: Doubleday, 1993.
Finnis, John. *Aquinas: Moral, Political, and Legal Theory*. Oxford: Oxford University Press, 1998.
Frankfort, Henri. *Kingship and the Gods*. Chicago: University of Chicago Press, 1948.
Gilson, Etienne. *The Spirit of Medieval Philosophy*. Notre Dame: University of Notre Dame Press, 1991.

39. Lewis, *Poetry and Prose*, 47.
40. Hobbes, *Leviathan*, 26.5–6.

Gregory I. "Pastoral Rule, Part 2." In *From Irenaeus to Grotius: A Sourcebook in Christian Political Thought*, edited by Oliver O'Donovan and Joan Lockwood O'Donovan, 196–200. Grand Rapids: Eerdmans, 1999.

Hobbes, Thomas. *Leviathan or The Matter, Forme and Power of a Commonwealth Ecclesiasticall and Civil*. Edited by Edwin Curley. Indianapolis: Hackett, 1994.

Hooker, Richard. *Of the Laws of Ecclesiastical Polity*. Edited by Arthur Stephen McGrade. Cambridge: Cambridge University Press, 1989.

Klosko, George. *Ancient and Medieval*. Vol. 1 of *History of Political Theory: An Introduction*. Oxford: Oxford University Press, 2012.

Lactantius. *Divine Institutes*. In *From Irenaeus to Grotius: A Sourcebook in Christian Political Thought*, edited by Oliver O'Donovan and Joan Lockwood O'Donovan, 48–55. Grand Rapids: Eerdmans, 1999.

Lewis, C. S. *Poetry and Prose in the Sixteenth Century*. Oxford: Oxford University Press, 2002.

MacIntyre, Alasdair. *After Virtue: A Study in Moral Theory*. 3rd ed. Notre Dame: University of Notre Dame Press, 2007.

Oakley, Francis. *The Empty Bottles of Gentilism: Kingship and the Divine in Late Antiquity and the Early Middle Ages (to 1050)*. New Haven: Yale University Press, 2010.

———. *The Mortgage of the Past: Reshaping the Ancient Political Inheritance (1050–1300)*. New Haven: Yale University Press, 2012.

O'Donovan, Oliver, and Joan Lockwood O'Donovan, eds. *From Irenaeus to Grotius: A Sourcebook in Christian Political Thought*. Grand Rapids: Eerdmans, 1999.

Plato. *Apology*. In *The Collected Dialogues of Plato*, translated by Hugh Tredennick and edited by Edith Hamilton and Huntington Cairns, 3–26. Bollingen Series 71. Princeton: Princeton University Press, 1961.

———. *Crito*. In *The Collected Dialogues of Plato*, translated by Hugh Tredennick and edited by Edith Hamilton and Huntington Cairns, 27–39. Bollingen Series 71. Princeton: Princeton University Press, 1961.

———. *Republic*. Translated with an introduction by C. D. C. Reeve. Indianapolis: Hackett, 2004.

Rahner, Hugo. *Church and State in Early Christianity*. San Francisco: Ignatius, 1992.

Steinberger, Peter J., ed. *Readings in Classical Political Thought*. Indianapolis: Hackett, 2000.

Suarez, Francisco. *A Treatise on Laws and God the Lawgiver in Selections from Three Works*. Edited by Thomas Pink and translated by Gwladys L. Williams, Ammi Brown, and John Waldron, with revisions by Henry Davis. Indianapolis: Liberty Fund, 2015.

Wilken, Robert Louis. "The Christian Roots of Religious Freedom." In *Christianity and Freedom, Volume 1: Historical Perspectives*, edited by Timothy Samuel Shah and Allen D. Hertzke, 62–89. Cambridge: Cambridge University Press, 2016.

Wright, N. T. *Pauline Perspectives: Essays on Paul, 1978–2013*. Minneapolis: Fortress, 2013.

———. *Simply Good News: Why the Gospel is News and What Makes It Good*. New York: HarperCollins, 2011.

6

Finding Wisdom in Literature
Leland Ryken

With all your getting, get wisdom, the ancient teacher told his students (Prov 4:7). That advice falls strangely on the ears of our contemporary culture. After all, we live in the information age. The concepts of wisdom and folly that formed the basic template of life in ancient cultures mystify people today. Writing prophetically in 1934, British poet T. S. Eliot asked, "Where is the wisdom we have lost in knowledge? Where is the knowledge we have lost in information?"[1]

This essay will explore how Christian readers can find wisdom in literature. Wisdom is not the customary term that literary scholars use to describe their enterprise, but it proves to be an illuminating approach. Interestingly, some towering literary figures from the past have anticipated me in thinking of their work in terms of wisdom. English Romantic poet Percy Shelley spoke of poetry as "a fountain for ever overflowing with the waters of wisdom and delight."[2] American poet Robert Frost used the same pair of words when he said that a poem "begins in delight and ends in wisdom."[3]

These two qualities are ascribed to literature already in the Bible. Near the end of the book of Ecclesiastes, the author expresses in kernel form not only his own philosophy of composition, but one that all the writers of the Bible would probably endorse. "Besides being wise," the author tells us, he also "sought to find words of delight" (Eccl 12:9–10, ESV). Wisdom and

---

1. Eliot, "Choruses from *The Rock*," 147.
2. Shelley, *Defence of Poetry*, 372.
3. Frost, "Figure a Poem Makes," 132.

delight are the domain of literature. The essay that follows will focus on half of that equation, though not to the exclusion of the other.

Wisdom enters our thinking about literature in two ways. It first names an inherent quality of literature, most naturally associated with its content rather than its form. Wisdom also applies to the reader who assimilates literature, whom I will call the wise reader. Formalist literary theory (with its focus on the text) undergirds the first aspect, and reader-centered theory the second. Another important duality on which I have based this essay is that a Christian approach to literature consists of two things—a Christian defense of literature and a methodology for assimilating literature in a Christian way.

I have been guided in my exploration by the evocative question raised in Job 28:12: "Where can wisdom be found?" Where can wisdom be found in the literary enterprise? The answer: in the text and in the reader.

Truthfulness to Human Experience

Our quest to find wisdom in a literary text begins by acknowledging the time-honored distinction between form and content. Form consists of *how* authors express or embody their content, and content consists of *what* is expressed by means of that form. Wisdom in literature is found in the specific forms of knowledge and truth that literature embodies and imparts.

We can begin where the classical tradition began—by noting that literature takes human experience as its subject matter. The formula that the ancients used was the concept of imitation: the author imitates reality (also called nature). This formula acknowledges that when we assimilate a work of literature, we are looking at life as selected and organized by an author. That view of art went unchallenged for more than twenty centuries. It remained for the Romantic movement of the early nineteenth century to dethrone the concept of imitation and replace it with the imagination as the key to everything that happens in literature and the arts. But the Romantic theory of the imagination retained an essential ingredient of the classical theory of imitation, namely, a belief that the subject of literature is human experience, rendered as concretely as possible.

The word *imagination* contains the word *image*, so we can say that literature is an *embodiment* or *incarnation* of reality and human experience. Shelley famously called literature "the very image of life expressed in its eternal truth."[4] More than a century later, Dorothy L. Sayers wrote, "Suppose, having rejected the words *copy*, *imitation*, and *representation* as inadequate,

---

4. Shelley, *Defence of Poetry*, 360.

we substitute the word *image* and say that what the artist is doing is to image forth something or other."⁵ Literature is truthful to life.

Literary authors have confirmed this view of the writer's task. In what is perhaps the most famous statement, Flannery O'Connor said that "the writer should never be ashamed of staring."⁶ Writers are gifted with powers of observation, and what they observe is human experience as lived. Additionally, Ralph Waldo Emerson was right when he said that "all [people] . . . stand in need of expression" of their experiences and insights. "Notwithstanding this necessity," Emerson added, "adequate expression is rare." Writers "are natural sayers, sent into the world to the end of expression."⁷ I will note in passing that writers record and illuminate experience in three primary spheres as they write about God, people, and nature. Literature as a whole is the human race's testimony to its own experience. Every culture demonstrates that people are created with an urge and capacity to express their affirmations and denials, their longings and experiences, in the form of stories, poems, and visions. It is therefore no wonder that God gave us a literary Bible. The Bible conveys truth and beauty in the way people most naturally assimilate them.

What I have said thus far delineates the literary enterprise from the writer's perspective. If we shift our focus to the readers of literature, we can say that they acquire wisdom from literature by appropriating what writers put before them. Flannery O'Connor's dictum that the writer is never afraid of staring is often and correctly applied to readers of literature and the Bible. Readers as well as writers should never be ashamed of staring. A towering literary critic of a bygone age said that the writer's task "is to *stare, to look at* the created world, and to lure the rest of us into a similar act of contemplation."⁸

The first type of truth that literature imparts is thus truthfulness to reality and to human experience. When literary critic Louise M. Rosenblatt surveyed college students to ascertain why they valued literature, she found that "students value literature as a means of enlarging their knowledge of the world, because through literature they acquire not so much additional information as additional experience."⁹ Truthfulness to life as we experience it in the world is the particular forte of literature and the arts. We might think of it as experiential knowledge as distinguished from abstract ideational

5. Sayers, "Towards a Christian Aesthetic," 78.
6. O'Connor, *Mystery and Manners*, 84.
7. Emerson, "Poet," 531.
8. Scott, *Modern Literature and the Religious Frontier*, 52.
9. Rosenblatt, *Literature as Exploration*, 38.

knowledge and information. To quote again from Rosenblatt, "Literature provides a living-through, not simply knowledge about: not the fact that lovers have died young and fair, but a living-through of Romeo and Juliet."[10] In a similar vein, Flannery O'Connor repudiated "the notion that you read the story and then climb out of it into the meaning," insisting rather that "the whole story is the meaning, because it is an experience, not an abstraction."[11]

What kind of knowledge or truth does this yield? It stands to reason that if we stare at the human experiences that the writer places before us, we come to see them clearly and thereby understand life better. This is knowledge in the form of right seeing. When Robert Frost wrote that literature "begins in delight and ends in wisdom," three sentences later he substituted the formula "clarification of life" for the term *wisdom*.[12] The wisdom of literature lies partly in its ability to clarify life. Earlier I used the label *experiential knowledge* for literature, and this is exactly how biblical wisdom literature is often defined. Scholars also speak of biblical wisdom as *skill for living*, and again we can see the link between literature and wisdom. Kenneth Burke wrote a well known essay entitled "Literature as Equipment for Living." In it, Burke began by noting the traits of proverbs and then offered the view that "works of art [can] legitimately be considered . . . as 'proverbs writ large,'" adding that both proverbs and works of literature "are *strategies for dealing with situations*."[13]

Ideational Truth

Literary authors do more than record human experience. They also offer interpretations of the experiences they present. A second type of literary truth leading to wisdom is thus ideational truth. Literature embodies themes and ideas. These ideas are not always true, and to discern true ideas from false ones is a chief task confronting the wise reader of literature, as I will later assert.

Nonetheless, it is important that Christians value and nurture a common bond with the human race at the level of general truth (as distinguished from a specific, ultimate, and worldview category of truth). Before the contemporary assault on Christian belief and morality, most works of English and American literature expressed ideas that the mass of people could affirm at a general level. We might think of these ideas as the shared

---

10. Rosenblatt, *Literature as Exploration*, 38.
11. O'Connor, *Mystery and Manners*, 73.
12. Frost, "Figure a Poem Makes," 132.
13. Burke, *Philosophy of Literary Form*, 296.

wisdom of the human race, bestowed by God as part of his common grace that falls like a benediction on humanity generally.

Literature and the other arts are a leading means by which the human race grapples with reality and interprets it, and a lot of wisdom is generated by that grappling. Even the list of topics and experiences that authors select for observation and recording yields a kind of wisdom about what the human race values. We might think of it as wisdom about what *matters* to people. The most influential literary scholar of an earlier era, Northrop Frye, believed that literature as a whole is the human race's record of what it desires (human longings) and the things that get in the way of that vision (human fears). Literature expresses what the human race wants and does not want. This yields a wisdom worth having—a knowledge of essential humanity.

One dimension of this wisdom about what it means to be human is the presence in literature of archetypes—the universal plot motifs, character types, settings, and images that make up the foundation of the literary imagination as of life. I offer the following statement by the early champion of archetypal theory Carl Jung as a helpful slant on the subject I am considering: archetypes "make up the groundwork of the human psyche. It is only possible to live the fullest life when we are in harmony with these symbols; *wisdom is a return to them*" (italics added).[14]

Summary: Wisdom in the Text

I have provided one answer to the question of where wisdom can be found in literature. It can be found in the text. The wisdom in the text consists partly of embodied experiences that we come to see clearly as we stare at the text and assimilate what the author places before us. An additional overlay is the ideational framework that authors impose on the embodied experiences. These ideas exist on a continuum. On one end is general wisdom—ideas that we formulate in such broad terms that virtually the whole human race can affirm them. We can think of this as the shared wisdom of the human race, enabled by God's common grace. As we move toward more specific ideas and, finally, an entire worldview, we find a greater margin of error, but much of the time we find truth as Christians believe it. Here wisdom consists of the great ideas by which humanity has lived. In summary, wisdom in literature consists of truthfulness to life and ideas that are true.

---

14. Jung, *Psychological Reflections*, 47.

The Wise Reader

As I turn now from the text to the reader, I will be building on a theory of literature known as reader-response criticism. That theory is based on the obvious fact that readers assimilate a work of literature in terms of who they are and what they bring to a text. All readers belong to one or more interpretive communities—groups with whom they share a common core of ideas, attitudes, and beliefs. Christian readers are an interpretive community and should feel entirely free to be themselves when they read or view literature. They need not apologize for being citizens of their community. In the discussion that follows, I will be defining what I regard as the ideal Christian reader. I will call that reader the wise reader. My guiding principle is that literary wisdom resides in readers as well as texts.

Valuing Literary Form and Beauty

To begin, the wise reader values literary form and beauty. Earlier in this essay I explored the content of literature—*what* the writer expresses. But content makes up only half of a work of literature; artistry, creativity, and beauty make up the other half. The wise reader recognizes this and gives form and beauty their due. We can profitably consider this from three angles—the inherent nature of literature, statements by writers about their craft, and the Bible's teaching on art and beauty.

No work of literature is devoid of form and beauty. Along with content, form is what constitutes a work of literature. This beauty of form begins at the level of words, so we would do well to think of the creation of verbal beauty as a primary skill of a literary author and trait of literature. Starting with the very words, literary form then reaches outward to larger features, such as the genre and organization of a work. A utilitarian outlook tries to squeeze the artistic aspect of literature out of the picture and privilege ideas over artistry and beauty, but works of literature refuse to let that happen.

C. S. Lewis correctly claimed that "one of the prime achievements in every good fiction has nothing to do with truth or philosophy . . . at all."[15] A literary work, added Lewis, "is not merely *logos* (something said) but *poiema* (something made)." Elsewhere Lewis offered the opinion that two things that we demand of a great work are wisdom (so that "after reading it [we] understand things . . . better than we did before") and deliciousness ("what the older critics often called simply 'Beauty'").[16] Another literary scholar

---

15. Lewis, *Experiment in Criticism*, 83.
16. Lewis, *Williams and the Arthuriad*, 374.

surveyed the areas where modern criticism has found value in literature and identified one of these as "a group of closely related ideas about form [viewed as] a function of the imagination: beauty, form, art, style, craftsmanship, structure, and the perfect and isolated object."[17]

Writers themselves confirm the importance of form and craftsmanship in the literary enterprise. They lavish their time and skill on the formal aspect of their stories and poems. Their surviving manuscripts show how painstakingly they revise—not to improve the ideas but to refine the artistry. Ernest Hemingway rewrote the ending of *A Farewell to Arms* some 47 times in a determination "to get it right."[18] Robert Frost called a poem "a performance in words,"[19] implying that authors intend to entertain us with their display of technique the same way a musician or athlete does. Welsh poet Dylan Thomas wrote, "I like to treat words as a craftsman does his wood or stone . . ., to hew, carve, mold, polish, and plane them into patterns, sequences, sculptures, fugues of sound."[20] The writer of Ecclesiastes "sought to find words of delight" (12:10), reminding us that the function of the artistry that we find in literature is pleasure and enjoyment.

I have space only to summarize how the artistic beauty that authors place in their works for our pleasure relates to Christian thinking about literature. Here is that summary:

1. God is a creative God who delights in beauty;
2. this creative God made people in his image, endowed with an ability to create works of beauty;
3. the Bible by its very example confirms the importance of literary form and beauty;
4. the Bible endorses beauty and pleasure.

We can allow a statement by Abraham Kuyper to clinch the point: "As image-bearer of God, man possesses the possibility both to create something beautiful and to delight in it."[21]

---

17. Kernan, "Idea of Literature," 35.
18. Hemingway, *Farewell to Arms*, 303–22.
19. Frost, as quoted in Drew, *Poetry*, 84.
20. Thomas, "Poetic Manifesto," 185–86.
21. Kuyper, *Lectures on Calvinism*, 142.

The Discerning Reader

In addition to reading literature as art and entertainment, the wise reader is a discerning reader at an intellectual and moral level. There are several ways in which this applies, including what type of literature we choose to read or view and how much time we devote to it. But my concern here is the methodology by which Christian readers discern truth from error in the literature they read or view. Reading literature Christianly is an exercise in discernment.

Such discernment is required by the fallen nature of our world. Literature did not escape the effects of the fall. The embedded ideas in a work of literature can be false as well as true. Discerning one from the other is a prime task facing the wise reader. The methodology by which this is accomplished is a two-stage process that begins by letting an author and work say what they have to say. Receiving what a work expresses is an obligation that we owe to an author—a literary application of the golden rule, not foreclosing on the possibility of finding truth and beauty in a work of literature, just as we do not like having people foreclose on us. C. S. Lewis has written with his usual good sense on the need to begin by receiving what a work of art offers to us. "The first demand any work of any art makes upon us," writes Lewis, "is surrender. Look. Listen. Receive."[22]

But after we have received, we need to judge. The best statement on this comes from T. S. Eliot, in a sometimes reprinted essay entitled "Religion and Literature." It was Eliot's conviction that "literary criticism should be completed by criticism from a definite ethical and theological standpoint. . . . What I believe to be incumbent upon all Christians is the duty of maintaining certain standards and criteria of criticism over and above those applied by the rest of the world; and that by these criteria and standards everything that we read must be tested."[23]

Eliot's statement bears unpacking. Obviously he envisions a two-stage process. The first stage is to receive what a work of literature stands ready to offer. By God's common grace, virtually all works contain some beauty and truth that a Christian can affirm. Even when the embodied ideas are false, there is a whole other level of truth, namely, truthfulness to reality and human experience. Nonetheless, at the level of specific ideas, moral vision, and worldview, literature often misses the mark. At that point a Christian reader weighs the truth claims of a work in the balance of biblical truth. We might think of it as intellectually testing the spirits to see if they are from

---

22. Lewis, *Experiment in Criticism*, 19.
23. Eliot, "Religion and Literature," 388, 399.

God (1 John 4:1). The ethical and theological standards that Eliot mentions are those of Christianity, based ultimately on the Bible.

At points where a work of literature deviates from the truth, wisdom does not reside in the text but in the Christian reader. The process of discernment that I have described actually produces wisdom about the Christian faith: in the very process of disagreeing with an author's perspective on life, we come to see and embrace the Christian perspective more fully. Early in my career I was fortunate to run across the following statement by Harry Blamires, who was once a student of C. S. Lewis at Oxford University: "There is nothing in our experience, however trivial, worldly, or even evil, which cannot be thought about christianly."[24] We can find evidence of this in the Old Testament book of Proverbs, where the author shows us how to think wisely about what is foolish, worldly, and evil.

Still, we should not overstate the proportion of unbelief in literature. Before the modern age, English and American literature was broadly and often specifically Christian in allegiance. Most of the literature that I have read and taught through the years can be read devotionally. This is not to say that the authors always intend the material to be read devotionally, but rather that a wise reader can appropriate it that way. Certainly imaginative literature has been a primary input into my spiritual life from a very young age.

Literature and the Quest for Wisdom

Literature serves multiple functions for individuals and societies. It places human experience before us in a way that allows us to look at it carefully and come to see it clearly. Literature gives expression to our fears and longings and thereby satisfies the human urge for expression. Literature intensifies our involvement with life. Authors also offer interpretations of the experiences they present, and the resulting ideas can accurately be called a repository of the great ideas by which the human race has ordered its intellectual life. Because literature is a leading means by which the human race grapples with reality, we can assuredly say that literature leads us to ask the right questions about life, even when a given work does not answer the questions correctly. Asking the right questions is a form of wisdom.

A further dimension of literature resides in its status as art and recreation. Authors create verbal beauty to enrich our artistic life, and the stories and poems they compose provide the material and occasion for enlightened leisure.

24. Blamires, *Christian Mind*, 45.

Although the following statement by Annie Dillard lacks a specifically Christian slant on why and how literature matters, it is an admirable summary of what literature can impart to any person's life:

> Why are we reading, if not in hope of beauty laid bare, life heightened and its deepest mystery probed? Can the writer isolate and vivify all in experience that most deeply engages our intellects and our hearts? Can the writer renew our hope for literary forms? Why are we reading if not in hope that the writer will magnify and dramatize our days, will illuminate and inspire us with wisdom, courage, and the possibility of meaningfulness, and will press upon our minds the deepest mysteries, so we may feel again their majesty and power?[25]

Of course literature can provide no more than the *potential opportunity* for exercising the true, the good, and the beautiful in the ways I have delineated. It is our responsibility as wise readers to make sure that we assimilate literature in ways that are edifying rather than contaminating, and ways that represent a good use of leisure time rather than a foolish waste of time. Jesus' parable of the talents shows that God loves to see his creatures seize good opportunities and is disapproving of missed opportunities. The choice is ours, as in the motif of the two paths (wisdom and folly) in biblical wisdom literature.

Bibliography

Blamires, Harry. *The Christian Mind*. London: SPCK, 1966.
Burke, Kenneth. *The Philosophy of Literary Form*. Baton Rouge: Louisiana State University Press, 1941.
Dillard, Annie. *The Writing Life*. New York: Harper & Row, 1989.
Drew, Elizabeth. *Poetry: A Modern Guide to Its Understanding*. New York: Dell, 1959.
Eliot, T. S. "Choruses from *The Rock*." In *The Complete Poems and Plays of T. S. Eliot*, 147–67. London: Faber & Faber, 1969.
———. "Religion and Literature." In *Selected Essays, 1917–1932*, 388–401. 3rd ed. London: Faber & Faber, 1951.
Emerson, Ralph Waldo. "The Poet." In *Major Writers of America*, edited by Perry Miller, 1:530–40. New York: Harcourt, Brace & World, 1962.
Frost, Robert. "The Figure a Poem Makes." In *The Collected Prose of Robert Frost*, edited by Mark Richardson, 131–33. Cambridge: Harvard University Press, 2007.
Hemingway, Ernest. *A Farewell to Arms*. New York: Scribner's, 2012.
Jung, Carl. *Psychological Reflections*. Edited by Jolande Jacobi. Princeton: Princeton University Press, 1953.
Kernan, Alvin. "The Idea of Literature." *New Literary History* 5 (1973) 31–40.

---

25. Dillard, *Writing Life*, 72–73.

Kuyper, Abraham. *Lectures on Calvinism: The 1898 Stone Lectures.* Grand Rapids: Eerdmans, 1931.

Lewis, C. S. *An Experiment in Criticism.* Cambridge: Cambridge University Press, 1967.

———. *Williams and the Arthuriad.* Grand Rapids: Eerdmans, 1952.

O'Connor, Flannery. *Mystery and Manners.* New York: Farrar, Straus & Giroux, 1957.

Rosenblatt, Louise M. *Literature as Exploration.* New York: Noble & Noble, 1976.

Sayers, Dorothy L. "Towards a Christian Aesthetic." In *Christian Letters to a Post-Christian World*, edited by Roderick Jellema, 69–83. Grand Rapids: Eerdmans, 1969.

Scott, Nathan A., Jr. *Modern Literature and the Religious Frontier.* New York: Harper, 1958.

Shelley, Percy B. *A Defence of Poetry.* In *Criticism: The Major Statements*, edited by Charles Kaplan, 355–80. New York: St. Martin's, 1975.

Thomas, Dylan. "Poetic Manifesto." In *The Poet's Work*, edited by Reginald Gibbons, 184–90. Boston: Houghton Mifflin, 1979.

7

The Feminine Quality of History
Rick Kennedy

Imagine the situation: a group of six or so students conversing at a round table while eating lunch in the cafeteria, each of whom has come to a Christian college wanting more than just a degree, wanting to live and think deliberately for Christ, wanting to give their utmost for God's highest. Among them a pleasant young first-year student, small with wild hair, not yet sure what to major in, wanting to spark a fun conversation, asks a provocative question: "Wouldn't the earliest apostles, if they were picking a major, choose history?" At this, most at the table are taken aback and turn to look at her. The first-year, enjoying the fact that she has sparked interest, leans in and puts a finger on the edge of the table saying: "The first speech by Peter after the ascension was a history lesson. He told a crowd in Jerusalem that they were eyewitnesses to actual events performed by God that were historically linked to long dead people, long past events, and things written down long before! Luke and Paul were a traveling tag-team of historians. Luke, the researcher and writer, tells us about his investigations and his pursuit of historical accuracy. Paul adamantly told his readers in Corinth that he was not a wandering wise man; rather, he was a historian passing on testimony of Jesus' resurrection. He told them that if the resurrection was not true history, then all Christianity was bogus. The truth of Christianity depends first on its history, not theology. The gospel is news, not ideas. For Paul, to be an evangelist is to be a historian.

"It's obvious!" declares our first-year, triumphantly slumping back into her chair. "The first apostles, if they were going to college today, would choose to be history majors!"

Rallying to the conversation, a sophomore history major, an older, tall, short-haired, serious student who had recently returned from a stint in Afghanistan with the army, speaks in agreement. "More than just being history majors, the first apostles and early Christians helped create the modern discipline of history. In my Research Methods class we read a couple chapters from a book by two important scholars, Anthony Grafton and Megan Williams, that say that Eusebius of Caesarea, a great scholar-bishop and author of *The History of the Church*, consolidated and developed many of the most important methods still taught in the modern academic discipline of history." Our history major, trained by the military to be clear and concise, then names three examples, lifting a finger with each: "One, the way Eusebius was concerned with written primary sources and authoritative chains of hearsay. Two, the way he gathered extensive quotes and was concerned about corroborative situations. And three, the way he thought that the credibility of sources could be rated."

Seeing that several at the table were listening, the history major then reaches down into his backpack and pulls out Marc Bloch's *The Historians Craft*. "This book," he says to the lunch-table group, "was written by a historian of Jewish ancestry who was executed during World War II. Let me read you a great passage: 'Unlike others, our civilization has always been extremely attentive to its past. Everything has inclined it in this direction: both the Christian and the classical heritage. Our first masters, the Greeks and the Romans, were history-writing peoples. Christianity is a religion of historians . . . Other religious systems have been able to found their beliefs and their rites on a mythology nearly outside of human time. For sacred books, the Christians have books of history, and their liturgies commemorate, together with episodes from the terrestrial life of a God, the annals of the church and lives of the saints. Christianity is historical in another, and perhaps, even deeper sense. The destiny of humankind, placed between the fall and Judgment, appears to its eyes as a long adventure, of which each life, each individual pilgrimage, is in its turn a reflection. It is in time and, therefore, in history that the great drama of sin and redemption, the central axis of all Christian thought, is unfolded.'"

"Yes! But!" declares the court jester of the group. He too had not yet decided on a major. "Not every Christian needs to be a history major! For the rest of us, history need only be part of our general education."

It is true. All at the lunch table agree. All Christians should be historians, but all Christians don't need to be history majors.

"I am enjoying my GE history class," announces the business major, "but I am not changing my major. Ancient World Civilizations is actually my favorite class this semester."

"I don't have to take a history class," declares a chemistry major. "I took Advanced Placement history in high school."

"You are missing out!" laughs the business major, a big burley fellow, full of confidence, and a face with an easy smile. "College history is nothing like high school history! We read and discuss all sorts of great stuff. We don't just prepare for an AP test. In my class we spent a week reading "the father of history," Herodotus. He is a roller coaster of fun. He tells stories about Persians and Greeks both fighting about freedom, about different pursuits of good government, and about the fickleness of democracy. He has great stories about women such as Queen Tomyris who tells Emperor Cyrus to seek peace rather than war, about the Admiral-Queen Artemesia who fights for Xerxes but is more worried about her own men than winning the battle for Persia, and about Amazon women up on the Black Sea who marry men on their own terms, wanting to remain hunters and warriors. The heroes in Herodotus's book are often not the great, but rather the normal people who have wisdom and commonsense. There is a Persian guy, 500 years before Jesus, who tells Darius that equality for "the people" is important, that he prefers democracy to monarchy, and warns that power corrupts people, even the best of people." Looking around the table, he says, and all nodded in agreement, "High school was fun and good, but college is different and has so much more to offer."

"Check this out," the business major says as he pulls his class syllabus out of his backpack and reads out loud the professor's statement about why it is good to study history:

> First, God created it and put Jesus at the center of it. God has some purpose for time, and we historians are "time detectives." Second, within the fullness of God's time, there is the room for humans to create. For some reason the Creator encourages humans to be creators. We historians are the record-keepers and analyzers of human creativity: the arts, sciences, politics, religions, philosophies, all of it. Third, historians help encourage and perpetuate the communion of humanity: the living and dead, strong and weak, victors and victims. Listening is a historian's most useful tool. Empathy is our best method. Wisdom and understanding are our highest goals. Finally, historians are entrusted with a job both critical and judgmental. We look for errors, lies, unintended consequences, and misguided goals. We study the influence of Satan and the knots in which we tie ourselves. We honor the virtuous, disdain the irresponsible, and condemn the evildoers. We pass on to the next generation our criticisms and judgments in the hope of a better future.

Again, most everyone around the table agrees that history is obviously good to take as a general education class or elective in college. They all lean back in their chairs, satisfied, but then, as they all expected at some point in the conversation, their friend at the table, a philosophy major in her senior year, leans forward and adds her thoughts. Big-boned with deep intelligent eyes, she comes in loud and authoritative: "Yes, history is foundational for Christianity. Yes, history is important for all people to learn in general education. But there is a deeper reason for us to study history, whether as a major or in General Education. There is a servant quality, a listening quality, dare I say a feminine quality, in history that gives balance to the high-flying rhetoric about success and leadership promulgated by all that university literature sent to us when we were in high school."

Most everybody by this time is finished eating, but no one is going to leave now. They push their plates to the center of the table. This could get fun.

The philosophy major, a woman's studies minor who is well known for her keen sensitivity for gendered ways of thinking, is easily one of the smartest and well-read students in the college. As a senior, she has already been accepted at a hotshot graduate school. She is a bit pompous and insistent, but friendly too. Everybody likes her. She is interesting, and they had all come to college hoping to meet interesting people with interesting ideas.

"David Hume," she begins, reaching both arms out onto the table with her palms flat and fingers splayed, "one of the great thinkers with one foot in philosophy and the other in history, wrote in 'Of the Study of History' that women should study history because it is the discipline best suited to their sex. This sounds demeaning if you think it means women should not study math or science; however, what Hume was tapping into was a long tradition in which historians pleasantly depict themselves as practicing a feminine way of thinking. Eusebius, for example, depicted himself as a flower-gatherer. In the language of the Middle Ages and Renaissance, historians wrote what were called, in Latin, *florilegia* and, in Greek, *anthologies*, both terms meaning 'flower arrangements.' History has feminine qualities similar to flower arranging. For Hume, philosophy and science are masculine. Plato had described philosophy in erotic terms of male desire, and there is a long tradition of philosophy and science being gendered as male: rigorously logical, anti-authoritarian, heroic, and even voyeuristic in their desire to see what is hidden."

"Wait!" calls out the chemistry student. She is also a senior, tall, thin, very smart, and already has a job waiting for her after graduation. "None of this needs gender-talk. You are simply saying history is like botany—gathering specimens, organizing, and categorizing. You are just giving a gendered spin to analysis and synthesis, the cutting up and putting back together that we all learned as 'critical thinking.'"

Our philosophy major, a pleasant soul, leans over and lightly grabs the chemist's thin wrist. "No. Botany is not like history. Botany can be done alone. A botanist can also be more confident in her work than a historian." She looks up, as if teasing something out of her brain, then continues. "It is not that history gathers actual flowers, but rather that the field of flowers it gathers from is, for the most part, human. History is a literary field of people, living and dead, flower-picking and being flowers, communicating and being communicated to, always tainted by the limits of being social."

The philosopher lifts her hand from the chemist's wrist, pauses, and looks around the table. She knows she is dominating conversation and has turned it in an awkward direction. The history major, slow to speak this time, looks at the philosopher and replies: "I don't have any problem with thinking of history as feminine, especially if feminine is associated with being more social than individualistic. However, I think it may be better to say that history is necessarily a more humble discipline than most. Instead of flower-gathering, it may be better to say that history relies mostly on listening. History is more passive than active, more process-oriented than goal-oriented, less assertive of its truth and more conscious of the need for faith.

An awkward moment of silence follows, but the philosophy major blurts: "Excellent! We are talking about why history is so important as a subject of college education, of education above and beyond mere high-school AP tests, of especially Christian education, most especially whether it is the kind of education that the apostles would want us to have!"

"And you, my historian friend," she said while fixing his eyes with hers, "have spoken the essential truth. History is a different way of thinking than most, yet still essential to the whole of the university's pursuit of truth."

"There is," she continues, turning her eyes back to the rest, "a much respected philosopher named Alasdair MacIntyre. He says the first step in Christian education should be 'obedient trust,' 'faith in authority,' and 'conformity.' These are the feminine qualities we have been talking about. Paul in the New Testament used the word, *tapeinophrosune*, a word we can translate as "humblethink." Paul wrote to the Ephesian and Philippian churches that he desired them to practice humblethink, and in *Acts* he reminded the Ephesian elders that he, himself, practiced it. Humblethink is an art of thinking, an art of trust, faith, and conformity that MacIntyre thinks is the first step in Christian education. Humblethink is optimistic in that it believes that most people, most of the time, want to tell the truth and that truth tends to show itself over long periods of time among large and long-lasting fellowships of people."

On a roll, she stretches both arms out again on the table with palms down. "St. Augustine wrote that the beginning and end of Christian education is humility." ... "Let us beware of [the] dangerous temptations of pride," he declared. "Man fell through pride, humility restored him."

The jester, still leaning back in his chair, interjects with a wry smile: "So history is a social discipline because it depends on faith, obligation, and submission, while philosophy and the sciences are individualistic because these disciplines can theoretically be done alone?"

"Sort of," replies the philosopher. "I am saying only that the traditional ways of thinking that sustain the center of the discipline of history are social and are traditionally gendered as female. The traditional ways of thinking that sustain the center of philosophy and the sciences are individualistic and traditionally gendered as male. Different professors do different things, and all majors are complicated. If we go back to the question of what major the apostles would, in general, choose, I am agreeing with our first-year friend that the apostles would find their best help in history—not philosophy or the sciences. A critical thinker, using hard logic and scientific method, will never come to the conclusion that Jesus rose from the dead. Only a social thinker, using traditional historical methods, humble methods of listening, will be able to promote, at a university, the reasonableness of the gospel accounts of the resurrection."

The business major, gathering up his gear, agrees: "That is why the Jewish historian wrote during World War II that Christianity is a fellowship of historians."

As the others begin to gather their gear and stack their dishes, the first-year turns to the former soldier and asks: "What do you plan to do with your history major?" Unbending himself out of the chair, the man replies: "As for a job, I will probably go back into military service. The history major, I hope, makes me better and wiser."

8

Word Made Flesh

The Transformational Power of Theatre

ANGELA KONRAD

EARLY IN MY TEACHING career, during an open question session I call "instructor hot seat," a fresh-faced undergraduate looked up at me with huge, innocent eyes and asked, "When did you first know that theatre was for you?" With some effort, I silenced the evil twin on my shoulder whose cheeky response was "I'll let you know." I don't recall my actual answer, but I still identify with that evil twin; theatre is a not an easy path and its place in contemporary culture, and in academia, is ever insecure. A strange discipline that seems to have more in common with extracurricular sports than serious intellectual pursuits, theatre is at best seen as "fun" or "entertaining" but certainly not essential. And given the longstanding mistrust of theatre by the church, the presence of a theatre department and theatre artists within a faith-based school is nothing short of perplexing. What on earth has theatre to offer the university? The Christian church? Culture as a whole? I hope to answer these questions and perhaps even convince you that, properly practiced, theatre can change the world.

Why Is Theatre Worth Doing?

Theatre Is Incarnational

When I was an undergrad, I was a major in Theatre and a TA in the English Department. I loved English because I loved story and I loved Theatre because we brought the stories literally to life. This is absolutely central to theatre's power. A few years ago I directed a play called *Grace* in which several characters were shot on stage. There is something inescapably affecting about hearing the blast of the gun, smelling the gunpowder, and watching each character fall heavily to the floor. Somehow, these deaths are more real than bloody murders on the silver screen, despite our certainty that the actors will get up in a moment to take a bow. We are all aware that our appreciation of acting is increased by our knowledge that the actor both *is* and *is not* the character. Thanks to this incarnation, we recognize them most fundamentally as people; like us, neither fully good nor fully evil; like us, struggling to make sense of their lives.

If theatre holds a mirror up to nature, it must reveal a reflection that is true and more than true. Life is complex and difficult, a place where resolution is not always possible and reconciliation is sometimes reserved for the next world. When we see on the stage a reflection of the darkness we know in our own lives, we are willing to examine those lives, to accept the possibility that the embodied "reality" in front of us has wisdom to speak into our brokenness. It can be argued that the current proliferation of "reality programming" is fed by a demand for truth-telling. We long to see others like ourselves—people who live in the real world where problems are not easily solved, hurts healed, or wrongs forgiven. The irony is that reality television has become the most unreal, a mockery of both critical and commonplace concerns, transparently manipulating our emotions, even while it claims to be unscripted. Theirs is a funhouse mirror, minimizing features of substance and exaggerating minute details. In theatre, the mirror shows us real human beings whose existence requires the very air that we breathe.

But that "happening right in front of us" sense is not only effective for dark stories, it's also the place where stories with light and hope really deliver. Sometimes our own lives are too much for us and we simply cannot handle the real world. In these moments, a fictional world has the ability to transport us beyond ourselves. And because theatre requires that we leave our homes and experience that story with others, and because that story is incarnated before our very eyes, it can save us from despair and give us the perspective we need to reenter our own lives. Recently, I directed John Patrick Shanley's transcendently beautiful play *Outside Mullingar*. Set in Ireland, the story is no stranger to darkness, but its heart is pure joy. The opportunity to meet the characters had this effect on one critic:

> Watching playwright John Patrick Shanley's *Outside Mullingar* opens your heart and makes you giddy. The experience is kind of like falling in love. It's as if you can smell the spring leaves

more keenly on your way home from the theatre. You're more hopeful and awake. And you want to kiss somebody.... It's not often that a play makes you happier to be in your body, but this one does.[1]

This is escapism at its finest. Entering into the world of the play, the critic's perspective is transformed—one might say redeemed—by the living beings he has had the privilege to meet, and he emerges awakened to the wonders of his own life.

Theatre Is Communal

Theatre is an intensely communal experience. There's a sense of "being in this together" at the theatre, so patrons actually speak to one another before or after the show, and they laugh, gasp and applaud as an ensemble. Moreover, the audience has a vital role to play in the production. I often refer to the audience as "the final cast member." Their response to the action can change the intensity of the action; their belief in the characters increases the belief of the actors; their appreciation for the play enhances the appreciation of those around them. So theatre patrons are not passive observers; they are participants whose mere presence can alter the play.

A lot of people are concerned about advances in technology, the prevalence of screens, the fact that we can get our entertainment anywhere we are. They think this reality might kill theatre. That theatre is antiquated and attended only by octogenarians. That soon no one will bother. To those people, let me offer the wisdom of John Steinbeck: "The theater is the only institution in the world which has been dying for four thousand years and has never succumbed. It requires tough and devoted people to keep it alive."[2]

I am among those tough and devoted people, and we think the reverse is true. In a world where technology races to replace human contact, live theatre remains incredibly *live*. Having to leave the comfort of our living rooms and join others in a communal experience might require effort, but it has tangible rewards. As a species, we are wired for relationship, designed for community. There's a reason that Canadian playwright Daniel MacIvor calls theatre his church—it appeals to our need for belonging and shared purpose. And that need is not going away, no matter what Apple comes up with next.

---

1. Thomas, "Outside Mullingar."
2. Steinbeck, *Once There Was a War*, 23.

This gathering together involves not just other audience members but the performers as well. There is unmistakable power in sharing the same room, breathing the same air, as the characters in the story, particularly when those characters are people you would normally cross the street to avoid. Coming face to face with others you might not normally meet expands our understanding of humanity, increases our compassion, and makes the communal connection more acute. In the words of Pulitzer Prize-winning playwright and novelist, Thornton Wilder, "I regard theatre as the greatest of all art forms, the most immediate way in which a human being can share with another the sense of what it is to be a human being."[3]

Theatre Is Challenging

Statistics gathered by major film companies will tell you we all love a happy ending. Many a producer has headed back to the studio to reshoot a final scene that is too sad or uncertain for preview audiences to approve. Television sitcoms regularly provide a problem, complication, and resolution in approximately twenty-two minutes. And in theatre, only musical comedy–the genre in which protagonists not only conquer all obstacles but do so while singing–consistently makes money at the box office.

While all theatre has an obligation to be entertaining (boring is the unforgivable sin, in my opinion), it rarely offers only escape. Rather than inviting you to "sit back and enjoy the show" the most influential theatre demands that you "sit up and pay attention." The best plays push us out of our comfort zones, challenging our views and shunning easy answers.

Understandably, this doesn't always win us friends. In Christian circles, it is especially troublesome as expectations of the audience frequently reflect a particular understanding of valuable theatre. "Positive," "uplifting," "edifying," "inspiring"—these are adjectives used to describe productions many faith-based audiences consider worthwhile. When we think of theatre as solely entertainment, or mere escapism, or an enacted sermon, we stay away from plays with difficult subjects. Therefore, theatre companies and departments that choose to stage demanding or dark pieces run the risk of not being able to pay the bills.

But a steady diet of easily-digestible stories means we never graduate from the theatrical equivalent of pabulum. Patrons who know what to expect learn to check their brains at the door of the theatre, losing their ability to think for themselves and winding up like college freshmen insisting *we* tell them what the story means. These simple scripts sometimes tell

---

3. Bryer, *Conversations with Thornton Wilder*, 72.

the truth, but never the whole truth. If theatre is to express the breadth of the human experience, we must tell stories that reflect our own lives, lives in which suffering is not easily explained and relationships are sometimes irreparably damaged.

Dark, difficult plays plunge us into a universe of uncertainty and ambiguity, a world where we cannot expect solutions to be easy or stories cheerful. But that is the world where we live. The most memorable productions are those that meet us where we are, and take us beyond. As we relate to characters who know our pain, we gain insight for our own lives by sharing in theirs. In that transcendent place, we can simultaneously experience and examine, a luxury we can rarely afford in our real-life dramas. While there is nothing wrong with uplifting entertainment, theatre's highest goal is not positivity but redemption. And as Christians know well, the path to redemption is often painful.

Why Teach Theatre?

This is not an idle question, I assure you. I cannot tell you the number of students I have had in my office, weeping because they feel called to the theatre yet their parents are pushing them to pursue something "worthwhile," "responsible," or at least "lucrative." My colleagues can be very supportive of me personally and interested in the plays we stage, but as an academic discipline, theatre's value is frequently questioned. One colleague, learning that his child had failed my class, remarked congenially, "I mean, how can you FAIL a drama class?" I'm pretty sure he expected me to agree.

Not only do I believe that theatre has a vital role to play in the academy, I am so passionate about actor training that I think it should be part of every undergraduate degree. And I have been known to say—without irony—that I think theatre is the best possible undergraduate major, regardless of potential career path. Let me give you a sense of why.

Know Thyself

I frequently refer to university as "the real formative years." This is a time when students are figuring out who they are, separating from their parents, preparing for the real world, forging friendships that will last a lifetime. I would argue that this passage is the most important thing that happens—or should happen—while in college. And if that's the task, theatre is the path.

Theatre is a discipline in which the primary source for study is the human being. Actors must know themselves, and they must learn to know others. They must study how people think, choose, respond, speak, and move. They must understand what makes one person angry and another sad; one joyous, another complacent. They must understand how relationships and communication work. Or don't. The best actors are students of psychology and human nature. They devour philosophy, religion, and literature for their insights into the human psyche. And they must apply all this knowledge to themselves, unflinchingly examining their weaknesses, fears, and biases; acknowledging and developing their strengths; honing their physical and vocal dexterity; and courageously revealing who they are to the world.

Not for the faint of heart, I tell you.

This study means that actors have to learn to access, appreciate, and express emotion, and to do so with their whole selves. This is a particularly tricky area for conservative Christians—in fact, for all of us. Part of the "civilizing" force of Western culture is to teach us to control our emotions and stifle our impulses. Those who laugh loudly or cry openly are suspect. Those who physicalize anger are feared (and often rightly so). Yet one of the things I must teach my students is to follow their impulses, and this sometimes means we need to undo twenty years of socialization. Many of my students–possibly because they have grown up in homes where strong emotions are frowned upon–cannot even identify their impulses. It's fascinating to discover how many dear young people cannot yell convincingly. Or skip with joy. But the truth is that feeling deeply is part of being human. And as vulnerability researcher Brené Brown has told us, we cannot selectively repress emotion. So if we want to experience fully, we must be willing to feel fully. This is a reality the actor understands very well. And it's closely related to an ability to appreciate all of life, in all its complexity.

Our Town is one of the most produced plays in the world and it contains one of my favorite scenes. After dying in childbirth, Emily is given the opportunity by the stage manager/narrator to go back and relive a single day of her life. She ignores the advice of others to choose an ordinary day and instead chooses her twelfth birthday. It's a winter morning in 1899 and nothing much happens. But watching the day unfold in all its exquisitely mundane beauty, Emily can handle only a few minutes and begs the stage manager to take her back to her place in the cemetery. She asks him, "Do any human beings ever realize life while they live it, every minute?" And he replies, "No. The saints and poets, maybe–they do some." That's part of what theatre training does: it prepares us to pay attention to our lives; it teaches us the beauty in the sadness; it takes us a step or two closer to the saints and poets.

Theatre Has Many Parts

Of all the arts, theatre is the most collaborative. In addition to the actors, most productions involve countless numbers of people working in many unseen capacities to create a public art. From the moment a play is chosen, every decision is made in collaboration. Even opinionated and visionary directors must consult with designers, compromise with business partners, and communicate with publicists. Rehearsal is a continual process of discovery and negotiation, as actors, designers, builders, and director work together to realize a common goal. The greater the passion and creative energy, the greater the need for careful listening and open dialogue. Once the play is in production, performers rely on stage managers, running crew, and front of house in order to bring the story to life. Even strike—when the set is dismantled and the theatre returned to basic black—involves everyone working together.

Therefore, each production is a new opportunity to assist my students in living as a community, helping them to understand and value the contribution of each person. Those who work on a play are a team, and when each member's contribution is respected and valued, the whole production is much greater than the sum of its parts. Those working on a production spend a great deal of time together, and they must cultivate a gracious, forgiving, and teachable spirit in order to thrive and grow. This means that the skills developed working on a play can be applied to far more than the world of theatre; they are used in every circumstance where people are required to work together in harmony.

Theatre Is Dangerous

Theatre is scary stuff. Society has been suspicious of theatre and theatre people since the Greeks, and theatre's relationship with the church has been particularly problematic. In evangelical circles, it's still easy to find those who are afraid of what they might see or hear onstage, the sorts of behaviors theatre artists participate in (on stage and off), and the lack of moral compass–or uplifting theme–in modern plays. And the reality is that even outside Christendom, theatre is seen as a formidable force. A quick Google search will uncover any number of productions–not just in countries under non-democratic governments–that have been closed down because of fears they would incite some sort of undesirable action.

Isn't that exciting?

Theatre exposes us to situations and language and ideas that push our buttons and make us uncomfortable. Rather than sewing things up tidily at the end, theatre often leaves us scratching our heads, questioning our opinions, debating its meaning. I consider my work in the theatre a failure if the most pressing question patrons ask at the end of the production is, "Where do you want to go for pizza?"

All the arts love to ask hard questions, and university is big on questions as well. But the real challenge in the theatre—and for theatre in the Christian academy—is not the mind, but the body. Remember, it's incarnational. A beloved colleague told me that she considers her body to be simply the vessel required to transport her mind from class to class. A large portion of evangelical Christianity still considers things of the body to be suspect, unsavory, worldly—in opposition to things of the spirit. But the work of theatre is unapologetically embodied. You cannot get away from the fact that the character does not exist unless the actor gives him life. And to do so, the actor has only her own self-imagination, emotions, intellect, voice, and *body*-to make that happen. Performed in real time, live performance has penetrating relevance for the actor and the audience. If a piece is strongly political, there's a legitimate risk that the audience-spurred on by the characters sharing that physical space-will take to the streets in protest.

We are discouraged from presenting works that might incite riots at my university, but we still manage to upset a lot of people. As disheartening as it can be to deal with, the file of complaint letters I have is evidence that theatre is dangerous. If it isn't, what are they worried about? And if it is, what can we accomplish?

How Can Theatre Change the World?

A Theology of Actor Training

I once saw a stage adaptation of Harper Lee's remarkable novel *To Kill a Mockingbird*. Early in the story, Atticus tells Scout, "You never really understand a person until you consider things from his point of view—until you climb into his skin and walk around in it." That is what the actor must do. Acting theory requires that the student quite literally put on the shoes of another. To be successful, the actor must not judge the character but must know what led that person to make specific—and sometimes tragic—choices. There is a common misconception that the actor's job is to put on a mask, to cover up their identity, and to pretend to be someone else. But much to the dismay of many a beginning actor, the reality is that acting requires getting naked—metaphorically, at least. In order to identify with the other, the actor is called upon to expose parts of himself that he chooses to cover up quite neatly most of the time. Because of this, acting is terribly vulnerable work. Any truly meaningful, moving portrayal requires investment of the most personal sort, as the actor digs deep within to uncover a common humanity. This is why I have immense respect for actors. The path to self-revelation is a difficult one, yet the actor's gift is the ability to let us see into his soul, to express the heights and depths of the human experience. Within each of us is the capacity for both evil and greatness beyond what most will experience. To walk another's path—not just with them but *as* them—can engender compassion with revolutionary potential.

Opening students' eyes to the importance of identifying with the other is at the core of an effective approach to teaching acting, and it is a goal with deep theological underpinnings. Jesus made it clear that next to loving God, loving others as ourselves is our most important task (Matt. 22:37–40). The deep identification of actor with character is perhaps the most profound way to understand this call.

At the end of *To Kill a Mockingbird*, Scout and her brother Jem have grasped her father's lesson more completely than they would have hoped or imagined. They have come to understand people they would not have spoken to previously; they have experienced life in ways many grown-ups never do. And Scout's response to her summer is to say, "There wasn't much else left for us to learn, expect possibly algebra." The education of the actor is so much more than graceful movement and eloquent articulation: it is an education in humanity.

Growing Empathy

This ability to take people beyond themselves is the power of theatre, and it is extended to audience as well as participant. To see a story come to life in front of us, and to take the journey with the actors, provides us with the great privilege of a genuine encounter with fellow human beings—people who are both fictional and real, both actual and imaginary—and this duality makes the experience richer and more fulfilling. Just as the actor cannot judge the character she plays, participating in the stories of people far outside our circles—or sometimes buried within them—helps us to understand the perspective of the other and increases our compassion. There are few forces in the world more potent than empathy, and empathy is the heart of the theatre.

Empathy begins with a basic understanding that we are all the same—as children of God, we are created in love, designed to be lovable and loving. But circumstances and choices shape who we become. As we identify with others on stage—people who are not two-dimensionally represented on a silver screen or buried within the pages of a book, but living and breathing right in front of us—we are confronted with our common bond. We can no longer judge the "characters" as we consider the world from their point of view. As we watch a play, we are transported into another's story, walking alongside and sharing in the joy and pain of a fellow human. One of the most damaging forces at work in our world is the demonizing of the "other." Whether separated by trauma, social standing, religion, race, sexual orientation, geography, age, or gender, breaking down barriers begins with a willingness to see beyond labels. As we come face to face with another's perspective, without judgment, we are empowered to act in love. And that action can ignite a compassionate revolution.

The Strength of Story

We might be people of the book, but we are unquestionably people of the story. We work to make sense of our lives through story. Jesus taught with stories. Stories are a primary mode of human communication. Stories help us understand each other and our place in the world. And people's stories matter. One of my favorite quotations about story is from Frederick Buechner: "My story is important not because it is mine, God knows, but because if I tell it anything like right, chances are you will recognize that in many ways it is also yours . . . If this is true, it means that to lose track of our stories is to be profoundly impoverished not only humanly but also spiritually."[4]

This idea applies to all stories, in print and on stage. But theatre provides a unique platform to tell personal stories. For people crippled by shame or corroded by anger, the opportunity to share their pain can be life-giving. Research shows that those who endure harmful experiences are greatly assisted by telling their stories because human connection is central to healing. Theatre is an intensely collaborative process, which immerses participants in the realization that they are not alone. Giving voice to those who do not feel heard and bringing to life experiences that might otherwise remain hidden grows empathy for both actors and audience.

---

4. Buechner, *Telling Secrets*, 42.

A Case Study—disPLACE:
Refugee Stories in Their Own Words

In the fall of 2016, I directed the inaugural production of my company Dark Glass Theatre. An initiative of the Humanitas Anabaptist-Mennonite Centre, the theatre grew out of the ideas in this essay, and its first production offers a concrete example of the principles I've outlined. *disPLACE: Refugee Stories in Their Own Words* is an original theatre production based on personal interviews I conducted with refugees to Canada. Audio recordings of the interviews were used to craft a ninety minute play that combines original music, short scenes, and verbatim testimony into a moving exploration of the refugee experience.

Transforming the Individual

The undergraduate student actors in *disPLACE* had no idea when they auditioned for the play how demanding—and how transformational—the process would be. Their knowledge of refugees grew from research, but it grew exponentially more from the myriad exercises we did to enter into the refugee experience. In one instance, for example, I led the students on a walk into the woods on campus, encouraging them to look at everything as if they had never seen it before, as if this was a place and a culture they had never encountered. When we got to the destination deep in the forest, I told them they were running from their persecutors, and I released them one at a time with the directive to get back to the rehearsal hall without being seen. This exercise was one of many that effectively moved their understanding from the head to the heart. It also increased the students' appreciation for the richness and mercy of their own lives, honing their powers of observation and increasing their capacity for gratitude. As one might expect, the effect of this production on the actors was deep and profound. At one talkback, as I listened to each student answer a question about how the production had changed them, I was struck by the realization that their experience alone was sufficient justification to do this show. The growth in empathy for each one will alter the course of their lives.

Transforming the Community

Actors have a unique opportunity to understand what it means to love our neighbor as ourselves since their work involves identifying with the "other" in a complete and visceral way. This is effectively illustrated by the rehearsal experience of embodying the refugees merely by listening to audio recordings. Wearing headphones, with no visual cues, the actors spoke the text at the same time as their character, listening intently to match the melody of the words, the substance beneath the words, and the impact behind the words. As they assumed the other's identity, they found themselves literally moved by what they were speaking. Gestures emerged organically alongside exclamations, postures transformed naturally as the individual's spirit was assimilated. The resulting portrayals were remarkably sophisticated for undergraduate actors, and surprisingly true to their subjects. At a special performance marking the launch of Dark Glass Theatre, refugees and students were able to meet and the experience was electric. Despite differences of age, race, and culture, the students communicated the essence of each individual, prompting the mother of one refugee to say, "It was like watching my daughter." Another remarked to her double, "You know me. You know my heart." She then turned to her husband and said, with a twinkle in her eye, "You have two wives now." Cultures were bridged in a way that global summits can only envy.

Transforming the World

Theatre is dangerous because of its power to provoke change. The more substantial the question, the more inflammatory the potential response. By this measure, *disPLACE* is indisputably volatile, as it confronts one of the most pressing social issues of the twenty-first century, one that is complex and polarizing. Consequently, the opportunity for the audience to develop empathy is heightened; the more unlike ourselves the characters are, the more profound the potential shift in perspective. *disPLACE* challenges preconceptions, pushing people to examine their attitudes and reconsider their behavior. Rooted in the story of a Mennonite woman who escaped Stalinist Russia, and depicting individuals from South America, the Middle East, and Africa, the show seeks to enlarge our image of refugees and to expand our understanding of their struggles. There are no easy answers, and the play does not attempt to provide them. Rather, sitting shoulder-to-shoulder to watch the story live, patrons must face the issue directly, sharing the sense of responsibility and looking together towards a solution. Because *disPLACE* tells stories of real people, because they are people we might not otherwise meet, and because their treatment is a concern of global significance, any resultant empathy is both meaningful and important. We observed this outcome after every performance. Patrons talked about how the production had deepened their understanding and changed their position on refugees.

Each talkback featured lively discussion about what can be done, how to sponsor refugees, and ways to make Canada a more welcoming new home. And the most common question afterwards was, "When are you doing this again?"

When I first talked about the idea for this production, many questioned whether refugees would want to talk about their experiences, whether it would be too painful to discuss war, homeland, hardship, and loss. Certainly, the reports were challenging, to hear and to tell, and not everyone we approached agreed to be involved. But those who did were gracious and generous, sharing their stories, their homes, and their hearts with us. When I asked why they were willing to participate, they spoke of the potential for their stories to help other refugees, to teach about their country or culture, to make a difference to those left behind. When they came to see the show, the response was overwhelming; I was completely unprepared for the depth of their gratitude. Each one talked about how meaningful it was to hear their story told and to watch it move others. They spoke of the commonality across the narratives and how encouraging it was to know they are not alone. And they built bridges within their own families and communities, who were emboldened to have new conversations by the revelations on stage.

The wisdom to be found in theatre, and taught through theatre, demands an appreciation for the razor-thin line between the beauty and horror of life. Theatre's effectiveness is rooted in the recognition of the *imago Dei* in each of God's children, as they are incarnated in front of us, confronting our prejudices, overturning our judgments, and requiring we meet them face to face. And this encounter can change the world.

Bibliography

Bryer, Jackson R. *Conversations with Thornton Wilder.* Jackson: University Press of Mississippi, 1992.
Buechner, Frederick. *Telling Secrets.* New York: HarperCollins, 1991.
Steinbeck, John. *Once There Was a War.* New York: Penguin Classics, 2007.
Thomas, Colin. "Outside Mullingar Is Food for the Soul." http://colinthomas.ca/2017/05/21/outside-mullingar.

9

Becoming a Soulful Wordsmith

Jeffry C. Davis

They constantly swirl around us, shaping how we think and what we do. From the first moments after we wake—often spent texting, emailing, or browsing—until our last minutes of consciousness—possibly relaxing with a good book or reflecting in a journal about the day: words abound. In various forms, colors, and media, they surround us, occasionally confound us, and sometimes astound us. Words both create and help us navigate the world in which we live.

Words in Social Media

Precisely because they are so pervasive in new technologies, words do not always receive the careful attention that they deserve. In our fast-paced, multitasking Digital Age, most people ignore the importance of words and their best use. This is understandable, given that according to one study conducted at the University of California, San Diego, the the average American media consumer views over 100,000 words per day.[1] We have become deluged by words.

This sort of word hurricane simply does not allow the typical viewer/reader the time, energy or ability to absorb the meaning of individual words (semantics) and how they are combined to create sentences of coherent thought (syntax). Both of these practices find their roots in the study of the structures of language (grammar), the first of the seven liberal arts that

---

1. Bohn and Short, "Measuring Consumer Information," 980.

students traditionally focused their energies on to improve their analytical skills and to promote their critical judgment. In ancient times, grammar encompassed more than just rules; it included a serious consideration of the best use of words, and the personal disciplines needed to foster such practices. Rational expression required regular, self-aware skill-exercises with words.

Alarmingly, some technology critics are now arguing that few individuals exercise sufficient personal discipline when it comes to their hand-held gadgets, especially when navigating the realm of words and images in social media. In *The Power of Off*, Nancy Colier reveals that most people check their smartphones 150 times a day, and not enough of us believe this is a serious concern; moreover, when a "technology-fueled mind is consulted as if it were a wise sage," she argues that we set ourselves up for believing lies, such as, the more information we consume, the more interesting life becomes.[2] As so-called "smart" devices have taken on a primary role, notably in the "ordinary" regimen for Post-Millennial college students, we have to ask, "Are these devices, and the behaviors they instill, actually making us smarter and more wise?"

Some experts remain unconvinced, and even dubious, about the promises of a plugged-in life. Eric Andrew-Gee reports that the research on personal technology continues to suggest that "smartphones are causing real damage to our minds and relationships, measurable in seconds shaved off the average attention span, reduced brain power, declines in work-life balance and hours of less family time."[3] Digital distractions, and the habits resulting from regular rapid task-shuffling and search engine dependence, may not be promoting the thoughtful mental abilities we need for the critical reception of meaning that is conveyed by words. Nicholas Carr, a technology researcher nominated for the Pulitzer Prize, laments that we have arrived at an intellectual and cultural crossroads, and human thinking is changing quickly: "Calm, focused, undistracted, the linear mind is being pushed aside by a new kind of mind that wants and needs to take in and dole out information in short, disjointed, often overlapping bursts—the faster, the better."[4] This is a time when the ability to discern between what is important and what is trivial online is increasingly difficult. As neuroscientist Mary Helen Immordino-Yang cautions, technology-driven activities

---

2. Collier, *Power of Off*, xii, xv.
3. Andrew-Gee, "Your Smartphone is Making You Stupid," para. 6.
4. Carr, *Shallows*, 10.

are quite possibly rewiring the networks of our brains, inclining us to desire entertainment rather than deep thinking.[5]

The ultimate danger from a regular torrent of icons and text is the devaluation of words, with consumers perceiving words mainly as promotional symbols with a purpose much like a sales pitch, one that can misrepresent and manipulate. According to a recent Pew Research Center survey on social media use, approximately two-thirds of the public uses more than one social media platform regularly; yet, only three percent of users trust the information they access on these sites.[6] This does not bode well for words in social media contexts, or for the people who encounter them there. When written words are generally perceived to be untrustworthy—lacking in their ability to carry the freight of truth—our view of their importance diminishes.

As never before, words can produce a profoundly positive or negative impact. This reality should heighten our awareness of, and longing for, their best and proper use. Words can be used for a number of diverging purposes, through social media and beyond: to elucidate a meaning or to obfuscate a motive; to defend an argument or to rebut a claim; to build up a relationship or to tear one down; to support a friend or to curse an opponent. These are just a few instances of lexical possibilities that warrant shrewd reflection. In the everyday exchange of ideas and emotions, word use has never required more prudence—the ability to discipline oneself with sound reasoning.

Writing in his personal notebook on the potential influence of words, the great American writer Nathaniel Hawthorne penned this sentence to himself: "Words, so innocent and powerless as they are, as standing in a dictionary, how potent for good or evil they become, in the hands of one who knows how to combine them."[7] Hawthorne obviously believed that all human beings possess the very real tendency to abuse others, as Hester Prynne's scarlet letter signaled her own social mistreatment by the Puritans of the Massachusetts Bay Colony. His writing stands as a challenge to his readers to become more responsible for living, and for using words charitably in relation to others. Such a commitment requires a belief in something greater than oneself.

---

5. Heid, "You Asked," para. 10.
6. Smith and Anderson, "Social Media Use in 2018," paras. 19, 22.
7. Hawthorne, "Passages from Hawthorne's Note-books," 690.

A Theology of Words

It is important to remember that we use language because our Creator used language first. After all, we have been created in his image. The ancient Israelites believed that Yahweh fashioned the heavens and the earth not from pre-existing matter; rather, he actually made the cosmos out of nothing—*ex nihilo*—calling forth every known thing into being with words. Integral to the work of God, words have spiritual power and significance. This truth is often overlooked. Nevertheless, words are vital tools that should be respected and used carefully by all believers, especially those in college. Without question, how we choose to handle words really matters to the divine Wordsmith of our world.

Few Christians spend much time thinking about words, much less developing a theology about them. As Justin Taylor rightly observes, "If you wanted to construct a biblical theology of words, you could get pretty far in just the first few pages of your Bible. The early chapters of Genesis are replete with God using words to create and order, name and interpret, bless and curse, instruct and warn."[8] By developing a theology of words, we gain a better understanding of the mind of our Maker. And we remind ourselves of our best aims with language, seeing the inherently spiritual significance of our verbal expressions, all to honor and worship God.

Serious students who seek *higher* education, the sort of liberating experience of life-changing learning that comes as a result of pursuing the heavenly wisdom of God, should remember this basic Christian truth: the reality we study, examined through the lens of each academic discipline, came into existence because of the Lord's powerful linguistic declarations. As the ancient and mysterious One repeated his bold command—"Let there be!"—during those initial six days recorded in Genesis, the crackling sound of creation erupted with myriad new forms. From words, the universe emerged, full of galaxies, suns, stars, meteors, moons, planets. And because of words, life on earth began.

It's no surprise, then, to see how Scripture reveals that the ability to use words well represents both an abiding characteristic and a prevailing concern of our God. For instance, Psalm 33:4–9 describes the clear connection between God's word, his creation, and his character:

> For the word of the Lord is right, and all His work is trustworthy. He loves righteousness and justice; the earth is full of the Lord's unfailing love. The heavens were made by the word of the Lord, and all the stars, by the breath of His mouth. He

---

8. Taylor, *Power of Words*, 16.

gathers the waters of the sea into a heap; He puts the depths into storehouses. Let the whole earth tremble before the Lord; let all the inhabitants of the world stand in awe of Him. For He spoke, and it came into being; He commanded, and it came into existence.[9]

As this passage shows, the language, action, and essence of Yahweh cannot be separated. His attributes remain interconnected. God's words and deeds prove to be consistent, coming from his own being. All the people of the earth should be encouraged to recognize the integrated nature of the Lord's divine traits. We ought to be filled with wonder, awed by his uniqueness.

By definition, "awe" combines reverence and fear. At a fundamental level, this quickening, this humbling realization about the holy otherness of God, can be understood as "the fear of the Lord," which is the beginning of true wisdom. Without a proper awareness of the very person of God, which appropriately links all his righteous attributes, we cannot even start to attain wisdom. The first step to lifelong learning, then, is to carefully consider the character of God. And such a consideration reveals how central language is to the work of the Wordsmith.

One of the core teachings of the Bible is that we who love our Creator are to become like him. The spiritual principle of *godliness* is predicated on a loving relationship that transforms our hearts and minds, moving us toward his greater influence so that we will emulate him. Solomon writes, "Blessed are those who keep my ways. Listen to my instruction and be wise; do not disregard it. Blessed are those who listen to me, watching daily at my doors, waiting at my doorway. For those who find me find life and receive favor from the Lord" (Prov 8:32–35). Righteous living involves waiting expectantly for God, heeding his voice, receiving his instruction, and walking in his steps. And what is the end result? We will become wise and receive God's blessing.

God's character and actions are inseparable from his words, as we have already seen, and the same should be true for us. To put it another way, when we allow ourselves to be directed by the living Word, Jesus Christ, we become his message bearers, through our being, our deeds, and our words. And as we collaborate with Christ's indwelling Spirit, we manifest his presence in the world. This is the remarkable work of God, through the Word in us, as Paul reminds us: "God chose the lowly things of this world and the despised things—and the things that are not—to nullify the things that are, so that no one may boast before him. It is because of him that you are in Christ Jesus, who has become for us wisdom from God—that is, our

---

9. Ps 33:4–9, HCSB.

righteousness, holiness and redemption" (1 Cor 1:28–29). The Word is our ultimate source of wisdom.

Becoming Soulful Wordsmiths

As followers of Christ, we have welcomed Jesus to dwell within the deepest part of our eternal being—our souls. The term for "soul" in the Old Testament is *nephesh*, which can be translated as "living being." Some scholars clarify that the soul is actually not *part* of who we are, but more accurately it represents our whole and truest self. This includes our life passions, moral compass, and rational thoughts. Therefore, Jesus—the Word—resides in our innermost self, understanding who we are better than we do. In this sense, he is indeed wise to us.

Liberal arts learning has always emphasized the importance of discovering who we truly are, over and above acquiring practical skills that can be applied in a work context. Students who are dedicated to liberal arts learning, from a Christian perspective, will develop an enduring interest in their souls, especially as they are enlivened by the living Word Jesus. To be soulful, biblically speaking, is to be aware of, and participate in, the transforming work of redemption by the LORD who promises to bring life, and bring it "more abundantly" (John 10:10). This is the Christian version of seeking "the good life," which is the prime directive of secular liberal arts. With Jesus as our foundation for wisdom, college rightly turns into *higher* learning.

One of the obvious implications of this approach is that we should desire to become soulful wordsmiths—image-bearers who strive to use words well, in a manner that honors the Word. As a Christian English teacher dedicated to helping students become better writers, I suggest three essential elements for composing soulfully: purpose, passion, and process.

Purpose

The great African American novelist Zora Neale Hurston explains, "Research is formalized curiosity. It is poking and prying with a purpose. It is a seeking that he who wishes may know the cosmic secrets of the world and they that dwell therein."[10] Effective writers must have a purpose that moves them—a reason for expressing themselves that literally gets the brain thinking and the fingers clacking. The ancients called it a *telos*, an ultimate

---

10. Hurston, *Sweat*, 43.

objective for doing something. Ironically, it is this end that is the starting point. By having a target to aim at, you gain a better sense of the distance, along with the best strategy to shoot the arrow in the right direction. Generally speaking, writers have four basic strategies when they write with purpose.

The first is to *describe* something so that it creates a vivid impression in the mind of the reader. To do this well, students must try to think in terms of sensory language, reflecting on the five human senses when capturing into words a person, place or thing in God's created world. I am regularly surprised at how often students forget that the reader is a real human being who wants to see, hear, taste, touch or smell something . . . in the mind. If you are going to err, I tell my students, give more—not less—description.

The second is to *narrate* a plot, with a setting, characters, and action. Jerome Bruner says that there are really only two categories of stories: those that are common to human experience and those that are not.[11] One of the most universal inclinations is to tell another person a tale with a compelling beginning, a developed middle, and a satisfying end, especially when asked "What happened?" To tell a story well, you need to portray a credible conflict that mimics actual lived experience. And the better narrative uses lots of description.

The third is to *explain* an idea or a process, which usually involves systematically breaking a whole thing into its respective parts and then analyzing each one in order. This kind of mental work requires painstaking concentration and effort, thinking logically in order to render the complexity of a thing to someone who wants to understand. Clarity represents the most important trait of this type of writing. Like narration, exposition is best done with lots of rich description. The writer's goal is to assist the reader in comprehending reality.

And fourth, is to *persuade* someone to believe or to do something. Historically, "the art of persuasion" represents the last and arguably the most important "art" of the liberal arts: rhetoric. Over the centuries, it has been considered the supreme skill of human expression. Aristotle asserted that every effective piece of argumentative writing employs three key modes: ethos—an appeal to authority, usually of an expert; logos—an appeal to facts and information; and pathos—an appeal to the emotions of the audience. Persuasive writing makes the reader believe in something that was initially only perceived as probable, not certain.

---

11. Bruner, *Acts of Meaning*, 48–49.

Passion

"If passion drives you," exclaimed Benjamin Franklin in one of his famous aphorisms, "then let reason hold the reins."[12] A scientist, statesman, printer, postmaster, activist and author, Franklin was arguably the most creative and industrious person living in colonial America. He possessed an appreciation for the meaning of hard work, and failure, and demonstrated the remarkable virtue of resilience—the ability to try again after not succeeding. His homespun wisdom became recognized as quintessentially American. Franklin expresses a profound insight in the proverb above: passion is vital to creative work, but it also requires rational oversight.

My writing students hear a similar sort of proverb from me on the first day of class: "All good writing begins with passion, but it must move toward structure." I want them to understand that passion—a powerful sensation of excitement toward some subject or skill—drives the engine of structure; conversely, structure regulates passion in a purposeful way. Without passion, you run out of gas. And without structure, you never arrive at your intended destination.

Too many student writers do not allow themselves sufficient time to locate their passions; instead, they begin with dread. Often they fail to give themselves permission to explore options before landing on a topic. Feeling rushed by a looming deadline or other competing demands in other courses, they panic. If a list of possibilities is provided by the instructor, they often succumb to the temptation of just choosing something, anything, to get on with it. The sad thing is that if a writer makes a mistake at the beginning, the consequences have negative and often irreversible ripple effects. Possibly the most important step is the selection of a subject to write about. Why? Because you write best about things for which you care most deeply.

So how do you find a passion that reflects your own soulful self? Here are three tips for discovering your personal and authentic concerns:

1. Identify Your Holy Loves: Saint Augustine asserts that followers of Christ should become mindful of what they love. What we love moves us, and we tend to order our lives according to the things that really matter. Yet, many people don't fully pay attention to these things. Augustine states in his sermon on love, "Love [God], and do what you will."[13] The challenge, here, is to reckon with your loves before the living LORD, allowing Him to purify or purge what you allow yourself to cherish.

---

12. Franklin, "Pennsylvania Gazette," para. 31.
13. Augustine, *Homily 7*, para. 8.

2. Consider the Things that Upset You: A form of passion that is overlooked, especially by Christians, is the kind which disturbs us. Yet, David expressed feelings of hatred towards the enemies of God (Ps 139), Nehemiah became irate towards the rich who exploited the poor (Neh 5), and Jesus exhibited anger toward the Pharisees hardheartedness (Mark 3). Lisa Harper concludes, "As Christ-followers, we're totally appropriate getting upset over sin, too. Evils such as abuse, racism, pornography, and child sex trafficking should incense us."[14] Negative passion can create interesting prose.

3. Meditate on Things God Cares About: In Philippians 4:8, Paul exhorts us: "Finally, brothers and sisters, whatever is true, whatever is noble, whatever is right, whatever is pure, whatever is lovely, whatever is admirable—if anything is excellent or praiseworthy—think about such things." Meditation is the ancient Christian discipline of reflection on a specific thing, such as a Scripture passage or theme, with the goal of gaining a deeper and lasting appreciation for God's revelation and perspective.

Process

Knowing how to craft written words for a constructive purpose represents one of the traits of a wise person. It also serves as one of the valued goals of a liberal arts education. Furthermore, four of the distinguishing qualities of a person who has attained a real liberal arts education are represented by the following literacy skills: 1) listening with critical engagement; 2) speaking with expressive eloquence; 3) reading with interpretive understanding; and 4) writing with persuasive clarity. These are the sorts of learning traits that make a person *free* (liberal) through intentionally developed *practices* (arts).

Quintilian, a first-century Roman writing teacher who was a contemporary of the apostle Paul, believed that writing was the most significant of the word-based skills. "It is in writing that eloquence has its roots and foundations."[15] Why? Because when you write, you actually do all the other skills as well: you read your own writing, either out loud or in your head, and in so doing you hear your voice and listen carefully. No other literacy skill requires all of the others.

Quintilian elevates writing as a supreme skill that dictates a deliberate instructional process, as follows.

---

14. Harper, "What is 'Righteous Anger'?," para. 7.
15. Quintilian, *Orator's Education*, 10.3.

First, students should begin by studying models of good writing, samples that address ethical issues; this sort of writing provokes student passion, and it helps form moral judgment. Second, students should learn from each other, sharing their work with others in class; this promotes healthy peer awareness and competition. Third, teachers should be aware that all the language skills mutually reinforce competence; therefore, speaking, listening, reading, and writing should be carefully attended to for precision in class. Fourth, students should learn to write quickly but conscientiously; thoughts should flow without restraint from over-deliberation. Fifth, a variety of assignments should be completed, moving from simple to complex skills; and the writing should have relevance to the world beyond the classroom. And last, revising is an important aspect of the writing process; students should be encouraged to delete and add words, after careful review.

Jesus the Writer

Students at first are taken aback when I tell them that Jesus was a writer. In an easy-to-overlook passage from John 8:1–11, Christ is portrayed as completing what appears to be a difficult writing task. While he is teaching in the temple courts, the Pharisees bring a woman caught in adultery to him, making her stand in shame before everyone. They tell Jesus what she has done, and they remind him what the Law of Moses commands—that she be stoned. "What do you say?" they ask, intending to trap him. The text describes what he does next: "Jesus bent down and started to write on the ground with his finger" (John 8:6). Then, after a few moments, as they question him again, he stands up and says, "Let any one of you who is without sin be the first to throw a stone at her" (8:8). Afterwards he stoops down again to write, and eventually the accusers walk away.

Scholars debate about what exactly Jesus wrote. Some speculate that he wrote down a verse from the Old Testament: "People who quit following the LORD will be like a name written in the dust, because they have left the LORD, the spring of living water" (Jer 17:13). Others think that he might have written down some of the sins that the Pharisees had been guilty of themselves. Still others think that all he needed to do was write a list of their names.

Whatever Jesus wrote, his words were effective. And they were obviously consistent with his character and actions. His writing moved a mob of hypocritical accusers to feel convicted, and then to disperse, and it dramatically demonstrated mercy and forgiveness to a woman broken by her own sin. This Wordsmith revealed the truth and grace of the kingdom of God at just the right moment.

May we aspire to do the same with our words.

Bibliography

Andrew-Gee, Eric. "Your Smartphone is Making You Stupid." *Globe and Mail*, January 6, 2018. https://www.theglobeandmail.com/technology/your-smartphone-is-making-you-stupid/article37511900/.

Augustine. *Homily 7 on the First Epistle of John*. http://www.newadvent.org/fathers/170207.htm.

Bohn, Roger, and James Short. "Measuring Consumer Information." *International Journal of Communication* 6 (2012) 980–1000.

Bruner, Jerome. *Acts of Meaning*. Cambridge: Harvard University Press, 1990.

Carr, Nicholas. *The Shallows: What the Internet Is Doing to Our Brains*. New York: Norton, 2011.

Collier, Nancy. *The Power of Off: The Mindful Way to Stay Sane in a Virtual World*. Louisville, CO: Sounds True, 2016.

Franklin, Benjamin. "Pennsylvania Gazette." https://sites.google.com/site/kondabhaskarreddy/benjamin-franklin-pennsylvania-gazette.

Harper, Lisa. "What is 'Righteous Anger'?" https://www.christianitytoday.com/biblestudies/bible-answers/theology/righteousanger.html.

Hawthorne, Nathaniel. "Passages from Hawthorne's Note-books." Boston: Ticknor and Fields, 1866.

Heid, Markham. "You Asked: Is My Smartphone Making Me Dumber?" *Time*, February 8, 2017. http://time.com/4663458/smartphone-brain-dumb/.

Hurston, Zora Neale. *Sweat*. New Brunswick: Rutgers University Press, 1997.

Piper, John, et al. *The Power of Words and the Wonder of God*. Carol Stream: Crossway, 2009.

Quintilian. *The Orator's Education, Volume 4: Books 9–10*. Edited and translated by Donald A. Russell. Loeb Classical Library 127. Cambridge: Harvard University Press, 2002.

Smith, Aaron, and Monica Anderson. "Social Media Use in 2018." http://www.pewinternet.org/2018/03/01/social-media-use-in-2018/.

Taylor, Justin, and John Piper, eds. *The Power of Words and the Wonder of God*. Wheaton: Crossway, 2009.

10

The Wisdom of Art

Cameron Anderson

Hope . . . aims at reunion, at recollection, at reconciliation: in that way, and in that way alone, it might be called a memory of the future.

—GABRIEL MARCEL, *HOMO VIATOR*

We are meaning-makers, not just image makers. It is not just that we recognize images . . . it is that we are constructed to make meaning out of things, and that we learn from others how to do it.

—KIRK VARNEDOE,
PICTURES OF NOTHING: ABSTRACT ART SINCE POLLOCK

Perhaps it was your birthday, maybe Christmas, and a parent or grandparent presented you with a fine set of oil pastels. Neat in their rows, the package of brilliantly hued crayons may have seemed too special to open. But laying down a stroke or two of buttery color on clean paper would prove more urgent and, in that young moment, drawing and its potential opened wide. Perhaps you arrived to the art world through some other door—the lessons of an inspiring teacher, tinkering on a model at home, an aunt who took you by hand to a museum. Whatever first brought you to art, it captured your heart and mind and did not let go.

If, like me, you belonged to a conservative Protestant church, your new impractical love would soon need to be defended. In fact, these Bible-believing communities had little interest in the art world, not least because to them, it appeared brazen, bizarre, and elite. Adding to this sense of disconnection, artists belonging to these congregations were ill-equipped to provide art suitable either for worship or teaching. The art departments and academies where they studied (not least, church-related colleges and universities) had no interest in such things. Consequently, for the twentieth century and beyond, the social and aesthetic divide between the church and the art world appeared intractable.[1]

In conservative Protestant communities there was, however, at least one means to address the awkwardness that inevitably accompanied a calling to the arts: the artist could establish a *biblical basis* to defend it.[2] Searching chapter and verse in support of one's calling can be spiritually rewarding, but where the visual arts are concerned, discouragement is close at hand.[3] For if the two testaments make regular mention of rulers and warriors, prophets and priests, shepherds and vintners—even widows and lepers—then they are mostly silent about painters, potters, weavers, sculptors, and architects.[4] Still, those who persist will eventually learn of Bezalel.

> The LORD spoke to Moses: "See, I have called by name Bezalel son of Uri son of Hur, of the tribe of Judah: and I have filled him with divine spirit, with ability, intelligence, and knowledge in every kind of craft, to devise artistic designs, to work in gold, silver, and bronze, in cutting stones for setting, and in carving wood, in every kind of craft." (Exod 31:1–5)

The artist of faith who discovers this passage and its echo in Exodus 36:1–2, may sense that he has met the lost founder of his tribe. In this instance, an artist equipped by God's Spirit to build Israel's tabernacle. In the quest to establish a biblical basis for a calling to the visual arts, Bezalel is exemplar.

---

1. See Anderson, *Faithful Artist*, and Elkins, *On the Strange Place*.

2. Hence the title of H. R. Rookmaaker's *Art Needs No Justification* and Francis Schaefer's *Art and the Bible*.

3. In their most regrettable form, these searches become "name it and claim it" operations that pay no heed to the biblical or theological context from which such texts have been excised.

4. Although visual artists are scarcely mentioned in the Bible, the Good Book abounds with images that send the mind's eye of the reader rushing from creation accounts in Genesis to the prophet Ezekiel and from Jesus' parables to John's Apocalypse.

I

The story that surrounds Bezalel is epic. Having resided in Egypt for more than 400 years, the children of Israel had grown in size and power, thereby posing a tangible threat to Pharaoh and his empire. Mercifully, God—I am who I am—heard the cry of his people. To rescue the children of Israel from the land of Egypt, God called Moses, appearing to him in a burning bush that would not be consumed. Aided by his older brother Aaron, Moses returned to Egypt to plead for Israel's release. But Pharaoh would not relent, and so God set ten plagues on Egypt. Finally, with the death of his firstborn son, Egypt's broken-spirited ruler yielded to Moses' demand.

As Israel, a nation of 2.4 million people, advanced toward Sinai, God's presence went before them. He parted the Red Sea. He provided a pillar of cloud to guide them by day and a pillar of fire to lead them by night. Manna, quail, and water would follow. Yet, in his mercy, God desired something more: the construction of a sacred tent grand enough to contain his glory. At this point, Bible readers typically bypass the description of the tabernacle's design, construction, and function; recorded first in Exodus 25–31 and then again in Exodus 35–40, it is a tedious read.[5] Nonetheless, patient readers will be rewarded with considerable insight into the calling of artists in ancient Israel. In this regard, six observations follow.

The first observation of note is that the *tabernacle* is God's idea. It was during Moses' forty-day sojourn atop Mount Sinai that God revealed his plan for the tabernacle, and on the prophet's descent he shared this plan with the children of Israel. The collaborative venture commenced.[6]

Second, Bezalel was charged to oversee the project. Doubtless, his reputation as a master craftsman and project manager was widely known. But how did this maker achieve such marvels? The answer can only be that he was apprenticed to his trade in Egypt. Given his superior skills, perhaps he served in Pharaoh's court? Whatever notoriety Bezalel may have enjoyed, the Exodus account does not present him as an *artist-genius*, nor is his divine commission described as an opportunity for *personal expression*. More practical matters consumed Bezalel's attention. Tools in hand, he would

---

5. Thirteen of the forty chapters in Exodus—nearly a third of the book—are devoted to the design, construction, and function of the tabernacle. By contrast, only five chapters are devoted to the giving of the law, also delivered to Moses during his retreat on Mount Sinai.

6. In our modern era, we are inclined to regard art-making as a solitary pursuit. For an explanation of how theologians, patrons, merchants, and artists, chiefly during the Renaissance, collaborated to produce objects and build spaces in service to their communities, see Skillen, *Putting Art (Back) in Its Place*.

need to establish a foundry, a carpenter shop, and spaces for weaving and metal work.

Third, so that Bezalel might be equipped to construct a holy house for God, God's Spirit filled him. Perhaps Moses, the one who spoke to God face to face, had also been filled by the Spirit. Yet Bezalel's filling is the first mention of such an event in the Old Testament.

The fourth notable detail is the array of richly dyed fabrics of purple, blue, and crimson, and the silver and gold used to adorn the tabernacle, its furniture, and priestly garments. This was all Egyptian plunder, not taken by force, but rather given to the Hebrew women by their Egyptian masters and then carried into the wilderness, often as jewelry. The Israelites released this wealth to support the construction of the tabernacle, and following the folly of the golden calf, their offerings exceeded the need. When completed, the tabernacle would be a place of remarkable beauty in service to God's greater glory. According to God's plan, the treasure of Egypt's empire had been repurposed.

Since the tabernacle was a place where Divine desire could meet human need, a fifth observation is salient: When compared to Egypt's monumental pyramids erected centuries earlier, the scale of the tabernacle hardly bears mention. But if the pharaohs' tombs had been designed to deliver their deceased god-men to a hoped-for afterlife, the tabernacle hosted the glory of a living God. At its completion, the same Spirit that filled Bezalel would invade the tabernacle, causing priests and worshippers alike to encounter the real presence of the LORD. Modern minds will be tempted to imagine a series of cinematic special effects. The events surrounding the tabernacle were not, however, a virtual brush with an imaginary God, but instead an actual encounter with sounding trumpets and penitent worshippers, animal sacrifice and spattered blood, perfumed incense and burning flesh.

Sixth and finally, since the Jews were a wandering people, a worship space suited to their purposes had to be portable. New Testament readers will recognize that the itinerant character of the tabernacle anticipates the ministry of Jesus. Matthew and Luke record Jesus' claim that, "Foxes have holes, birds have nests, but the Son of Man has no place to lay his head" (Matt 8:20/Luke 9:58). According to John's Gospel, Jesus of Nazareth "tabernacled" with us; the fullness of God dwelling in Christ and his body becoming God's new temple. Further still, the writer of Hebrews points out that Jesus is both the unblemished sacrifice and our sinless high priest. Together, these signs anticipate the coming rule of Christ.[7]

---

7. Through the centuries, more sacramental traditions have maintained a physical space for the tabernacle in their houses of worship to contain the host, the body of Christ.

Remarkably, it was Bezalel, Oholiab, and their band of makers who fashioned the tabernacle that foreshadowed the coming Son of Man. A striking coda to their calling is Solomon's request to Hiram King of Tyre to provide Israel with a gifted artisan to oversee the building of the temple in Jerusalem 485 years later. Hence, King Hiram's response:

> I have dispatched Hiram-abi, a skilled artisan, endowed with understanding, the son of one of the Danite women, his father a Tyrian. He is trained to work in gold, silver, bronze, iron, stone, and wood, and in purple, blue, and crimson fabrics and fine linen, and to do all sorts of engraving and execute any design that may be assigned him, with your artisans, the artisans of my LORD, your father David. (2 Chr 2:13–14)

To grasp the scope of Hiram-abi's appointment, some context is needed. David, Solomon's father, and Israel's second king, longed "to behold the beauty of the LORD, and to inquire in his temple" (Ps 27:4). In this regard, it troubled David that he occupied a splendid palace, while God's place of dwelling was a tent. David was eager to construct a temple for God, but God forbade it and the opportunity fell instead to Solomon. As the reign and wealth of Israel's third king increased, his work on two ambitious projects commenced: a royal palace, taking thirteen years to construct and a holy temple, requiring seven more. Again, Hiram King of Tyre—a friend and advisor to David—enters the story supplying vast quantities of cedar, cut stone, and gold. To aid the effort, Solomon "conscripted seventy thousand laborers and eighty thousand stonecutters in the hill country, with three thousand six hundred to oversee them." Remarkably, the cedar and cypress they felled and the stones they quarried were prepared with such precision "that neither hammer nor ax nor any tool of iron was heard in the temple when it was being built" (1 Kgs 7:1).

Once completed, worshippers entering the temple would encounter terrestrial and celestial glories—pomegranates and palm trees, lions and oxen, flowers and wreaths, and winged cherubim.[8] Moderns viewing the restored lapis lazuli fresco on Giotto's starry ceiling in the Scrovegni Chapel (c. 1305), or even Vincent van Gogh's comparatively small *Starry Night* (1889) painted a half century later, might gain a sense of the cosmological glory present in the precious stones, silver, gold, and richly dyed fabrics that adorned the temple. Theologian G. K. Beale writes:

---

8. Notably, Solomon was a naturalist (1 Kgs 4:33), and so it should be no surprise that elements of the natural order, creation, appear abundantly in the design and construction.

> [The] temple as a small model of the entire cosmos is part of the large perspective in which the temple pointed forward to a huge worldwide sanctuary in which God's presence would dwell in every part of the cosmos. The conception also is a linchpin for a better understanding of why John later pictures the entire new heavens and earth to be on a mammoth temple in which God dwells as he had formerly dwelt in the holy of holies.[9]

On the day of its dedication, the temple's every detail culminated in such splendor that we read, "the priests could not stand to minister because of the cloud; for the glory of the LORD filled the house of God" (2 Chr 5:14). This achievement was unequaled in Israel's history and yet, even in that moment, Solomon would be left to wonder, "Will God indeed dwell on the earth? Even heaven and the highest heaven cannot contain you, much less this house that I have built!" (1 Kgs 8:27).

The central interest of this essay is the artist's vocation and its relationship to wisdom. For good reason, ancient projects like the tabernacle and the temple rightly capture our religious imagination, and clearly God's call to Bezalel and Hiram-abi confirms that the humble service of gifted artisans can be a vital means to host God's glory.

But what relevance, if any, does this pair of accounts have for today's artist of faith? On the one hand, some in the church long to return to creating objects and spaces that celebrate the glory of God. In this regard Orthodox Christians have remained constant. On occasion, iterations of the temple's grandeur have appeared to us in modern life, none more impressive than Antoni Gaudi's *La Sagrada Familia* in Barcelona. Begun in 1883, the estimated completion date of this soaring wonder is 2026, the centenary of Gaudi's death.

On the other hand, while smaller but equally imaginative sacred projects dot the globe, in the modern West an achievement like Gaudi's is exceptional, anomalous. Today no revered prophets call us to such actions, no startling theophanies draw us in, no theocracies sponsor the construction of a high holy place for God. For all its reach and innovation, the church today is mostly an aesthetic wilderness, and artists hoping to respond to our global situation are diverted to substantially different kinds of work.

II

In the long arc that stretches from Bezalel's tabernacle to, say, Frank Gehry's Guggenheim Museum in Bilbao, the landscape of making and meaning

---

9. Beale, *Temple and the Church's Mission*, 48.

has shifted. As early as the first century and then through the Renaissance and beyond, much of the art and architecture fashioned in the West was made in service to a Christian vision of the world—Europe's cathedrals being Christendom's grandest achievement. Inside and out, the design of each featured a complex theological program articulated by frescoes, altarpieces, carved reliefs, statues, mosaics, stained glass, and liturgical objects.[10] Alongside thousands of monasteries, libraries, schools, civic spaces, and smaller churches, these grand spaces were built by stonemasons, carpenters, sculptors, furniture makers, goldsmiths, and painters who, like Bezalel and Hiram-abi, belonged to guilds where they learned their trade and labored together in service to the vision of a master architect and/or wealthy patron. These artisans were among the most skilled makers of their day, and surely their strong hand and imagination was present in each completed task. How could it be otherwise? Nonetheless, their daily work was not primarily an opportunity for personal expression nor the occasion to establish their renown. If a few artists and artisans did grace the parlors of popes, princes, and wealthy merchants, most remained anonymous.

As Christian art and the humanities flourished, especially during the Renaissance, a subtle inflection occurred that would alter popular perceptions of art-making: the *artist-genius* emerged.[11] At first, many of these artists maintained their religious devotion, but in the closing decades of the seventeenth century, the philosophical lineaments of Western thought were being recast. Alternately termed the Age of Reason or the Age of Enlightenment, the rise of modern science, secular thought, and heady notions of personal freedom became a gathering force.[12] By the end of the century that followed, the theological engine that had powered Christian art began to sputter. With this, a romantic, spiritually-toned understanding of the artist emerged. Summarizing the moment, David Lyle Jeffrey writes:

> They [William Wordsworth and Caspar David Friedrich] turned to nature, especially nature in its most awe-inspiring manifestations, seeking there a replacement for the failed glory of an ancient faith from which the sensibilities of the Reformation had cut them off both aesthetically and spiritually. Needing a place marker for the holy, they sought it outwardly in nature

---

10. The scale of Christian art was not always monumental. In fact, smaller, more intimate chapels, handheld icons, illuminated prayer books and Psalters, reliquaries, and a bounty of other devotional objects occupied a central place in the worshipping community.

11. Written in 1550, the first serious effort to record the stories of individual artists is usually attributed to Vasari, *Lives of the Artists*.

12. For a thorough examination of secularism, see Taylor, *Secular Age*.

rather than in nature's God, but finally found it in their own imaginations.[13]

Political and social revolutions would follow, artist manifestoes were drafted, and conventional approaches to art-making overturned. On entering the twentieth century and hardened by the carnage of two world wars, "the shock of the new" advanced, first in Europe and then in the United States.[14] A new modern art world was born, and with it a full complement of museums, university art departments, galleries, publishers, patrons, and collectors. The perceived constraint of tradition would now leach away, and its corresponding wisdom would be relegated to the margins of contemporary life.

My summary of this broad sway is admittedly thin, but the larger point stands: If artistic brilliance and facility had once been the handmaiden of the church, the church's piety and iconoclasm would cause her to become art's enemy. Once celebrated as the central patron of the arts, she would be regarded now as art's oppressor, a posture of resistance grounded substantially in the thought and action of the Protestant Reformation. Imagined to be a liberating vanguard, irreligious prophets, priests, and poets invaded the cultural scene, and in more progressive quarters the *idea* of the artist gained unparalleled esteem.[15] In this new world, fresh imagination and magical creations abounded, but so also did a hunger for personal aggrandizement and an admiring public. Amid it all, romantic conceptions of the artist prevailed.

At this point, our account takes an unexpected turn. Self-proclaimed atheist Alain de Botton is forthright in observing that, while belief in God (worse still, organized religion) has fallen out of fashion, contemporary men and woman are unwilling to let go of religion's benefits. Writes de Botton, "I recognized that my continuing resistance to theories of afterlife or of heavenly residents was no justification for giving up on the music, buildings, prayers, rituals, feasts, shrines, pilgrimages, communal meals and illuminated manuscripts of the faith."[16] We are, it seems, eager to occupy God's house of devotion, wonder, and story, but only while he is away on holiday. The human longing for transcendence holds. We look up and beyond to refined aesthetic encounters, the wonders of nature, and the mystery of the

---

13. Jeffrey, *In the Beauty of Holiness*, 251.
14. Hughes, *Shock of the New*.
15. Deresiewicz, "Death of the Artist."
16. de Botton, *Religion for Atheists*, 14.

cosmos, but no spiritual solace greets de Botton's "non-believers."[17] They are alone in the cosmos.

As we did at the close of the first section of this essay, we pause to ask what bearing the modernist disenchantment considered here may have on the artist's vocation. Jacques Barzun provides a clear answer: "The power of art to evoke the transcendent and bring about this unity is what has led artists and thinkers in the last two centuries to equate art and religion, and finally to *substitute art for religion*."[18]

III

Ed Meadors, the editor of this book, has undertaken a noble task: to celebrate wisdom, especially as it may be found in the academic and professional disciplines. Regarding wisdom, our longstanding practice has been to mine it from troves of canonical art, music, literature, philosophy, and theology. But in the wake of postmodern ambiguity and its modernist antecedent, social and cultural conditions have been radically reconfigured. As early as the 1960s, Canadian futurist Marshall McLuhan forecast that our world would become a global village. It has. But if the world is now a fascinating mélange of diverse callings, cuisines, customs, manners, and identities, it is decidedly not a unity. Our global village is a discordant plurality wherein the poor and the powerless are displaced in record number, environmental degradation heads to code red, the penchant for greed and violence holds fast, and personal anxiety seems to know no bounds.

Amid the clamor and anxiety of these ever-shifting boundaries, one reality does cohere—consumption. Our lives are given to produce goods and services and to consume, the same obligations that have been native to every human economy. What has changed in this brave new world is the conviction that every dream we can imagine should come true. We are entitled to receive nothing less. The pulsing heart that gives life to this global enterprise is a socially mediated, dazzling (mostly digital) spectacle that cleverly converts symbols into promises and wants into needs. Magnificent temples surround us, but they are erected mostly in service to commerce, sports, and the arts.

A disturbing byproduct of our information-laden technological world—its breathtaking benefits notwithstanding—is its ability to keep us preoccupied, distracted. In the shadow of this deceit, the dramatic

---

17. Hubble telescope's Ultra Deep Field has led astronomers to estimate that the observable universe contains about 200 billion galaxies.

18. Barzun, *Use and Abuse of Art*, 26. Italics mine.

convenience of our automated, wireless, sensor-riddled world invites a steady retreat from the vital experiences that make us human. Tactile learning subsides, social engagement embodies thin solutions, critical thought dissipates, the celebration of common life flies away. Is it possible, we wonder, to sort out the difference between information and knowledge or knowledge and wisdom?

Fortunately, our conspicuous consumption is incapable of sating the appetite we have for meaning. The weighty existential questions still dog us. What, after all, does it mean to be a feeling and thinking being? To what degree am I free to make and act? What, if any, moral obligation does this freedom entail? Will the world's injustices be righted? When breathing my last, will I, at least in some essential form, continue to exist? Is there some supernatural being, a god, who superintends all things?

For the third time in this essay, we return to our central question: In the swift eddies of information and consumption that surround us, how shall we understand the artist's vocation? At this point in the human story, the artist's best gift to us may be their *critical distance*. Now more than ever, we need artists to create and not merely to consume. We need them to exercise their agency as resistance to the hyper-mediated world that engulfs us. According to artist Olafur Eliasson, "Art . . . encourages us to cherish intuition, uncertainty, and creativity and to search constantly for new ideas; artists aim to break rules and find unorthodox ways of approaching contemporary issues."[19] But how exactly is such work enacted? Religious or not, consider three arenas: making, meaning, and being.

Making. Of central interest to the contemporary art world is the way that makers make. *Homo sapiens* need water, food, clothing, and shelter to survive, and to that end we harvest materials, invent tools, and master techniques. The labors ease suffering and extend leisure but, as anthropologists will attest, the skill and handiwork they require are seldom limited to their utility. Beyond the demand of function, we embellish our forms—finely worked filigree on sword hilts, stitched logos on shirt pockets, geometric patterns woven into Navajo blankets. We carve, weave, glaze, and paint symbols, tales, and histories.

Consider the painter. Paint, her medium, possesses remarkable utility, protecting objects and spaces from exposure to the elements and daily wear. Whether applying sleek lacquer to a new car or scumbling paint plein air on a canvas, the painter's need is to finish a surface. To achieve this, she learns how paint responds to the push and pull of a brush, how it yields to solvent, how it conforms to a surface. In time, this knowing *how* and knowing *about*

---

19. Eliasson, "Why Art Has the Power," para. 6.

become enfleshed muscle memory, gross and fine. Painting also presents considerable aesthetic potential, a means, say, to intercept the shape of a late afternoon shadow and the blue-gray light of the dawn that follows. In that moment, the painter sorts the uncanny relationship between likeness and abstraction; she probes the nature of reality itself.

> [L]ike the history of representation, the real history of abstract painting shows the continuous evolution of a new language for art that, through the slow growth and accretion of symbolic meaning—so that a *splash* might come to suggest freedom, and a *scrawl* the Self—would capture truths about the world and about modern existence.[20]

Plying these media, old and new, these acts of making are nothing less than the restoration of our humanity. In this regard, Christians might hope for more, but we certainly do not hope for less. As ones created to bear the image of God, we are *homo faber* who, in actions large and small, are called—commanded, even—to deploy the creative triunity of mind, eye, and hand to good cause.

Meaning. If the material world is able to bear meaning, then it follows that those who create objects and spaces have the capacity to be meaning makers. For the spiritually inclined, this proposition can be problematic, not least because every major religion rightly instructs its followers to avoid worldly entanglements. "Do not store up treasures for yourselves on earth, where moth and rust consume and where thieves break in and steal," says Jesus (Matt 6:17). Possessing things is not our problem, rather it is that we are charmed and seduced by them. The prophet Isaiah cleverly outlines the problem:

> He [the carpenter] cuts down cedars or chooses a holm tree or an oak and lets it grow strong among the trees of the forest. He plants a cedar and the rain nourishes it. Then it can be used as fuel. Part of it he takes and warms himself; he kindles a fire and bakes bread. Then he makes a god and worships it, makes it a carved image and bows down before it. Half of it he burns in the fire; over this half he roasts meat, eats it, and is satisfied. He also warms himself and says, "Ah, I am warm, I can feel the fire!" The rest of it he makes into a god, his idol, bows down to it, and worships it; he prays to it and says, "Save me, for you are my god!" (Isa 44:14–17)

---

20. Gopnik, "Preface." Italics mine.

The idol maker's critical error is misrepresentation, bearing false witness. Consider this, Israel's gold calf *did* represent a god, but it *did not*, as claimed, represent Israel's god (who forbade such representations).

In fact, the Bible upholds the belief that the material world *means* and rejects, therefore, the spiritual/material dualism that appears to be the mainstay of contemporary Christianity. Our difficulty in getting after the significance of things is that they either mean *too little* or mean *wrongly*. To redress this, artists in the Christian community need a theology of making that celebrates the "stuffness" and "thingness" of the world. Ben Quash puts it like this, "Imagination works in history, and the particularities of material creatures, to make analogical connections between things and to disclose the binding of the world which is its God-given state."[21] Indeed, the material world—the creation, the incarnation, the community of God's people gathered, and, in most Christian traditions, the sacrament—bears witness to a greater spiritual reality.

It follows that, in her studio practice, the artist of faith bears witness. In part, the wisdom we so desperately need resides in material making and artists are those (so also scientists and others) who can *show* it to us. Wisdom's beauty greets us as a signpost, a lens, a window, and the visual arts can, as they have, incline us toward the sacred, narrate the salvation story, and enrich our liturgy.

Being. Acts of making paired with the pursuit of meaning contribute to the formation of a self—the cognitive, aesthetic, and spiritual dimensions of being. Art making, in its most popular sense, is primarily thought to be an act of personal expression. Without question, drawing, model making, and photography are ways to pay attention, to keep track. At the same time, clinging to an older atomistic notion of the self—an isolated mode of being associated with the Enlightenment—now appears naïve. Now more than ever we must reject the impossible idea that we occupy the world alone and with this resist the insufficient idea that art-making is primarily a vehicle for self-adulation, sustained adolescent "specialness."

Art exists in a discursive environment; it always has. And it follows that the relationship between personal expression, existential meaning, and responsible social action is neither linear nor neat. Genuine discourse is a sequence of short cuts, switchbacks, and cross references. It bobs and weaves, shifts and dodges. It invites participation and critique. And where material making is concerned, haptic and cognitive operations interpenetrate, artifact histories are consulted, and creative potential is explored. These matters are not, however, endlessly fluid. In the end, the one who

---

21. Quash, *Found Theology*, 30.

hopes to make, mean, and be must commit to beliefs, values, and practices. At its best, our discursive nature inclines us to the reciprocal pleasures of deep friendship.

Considering the several issues presented in this essay, how shall Bible believing people who sense a calling to the visual arts respond? Two directions seem possible. On the one hand, some among us are called to exercise our creative abilities in service to the worshipping communities to which we belong. Like Bezalel and Hiram-abi, this kind of work requires nothing less than excellence and humble service. On the other hand, today's artists, especially those participating in the world of contemporary art, are called to something more prophetic. Since the Judeo-Christian tradition is prophetic, the posture of *critical distance* mentioned earlier should ring familiar. Neither the Old Testament prophets nor the New Testament apostles were accommodationists. In fact, those who drew near to God—that "great cloud of witnesses"—are also those set apart. This prophetic call equips the believing artist to critique the existential crisis of Modernism, to name the idols of today's consumer culture, and even to challenge the hubris of Christendom. In the end, the true source of wisdom is our all-wise God, the maker of heaven and earth who calls us to pursue truth, goodness, and beauty even as his Holy Spirit continues our transformation back into the *imago Dei*.

Bibliography

Anderson, Cameron J. *The Faithful Artist: A Vision of Evangelicalism and the Arts*. Studies in Theology and the Arts. Downers Grove: InterVarsity, 2016.

Barzun, Jacques. *The Use and Abuse of Art*. Bollingen Series 35. A. W. Mellon Lectures in the Fine Arts 22. Princeton: Princeton University Press, 1975.

Beale, G. K. *The Temple and the Church's Mission: A Biblical Theology of the Dwelling Place of God*. New Studies in Biblical Theology 17. Downers Grove: InterVarsity, 2004.

de Botton, Alain. *Religion for Atheists: A Non-believer's Guide to the Uses of Religion*. New York: Vintage, 2012.

Deresiewicz, William. "The Death of the Artist—and the Birth of the Creative Entrepreneur." *The Atlantic*, January/February 2015.

Elkins, James. *On the Strange Place of Religion in Contemporary Art*. New York: Routledge, 2004.

Eliasson, Olafur. "Why Art Has the Power to Change the World." https://www.weforum.org/agenda/2016/01/why-art-has-the-power-to-change-the-world/.

Gopnik, Adam. "Preface." In *Pictures of Nothing: Abstract Art Since Pollock*, by Kirk Varnedoe, ix–xvi. Princeton: Princeton University Press, 2003.

Hughes, Robert. *The Shock of the New: The Hundred-Year History of Modern Art—Its Rise, Its Dazzling Achievement, Its Fall*. New York: Knopf, 1987.

Jeffrey, David Lyle. *In the Beauty of Holiness: Art and the Bible in Western Culture.* Grand Rapids: Eerdmans, 2017.

Quash, Ben. *Found Theology: History, Imagination, and the Holy Spirit.* London: Bloomsbury, 2014.

Rookmaaker, H. R. *Art Needs No Justification.* Downers Grove: InterVarsity, 1973.

Schaeffer, Francis A. *Art and the Bible.* Downers Grove: InterVarsity, 1993.

Skillen, John. *Putting Art (Back) in Its Place.* Peabody: Hendrickson, 2016.

Taylor, Charles. *A Secular Age.* Cambridge: Harvard University Press, 2007.

Vasari, Giorgio. *The Lives of the Artists.* Translated by Julia Conaway Bondanella and Peter Bondanella. Oxford World's Classics. New York: Oxford University Press, 2008.

11

The Wisdom of Music
Tony Payne

Give thanks to the L‍ord with the lyre; Sing praises to Him with a harp of ten strings. Sing to Him a new song; Play skillfully with a shout of joy.

(PS 33:2–3)

Introduction: The Wisdom of the Arts

Across the spectrum of the liberal arts, educators communicate meaning almost exclusively in words. Yet careful reflection reveals a yearning for meaning that exceeds their power. The arts lie beyond words, yet help us understand their subtler meanings. This is why the wisdom of the arts is such a beautiful idea. I have experienced it standing before Ivanov's painting, "The Apparition of Christ," in Moscow's Tretyakov Gallery. I have heard it on many Christmas Eves, sitting at the organ, playing, "O Come, All Ye Faithful." Coming to the verse that begins, "Yea, Lord, we greet thee," the hymn ascends until, almost too glorious to bear, the congregation sings, "Word of the Father, now in flesh appearing."

And I have seen it watching the film *Babette's Feast* as Axel patiently reveals Babette's true character. Babette, a celebrated French chef, proclaims, "Throughout the world sounds one long cry from the heart of the artist: Give me the chance to do my very best." Daniel Treier writes that wisdom "involves both the communication of tradition and reflective enquiry about its ongoing viability. In Scripture, wisdom is the tree of life to which human beings cling so that by embracing God they may know how to live well" (Prov 3).

Words spew out everywhere, every day, but wisdom pauses to reflect. It's not that words are absent from the arts, rather they can be clues to transcendent meanings. Poetry, for example, shares a kinship with everyday words, but the poet often rejects those everyday meanings. In his *War Requiem*, a towering choral/orchestral work of the twentieth century, composer Benjamin Britten employed the poetry of Wilfred Owen, a Welshman who died fighting during World War I just a week before the Armistice:

> Bugles sang, saddening the evening air;
> And bugles answered, sorrowful to hear.
> Voices of boys were by the river-side.
> Sleep mothered them; and left the twilight sad.

The sculptor takes raw materials—a block of wood or marble, a lump of clay, and creates a work of art with it. Gaze upon such an object and you will find your own meaning; words may not help at all. Stand before the baptistery window in Coventry Cathedral, and you will understand that words are sometimes useless. This is the ineffable reality of wisdom.

Alongside the visual arts, music has the potential to help us interpret the world around us, but not as an exact science. It was the philosopher and mathematician Gottfried Leibniz, a contemporary of J. S. Bach, who wrote, "Music is a hidden arithmetic exercise of the soul, which does not know that it is counting." J. S. Bach's music is widely considered to be the pinnacle of the western European music tradition, but it is also mathematical in the sense that Leibniz described. As a composer, Bach's mastery of theological symbolism and biblical imagery, dramatic gesture, numerology and mathematics were unparalleled. While it is certain that Bach intended to convey his Christian worldview through his music, it is unclear how Bach's music conveys wisdom embedded with truth claims. Hence, the challenge of the wisdom of music.

Recently, I heard the Chicago Symphony Orchestra perform Beethoven's Symphony No. 6—the *Pastorale Symphony*. I find Beethoven's imagery in this symphony convincing: meadows and flowers blowing in a light breeze, the babbling brook, the "merry gathering of country folk," the thunderstorm, and the "cheerful and thankful feelings" of the shepherds after the storm had past. For most, Beethoven's *Pastorale* imagery is easier to understand than Bach's symbolism. Yet, sacred music is just a part of Beethoven's catalog of works. You will find faith expressed in the *Missa Solemnis* based on the great mass liturgy. Beethoven gave the work evangelistic purpose when he said, "My chief aim when I was composing this grand Mass was to awaken and instill enduring religious feelings not only into the singers but also into the listeners."

In the 20th century, impressionist composer Claude Debussy painted a musical picture of a sunken cathedral in *La Cathédrale Engoultie* (*The Sunken Cathedrale*). In his letter to composer Paul Dukas (1901), Debussy writes, "I confess that I am no longer thinking in musical terms, or at least not much, even though I believe with all my heart that music remains for all time the finest means of expression we have." He continued, "There's no need either for music to make people think! . . . It would be enough if music could make people listen." Debussy highlights the contrast between rational thought and ineffable wisdom.

Audiences have always loved *Sleigh Ride* by Leroy Anderson for its ability to evoke realistic images of horse drawn sleigh ride on a snowy winter day. Sadly, it's because of Anderson's ability to inspire listeners with such vivid imagery that it is judged by some as trite. Among the most precise natural representations is the famous night music found in the music of Bela Bartok, but Bartok's music is far less popular than the more overt musical gestures of Anderson. Yet, the wisdom of music expresses itself in subtle gestures, ideas, and feelings.

Wisdom through Music

During my first year of college, I was enrolled in an ethnomusicology course. Our assignment was to transcribe the songs of remote New Guinea tribes onto music staff paper. Thanks to Professor Dr. Vida Chenoweth, that ethnomusicology class led to many other experiences that shaped my understanding of music in culture. Ethnomusicology provides a method of inspiring broader engagement with music beyond that which is most familiar.

For some, ethnomusicology helps to understand the Xhosa people of South Africa, for others it's jazz fusion or even Bach. Whether your cultural reference point is European classical or Hillsong Australia, it is natural to remain tethered to the familiar and skeptical of everything else. This is why ethnomusicology is such a valuable asset to the discovery of wisdom's embrace. It instills generosity and promotes inclusion.

It is probably ethnomusicology that led me to my life axiom: *Sing each other's songs*. I want other people, other tribes to feel that their songs matter and that their story is worth retelling. Singing each other's songs is rooted in a reconciling Gospel. John 3:16 famously declares God's love for the entire world. Because you are loved by God, your songs and stories matter!

Singing each other's songs becomes a mission of love, embracing cultural traditions and personal stories in fulfillment of the great commandment to love God and to love your neighbor as yourself (Mark 12:30–31). Throughout this chapter, my goal is to offer some examples of wisdom rooted in biblical tradition, even when they are shrouded in mystery. Sometimes wisdom is communicated *through* music and sometimes *because of* music. I encourage you to remain in conversation with wisdom and mine the benefits from this amazing discipline of music in all of its styles and colors.

Consider Samuel Barber's *Adagio for Strings*, arguably one of the most emotionally powerful string pieces of the 20th century. A listener might speak of the *Adagio's* soulfulness or its passion. It rises to an almost unbearably beautiful climax then gradually draws down to the melancholy beauty of its beginning. Can anyone explain the meaning of this iconic music? Does the tense climax in the upper register of the strings refer to death or resurrection? Does the conclusion of the piece speak of disappointment or resignation? What does this music mean *to you*? How does it speak wisdom?

In Job 28:20, Job asks, "Where does wisdom come from?" In v. 23, "God understands the way to it and He alone knows where it dwells." Perhaps music harbors wisdom's secrets. Who can say that a descending melody represents a sigh as it might in the music of Johann Sebastian Bach? Or that march rhythms are a call to war? Even if a listener appreciated the evocative or pictorial meaning of a musical idea, surely wisdom runs deeper.

It seems to me that both music and wisdom find their meaning in the ineffable—that is, they are not easily expressed in words. Former Archbishop of Canterbury, Rowan Williams, writes in *The Dwelling of the Light: Praying with Icons of Christ*, that "visual artists cannot depict the resurrection of Jesus Christ, they can only depict the results." Similarly, music may witness to the fruits of wisdom rather than wisdom itself. Ultimately, you will have to decide how the wisdom of music impacts your life!

Wisdom through music is found in sound and silence, feeling and response, haste and rest, complexity and simplicity, originality and imitation, tonality and abstraction, improvisation and literalism, and of course, in lyrics attached to music. Music also generates the wise virtues of humility, transparency, generosity, collaboration, community, originality, listening, and artistic courage.

I was a freshman in college when a shortage of bassoon players led the conductor to invite me to play in the college orchestra. In spite of our unsophisticated performance and my lack of experience as a bassoonist, I was awakened to the genius of Tchaikovsky's Symphony No. 6 in B minor—*Pathétique* and I realized why it ranks with the great orchestral works. This central theme is just one example:

The melodies, harmony, and the instrumentation of the *Pathétique* all possess spiritual power few would dispute. At the climax point, there is a transcendence to the music that elevates the spirit toward heaven. Think of an ascent to a climactic musical summit. Can you see the path you followed to get there? Likewise, in the music of Tchaikovsky, the composer's genius is evident on a musical journey that has been brilliantly mapped.

Hymn writers often refer to these journeys in hymns like John Newton's *Amazing Grace*, "Through many dangers, toils and snares I have already come: 'Tis grace that brought me safe thus far, and grace will lead me home." Or in Johnson Oatman's *Higher Ground*, "I want to live above the world, Though Satan's darts at me are hurled; For faith has caught the joyful sound, The song of saints on higher ground." Regardless of the music—a great symphony, or a simple hymn, genius emerges, and the inspiration transports us to higher grounds.

For me the satisfaction of experiencing Tchaikovsky is ineffably wise. Through the music, Tchaikovsky tugs at my heart and tightens my throat. The most compelling music tutors us about style and form, melody and harmony, clarity and obscurity, all quite apart from any consideration of text or word painting. Conductor Blair Skinner writes:

> The temporal nature of music necessitates form and structure—an Apollonian ideal—to constitute its place in the continuum of eternity. The composer of the music, or members of a band plot out a unique experience in time that comes only from the imagination of creative musing and openness to the inspiration of the present moment. The formation of melodies, harmonies, and textures is an act of creation mimicking the Creator in the formation of every unique facet of our Universe.

As a prized possession in the Scriptures, wisdom still runs deeper than any temporal set of conditions. In this respect, my earlier quotation of Daniel Treier bears repeating: "Wisdom involves both the communication of tradition and reflective enquiry about its ongoing viability. In Scripture wisdom is the tree of life to which human beings cling so that by embracing God they may know how to live well" (Proverbs 3).

I believe wisdom is not so much a fixed point as a navigational method. Scripture extols wisdom but does not explicitly define it in all of its variegations. Through the course of over 200 uses of the word wisdom in Scripture, one learns that wisdom begins with living in fear of God. But there's more! It's an attitude of learning and of receptivity to forces outside of ourselves. We're to learn wisdom from our elders (Job 12:12), to "get wisdom," (Prov 4:6–7), earn wisdom, (Eccl 2:26), and get to know Christ and with him the hidden treasures of wisdom and knowledge (Jas 3:17). Wisdom, like music and the arts, is shrouded in mystery, but among these 200+ verses about wisdom are numerous opportunities for wordless reflection.

Psychology Today offers a meaningful definition of wisdom drawing on principles rooted in God's Word and God's work in the world:

> Psychologists tend to agree that wisdom involves an integration of knowledge, experience, and deep understanding that incorporates tolerance for the uncertainties of life as well as its ups and downs. There's an awareness of how things play out over time, and it confers a sense of balance. It can be acquired only through experience, but by itself, experience does not automatically confer wisdom.

I think all Christians can agree that wisdom engenders the ability to draw deeper meaning from knowledge and experience and to apply this meaning toward the greater good of humankind as we celebrate the glory of God. It follows that any virtue of wisdom is virtue that leads us back to Scripture or illuminates Scriptural principals.

Hopefully, wisdom dwells along a continuum and provides strength and purpose to the open-hearted. For some, this means benefits that cannot be touched but can be felt, cannot be heard but can be received. This is ineffable wisdom. For others, wisdom has to be quantifiable to be valid, and tangible to the touch or the sight. We may call this empirical wisdom.

J.S. Bach stands out as a composer with an uncanny ability to word-paint, that is, to create musical sounds that describe the ideas in his lyrics. For example, in the cantata *Prepare the Paths and Byways* (BWV 132), the image of baptismal water drives the fast-flowing musical gestures. Bach gives us hundreds of other examples of his word-painting, and while he may be the pinnacle, there are certainly many, many other composers who have done the same.

There is music that describes a scene or an unfolding drama. And there is music that evokes common responses or shared feelings such as Sousa march or *The Representation of Chaos* for Josef Haydn's oratorio *Creation* or *Morning* from *Peer Gynt*, which offers an unmistakable portrayal of the glory of a sunrise.

There is a great deal of classical music from which no meaning is intentionally to be drawn at all. Many of the works of Beethoven and Brahms, for example are pure music like the former's *Symphony No. 5* in C minor. This is music for its own sake, music that is not encumbered with the burden of description, evocation or lyrics. I think this music also compels us to a higher realm of wise existence.

But the *Seventh Symphony* of Dmitri Shostakovich is an interesting anomaly. Numerous authors record that Soviet audiences wept when they first heard it performed. Why would an audience respond in such a fashion? Under the watchful eye of the Soviet regime, the composer was politically constrained. Yet, one instinctively feels that he is trying to communicate something. It's easy for a westerner to assume the wisdom of rejecting the authority of despotic regimes! But one astute Russian musician told me otherwise!

Wisdom about Music

Music cultivates a host of wise virtues:

Integrity, when defined as wholeness or coherence, exists almost universally in music. My son sees integrity in the Civil Wars' *The One That Got Away*. For me, it's *Yesterday* by the Beatles. If you're a music lover, you will have examples of your own. Any good analysis of Beethoven's *Symphony No. 5* in C minor or Sousa's *Stars and Stripes Forever* will agree to their fundamental integrity. Think of the music you love and why you love it. Of course, a great deal of music disappears in history. But the music that is remembered is remembered because it possesses qualities that garner positive critical acclaim. This coherence can be present in Schubert songs or the blues of B. B. King, in global songs or folksongs.

Humility may seem out of place in a list of the fruits of wisdom. But humility in music insures a link with the spiritual world. Does it seem strange to encumber our musical experiences with the burden of humility? Johann Sebastian Bach's inscription of "*SDG*" on his scores—*Sola Dei Gloria*, offer a powerful example of genius submitting to the greater authority of God. Bach also inscribed scores with "*JJ*" (*Jesu Juva*)—where one of the great musical masters of all time expresses the ultimate act of humility by explicitly acknowledging the need for God's help in completing a composition. George F. Handel possessed a similar humility over the experience of composing his famous *Messiah*. He believed that composing the *Hallelujah*

Chorus may have been an out-of-body experience, and responded to Lord Kinnoull, who had complimented him for the "entertainment" of *Messiah*: "I should be sorry if I only entertained them, I wish to make them better." This is similar to Beethoven's remark, quoted earlier, regarding the *Missa Solemnis*.

At age 67, legendary soprano Leontyne Price gave a gracious, deliberate curtsy to her audience at the beginning of her concert. Through this act of humility, Ms. Price predisposed the audience to receive her gift of music. This was her gesture to the audience that they were regarded and that the music was for them.

Ken Medema, blind from birth, has been known as a music therapist, keyboardist, singer, composer, improviser and storyteller. One particular gift that expresses Ken's humility is his making up songs based on the stories of audience members. He could exercise his genius in any number of ways, but he chooses to invest in the stories of others.

Transparency. Once, during a Chicago Symphony Orchestra performance of Mahler's Symphony No. 2 ("Resurrection"), soprano Sylvia McNair sat silently onstage for four long movements. I remember watching her for 45 minutes as she visibly reflected the glorious music with her bright, expectant face. She lived the music without singing a note. Finally, in the fifth and final movement, she stood and sang the soprano solo:

> Rise again, yes, you will rise again,
> My dust, after brief rest!
> Immortal life! Immortal life
> Will He, who called you, grant you.
> To bloom again, you were sown!
> The Lord of the Harvest goes
> And gathers like sheaves,
> Us, who died.

I have rarely observed such transparent engagement with music. Ms. McNair revealed her integrity by investing in the music, and her transparency by illuminating the music to the audience.

Silence. While silence may not be considered a virtue, it undoubtedly promotes virtue. Sometimes a person or a group is silenced by someone in authority. Wisdom can also be manifested through an individual's silence. Silence can be likened to waiting, such as, "In the morning, Lord, you hear my voice; in the morning I lay my requests before you and wait expectantly" (Ps 5:3).

Composers have been creative in making silence integral to their music. Silence enhances music and creates drama. Silence prompts us to ask what just happened or anticipate what is about to happen. Silence heightens anticipation and offers its interpretation, and words are not needed. Haydn uses silence for dramatic effect in his *String Quartet, Opus 33, No. 2* ("*The Joke*"). His witty *Rondo* displays a mastery of silence in creating both surprise and deception.

In the seventh-century hymn *Christian, Dost Thou See Them?* by Saint Andrew of Crete, there are two conspicuous beats of rest after the opening phrase of John B. Dykes's tune, following the opening question of Saint Andrew's text. Because Andrew's hymn is about spiritual warfare, the two beats must represent Dykes's attempt to allow a response to Saint Andrew's question. In those two beats of silence, the drama of the hymn heightens noticeably.

Community. Making music is almost always a community affair and nowhere has community music found more sustained practice than among the covenant people of God—from the exodus of the children of Israel to the corporate Psalms of the Old Testament to Jesus and the disciples at the Last Supper (Matt 26:30). The most glorious of all singing communities is the great apocalyptic gathering around the throne of the Lamb that was slain. In Revelation 5:11–12, where the angels alone number ten-thousand times ten-thousand, "every creature in heaven and on earth and under the earth and on the sea, and all that is in them, cry out: 'To him who sits on the throne and to the Lamb be praise and honor and glory and power, for ever and ever!'"

Imagine the power of community expressed in every choir and congregation in every Christian church gathered on any given Sunday, dating back to the early church. This is the ultimate expression of community music making. The Brooklyn Tabernacle Choir's powerful anthem *Pray!* beautifully exemplifies the phenomenon.

And while believing communities project the wisdom of music outward, collaboration offers musicians the opportunity to work together, to grow as musicians and to negotiate musical interpretations for inward benefits. This leads to an exciting vision of Christian unity as expressed in 1 Corinthians 12:12: "Just as a body, though one, has many parts, but all its many parts form one body, so it is with Christ." This wisdom comes from the very heart of the gospel and finds expression in the lives of musicians playing and singing together every day.

Artistic Courage. Artistic courage may be one of the most valuable qualities of all of wisdom's fruits. Artistic courage unlocks potential we may not realize. Artistic courage summons forth wisdom, embraces silence, thrives on transparency and promotes community. Mere use of the materials of music can have mundane results, but exercising artistic courage reaches for the transcendent. Artistic courage grants permission to the improviser and promotes independence from the printed score. It transforms a performance from common to sublime. Artistic Courage inspires the journey to the climactic musical summit referred to earlier. Artistic Courage defines the difference between breathless and breathtaking.

Originality. While God is creator *ex nihilo*, we are creators *ex aliquot*—creators out of something. Skinner refers to these acts as "procreation." We may strive for originality, but our originality is always subject to our *ex aliquo* limitations. Originality inspires wisdom through the pursuit of lifelong learning and continuous improvement. It reminds us of the real, palpable ministry of the Holy Spirit in our lives, where we experience the Lord's pleasure in our creativity, the exhilaration of exercising our creation in God's image.

Listening. Music cultivates the spiritual virtue of intelligent, patient listening. The more focused the listening the more vibrant the interpersonal communication. Hence, before performing Sylvia McNair entered into the first four movements of Mahler's Symphony by listening. Indeed, anyone singing or playing in a musical ensemble has to listen intelligently before performing capably. Music is for those who have ears to hear. On this score, C. S. Lewis's reflection on art bears repeating, "The first demand any work of art makes upon us is surrender. Look. Listen. Receive."[1] Music is remarkable in its ability to comfort the soul, lift the spirit, and refine the character. Music, *shalom*, abundant life, and joy pass from generation to generation as the stabilizing virtues of the truly wise. So it is that "A wise man will hear and increase in learning" (Prov 1:5). For these reasons it's not surprising that the word "listen" appears in the Bible over 400 times.

We conclude by affirming that the ultimate goal of music is the celebration of God as our heavenly Father. Through the gift of music, we are able to extol God through the incomparably wise direction of the Lord Jesus: "'Love the Lord your God with all your heart and with all your soul and with all your mind" (Matt 22:37). This indeed is the noble end of great music—to express with and without words the love of God and the love of neighbor—the inherent beauty, glory, and peace of God's sovereign design. To comprehend this truth is to discover the wisdom of music.

---

1. C. S. Lewis, *An Experiment in Criticism*, 19.

12

The Joy of Mathematics
Jim Bradley and Russ Howell

In the Oscar-winning blockbuster *Chariots of Fire*, Scottish missionary Eric Liddell explains to his sister Jennie the spiritual value of training for the 1929 Paris Olympics—a commitment of time and resources that will delay his travel to China. He remarks, "I believe God made me for a purpose—for China—but he also made me fast. And when I run I feel His pleasure."

Liddell reveals a deep truth: humans experience joy when exercising their God-given potentials. In this chapter, we explore that joy as it relates to two potentials we all possess to some degree: the capacities to engage in mathematical activities, and to reflect on them. The claim that there is joy in mathematics may seem odd to those for whom it is a cold, dull subject filled with rote memorization and computation. But that is not the judgment of those who know the field well. The logician Augustus De Morgan wrote, "The moving power of mathematical invention is not reasoning but imagination." A main thesis of this chapter is that De Morgan was right: the practice of mathematics requires not only solid reasoning, but curiosity, imagination, and creativity. Those who utilize those capacities experience joy that can enrich their understanding and worship of God. How does joy relate to biblical wisdom, the overriding theme of this book? We will explore this question carefully as we go along.

But merely stating that mathematical practice can produce joy won't convince those predisposed to think otherwise. If you'll pardon the expression, they need proof! As a first step in this direction, let's look at a simple example. Afterwards we will discuss the notion in depth.

Suppose you are directing a single-elimination tennis tournament with 243 entrants. The tournament protocol matches people in pairs and give each twosome a new can of balls for each round. With 243 participants, someone will be left out of the first round, so you select a person randomly (or maybe the highest-ranked player) who will have a bye. The winners, plus the person who had a bye, continue to subsequent rounds. That is, at each round the remaining players get matched in pairs, with someone getting a bye if there are an odd number of players remaining. You now have a simple question to answer: how many cans of tennis balls are needed for the tournament?

There is a dull, computational way to solve this problem. With 243 participants, one gets a bye for the first round, resulting in 242 pairs. So initially you need 121 cans of tennis balls. The player with the bye then joins the winners from round one. Those 122 people are paired, so you need 61 cans of tennis balls. For the third round, one person from the 61 winners gets a bye—you need 30 cans. At the start of the fourth round the person who had a bye from the third round joins the 30 winners, so there will be 31 left. Again, someone gets a bye, so you need 15 cans. The fifth round will then have 16 players (the 15 winners plus the bye). Fortunately, this round and all the remaining rounds now have an even number of players. You thus need 8 cans for the fifth round, 4 for the sixth, 2 for the seventh, and 1 can for the championship match. All together, then, you need 121+61+30+15+8+4+2+1=242 cans of tennis balls. Whew!

That was tedious, something you would not like to repeat if there were unanticipated last-minute entries. You would like a simple formula that tells you how many cans you need regardless of the number of people participating. There is such a formula, but arriving at it requires creative "out of the box" thinking. It comes from focusing on the losers rather than the winners. Winners continue in the tournament, but once a loss occurs, the loser is eliminated. In a tournament with 243 players, there will eventually be 242 losers, and that observation tells you the number of tennis ball cans you need—just imagine giving each loser the can of tennis balls used for that match as a consolation prize. With 243 entrants, you would thus need 242 cans, one for each loser. If there were n participants, then, you would need $n-1$ cans. Neat!

Neat, yes, but imagine that you discovered this solution by yourself. Would you experience some degree of joy? Probably so! Further, what would have caused you to see a one-to-one correspondence between the losers and the number of tennis ball cans required? Answering that question is not easy, as the revelation you experienced involved a "creative insight" of sorts. The Princeton mathematician Andrew Wiles attempted to offer an explanation for such insights in a PBS interview. He described what he thinks when he engages in mathematical research.

> I start trying to find patterns, really, so I'm doing calculations which try to explain some little piece of mathematics, and I'm trying to fit it in with some previous broad conceptual understanding of some branch of mathematics. Sometimes, that'll involve going and looking up in a book to see how it's done there. Sometimes, it's a question of modifying things a bit, sometimes, doing a little extra calculation. And sometimes, you realize that nothing that's ever been done before is any use at all, and you just have to find something completely new. And it's a mystery where it comes from.

Later in the interview he described the joy he experienced when an idea that was the key to solving a difficult research problem came to him. "I was sitting here at this desk, when suddenly, totally unexpectedly, I had this incredible revelation . . . It was so indescribably beautiful; it was so simple and so elegant, and I just stared in disbelief for twenty minutes."

Why did Wiles think his insight was indescribably beautiful? What brought him such joy? To find out we will look in detail at a classical result that many scholars have found beautiful.

We are going to explore a proof from Euclid's *Elements of Geometry*—that there is an unending supply of prime numbers. In modern terms, we would say there are *infinitely many* prime numbers. So, let's review what a prime number is. Consider the numbers 2, 3, 5, and 7. We can write $2 = 2 \times 1$, $3 = 3 \times 1$, $5 = 5 \times 1$, and $7 = 7 \times 1$. For each of these numbers, the only way to write it as a product of two whole numbers is to write it as itself times 1. Now consider the numbers 4, 6, and 8. They can be written, respectively, as $4 = 2 \times 2$; $6 = 3 \times 2$; $8 = 4 \times 2$. In each case there is a way to write the number as a product of two numbers without using itself. The numbers that make up such a product are called *factors*; for example, in the case of 6, 3 and 2 are factors. Numbers like 2, 3, 5, and 7 are *prime*; numbers like 6 and 8 are *composite*. Stated precisely, a *prime number* is a whole number greater than 1 that has only 1 and itself as whole-number factors.

Prime numbers have fascinated people for ages. The Fundamental Theorem of Arithmetic establishes that every whole number is a product of primes. If we don't care what order they are written in, it tells us that there is only one way to write that product. (Recall that 1 is not a prime.) We are not going to prove this theorem, but it points out that primes are basic building blocks—all whole numbers can be built from them. They are to numbers what atoms are to molecules. So, people who have thought about primes have asked many questions:

- How many primes are there?
- If we can form every whole number by multiplying primes, can we also form them by adding primes?
- Are primes common or rare among the whole numbers?
- Is there a formula that we could use to find primes? Suppose we wanted the tenth prime, could we enter the number 10 into our formula and find the tenth prime?

Euclid answered the first question—he showed that there are infinitely many primes. Here is a modern version of his proof:

Suppose there are only finitely many prime numbers; call them p_1, p_2, ..., p_n. We will show that there must be at least one more prime number not in this list. Let P be the product of all the prime numbers in the list, that is, $P = p_1 p_2 \cdots p_n$. Let $Q = P + 1$. Then Q is either prime or it is not:

If Q is prime, then there is a prime, namely Q, not in the list since Q would be larger than any number in the list.

If Q is not prime, then one of the primes (call it p) divides evenly into Q. Since P is the product of every prime, p must be in the list. It divides evenly into P also. Since $Q = P + 1$, we can write $Q - P = 1$. Since p divides evenly into Q and P, p divides evenly into Q - P which equals 1. But p cannot divide evenly into 1 since no prime number divides 1. This is a contradiction—so p cannot be in the list.

These observations tell us that at least one more prime number exists beyond those in the list. But we assumed that there are only finitely many prime numbers—we named and listed them all—p_1, p_2, ..., p_n. Thus, any finite list of primes necessarily misses at least one. Therefore, there are infinitely many prime numbers.

Why would someone enjoy reading this proof? Following are some reasons that seem plausible. Note that they all relate in some way to exercising our creative faculties.

Surprise: Imagine a magician making a rabbit disappear. Everyone in the audience laughs. Why? Because surprise, when it is not harmful, is a source of pleasure—the humor in most jokes depends on surprise. The use of Q and P in Euclid's argument brings the argument to a conclusion in so few steps that it almost seems like a magician's trick.

Experiencing discovery: Why would someone ask how many primes there are? Today, primes are important in creating codes used by financial institutions and the military. But in Euclid's time they had no financial or military value. So, the question originated in someone's curiosity. Resolving a puzzling question gives the sense of having grown in the process and of having more control of the world around us.

Finding a simple insight into something profound: The word "profound" suggests complexity, depth, and richness of meaning. But what concept could be more profound than infinity? And yet, this proof can be produced with a few short sentences. It seems to bring the infinite closer to our reach.

Gaining certainty: Euclid's argument is compelling. When it is fully understood something within us says, "Yes, that is right. I'm sure of it." The move from uncertainty and confusion to clarity and confidence is a source of joy.

Intellectual pleasure: Solving a problem, thinking through a question, using our imagination in a creative way, or organizing something that is disorderly is often a source of pleasure. There are many examples of people experiencing such pleasures: solving crossword or Sudoku puzzles, playing chess, or puzzling over a riddle. If you were to ask a typical mathematician why he or she does mathematics, you might expect an answer like, "It's so useful," or "It's necessary for engineering and science," or "It underlies technology, the principal driver of our economy." But that is typically not the answer you will get. More likely, the mathematician will say "It's so beautiful" or "I find such pleasure in it." Indeed, those were the judgments of Andrew Wiles, whom we quoted earlier.

But what about the other three questions? We're going to answer each of them—as far as possible—but without proof because the proofs require more knowledge of mathematics than we are assuming for this chapter. But, as we will soon see, the answers themselves are a source of joy and can give us some new insights into the joy of mathematics.

If we can form every whole number by multiplying primes, can we also form them by adding primes?

As written, the question is neither interesting nor challenging. Why? For 2 and 3, the answer is obviously 'no' since they are the smallest primes, so cannot be formed by adding others. But for any number greater than 3, the answer is equally obviously 'yes'—if the number is even, add 2's until you get it, if odd, start with 3 and again add enough 2's to form the number. Let's refine the question. For every number greater than 2, can we obtain it by adding *exactly two* prime numbers? But again, the answer is too easy for the question to be interesting. If the number is odd, the answer is 'no.' For the sum of two numbers to be odd, one of them must be even. But the only even prime is 2, and it is easy to find odd numbers that are not the sum of 2 and a prime—the smallest example is 11. Let's refine the question again:

Can every even number greater than 2 be written as the sum of two primes?

The answer is unknown! The conclusion that the answer is 'yes' is called Goldbach's conjecture, after Christian Goldbach who formulated the conjecture in 1742. It is probably the oldest and best known unsolved problem in mathematics. So how does it illustrate the joy of mathematics? Well, first there is the process of refining the question. It is like exploring—a few false starts, a few dead ends, and then the discovery of a gem. But there is another type of joy taking place here, one that is rooted in a sense of wonder and awe—that a question so simply stated can be so subtle that its solution has eluded the efforts of all the brilliant mathematicians that have tried to answer it. This is a kind of joy one experiences in confronting mystery when the question is easy to understand and the answer is subtle or elusive—a similar stimulation to that found in good detective novels.

Are primes common or rare among the whole numbers?

This question has been clearly answered—informally, they are common among small numbers and become increasingly rare as the numbers we are searching through get larger. More precisely, the prime number theorem tells us that the fraction of primes between 1 and some number n is approximately $1/(\log_e n)$, where "$\log_e n$" denotes the logarithm to the base e of the number n.

The expression may look formidable but it is not. The number e has the value 2.71828 ... and is a number that arises often in calculus. The quantity measures the power to which e must be raised to get n. To illustrate, the following table gives a few values of n and the approximate value of $\log_e n$.

n	$\log_e n$
10	2.303
100	4.605
1000	6.908
10,000	9.210

The key thing to notice is that $100 = 10^2$ and $\log_e(100)$ is twice as large as $\log_e(10)$; $1000 = 10^3$ and $\log_e(1000)$ is three times as large as $\log_e(10)$; and $10{,}000 = 10^4$ and $\log_e(10{,}000)$ is four times as large as $\log_e(10)$.

We can count the number of primes between 1 and 10—there are four—2, 3, 5, and 7. So 40 percent are prime. Therefore, between 1 and 100, we would expect the percentage to be about 40/2 = 20 percent; between 1 and 1000, the percentage will be about 40/3 = 13.3 percent; between 1 and 10,000 the percentage will be about 40/4 = 10 percent. Today, using computers we can count the exact number of primes up to large but finite values. The following table gives the exact number of primes between 1 and various values and the estimate generated by the prime number theorem:

n	# primes	estimate	% error
10	4	4.34	-8.5
100	25	21.71	13.2
1000	168	144.76	13.8
10,000	1229	1085.74	11.7
10^{10}	455,052,511	434,294,482	4.6
10^{18}	24,739,954,287,740,860	24,127,471,216,847,300	2.5

If we continued this table on to larger values of n, the percentage of error would continue to drop.

This theorem seems rather technical. Where's the joy in it? We see it in two places. First, note that if we start with 10 (the number 1 with one zero after it), we get an estimate of 4.34. If we start with 1 and put two zeroes after it, the percentage drops by 1/2; with three zeroes after the 1, it drops by 1/3; with four zeroes, by 1/4. This result is amazing and completely surprising. But as we saw earlier, surprise and the discovery of simplicity amid complexity can be sources of joy. Also, many people would say that a simple pattern found amid complexity is beautiful. The perception of beauty is often a source of joy.

Furthermore, there is a type of joy that arises here that we did not note earlier—seeing and appreciating some of the amazing things humans have accomplished. For example, both authors of this article have traveled in Italy and seen Michelangelo's sculpture of David in Florence and the Pieta in St. Peter's Cathedral in Rome. Although we did not see them together, our experiences were much the same—a sense of wonder and awe, of great joy in seeing such beauty, of feeling a bit prouder of being human—of belonging to a race of people able to accomplish such wonders. This theorem was first conjectured in AD 1797 or 1798 by Adrien-Marie Legendre, even though primes had been thought about before Euclid in 300 BC. It was worked on by many great mathematicians during the nineteenth century, and was finally proven independently by Jacques Hadamard and Charles Jean de la Vallée-Poussin in 1896; their proofs were subsequently improved several times in the twentieth century. For many people, this result is to mathematics what David and the Pieta are to art.

> *Is there a formula that we could use to find primes? Suppose we wanted the tenth prime, could we enter 10 into our formula and find the tenth prime?*

The answer seems to be 'no'—while people have devised various formulas, they are impractical, inefficient, or in some sense, artificial. This outcome is significant. A formula expresses a pattern. Saying there is no formula for finding the nth prime is saying that the location of the primes does not follow a pattern, that their locations are random. Putting it differently, it looks like there is no finite way to describe the location of the primes. To illustrate, consider the decimal number 0.2323232323 . . . We could not write out the digits to the millionth place in any reasonable length of time, but we know that the millionth digit will be 3 because one million is an even number and every even numbered place receives a 3. We can reduce the description of this infinite list to something finite. But the location of the primes apparently cannot be reduced to anything finite—only an infinite mind could comprehend the location of all of them.

How is the latter observation a source of joy? Well, it brings us face to face with our finiteness. It introduces humility into our lives. In the garden of Eden, the serpent's temptation of Eve was, "You will be like God." Instead of yielding to that temptation, affirming our finiteness is one way of saying, "No, I am not like God and never will be." Accepting who we are as finite beings is a source of contentment and joy.

How can understanding the joy of mathematics enrich our understanding of God? To address this question, we need to talk a bit about the nature of mathematics.

Up to this point, an atheist or agnostic would likely find little with which to disagree. This is not surprising—there is nothing in the definition of a prime number or the other mathematical concepts used to study them that seems to depend on God's existence or nature. Thus, believing mathematicians can fully collaborate with unbelieving mathematicians, work on the same problems, use the same methods, and share the same mathematical assumptions. But suppose we step back and begin to ask more philosophical questions: What are numbers? What do they mean? Do they have a purpose? In addressing such questions, secular and Christian mathematicians begin to part ways.

In philosophy, ontology refers to the study of the nature of things. It derives from the Greek word *ontos*, meaning *being*. Probably the clearest place where secular and Christian mathematicians might differ is in thinking about the ontology of mathematical objects such as numbers. The ontology of mathematics is subtle. Children learn to count before they go to pre-school. And yet, people who think philosophically about mathematics are far from agreeing on an answer to as simple a question as "What is the number 5?" There are many answers, but here are four that have been widely held by various secular scholars in the past century or so:

- Numbers have no meaning. They are simply symbols that are manipulated according to formal rules.
- Numbers are linguistic conventions that facilitate conversation.
- Numbers do have a meaning, but that meaning is internal to our own minds. That is, human beings have largely the same neurological structure. Numbers are tools we use to organize our perceptions of the material world. Primarily, then, numbers tell us something about how our minds work.
- Numbers are a shorthand notation used to describe patterns in nature.

Note that in none of these answers do numbers have any transcendence—that is, they either point to nothing beyond themselves, or to things in the material world. But for Christians everything finds its meaning in Christ. Indeed, Augustine wrote that we do not understand anything properly until we understand its relationship with Christ. Thus, for Christians, numbers (and in fact everything in mathematics) must in some way point toward Christ. Other meanings of numbers may be true and understanding them may be helpful, but by themselves such meanings are incomplete.

How do Christians see the ontology of mathematical objects like numbers, equations, and geometric figures? What makes this question challenging is that mathematical objects are abstract—they do not have a concrete existence like rocks or trees—they exist in a different way than do physical objects. There are two principal ways of looking at their nature—some Christians see them as entities created by God and some see them as uncreated objects that participate in God's nature. Let's explore each of these views.

If mathematical objects were created, part of God's purpose was that intelligent beings could exercise stewardship of creation; human minds and the physical laws that govern nature were made compatible so that humans can understand what they are stewarding. Furthermore, the laws of nature and the structure of the human mind could have been different from what we know them to be—God is free to create the world as God chooses. Thus, from this perspective, God is not bound by the laws of logic or arithmetic since they are created entities. In studying mathematics, a person is studying God's creation, a very appealing calling.

The uncreated approach says that God has always apprehended mathematical truths. From this perspective, the laws of mathematics are necessary truths—they cannot be otherwise than they are and would hold true in any creation that God has made or will make. Logic is closely linked with mathematics; in fact, starting with one basic principle of logic—the law of non-contradiction—the whole numbers can be derived. This approach sees logic as originating in God's consistency and thus God cannot violate the laws of logic or arithmetic. Theologians resist saying that mathematical objects are part of God since God is not typically seen as having parts—if so, those parts would be more basic than God just as atoms are more basic than molecules. Nevertheless, in studying mathematics and logic, we are not simply studying creation—we are studying something that, in a mysterious way, originates in and is consistent with God's nature and that God has apprehended from eternity.

The astronomer Johannes Kepler, who discovered the elliptical orbits of the planets in our solar system, articulated one classical approach to this mystery. He described geometric objects as "ideas in God's mind." Kepler did not mean to suggest that God has a mind in the same sense that we do. Rather he was using this phrase as a metaphor to convey the concept that God has always apprehended geometric objects and used them as patterns in creating the universe.

The choice between the created and uncreated views of mathematics arises from two different perspectives on God's nature. If someone primarily emphasizes God's sovereign will, that person would not accept the idea that there can be constraints on God's freedom. It would have to be the case that the laws of logic and those of mathematics could be other than they are. However, people who primarily emphasize the love of God are more willing to accept the idea that God's own nature can constrain God's freedom. That is, they would say that God *cannot* do evil, not merely that God *chooses* not to do evil. Similarly, they are comfortable with the idea that the laws of logic originate in God's consistency—since God cannot be self-contradictory, God acts consistently with the laws of logic. It's not that God is bound to obey the laws of logic, but rather that the laws of logic express God's nature. The authors of this article have found the position that numbers are uncreated to be the more compelling of the two perspectives because of its compatibility with the notion that the laws of arithmetic are necessary truths, and because the view that primarily emphasizes God's sovereign will does not strongly enough affirm God's goodness—rather it leaves open the possibility that God could have chosen to be evil.

The origin of mathematics and its relationship to God is a deep mystery. But we would like to suggest a possibility we think is worth considering. The Gospel of John identifies Jesus Christ with *logos*, the eternal Word. *Logos* includes many ideas but among them are reason, order, principles, and thoughts. Although it is not commonly pointed out, it could be understood as including mathematics. The Nicene Creed speaks of "one LORD Jesus Christ, the only Son of God, begotten from the Father before all ages, God from God, Light from Light, true God from true God, begotten, not made; of the same essence as the Father." Perhaps that begetting of the second person of the Trinity also includes the origin of mathematics.

Let's return to our main topic—the joy of mathematics. What does it tell us about God? First, let's reflect on the concept of joy.

For the apostle Paul, joy is a fruit of the Spirit. It is closely tied with love. It can be defined as a positive emotional state associated with a deep-rooted confidence in God's love for oneself and a trust in God's providential care that is stronger than whatever negative emotions might arise from one's circumstances. When we speak of the joy of mathematics, we are not speaking directly about that kind of joy, but rather about a kind of natural pleasure and satisfaction that arises from the kinds of experiences we discussed earlier in this chapter. The joy of mathematics is related to the joy that originates in the Spirit; however, it is not the direct fruit of God's Spirit. Those holding the uncreated view would suggest that it is an apprehension of some aspect of God's nature mediated through our intellect. From this perspective, everyone who experiences the joy of mathematics is experiencing joy in God's nature, even though may not know it. This idea is not new. For instance, in his eighteenth-century book, *The Nature of True Virtue*, Jonathan Edwards wrote, "All beauty to be found throughout the whole creation is but a reflection of the diffused beams of that being, who hath an infinite fullness of brightness and glory."

Let's review the ways in which we experience the joy of mathematics and observe how each of them can point us to God, to God's will for us, or to what it means to have Godly character.

- Surprise—God is infinite and we are finite. Thus, there is always infinitely more of God than we have apprehended. For eternity, God will always be surprising us. Furthermore, God is creative and has made us in his image. Thus, acts of creativity and discovery are God's will for us.
- The experience of discovery—One of God's attributes is wisdom, and God has created us with the capacity to obtain wisdom and the desire for it; curiosity and the desire to discover new truths are God's gifts.
- Simple insight into something profound—Jesus said, "I praise you, Father, LORD of heaven and earth, because you have hidden these things from the wise and learned, and revealed them to little children." In this, we see God's delight in connecting simple insights with profound truths. When we experience this kind of joy, we experience something of God's pleasure.
- Gaining assurance—God has given everyone a hunger for truth and a desire to be confident in that truth. The joy we find in mathematical proof arises from satisfying that desire. In earlier generations, mathematical truth was often used as a sermon illustration for the confidence in God's truth we can have by faith.
- Apprehension of beauty—Scripture consistently teaches that God is the source of all that is good and beautiful. Thus, all beauty originates in God and points toward him.
- Intellectual pleasure—Psalm 16:11 says "You make known to me the path of life; you will fill me with joy in your presence, with eternal pleasures at your right hand." Finding joy in apprehending God's nature and God's creation is his will for us for eternity. It points us to God's goodness and our hope in him.
- Awe and wonder—We are created for worship—that we should love God with all our hearts. When we experience awe and wonder at some aspect of mathematics (or any other truth), the joy we find is a taste of who we were created to be.
- Finding simplicity in complexity—Humans were created to be stewards of God's creation. This requires understanding it. Finding simplicity in complexity gives us a taste of control, mastery, and autonomy. That is, we are experiencing our true identity—who we were created to be. In that, there is great joy.
- Appreciation of great achievements—The joy we find here is another aspect of the sense of awe and wonder. It also expresses gratitude—in

these achievements we recognize God's generosity in giving amazing gifts to humanity.

- Recognition of our finiteness—Great contentment can come from recognizing how small and temporary we are and accepting that with gratitude to God for caring about us anyway.

Conclusion

Putting this all together, what can we say? We have argued that mathematics originates in God's nature and understanding it can enrich one's appreciation of God. We have also argued that the joy found in doing mathematics is an experience of God's wonder even if we do not recognize our experience as that. In a speech in Athens (Acts 17:28), the apostle Paul said, "For in him we live and move and have our being." In this chapter, we are suggesting that when we experience the joy of mathematics and see how it points to God, we participate in one aspect of that truth that Paul celebrated in the Areopagus.

13

The Biological Sciences

Living Testimony to the Wisdom of God

DOROTHY F. CHAPPELL

> *How many are your works, LORD!*
> *In wisdom you made them all*
> *The earth is full of your creatures.*
> *There is the sea, vast and spacious,*
> *teeming with creatures beyond number—*
> *Living things both large and small.*
>
> (PS 104:24–25, NIV)

Intrigue with God's Design and Creation of Everything!

ONE CANNOT HELP BUT be impressed with God's great wisdom and charisma as the designer and creator of all creation. Serious purveyors of nature rejoice that creation fulfills the purposes of God and "glorifies God by carrying out his will."[1] Christians marvel at the beauty of animate and inanimate parts of creation and that God's design of our senses allows us to experience the glory of God in the grandeur of creation. In fact, our God-given senses inform our blessed encounters with God as we worship him, especially as we perceive his glory in creation. Even when our human senses fail, the beauty we have discerned in form and function in creation is secure

---

1. Erickson, *Christian Theology*, 373.

in precious memories that are not easily corrupted. When on the journey of seeing beauty in large vistas or in the vast array of intricacies in creation, and in the sounds that accompany God's voice in nature, it is important that we maintain the fidelity of worship of God as the Creator and not worship the creation. It is also significant that we assume our role as stewards of creation including service to alleviate suffering of those who are made in God's image.

God, in his wisdom, designed and endowed humans with life and unique abilities to perceive beauty in creation through sight, sound, smell, and touch. We bask in the presence of our Lord and, as living humans made in his image, are aware of his creative genius as we use our senses to experience the environment in which we live. We discern something of our Lord's beauty because he made us in his image, including providing us with rational minds and sensitivities that discern his incarnate existence. Even so, we must remember that we are made in God's image but are not divine. God's plan is perfect, and his wisdom in designing life allowed for his miraculous entry into creation as a living human for witnesses with rational minds and sensitivities to discern his incarnate existence and record those trustworthy encounters for our study and worship of him. His holy Word testifies to his existence as the living God.

Biblical theology provides the basis for scientific study of creation, especially living organisms, including human beings, who alone have the distinction of being created in God's image. God's providence includes both creation and the sustaining narrative of creation, fall, and redemption. It is within God's providence that our redemption is won through Christ's death and resurrection, our hope for redemption is fulfilled in Christ, and that we are able to dwell with God and worship him forever.

This author joins other scientists who are Christians in affirming that in Jesus Christ all things were created. This creative activity includes the physical, spiritual, and moral dimensions of the entire universe (Col 1:15–17). As God's image bearers, we cherish our relationship with God including our worship of him and stewardship of his creation.

What Can Fallen Creatures Discern in Creation?

We recognize our place of privilege and ability to seek the Holy Spirit's enablement while striving to be faithful to our Creator, anticipating and reflecting the faithfulness of Christ to all of his creation. God-given wisdom is required to steward well what we know of and have access to in God's world. In addition to enjoying a rational relationship with God and reveling in the gift of wisdom required to worship God, we also have been given wisdom in our rational capabilities to perform works of stewardship. Those works require wisdom and include stewarding the well-being of the various life forms God has created. Christians affirm, with the Scriptures, that knowledge of creation can be gained by studying creation (Isa 28:23–29; Prov 27:23–27). Given that the human intellect is affected by the fall, we can know in part but not in full. Thus one dimension of scientific wisdom is to approach science humbly and with utmost care.

Full knowledge of the complexity of creation exceeds the limits of human understanding. However, even our limited understanding of "general revelation" with apprehension of some of God's glory allows believers opportunities to enhance worship and enjoy our Redeemer. Such is the nature of thorough study and understanding of living organisms and the amazing phenomenon of life. There are thousands of species of life on Earth and each is distinctive. Yet each is subservient to God.

Theologically, there are many interesting distinctions about God's life as differentiated from other forms. Among them is that "the continuation of God's existence does not depend upon anything outside of himself. All other creatures, insofar as they are alive, need something to sustain that life. Nourishment, warmth, protection, all are necessary."[2] God, though, is not dependent upon the things essential to the life he created. Scientists who are Christians, aware that God has created us and not we ourselves (Ps 100:3), are alert to the danger of self-worship and the danger of worship of science, what philosophers call scientism.

The effects of the fall are immense. The apostle Paul taught that creation groans in brokenness and decay (Rom 8:22–25). Like us, it awaits the final redemption, the ultimate healing of all that is fallen. Hence, as Christian biologists, we are called to participate in healing activities through employment of scientific methods in response to God's call to steward creation. In this endeavor, Christians who study creation can see glimpses of God's glory in its exquisite details and vast expanses of beauty. Studying life opens our eyes to God's spectacular creativity and wisdom. Upon this discovery, led by the Holy Spirit, Christians can advance in faith and understanding of the responsibilities required of us in service to our Lord.

How Does Study of Creation Deepen Christian Worship?

God's wisdom as designer and creator of life is stunning. Our devotion to God enhances with the knowledge we have of his work in creation and his

---

2. Erickson, *Christian Theology*, 271.

devotion to his creation. God, in his great wisdom, designed humans and endowed us with life and unique abilities to perceive beauty in creation through sight, sound, smell, and touch. His plan included developing complex senses. He provided complex brains to help us process these senses and act upon what we experience. The complexity and exquisite splendor of his creation beckon us to see something of his majesty and glory in it and to be his stewards in maintaining it. In these discerning processes we are able to detect evidence of God's wisdom, because creation's detail, complexity, and beauty transcend us.

Scientists or not, part of our intellectual experience, by God's design, is to discover that "wisdom has to do with the theology of everything." God's wisdom prevails as we interface with and acknowledge our special place in creation. God has given us the mental and physical capacities to explore and discover the wonderful intricacies of his handiwork. Along with delighting in God's creation, we have the foundational responsibility to worship him and tend creation wisely with optimal scientific intelligence. Doing so evidences our devotion to and worship of God.

The Astonishing Phenomenon of Life!

The relationship of the Triune God to his creation is well chronicled throughout the Bible. Life, by design and with God's help, is able to consume some of its environment, and with distinct blueprints, is capable of at least two remarkable activities—making more of itself in its ontogenesis and intergenerational survival in asexual and/or sexual replication. The phenomenon of life is a feature exhibited by God who is the author of life and is life himself. Unlike humans, whose lives are tied to time, God's life is eternal. "Everything happens when it happens because God is sovereign over time as well as eternity."[3] With this statement, Philip Ryken captures well the meaning of God's authority over space and time. He reminds us of God's sovereignty over time with seasonal changes on earth and in life. "The initiation, duration, and termination of our existence are all under his authority . . . as the Creator God, Jesus ordered the rhythms of creation."[4] These rhythms, by God's wisdom, are perceivable to us because we are made in God's image, are alive, and have rational minds, consciousness, and senses to perceive. God, in his wisdom, made us in his image, so that we have the ability to measure our stages of growth. This gives us the opportunity,

3. Ryken, *Ecclesiastes*, 80.
4. Ryken, *Ecclesiastes*, 83–84.

though finite and fallible, to choose the wisest courses available for our own growth intellectually, physically, and spiritually.

Game Changers—Biologists Transfer Knowledge into Life Changing Strategies.

Biology has immense value to people around the globe whose lives have benefitted from biological research. Our current understanding of diseases, food products, medicine, and environmental stewardship rely upon advances in biology. Today biologists practice the scientific method with state-of-the-art technology using empirical data that lend insights into the complexities of life. Integration with mathematics, computer science, and scientific technology pushes the frontiers of exploration in well-designed biological experiments and descriptions of tightly interwoven systems of life and their interactions with the abiotic environment. Biologists build bridges among careers in academia, industry, and research, and they study a wide gamut of topics from agriculture to medicine to ecosystems and beyond. Many Christians have found exciting and rewarding careers as biologists engaged in ground breaking research that sheds new light on the mysteries and intricacies of God's creation. James Houston reminds us that "the wisdom of Christ is not know-how by which to gain mastery of the world. It is obedience: to do the will of God in justice and the fear of the LORD. It is the moral exercise of relationships with God and man" (See 1 Cor 1:27, 29–30).[5] Indeed, we are called to be game changers and to transfer knowledge about God's world into life changing service.

Life Is Complex

Life is very complex even in the simplest of single celled organisms, multicellular organisms, and in networks of living organisms. Single celled organisms are complex in that they can do many of the functions that some organisms require many cells to complete. Each cell in a multicellular organism is alive and sophisticated and yet contributes to the overall functions of an organism. The human body is a cohesive and effective whole with interdependencies among its parts just as we see the coordinated and interdependent functions among the parts of all creation. All of the tissues in mammals, for instance, are dependent upon the delivery of oxygen to their cells by blood which is a part of complex circulatory systems. So it goes

---

5. Houston, *I Believe in the Creator*, 135.

with the many parts of the human body where intellect, digestion, nerve responses, reproduction, and many other functions occur. There is an interdependency of the systems in the organism which is essential to its life.

Ecosystems offer complex examples of interdependency of organisms, although the ecosystem is not alive *per se* as are organisms. Each living organism in an ecosystem plays a role in the success of the ecosystem. For example, aquatic systems are dependent upon a complex array of microorganisms, plants, and animals. When one part of the web of life in an aquatic system dies or is altered, it affects the survival and efficiency of the other organisms in the system and often other parts of the system cannot be sustained. We see extraordinary examples of this type of demise in organisms where food for animals may be limited, toxins may be introduced from many sources into a system through pollution, or waters become so dense that light cannot penetrate the water to sustain the microbial production of oxygen essential to organisms living there. Once the balance of life is upset, other organisms in the system cannot survive and the whole system is jeopardized. It is also important to note that organisms and ecosystems have resilience and can regain functional balance through restoration efforts of humans to reclaim their original functions.

Biological research includes the use of advanced technologies to study molecular components of life as well as the behaviors of living cells and organisms. Many biologists and chemists have studied the components of cells and elucidated nucleic acids, their replication and manufacture of proteins. Even though scientists are pushing the frontiers of how nucleic acids function within cells and many lifesaving discoveries have been made for multicellular organisms, no one has been able to create life. It is for this reason, among others, that biology should evoke humility and respect to our God who did create life. Only God is the author of life!

We Live on a Planet Teeming with Life of Unparalleled Beauty!

In God's wisdom and strategic planning, Earth hosts a wide variety of intriguing life forms. New species are still being discovered all the time. Complex in relationships and webs among life forms, organisms have diverse forms of metabolism. Some can capture light or chemical energy and convert it into other forms of energy. Other life forms are dependent upon ingesting food. Some organisms are single celled and others are multicellular and organized into systems that provide division of labor to accomplish essential functions. Regardless of their cellularity, they have phenomenal biochemical pathways that allow them to undertake complex cellular reactions, multiply, and take parts of their respective environment and make more of themselves—a feat that non-living things cannot achieve!

The organisms living on Earth share space with an environment of non-living solids, liquids, and gases where phenomena of matter and energy exhibit distinct, repeatable, and predictable reactions. Living organisms are composed of many of the same types of molecules found in non-living substances, but they have been endowed by God with life and have the ability to take in a variety of molecules from their environment and make more of themselves by adding volume and mass to their structures. In addition, they are distinct because of their ability to replicate genetic material and cells, the basic units of their existence. Genetic codes control much of their basic life functions as well as their replication which perpetuates the respective species. An asexual pattern of cell replication is the only and dominate means of reproduction for some species whereas many life forms can reproduce sexually by combining gametes and redistributing genetic information to offspring. Sexual reproduction provides remarkable advantages to species because of the survival benefits of redistributing genes that increase survival likelihood in organisms as environments change.

Unparalleled beauty is characteristic of God's creation. Christians who carefully study and contemplate his creation are drawn to worship him as they grasp something of the intricacies of the structures and functions found in creation. The sheer beauty of living organisms is not limited to their external appearances but rather include the intricate functions within their cells and bodies and their interrelationships with other parts of creation. Living organisms provide special glimpses of the complexities that exist in creation.

What Happens When the Delicate Interdependencies of Life Are Broken or Adjusted?

Interdependence is observed among living organisms and in the physical laws and units of creation. When a child pulls one block from the foundation of a stack of blocks, a major shift occurs in the blocks. A collapse of inordinate proportions can occur and, at best, leave the blocks in disarray. Similarly, if one were to remove the simple carbon atom from creation, life as we know it, would not exist. Likewise, if the molecule chlorophyll were removed from plants on the Earth, there would be catastrophic effects on the food sources for animals and plants because chlorophyll is the key molecule in capturing sunlight in the process of photosynthesis which leads to food production. If one removes a key organism in an ecological system, other organisms will be harmed by its absence, or if toxins are added to an environment, including the atmosphere, living organisms may not have access to the essential gases or molecules for their life functions. The production of carbon dioxide through industry is deleterious and shifts the gaseous balance essential for living organisms on Earth. The presence of toxins in aquatic systems causes untold damage not only to the organisms that live there but also to the organisms that use the water as a source for drinking. Recognizing and honoring interdependence among living organisms means that we do our best to maintain those relationships the LORD has ordained in his life systems. For these reasons and others, we commend wisdom and care for creation as prerequisite for biology.

Studying Science Should Inspire Christians to Tend God's Creation Intelligently

Scientists who are Christians have a responsibility to address the biological problems that threaten life. Some questions address the practical intricacies of structure function models in *knowledge for the sake of knowledge*, whereas other questions address human behaviors as they relate to caring for creation. Experiential learning, in internships and research, provides experiences that enable students to grasp the practice of science and the hard work of conducting well-conceived research, with operable hypotheses, practical experimentation, and valued outcomes.

Simple questions that science can address are things like what happens if an organism ingests too much salt? What happens to living organisms if the temperature on Earth continues to rise and the polar ice caps melt? How do scientists design and accumulate valid data and use data with integrity to address Christians' responsibility and response to human induced climate change? How are energy saving devices contributing to the welfare of life on the Earth? What is addiction and how does a mother's addiction affect the fetus? Are there any limits on how technology should be used to enhance human life? What is the role of diet and exercise in good health? Thinking Christianly about creation should lead one to think about these types of questions and more complex ones—like how can the provision of energy in the two-thirds world be provided without degradation of the environment? How can genetically modified foods contribute to solving food shortages? The task of Christians is to bring meaning and legitimacy wisely to the practice of science, paying particular attention to acts of mercy commensurate with God's concern for the hungry, sick, disenfranchised, and the environment.

When Crisis Meets Opportunity!

When sin entered the world, it not only affected our relationship with God, but it affected our abilities to steward the world. The effects of sin are immense, both in the world and in individual lives. Even the capacity to know truth has been adversely affected. Hence, Paul taught that creation groans in brokenness and decay (Rom 8:22–25) waiting for God's revelation of the children of God. Our response, as the children of God, is to steward and care for the physical world which God created. Learning about creation helps Christians toward this end. There are moral boundaries to our manipulative and intrusive examinations of the world, and we bear responsibility for the consequences of our practice of science. Christian faculty and students should be committed to best scientific practices based upon the highest ethical principles.

Fulfilling the responsibility of stewardship requires study to gain knowledge of God's world and to care for creation with practices that perpetuate the networks and interdependences of the living and non-living world. Crises in creation, whether induced through natural disasters, disease, or grave human thoughtlessness are met by Christians who treat them as opportunities to study and apply scientific knowledge to serve people and our holy and good God.

Wisdom in Living Things?

Proverbs appeals to disclosures of wisdom in living creatures: "Four things on earth are small, yet are extremely wise: Ants are creatures of little strength, yet they store up their food in the summer; hyraxes are creatures of little power, yet they make their home in the crags; locusts have not king, yet they advance in ranks; a lizard can be caught with hand, yet it is found in kings' palaces" (Prov 30:24–28). As in all things, this passage challenges and redirects our curiosity back to the wisdom of God, whose creation of life amidst the world of inanimate things challenges the best intellectual exercises we can muster for understanding the phenomenon of life. Try as we may, we can neither duplicate life nor can we fully understand what God did and continues to do to perpetuate this miraculous ongoing paragon. He has orchestrated the creation of life and clothed it in a rich array of garments we call cells. Some cells exist alone, or are colonized, and others act in unison in complex organisms. Life is so delicately balanced in cells that it is found persisting singularly or in multicellularity with close proximity to other cells and shared in intergenerational patterns. Coordination of living cells in multicellular contexts is vaguely understood and demonstrates vast mysteries of communication through tissues.

Life is also a truly remarkable phenomenon in the created order and deserves the best attention possible in humbly discerning how our God wisely works in creation. "Insofar as the creation reflects the beauty of the Creator, in its essence, the world continually manifests God's glory, majesty, simplicity, symmetry, order, power and elegance (Ps 8:1; Job 38–39; Ps 104). This beauty elicits our humble respect and appreciation. Because the world has its beginning in the God of truth and beauty, we also recognize in this beauty evidence of God's glory (Isa 40:5).[6]

Can Biologists See God's Providence in Miracles?

God's great wisdom extends well beyond what we know and understand about creation. Miracles are "special supernatural works of God's providence which are not explicable on the basis of the usual patterns of nature."[7] They are purposeful and in the biblical narratives are limited in frequency. God's providential work in living organisms is often recognized in health and disease. We assume that diseases arise from apparent natural causes and we have developed many cures achievable through surgery and pharmacological treatments like antibiotics for diseases. God has the primary role in administering healing through those means and we should praise and thank him for those recoveries just as much as we thank and praise him for the recovery of a paralytic. God is sovereign over nature and can alter creation as he wills. He has given us curiosity to explore curative techniques which work well. Millard Erickson reminds us that there are God-given purposes in miracles including "glorifying God," "establishment of the supernatural basis of the revelation that accompanies them," and meeting "human needs."[8] God's work is providential through processes and causal powers operative in creation and by means that are beyond those in the natural order and are supernatural. God, unlike humans, knows all the facts about his universe and his purposes for creation. In his omnipotence, he can act in miraculous ways that reveal his constant care for his creatures and all of

---

6. Chappell and Jones, "Natural Sciences," 11.
7. Erickson, *Christian Theology*, 406.
8. Erickson, *Christian Theology*, 409.

creation. We should give him praise for his work in natural law and secondary causes and for his miracles.

God's Grandeur in Creation Reminds Us of Our Humble Frame before God

Alister McGrath's *A Scientific Theology* reminds us that "If any genre of Old Testament writing places a premium upon the theology of creation, it is the wisdom literature. God did not merely create the world; it was created "in wisdom" (Prov 3:19). Wisdom is portrayed as searching for regularity within the world and appears to make no real distinction between the human, socio-historical, and the natural realms. The fundamental belief which undergirds the wisdom literature is that certain patterns may be discerned by the wise within the vast ambit of life, and that such discernment is profitable for human education and reflection."[9] For Christians, the goal of wise scientific inquiry is to understand what can be known of God's creation and to worship God more fully as we discern his glory and majesty. Nature has a created rationality that can be studied in a specific manner with proper doctrinal grounding for scientific inquiry. This doctrinal grounding presumes that the social and natural world is real and intelligible. God brought into existence a *reality* intended to be quite distinct from God. All of creation is dependent upon God for its being and sustenance, while having distinctive intrinsic properties, powers, entities, and structures. Investigating these natural features is the task of *scientific inquiry*, a fully human, admittedly fallible endeavor that facilitates a tentative grasp of social and natural reality. Studying living organisms, including human beings made in God's image, is inspiring and draws us to worship God, while allowing us to respond in service to those whose needs for food, medical care, pure water, and clean environment provide the opportunity to love others as God has loved us.

What Roles Do Life Sciences Play in Redemptive Acts?

The Earth, its environment, and living creatures are great gifts for which humans bear great responsibility. Much of what we steward is life itself and its environment. Creation brings glory to God, and we are called to cultivate it, and to use and sustain it wisely in service to both God and others. Scientific inquiry provides a valuable means by which to better understand the world and to more effectively participate with Christ in its restoration. Knowing

---

9. McGrath, *Scientific Theology*, 149.

about structures, functions, and living creatures in creation provides an occasion to acknowledge, thank, praise, and worship God. In knowing God, we enter into service as God's stewards of creation.

Biology is a science that can address many effects of the fall seen in living organisms. "In addition to the delights of worship and praise found in the study of creation, devout scientists recognize expressions of common grace to creatures and to all people everywhere regardless of whether they follow Christ."[10] Scientists use biology to help others in the plights of disease, impoverishment, and malnutrition among many other works beneficial to humans.

Towards these ends, biologists use other disciplines, especially chemistry, mathematics, and computer science to further knowledge about life. A wise scientist recognizes that science, as a means of studying God's revelation of truth in creation, will provide a significant and more comprehensive insight into reality itself. Wisdom among Christian educators involves mentoring effective methodological approaches to science, applications of science, examination of competing theories about creation, and examination of the relationship of the Creator to his handiwork in nature. These healthy approaches to science contribute to the transformation of students into competent, respected members of the larger scientific community where they may serve with integrity as salt and light.

Furthermore, the process of scientific inquiry stimulates the engagement of the insatiable gift of curiosity and coordinates critical thinking skills to undertake problem solving essential to scientific progress. It unleashes the innovative character of humans to design and construct technology used to examine the frontiers of knowledge, provide means of healing to living organisms, and help restore parts of God's creation.

Are There Limits to the Disciplines in which God's Wisdom Is Manifest?

It is within God's providence and wisdom that we have curious minds and talent to engage the process of discovery about the universe, especially the planet upon which we live. The LORD cares about his creation and we have special responsibilities to help in its maintenance. The traditional and applied natural sciences and mathematics definitely provide a legitimate realm of study for Christians. Exploration of God's universe has ignited the development of many fields of study offered in liberal arts colleges and universities. As our knowledge of life forms increases, so do the fields of study in

10. Chappell, "World of Discovery," 188.

the sciences, mathematics, and applied science fields. The career options for liberal arts students are immense and include disciplines like applied health sciences, astronomy, biology, chemistry, computer science, engineering, environmental science, geology, mathematics, and physics, among others. Most Christians who participate in the exploration of God's world are responding to a God-given "calling" to be scientists, engineers, computer scientists, and mathematicians. They know the joy of discovery about God's world and people. The task of Christian educators is to affirm students' callings to study the creation that bears the mark of its Creator.

Food for Thought and Practice— Where Wisdom May Be Found!

The study of natural science, including the study of biology, should be one of worship and punctuated with excellent learning experiences in classrooms, laboratories, field instruction, stimulating seminars, hands-on research, internships, and mentoring of the scientific process of testing hypotheses and theories. Students should discern the best practices in science for care of God's creation. Christians should enjoy the intersections created by training in science and growth in moral values, and they should have great influence on humanity's stewardship of creation, especially its life forms, through anthropological, economical, ethical, political, and sociological dimensions of science.

The joy of discovery and the development of technology are natural outcomes of God-given curiosity. A Christian worldview informs how biological studies may fulfill the vision of helping those who are in need and lack food, medical resources, clean water, and other material goods. Undertaking those studies in the context of science sets and protects the survival agenda for future generations in all societies. The social implications of the use of science are morally bound, and Christians have a voice in establishing the vision for the welfare of humanity. It is essential that Christians who intellectually engage their faith and the natural sciences continue to be a part of the global response to the LORD's mandate to steward the Earth.

We are made in God's image and have the privileges and responsibilities of being his redeemed children through the precious blood of his son Jesus Christ. That knowledge should inspire us to approach the God of the universe with humility and reverence. We worship and honor him through our study of life, our care of his creation, and our service to others. Christians with gifts in studying the biological sciences can respond to a calling to devote their minds to the study of life both for the discovery of

God's grandeur in creation and for the advancement of God's love through provision of compassionate health care, healthy foods, clean water and wise stewardship of the earth. Embracing biological studies reveals something about life—the foremost physical characteristic humans share with the Living God!

In him was life, and the life was the light of all mankind. (John 1:4)

Bibliography

Chappell, Dorothy F. "World of Discovery through the Natural Sciences." In *Liberal Arts for the Christian Life*, edited by Jeffry C. Davis and Phillip G. Ryken, 179–90. Wheaton: Crossway, 2012.

Chappell, Dorothy F., and Stanton L. Jones. "The Natural Sciences at Wheaton College: Understanding Their Significance in Light of Our Christian Educational Mission." https://www.wheaton.edu/media/admissions/TheNaturalSciencesAtWheatonCollege.pdf.

Erickson, Millard J. *Christian Theology*. Grand Rapids: Baker, 1996.

Houston, James M. *I Believe in the Creator*. Grand Rapids: Eerdmans, 1980.

McGrath, Alister E. *Scientific Theology: Nature*. Grand Rapids: Eerdmans, 2001.

Phillips, Elaine A. *An Introduction to Reading Biblical Wisdom Texts*. Peabody: Hendrickson, 2017.

Ryken, Philip Graham. *Ecclesiastes: Why Everything Matters*. Preaching the Word. Wheaton: Crossway, 2010.

14

The Wisdom Required for Global Health
Nathan Thielman

Profoundly disturbing disparities in health transcend medical specialties and borders.

- Roughly one in five children diagnosed with cancer in resource-poor settings survive their illness, compared to four out of five such children in high-resource countries.
- Three quarters of the deaths from AIDS occur in sub-Saharan Africa, yet sub-Saharan Africa comprises only 14 percent of the world's population.
- Of the 830 women who die each day from complications of pregnancy and child birth, 780 reside in sub-Saharan Africa or South Asia.

These are but three glaring examples, among countless others, of health disparities. The field of Global Health exists to reduce such health disparities by working to expand healthcare availability and to improve treatment outcomes for economically disadvantaged populations. For centuries, Christian healthcare professionals, motivated by the Great Commission and Jesus' example of compassion to heal, have aspired to serve the poor in global settings. More recently, especially over the past two decades, as a field of academic inquiry and research, Global Health has increased dramatically in popularity, including among those without a motivation based in any faith system. In the United States alone, over 60 academic institutions now offer formal instruction in Global Health—ranging from undergraduate certificates and majors to Masters of Science degrees to doctoral programs.

The Consortium of Universities for Global Health, established less than a decade ago, now includes over 150 institutional memberships worldwide. With deep roots in the fields of Public Health, International Health, and Tropical Medicine, Global Health, which is necessarily interdisciplinary, emphasizes health issues that cross borders, seeks to understand contextual determinants of health, and ultimately aims to reduce health disparities.

The Foundations of Global Health: A Deeper Dive into Human Dignity

The underlying motivational premise for Global Health is that the health of all individuals and populations matters regardless of race, socioeconomic status, gender, geography, or other such descriptors. As such, Global Health researchers and implementers seek to describe health disparities, understand their proximate causes, and design, implement, and evaluate evidence-based solutions to improve health outcomes. Why should infant mortality in Sierra Leone or HIV risk behaviors among mountain porters in Tanzania matter to those who live an ocean away? What should motivate students, faculty, and institutions to care about health disparities? Surely there are multiple layers of answers, but practically all responses at some level endorse the language of the United Nations Universal Declaration of Human Rights, which describes "the inherent dignity and the equal and inalienable rights of all members of the human family." Ultimately, within the realm of Global Health efforts to improve access to interventions that preserve or restore health, particularly those that address health inequalities, in the end promote human flourishing and elevate human dignity.[1]

Largely absent from the UN Declaration is any proposition regarding the origin of human dignity and worth. It is not our purpose here to explain how non-Christians may or may not argue for universal human dignity, but before presenting a Christian argument for human dignity, we briefly draw attention to three secular arguments for human dignity and human rights, described primarily in bioethics[2] and legal literature. In the classical era, Stoics believed human beings possessed dignity because they possessed reason; a dignified life to the Stoic was achievable for anyone who chose to live a disciplined, reflective life. Self-control could lead to dignity regardless

---

1. The discussion of healthcare (including what level of healthcare and what constitutes healthcare) as a human right is beyond the scope of this chapter, but the author posits that some level of healthcare for all persons in the 21st century is a basic human right.

2. See Schulman, "Bioethics and the Question."

of one's station. Like the Stoics, the German philosopher Immanuel Kant also believed that dignity was unique to humans and had a rational basis, but for Kant, human dignity was a reflection of human autonomy, and as such demanded respect for all persons to include prohibition of exploitation. Clearly neither the self-determined dignity of the ancient Stoics nor the rational dignity of the Enlightenment is the same dignity referenced in the United Declaration for Human Rights, nor is it the motivating force behind Global Health. While Kant's construction of human dignity is useful for bioethics, it is not an inspiring rallying cry to don gloves and gowns in order to care for infectious Ebola patients in West Africa. In the modern era, even less inspiring, if not disturbing, are the amorphous discussions of human dignity and human rights by the organization Human Rights Watch, which defines human rights in evolutionary terms: "Human rights evolve because new groups advocate for their rights."[3] Alan Dershowitz puts a finer point on this, arguing that rights are "nurtural" rather than natural—that they grow out of experience, usually gross injustices such as the holocaust, and that they are invented.[4] This begs certain questions: Do human rights devolve when interest and interest groups cease to exist? Is human dignity, then, inherent and inalienable, or is such language just a rhetorical trick to help justify certain preferences for rights?

For the Christian, a more satisfying and compelling understanding of human dignity and human rights is found in the arc of the Biblical narrative. In the Bible, God reveals to mankind his unchangeable nature—that he is not only holy, all-powerful, and all-knowing, but that he is also just, good, and loving.[5] And demonstrated throughout Scripture is God's *dignifying* love for humanity. From the outset, we learn that unlike any other created thing or being, God created humanity in his very image—his *imago Dei*: "Then God said, 'Let us make man in *our image*, after *our likeness*; and let them have dominion over the fish of the sea, and over the birds of the air, and over the cattle, and over all the earth' . . . So God created man *in his own image, in the image of God* he created him, male and female he created them" (Gen 1:26–27). Four times, in the space of two verses, the Hebrew writer unequivocally designates the unique place that men and women are given in the created order.

By choosing to live according *to their own image*, Adam and Eve fell into the indignity of sin, so that, aware of their nakedness, they hid in shame from God. But amazingly, in mercy and grace God made for his rebellious

---

3. Human Rights Watch, "Human Rights 101."
4. Dershowitz, *Rights from Wrongs*.
5. Jas 1:17; Rev 15:4; Jer 32:17; Isa 46:9–10; Deut 32:4; Matt 19:17; 1 John 4:8.

people garments of skin to cover their shame and restore their dignity. That this act required the slaughter of animals foreshadowed the sacrificial system of atonement for sins later established in the Levitical system. God was not looking the other way to restore dignity. His grace was not cheap. A by-product of the sacrificial system itself was that in restoring a right relationship with God, in atoning for shameful sins, God restored dignity to his image-bearers through sacrifice. One cannot read Psalm 51, in which David repents of a series of sins deriving from his lust for Bathsheba, without getting the clear sense that in repenting and receiving assurance of forgiveness of his sins, David's dignity is restored: "The sacrifices of God are a broken spirit; a broken and a contrite heart, O God, you will not despise" (Ps 51:17). In biblical theology Jesus' crucifixion, of course, climaxes God's redemption of his people from shame, as Jesus' naked public sacrifice made possible the restoration of human dignity.

Humankind is ultimately dignified through the incarnation—the action in which the creator God "emptied himself, by taking the form of a servant, being born in the likeness of men" (Phil 2:7). God's very entry into humanity in the form of a helpless baby, born to an unwed teenager in a stable-cave, ennobled all of humanity—including its most vulnerable populations. Moreover, repeatedly in his ministry on earth, Jesus elevated the dignity of the least-regarded of his day. By touching and healing ceremonially unclean lepers (Matt 8:2-4), by affirming the faith of the woman with 12 years of menorrhagia who touched his garment (Luke 8:43-48), by restoring sight to the blind beggar Bartimaeus (Mark 10:46-52), by reaching across racial, gender, and power divides to engage the Samaritan woman at the well (John 4:7-26), and by showing compassion to the Syrophoenician woman (Mark 7:26-30), Jesus' interactions brought value and dignity to those most deprived of societal value.

But God's primary purpose in taking on human flesh was not to draw attention to the plight of the downtrodden or to dignify the human experience by becoming one of us—God's chief purpose was to offer redemption to all of humanity by making himself the object of the sacrificial system foreshadowed in the Garden of Eden: "In this the love of God was made manifest among us, that God sent his only Son into the world, so that we might live through him. In this is love, not that we have loved God, but that he loved us and sent his Son to be the propitiation for our sins" (1 John 4:8). This is the pinnacle event in God's dignity-conferring lovingkindness for humanity: he valued humanity so much that in the person of Jesus he entered humanity in space and time two thousand years ago and died on a Roman cross to make atonement for our sins—to restore his image in us.

The entire arc of the Biblical salvation narrative, from creation to the cross, affirms God's gracious action to restore human dignity.

Thus, Christians who engage in Global Health have access to a deeper, fuller understanding of the human dignity that is promoted in the Universal Declaration of Human Rights: we understand its origin. We understand that persons are of infinite value because God created humanity in his own image, because in Jesus he became human to redeem us, and because he allowed himself to be sacrificed on the cross for the sake of humanity. And this value is both inherent and inalienable. This fundamental tenet of Christianity provides a sure-footed motivational foundation for Christians to engage in Global Health.

Christian Posture and Practice in Global Health

Christians motivated to practice Global Health by a consideration for human dignity should approach their tasks with diligence and a clear-eyed commitment to appropriate posture and ethical practices. Global Health is best approached by focusing on a specific problem—typically a difference in a health outcome or a difference in access to a health care intervention across populations.[6] Consequently, the Global Health researcher first seeks to understand the multiple domains and determinants that contribute to health or healthcare disparities. For example, in sub-Saharan Africa, across the broad domain of "social circumstance"—sound epidemiological evidence describes worse outcomes of Human Immunodeficiency Virus (HIV) infection among men, those who are younger, those who fail to disclose their HIV status, those who have to pay for antiretroviral medications, and those who have overall less social support. Under the domain of "environment and co-morbidities," having a mental illness, being co-infected with tuberculosis, and excessive alcohol use also portend poor HIV outcomes. Much of this is mediated by the manner in which such patients interact with the health care system and adhere to antiretroviral medications. Taken faithfully antiretroviral medications transform HIV infection from a nearly universally fatal disease into a long-term chronic condition. Seeking to understand the multiple narratives that are at play and how complex interactions between human behavior, social conditions, and other illnesses contribute to poor health is a key task of the global health researcher. A

---

6. Distinctions may be made between health inequalities and health inequities, with the latter considered to be unnecessary, avoidable, and unjust, but the domain of Global Health need not be restricted to health inequities. For detailed discussion on health-related inequalities and inequities, see Whitehead, "Concepts and Principles," 429–45.

second key task is to design and then evaluate appropriate interventions to improve outcomes related to a specific disease.

Below are five major lessons I have learned as a Christian engaged in Global Health research and training.

(1) Seek godly wisdom and understanding through Christ.

The Author of Truth is at the center of all that we seek to understand. "For by him all things were created, in heaven and on earth, visible and invisible, whether thrones or dominions or rulers or authorities—all things were created through him and for him. And he is before all things, and in him all things hold together" (Col 1:17–18). The problems taken on by a Global Health researcher (e.g. health outcomes of persons living with HIV infection) are complex and often involve interactions between biological systems, human behavior, the environment, location, economic circumstances, and prevailing health policies.

As such, the Global Health researcher is frequently tasked with trying to understand causality across vastly different disciplines. There is ultimate unity of all truth in Christ, and the believer has direct access to the Creator of the universe through prayer to seek wisdom and integrative understanding that begins and ends with the Lordship of Christ. This does not give the competitive Global Health researcher 'a leg up' compared to her non-believing peers and by no means does it suggest moral or epistemological superiority. Rather, this understanding of truth is a resource that Christians may draw on. Knowing that Christ is at the core of all truth and understanding, we can, in humble confidence, simply ask for wisdom.

(2) Methods matter.

Given the Christian's belief in absolute truth and conviction that all truth coheres through Christ, what we report to be fact must be unscrupulously true. It follows then, that the Christian Global Health researcher must conduct his research with the utmost integrity and cannot endorse sloppy methodology that is likely to result in misleading findings. Conducting rigorous research, particularly in resource poor settings, brings its own set of unique challenges, including lack of infrastructure and a paucity of trained research personnel.[7] Beyond ensuring that the research design is sound, the Global

---

7. For a detailed discussion of some of the challenges encountered in attempting to conduct clinical research in West Africa, see Thielman et al. "Ebola clinical trials: Five lessons learned and a way forward," 83–86.

Health researcher will often be charged with training research assistants, developing systems from the ground up to ensure data provenance, facilitating audits, and encouraging open discussion that invites critiques of study methodology, data security, and analytic plans. And the follower of Christ in Global Health must be vigilant to resist temptations to "spin" findings to fit a particular narrative that may be politically or professionally enhancing. In understanding that Jesus is the LORD of all truth, our goal as researchers is to dig for truth, to find it, and to present the facts as they are, with a robust statement of their limitations. Only then are we able to respond to the truth we discover in ways that promote human dignity and honor Christ.

(3) You cannot address complex Global Health problems on your own.

Interdisciplinary and interprofessional team efforts are required to meaningfully address the world's most pressing health inequities. A Christian liberal arts education that equips learners with the vocabulary of diverse disciplines, a Christ-centered worldview, and a hunger for truth is well-positioned to prepare the next generation of Christian Global Health researchers and practitioners.

Biological systems and disease pathology are infinitely complex in their own rights. Elucidating and integrating an understanding of key behavioral, socioeconomic, environmental, and geographical determinants of disease is still even more challenging. Take for instance the complex and variable behaviors that contribute to obstetric fistula in resource-poor settings. Fistulas are most commonly formed when obstetric labor is prolonged or obstructed, resulting in the death of tissues that maintain the integrity of the genital tract with respect to the urinary and/or intestinal tracts. Critical contributors to obstetric fistula include teenage pregnancy (teenagers have higher rates of obstructed labor because of smaller pelvis size), illiteracy, harmful traditional medical beliefs and practices, delays in referrals for Caesarean sections when labor is not progressing, and lack of facilities and personnel capable of performing Caesarean sections. Obstetric fistulae, which are extremely rare in wealthier nations, lead to a woman's inability to control the flow of urine and/or feces, resulting in devastating social isolation and stigma.[8]

To comprehensively address the problem of obstetric fistula and its many causes requires not only wisdom and sensitivity, but a diverse team

---

8. For a helpful description of this problem, see Kristof, "Lepers: Women with Fistula."

that could include gynecologic surgeons (to surgically correct defects), psychologists (to address emotional and psychological effects of stigma), anthropologists and social/behavioral scientists (to address harmful traditional medical beliefs and practices), clinical educators (to train community health workers on the need for prompt referral of women with prolonged labor), and policy/implementation researchers (to address delays in referrals for Caesarean sections from remote facilities). From a completely different context, the need for teamwork and the value of each team member is not unlike Paul's metaphor to the Corinthian church enumerating the multiple parts of the body working cooperatively together (1 Cor 12:14–26). In a sense, the multi-disciplinary team functions best then when it is comprised of like-minded, but not like-talented individuals.

(4) Cultivate and engage virtue.

It has been said that character is who you are when you are a thousand miles from home. There is a certain literal truth to this axiom for those pursuing Global Health activities abroad. True character is engrained in one's being, and it does not change with location or environment. Developed over time and out of habit, it is manifest when no one you really know is looking. The cultivation of Christian character or *virtue* is about forming right habits. N. T. Wright puts it this way, "Virtue, in this strict sense, is what happens when someone has made a thousand small choices, requiring effort and concentration, to do something which is good and right but which doesn't 'come naturally'—and then, on the thousand and first time, when it really matters, they find that they do what's required 'automatically,' as we say."[9] There is much more that could be said about Christian virtue (read N. T. Wright), but the point, as it pertains to interacting in the arena of Global Health is that when one is thousands of miles away from home, in a different culture, perhaps even isolated from one's faith community, the metal of one's character will be tested. So, *prepare now*. Develop virtuous muscle memory. Ask the Holy Spirit to cultivate and grow within you the fruit of the Spirit—love, joy, peace, patience, kindness, goodness, faithfulness, gentleness, and self-control (Gal 5:22–23). As a Christian, these traits plus a solid dose of generosity should be characteristic of your interactions with other persons—co-workers, trainees, mentors, research participants, patients, taxi-drivers—all of whom are of eternal interest to God and for whom the congruence of your behavior and beliefs can be a testimony of God's grace. Although the point of virtue is not to enhance one's likelihood

---

9. Wright, *After You Believe*, 20.

of success in her chosen Global Health endeavor, peace-loving persons[10] will respond favorably to these character traits. When a collaborator or colleague does not—run!

The list of virtues—Christian, classical, and otherwise—that could be accessed in the service of Global Health is beyond the scope of this chapter, but prudence deserves special emphasis. Global Health endeavors are fraught with unanticipated road-blocks, with multiple opportunities to misinterpret local contexts, and with foreign researchers and practitioners who are blind to their own and others' biases. Navigating these and similar issues requires prudence. As described by Josef Pieper,

> Prudence, then, is the mold and mother of all virtues, the circumspect and resolute shaping power of our minds which transforms knowledge of reality into realization of the good. It holds within itself the humility of silent, that is to say, of unbiased perception; the trueness-to-being of memory;[11] the art of receiving counsel; alert, composed readiness for the unexpected. Prudence means the studied seriousness and, as it were, the filter of deliberation, and at the same time the brave boldness to make final decisions. It means purity, straightforwardness, candor, and simplicity of character; it means standing superior to the utilitarian complexities of mere "tactics."[12]

Biblically, prudence might be likened to the shrewd manager of Luke 16 or Jesus' admonition to his followers to be "as wise as serpents and as innocent as doves" (Matt 10:16). Would that we, as his followers, engage in the tasks of Global Health with godly prudence.

Finally, doing Global Health well is wonderfully fulfilling and rewarding, but a caveat is in order. There is something inherently dangerous about professionalizing what we might consider to be 'good works,' and there is absolutely no excuse for putting on, receiving, or otherwise endorsing any sense of one's own virtue or, heaven forbid, moral superiority for this work. Global Health researchers and practitioners (and those engaged in other professions who seek to honor human dignity and promote equity) typically earn a good wage. Even as we conduct research and implement programs intended to improve health disparities, we need to ask ourselves hard questions: Am I trying to prove my righteousness (i.e., demonstrating self-righteousness) before God, or am I acting in a posture of thankfulness,

---

10. Akin to "a son of peace"; Luke 10:6.

11. By which he means that memories invoked in decision-making reflect a clear view of reality; as things really are.

12. Pieper, *Four Cardinal Virtues*, 22.

gratitude, and obedience? Am I looking for a pat on the shoulder ('Wow, what a great guy')? Do I quickly defer praise to God to whom I owe my next breath and heartbeat? Never underestimate the capacity to deceive yourself in this regard. Be transparent, honest, and real before God and others.

(5) Create virtuous cycles of informative research and service in a process of continuous improvement.

Bill Foege, former director of the CDC, and one of the pioneers in Global Health offered this observation: "Scientific knowledge becomes a mocking unused library without translation into action."[13] In other words, Global Health research has a purpose: to generate new knowledge that will improve the health of disadvantaged populations. The end of one's work is not to publish research findings in a high-profile journal (although that often is an important means to the end); the ultimate goal is to generate knowledge that will change health-related policies and practices, which in turn will improve health outcomes. Many who lead global health research projects lack formal training in health policy, and while this is a skill that can be learned, the deficit is perhaps best corrected by engaging health policy and communications specialists with one's project to help translate the knowledge generated into action.

But implementing research into practice is only half of the virtuous cycle. The other is collecting data to assess the efficacy of service delivery (see Figure 1). Where are the gaps? Who is not benefiting and why? Could uptake of a new intervention be improved? What is the cost-effectiveness of the intervention, and are there opportunities for improvement?

Let me illustrate. Widespread testing for HIV is the first step along a succession of events required to engage persons living with HIV/AIDS into care. Efforts to increase HIV testing, link infected persons to care, and ensure that they adhere to effective antiretroviral medications hold promise for ultimately controlling the HIV epidemic. In 2003, having secured several thousand dollars to help an HIV/AIDS service organization in Tanzania to begin offering HIV testing to their community, the organization leaders decided to charge clients approximately $1 per test, as fee-for-service HIV-testing was standard practice in the community at that time. The mean number of clients presenting for testing at this price was about 4 per day, and 17 percent tested positive for HIV infection. After discussion, the organization leaders decided to conduct a 2-week free HIV-testing campaign and the daily rate of HIV testing nearly quadrupled, and with the

---

13. GatesFoundation, "2015 Global Partners," 15:45.

greater turnout more persons were identified as HIV-infected. In a formal cost-effectiveness analysis[14] with sustained free-HIV testing, annualized over a year, the cost per HIV infection averted was estimated at $92 versus $170 per person in the fee-for-service model.[15] Based on these findings, and the ability to find additional resources, the leadership of the service organization decided to permanently offer free HIV testing. Later, as more HIV/AIDS funding became available across the region, free testing became standard. Had we not collected data carefully, including detailed cost information and logging the number of clients and HIV seropositivity rates, we would not have been prepared to conduct the analysis that led to changes in policy at the AIDS service organization. Data from service delivery should be captured and analyzed, and the research results should inform service delivery—a virtuous cycle.

Global Health and Eternity

Reducing health disparities and improving the well-being of disadvantaged populations is God-honoring and fulfilling work. We and our secular colleagues who engage in Global Health do so in overlapping yet different ways (see table below). Notable differences in epistemological understanding, scope of concern, and the posture or demeanor of Christians involved in Global Health should not be construed to confer moral superiority, better science, or even a more loving spirit towards one's neighbor. But Christians have a deep wealth of resources from which to draw as we seek to honor human dignity and human rights. And, our understanding of the origin of human worth differs: persons are of value because they are made in the image of God who purchased their redemption through the sacrifice of his Son. Those whose lives we seek to improve and prolong have had eternity set in their hearts by their Creator (Eccl 3:11). As ensouled persons, hardwired for eternity, each of them—along with you, me, our colleagues, and everyone with whom we have contact—will someday pass from this life to one eternal destination or the other. Writes C. S. Lewis in *The Weight of Glory*:

> It is a serious thing to live in a society of possible gods and goddesses, to remember that the dullest most uninteresting person you can talk to may one day be a creature which, if you saw it

---

14. Analysis which incorporated cost data for the HIV testing service and imputed the number of HIV infections averted through interruption of ongoing transmission once an infection is identified.

15. Thielman et al., "Cost-effectiveness," 114–19.

> now, you would be strongly tempted to worship, or else a horror and a corruption such as you now meet, if at all, only in a nightmare. All day long we are, in some degree helping each other to one or the other of these destinations. It is in the light of these overwhelming possibilities, it is with the awe and the circumspection proper to them, that we should conduct all of our dealings with one another, all friendships, all loves, all play, all politics. There are no ordinary people. You have never talked to a mere mortal. Nations, cultures, arts, civilizations—these are mortal, and their life is to ours as the life of a gnat. But it is immortals whom we joke with, work with, marry, snub, and exploit—immortal horrors or everlasting splendors.

The noblest end of our task, the greatest and best way we can serve humanity, is to play a role in moving these immortals towards a saving relationship with Jesus. As we submit our lives and our work to God in light of our unique gifts, aptitudes, and calling, this will look different for each of us from day to day. It requires sensitivity to the leading of the Holy Spirit and being prepared to make a defense to anyone who asks for a reason for the hope that is in us—doing so with gentleness and respect (1 Pet 3:15). We should be quick to partner with others who are called to evangelism. Nothing communicates respect for human dignity more than caring for the whole person, body and soul, and taking an interest in that person's eternal destiny. Charles Malik, Rapporteur of the United Nations' Commission on Human Rights, summed this up well: "The greatest thing about any civilization is the human person, and the greatest thing about this person is the possibility of his encounter with the person of Jesus Christ."[16]

May our own encounter with the person of Jesus Christ shape our understanding of the field of Global Health and the persons we seek to assist, and may those of us who are called to this field look to him with humble but sure confidence for the resources to do this job well.

---

16. Acton Staff, "Charles Malik," epigraph.

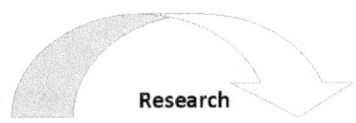

Research

- Define the service delivery
- Characterize end users
- Document outcomes
- Capture cost data

- Evaluate new/modified interventions
- Quantify and categorize service demand
- Identify disparities in uptake/outcomes
- Estimate cost-effectiveness

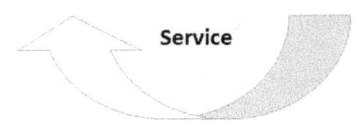

Service

Figure 1: A virtuous cycle: research with service / service with research

An Overview of Secular and Christian Approaches to Global Health

Table. An Overview of Secular and Christian Approaches to Global Health

	Secular	Christian
Goal	-Describe disparities in health -Explore/understand their determinants -Implement/evaluate solutions	
Method	-Interdisciplinary -Collaborative -Capacity-building -Appropriate and rigorous methodology	
Epistemology	-Truth is relative and fragmented	-Truth is absolute -All truth coheres through Christ (Col 1:17-18)
Scope	- Bodies	- Bodies and Souls (Eccl 3:11)
Posture	- Virtues	-Virtues – classical and Christian and the fruit of the Holy Spirit (Gal 5:22-23)
Rationale	Human dignity and human rights	
Origin of Human Dignity and Rights	-Reason and discipline -Autonomy -Experience-driven/"nurtural" rights -Others	- *Imago Dei* - God's dignifying acts toward humankind demonstrated through the arc of the Biblical narrative - God's law

Bibliography

Acton Staff. "Charles Malik." https://acton.org/charles-malik.

Dershowitz, Alan M. *Rights from Wrongs: A Secular Theory of the Origins of Rights*. New York: Basic Books, 2004.

GatesFoundation. "2015 Global Partners Forum—Bill Foege: 'Rewriting History?'" *YouTube*, May 11, 2015. https://www.youtube.com/watch?v=tbxOk6bh0UY.

Human Rights Watch. "Human Rights 101." https://www.hrw.org/human-rights-101.

Kristof, Nicholas. "The World's Modern-Day Lepers: Women with Fistula." *The New York Times*, March 19, 2016. https://www.nytimes.com/2016/03/20/opinion/sunday/the-worlds-modern-day-lepers-women-with-fistulas.html.

Pieper, Josef. *The Four Cardinal Virtues*. Notre Dame: University of Notre Dame Press, 1966.

Schulman, Adam. "Bioethics and the Question of Human Dignity." https://bioethicsarchive.georgetown.edu/pcbe/reports/human_dignity/chapter1.html.

Thielman, Nathan M., et al. "Cost-effectiveness of Free HIV Voluntary Counseling and Testing through a Community-based AIDS Service Organization in Northern Tanzania." *Am J Public Health* 96.1 (2006) 114–19.

Thielman, Nathan M., et al. "Ebola Clinical Trials: Five Lessons Learned and a Way Forward." *Clin Trials* 13.1 (2016) 83–86.

Whitehead, Margaret. "The Concepts and Principles of Equity and Health." *Int J Health Serv.* 22.3 (1992) 429–45.

Wright, N. T. *After You Believe: Why Christian Character Matters*. San Francisco: HarperCollins, 2010.

15

Chemistry, Christianity, and Wisdom
Stephen Contakes

Obtainable in quantities of 500 for around $14, the common plastic spoon is emblematic of chemistry's impact on our world. A marvel of chemists' ability to control matter's structure, these spoons are comprised of string-like polystyrene chains one to four thousand carbon atoms long (Figure 1A). Crucial to the spoon's strength and flexibility are flat hexagons of carbon protruding from every other atom along the chain. Since the hexagons dangle off the sides of the chain in an irregular fashion (Figure 1B) they prevent the chains from packing neatly so that the polystyrene forms a tangle of intertwined coils (Figure 1C). The ability of these coils to stretch allows polystyrene to deform without cracking (Figure 1D) while the imperfect packing of chains renders polystyrene easily melted, making it easy to produce spoons by injection of liquid polystyrene into industrial molds.

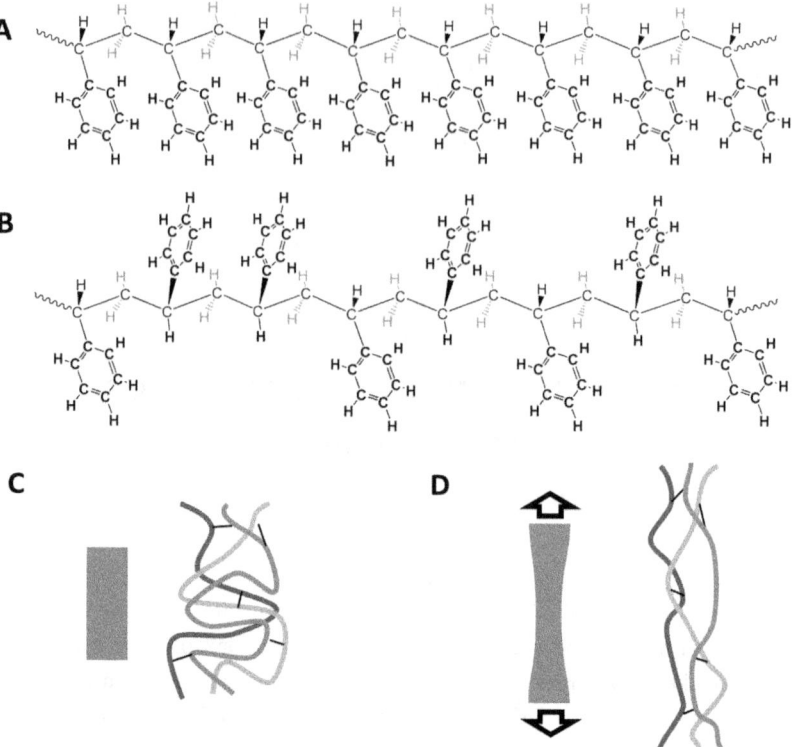

Figure 1. Relationship between polystyrene's structure and its behavior when stretched. The regular structure enabled by a consistent arrangement of polystyrene's hexagon-shaped side chains (A) is disrupted when the chains are irregularly arranged (B), giving a solid (grey) consisting of coiled chains at room temperature (C). When polystyrene is stretched the coils straighten and it lengthens without breaking (D).

Plastics are emblematic of chemistry's ability to transform the world. Along with inexpensive plastic cutlery, polymer chemistry provides us with easy to clean furniture, hygienic medical syringes, and the packaging materials that make it easy to organize, preserve, and protect many objects of everyday commerce. Because we take these products for granted today, it is difficult to appreciate the enthusiasm with which they were first received. In 1955 *Life* magazine celebrated their advent in a short article featuring a euphoric family standing around a large trash can with their hands raised as they toss a variety of pots, pans, plates, knives, forks, and spoons into the air.[1] Yet beneath that scene reads a title that seems less auspicious today—"Throwaway Living—Disposable Items Cut Down on Household Chores." Along with

1. LIFE, "Throwaway Living," 43–44.

wealth, hygiene, and convenience, chemistry also facilitates cultures of consumerism, waste, and low tolerance for inconvenience,[2] along with mountains of environmentally persistent plastic waste on land and in the oceans, the latter of which tends to harm the birds and fish which feed there.

Plastic cutlery illustrates the power and fragility of chemistry. Its knowledge of reality at the molecular level is so reliable and detailed that chemists can reliably design and synthesize compounds with precisely controlled properties. Through these products, chemists have the power to improve our quality of living. Unfortunately, chemists cannot always foresee how their work will impact human culture and the environment. They also cannot control how others ultimately use their discoveries. There is always some possibility that chemical products will be misused or cause unintentional harm.

Chemistry's potential for both creative progress and destructive catastrophe forms the backdrop to this chapter, where I will commend chemistry as a spectacular source of wisdom for Christians, but also a volatile science that requires patience, wise accountability partnerships, and uncompromising standards to protect humanity's long-term best interests.

Seeking Wisdom in the Molecular

The Bible portrays material creation as good, ordered, sustained by God, and subject to God's faithful control, with humanity imaging God within it as creation's caretaker. The material world is also treated as a valuable part of God's relationship with humanity. God forges and redeems an earthly people, dwells with them in a material tabernacle, places them upon a land, comes in the flesh to suffer and die, is bodily resurrected from the dead, and builds a new community that looks forward to Christ's bodily return prior to its own bodily resurrection. Christians then receive the call to follow Christ with their whole bodies in bodily fellowship with others, remembering Christ through sacramental objects like bread and wine. For the Christian, matter matters!

The Bible also gives Christians a theological foundation for valuing chemistry. If creation is orderly, as Genesis maintains, then there should be structure within matter for chemists to discover. If our "reason within and [God's] reason without are linked together by common origin in [God's] Rationality,"[3] then we can expect that it should be possible for us to at least partially understand that structure. If the precise form of matter's structure

---

2. These issues have recently been highlighted by Pope Francis in *Laudato Si'*.
3. Polkinghorne, "Cross Traffic."

depends on how God freely chose to create the cosmos, then just thinking about nature is not enough. Chemists should conduct experiments to determine how nature actually behaves.

These Christian expectations find affirmation through chemistry's success in revealing a cosmos of striking beauty, where molecules small and large move, collide, stick together, come apart, and react with one another. In these structures and their endless motion, there is interplay between order and disorder, regularity and irregularity. At the molecular level, some molecules are highly symmetric, while others seem to have no overall symmetry at all. Yet even then there is often a predictable local symmetry so that chemists can speak of the geometry of bonds in terms of octahedral metals, tetrahedral carbons, hexagonal aromatic rings, polyhedral cages, coil-like alpha helices, and zigzagging beta sheets (Figure 2). Symmetry amidst asymmetry also occurs in the way molecules twist, turn, fold, and stack. Row upon row, layer upon layer, molecules pack together to form crystals, cluster together to form supramolecular cages, and hook together into rings and chains. In the body, protein assemblies form as proteins work together to store and transport nutrients throughout the body, facilitate vast interconnected sequences of chemical reactions, and transmit and amplify the intercellular signals needed to control them effectively. To comprehend the molecular is to experience awe and wonder at the consonance between chemistry's picture of order emerging from seemingly chaotic motions of atoms and molecules and Genesis' picture of God bringing order to a chaotic creation.

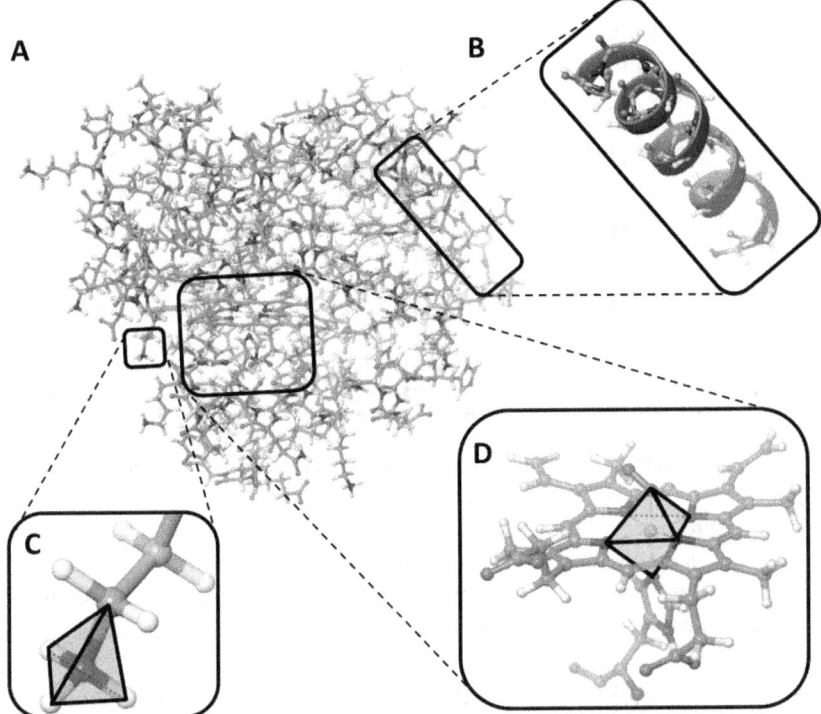

Figure 2. The protein oxymoglobin (A) has no overall symmetry but a closer look reveals the structure contains alpha-helices (B) and atoms with tetrahedral and octahedral bonding geometries (C and D, respectively). The image was prepared using coordinates from protein data bank entry 1MBO.

This consonance is also seen in the emergence of predictable properties from the seemingly random molecular motions and collisions which give rise to agglomerations, detachments, and reactions under the constraint of well-understood forces. A helium-filled balloon, for instance, contains a host of helium atoms moving about in different directions and at different speeds, undergoing occasional collisions with one another and the balloon wall, so that at the molecular level the whole system looks like a collection of bouncy balls let loose in a shaking room (Figure 3). However, all but the smallest chemical systems contain so many atoms the aggregate effect of all this chaos is so predictable the pressure generated by the collisions tracks with the volume of the balloon according to a simple mathematical relationship called Boyle's Law (Equation 1).

$$\text{Gas Pressure} \times \text{Gas Volume} = \text{constant} \tag{1}$$

While the consistency of these laws renders anomalies infrequent, their reliance on chance-fused motions, collisions, and rearrangements is highly significant. Without them molecular systems couldn't undergo the sort of changes needed to make the overwhelmingly probable real.

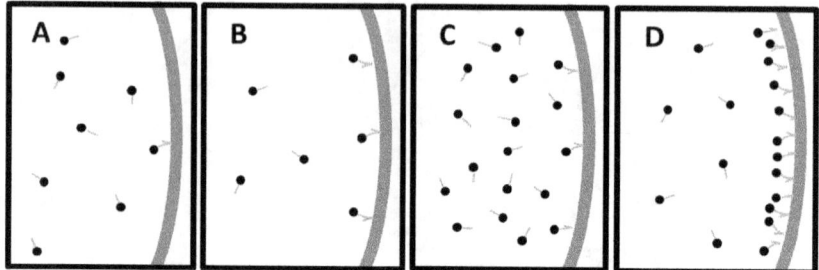

Figure 3. Molecules (balls) moving near the wall of a gas-filled balloon (gray) exert pressure as they strike the wall of the balloon. When there are only a few molecules the pressure expected from an average number of collisions (A) might be exceeded if several molecules collide with the wall at once (B). As the number of molecules increases (C), the number of simultaneous molecule-wall collisions needed to achieve similarly higher than average pressures becomes less and less probable (D).

Room for empirical fit between Christian and chemical conceptions of reality is also found in the "anthropic coincidences" in the cosmos' fundamental structure and properties which make Earth an uncommonly fortuitous place for the existence of life like ours. For instance, if the Boltzmann factor differed by less than a part per trillion, then life's central element, carbon, would not exist.[4] Although thorny questions remain over the significance of this and similar "fine tuning" in the properties of water and other compounds of biochemically-significant elements, such anthropic coincidences are consistent with Christianity's vision of a God-intentioned creation, which can give rise to the sort of life that can engage in a cognitively-aware fellowship with its Creator.

However, we should qualify that there may be limitations as to what we might learn from these anthropic coincidences. Their purpose is not to tease out Christian truths that originate in the special revelation of Scripture, the person of Christ, and the Holy Spirit. Chemistry is not the place to go for insights about the incarnation, atonement, and resurrection, but it is a legitimate domain for discovering the creative design of God "in the things that have been made" (Rom 1:20). Chemistry requires of the Christian the foresight and wisdom to resist either overstating or understating chemistry's

---

4. See Barrow and Tipler, *Anthropic Cosmological Principle*.

revelatory promise. Like all sciences, the revelatory potential of chemistry is subtle and complex, powerful and real, but theologically insufficient apart from the magnification of special revelation.

Humility is also needed to discern evidence of God's wisdom in the complex interlocking protein assemblies of biochemistry (Figure 4), which are sometimes offered as proof that an "intelligent designer" exists.[5] The eye of faith may indeed discern the work of a thoughtful Creator in these systems. However, their value as incontrovertible proofs for God's existence and the fallaciousness of Darwinism is tenuous, since other thinkers have offered these protein assemblies as evidence of evolutionary processes.[6] Moreover, to the extent these systems provide evidence for design, there remain questions about how we should think about chemical systems that appear to be designed. Such design might simply result from the fundamental laws of chemistry rather than spontaneous supernatural manipulations of matter. In the end, it really doesn't matter, since God could have designed the laws of chemistry just as creatively and intelligently to give rise to protein assemblies as he could have miraculously entered chaos to reorder events spontaneously. In either case, the confidence with which we assert our conclusions should be proportional to what science corroborates and theology demands. We should also resist dogmatic appeals to a "God of the gaps." According to the Methodist chemical bonding theory pioneer Charles Coulson, "either God is in the whole of nature, with no gaps, or He's not there at all."[7]

---

5. For arguments see Behe, *Darwin's Black Box*.
6. See Collins, *Language of God*, 181–96.
7. Coulson, *Science and Christian Belief*, 34.

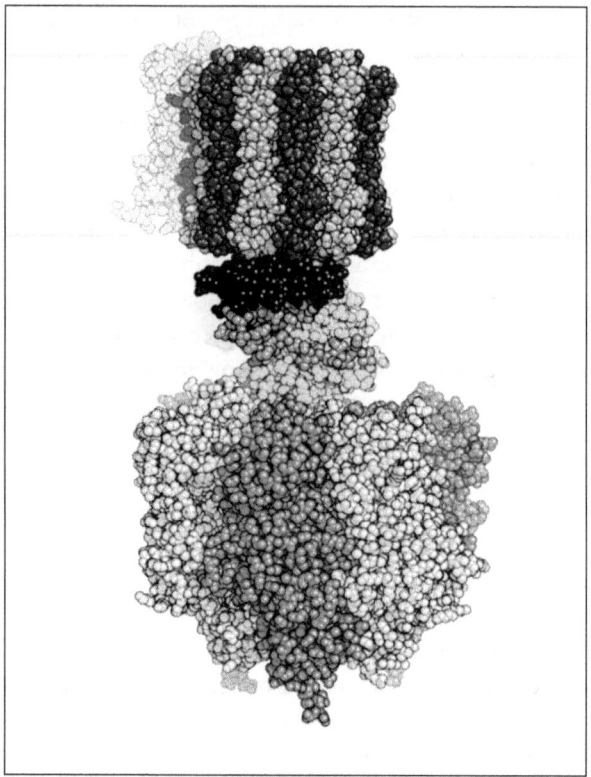

Figure 4. Part of the mitochondrial ATP synthase protein assembly used in energy metabolism. The different protein chains present are shown in various shades of gray. The image is adapted from Atp_synthase.PNG# by Alex.X licensed under CC BY-SA 3.0 (https://creativecommons.org/licenses/by-sa/3.0/deed.en).

Even if God is taken as present everywhere in nature, chemistry's picture of impersonal chance-driven processes giving rise to predictable outcomes can still occasion uncertainty, questioning, and doubt. For most of Christian history the idea that matter is comprised of randomly moving atoms was associated with Epicurus's belief that creation is purposeless and the Divine absent. Today the same reasoning forms part of a New Atheists' mythos in which science's success renders belief obsolete.[8] However, whatever challenge science may pose for certain ideas about God's guidance in natural history, chemistry's success in offering explanations in terms of physical and material causes is something Christians should continue to endorse. While chemistry might be a reliable guide to the impersonal workings of the

8. Stenger, *God and the Atom*.

molecular world, Christianity offers compelling answers to questions that science raises but cannot fully answer. Why is there something rather than nothing? Why is there order at all? Why is mathematics so "unreasonably effective" in science?[9]

For the average Christian, the issue is not about exhaustively explaining how God interacts with matter but in rationalizing suffering, death, and apparent waste in nature. There is something inadequate in explaining deaths caused by emission of carbon dioxide in the Lake Nyos natural disaster[10] in terms of God merely upholding, but not intervening in, the underlying molecular events. Here it can be helpful to realize that nature is only one of God's two books. Whatever chemistry reveals about God's wisdom and power, there is much it leaves undisclosed.

There are indeed times when the impersonal world disclosed by chemistry appears inimical to an optimistic world view in which God orders everything for good." In these cases, it is wise to acknowledge that scientific knowledge is limited to the fraction of reality that it is able to expose. Amidst the groaning of this present cosmos, faith enters in believing that God will, in his time, consummate this chaotic, impersonal, and terrifying natural world (Rom 8:22; Rev 21–22).[11] In short, we should not entertain chemistry as an alternative route to tidy theological answers. Chemistry is one complex dimension of God's comprehensive reality, now contorted by sin, in which God calls his people to live intelligently, all the while seeking understanding through faith.

Synthesis, Analysis, and the Need for Wisdom

Christianity's story moves from the cultivating and tending of a garden to the life and culture of a redeemed community characterized by the love of renewed hearts and renewed minds. In this story, humans created in the image of a creative and ordering God are called to care for, fill, subdue, and replenish the material world. Within the context of this so-called culture mandate, chemists have the calling of advancing science and innovation for the welfare of humankind and creation's ultimate good.[12] Seen in this respect, chemists can be a source of joy and benefit to humanity and the

---

9. Wigner, "Unreasonable Effectiveness of Mathematics."
10. Rouwet et al., "Cameroon's Lake Nyos Gas Burst."
11. McLeish, *Faith and Wisdom in Science*, 102–62.
12. Crouch, *Culture Making*; Monsma, *Responsible Technology*, 37–57; Hefner, *Human Factor*, 23–53; Brouwer, "Better Living through Chemistry?" For a historical perspective on the idea of chemists as created co-creators, see Brooke, "Chemistry."

Earth through their knowledge, know-how, and material bounties. Some chemists do this by controlling the course of chemical reactions to prepare interesting, beautiful, or useful materials. Others contribute in the realm of the theoretical by developing new strategies, methods, and procedures for understanding chemistry.

Equally significant, however, is chemistry's capacity for harm. Alongside countless beneficial drugs, devices, and sanitary products, chemistry's track record includes the Holocaust's only privately run concentration camp,[13] miracle pesticides later found to harm bird populations,[14] and weapons forged for use in a just cause that were later used indiscriminately against civilians.[15] A common response to chemistry's potential for bringing about both evil and good is to avoid it altogether, fearing synthetic chemicals and distrusting the corporations which make them. However, such a shirking of the culture mandate is not an option for those gifted with a passion for chemistry and the intellect, creativity, training, and grit needed to do it well. A better response is to accept that being responsible to God as a steward of creation and shaper of culture involves continual assessment of the values implicit in the trajectory of one's work. Every gift requires a controlling ethic for its optimal, benevolent usage.

In this regard, although it can be difficult to assess chemical work accurately, there are several guidelines Christians in chemistry might follow. The first involves right intent. Chemists should seek to use their passion and expertise to address the world's needs. Projects aimed at relieving human suffering or caring for the environment present obvious opportunities, while improving living standards has a role to play too.[16] To be sure, the culture mandate isn't limited to immediate technological applications. Chemists can legitimately pursue theoretical and technical problems as ways to uncover wisdom inherent within the natural world. Chemical synthesis and instrument design offer exhilarating opportunities for chemists to image God's creativity and beauty through the "design" of beautiful molecules and "elegant" syntheses. These activities are a Christian chemist's exercise of the *imago Dei*.

The second admonition is to avoid engaging in chemistry recklessly. Christian chemists should be careful to evaluate, disclose, and account for the possible adverse effects of their work. They should also follow safety

---

13. Jeffreys, *Hell's Cartel*, 276–336.
14. McGrayne, *Prometheans in the Lab*, 148–167.
15. Contakes and Jashinsky, "Ethical Responsibilities," 36–40.
16. Leegwater, "Loving the Kingdom."

and regulatory guidelines, undertake and account for risk-assessments, and employ industry-standard harm-mitigation strategies.[17]

In some cases, chemists might seek to avoid employers who unjustifiably cut corners and projects aimed at morally dubious ends. In rare cases, chemists may even need to expose wrongdoing.[18]

Third, chemists' efforts to shape culture should be infused with an awareness of human frailty. One approach is continual monitoring of the safety and environmental impacts of technologically important chemical processes. One example of what this might look like involves the pharmaceutical industry. Since even the most rigorous risk assessment cannot predict all side effects and other adverse impacts associated with a drug's use, responsible pharmaceutical companies continue to evaluate the safety of their products long after regulatory authorities require them to do so. Not all adverse impacts are due to unforeseeable consequences. Unjustifiable harms can also arise when chemical entities abnegate their moral responsibilities or when poor moral reasoning is used to navigate the calculus of harms and benefits associated with chemical experiments. In these cases an informed ethical dialogue can help Christians in chemistry avoid unjustifiable adverse impacts due to moral compromise. During the Second World War, the normally humane American chemist Louis Fieser would have benefitted from such an ethically steered collegial dialogue as he moved from an aversion to chemical warfare towards development of indiscriminate napalm bombs for use against Japanese cities.[19] This is illustrated by Fieser's later history when, amidst public ethical debate over how napalm was being used in Vietnam, Fieser indeed did publicly oppose the use of firebombs against civilians.

Moral dialogue within the church can help Christian chemists shape their field in ways that better reflect Christian ideals of human flourishing. In the 13th Century the Franciscan friar Roger Bacon offered the rational matter science of his day, alchemy,[20] both as a way to "give everyone what they wanted and . . . prolong life"[21] and as a source of chemical weapons that could be used against unbelievers "obstinate in their malice."[22] Fortunately, Bacon's enthusiasm for alchemical wealth, longevity, and security as a means

---

17. For examples see Rodricks, *Calculated Risks*.

18. On faith in whistleblowing see Glazer and Glazer, *Whistleblowers*.

19. Specifically napalm "Bat Bombs." See Contakes and Jashinsky, "Ethical Responsibilities," 38.

20. Then grounded in Aristotle's theory of matter.

21. Quoted from Bacon's *Opus Majus* in Power, *Roger Bacon and the Defence*, 119.

22. Power, *Roger Bacon and the Defence*, 96.

of advancing Christianity represented just one voice in the wider church, which also includes ascetic and peace traditions. Ultimately, questions of good stewardship and moral propriety played a determinative role. At various times in Bacon's era the Western Church sought to discourage its monks from undertaking alchemical investigations due to their expense, adverse health impacts, and association with fraud.[23]

Finally, Christian chemists should be sensitive to the broader narratives in which their work is embedded. Although overt attempts to promote materialism through chemistry are rare,[24] chemistry has sometimes become a locus for alternative gospels. Notably, its success as the workhorse science of the 20th Century sometimes led it to be treated as a sort of technological messiah, useful not only for bringing wealth and curing disease but also effective as a solution to complex social and geopolitical problems. The German physical chemist Fritz Haber is often cited as an exemplar of this tendency. After Haber developed a process for producing fertilizer from air, he turned his skills toward developing chemical weapons that Germany might use to break the stalemate of trench warfare. When that failed, he tried to isolate gold from seawater and use it to pay off Germany's subsequent war debt![25]

Chemical marketing campaigns have on occasion also portrayed chemistry as the giver of every good and perfect gift desired by those who seek the American dream of abundance, convenience, wealth, and long life. One way to address this is for Christians to present an alternative narrative in which chemistry is a science[26] that can bring "better things for better living" in ways that facilitate Christian charity along with wise stewardship of the earth—both acts being fully commensurate with God's commission.

Conclusion: Wisdom for a Life in Chemistry Well Lived

For those called to follow Christ, chemistry is rich in opportunities to discover, demonstrate, and practice wisdom. Chemistry's highs, lows, and

---

23. For a summary of 13th and 14th century Western Christian responses to alchemy, see Theisen, "Attraction of Alchemy."

24. Examples include Atkins and Ostwald. See Atkins, *On Being*, and Hakfoort, "Science Deified."

25. In these latter efforts, Haber was less successful. See Hoffmann, "Fritz Haber"; Stoltzenberg, *Fritz Haber*, 121–55, 241–48. For Christian reflections on the Haber story, see Brouwer, "Better Living through Chemistry?" and Charles, "Idol of Progress."

26. Chemistry is portrayed as a service in the oddly ambiguous work by the chemical industry promoter and Christian apologist Abraham Cressy Morrison, *Man in a Chemical World*.

everyday moral challenges present opportunities for spiritual growth. The creative joy of sketching out elegant sequences of reactions and ingenious analytical methods on paper is often tested in the real world, where reactions go awry and testing gives unpromising results. At times the chemist's life can seem to be a cycle of repeated planning, testing, rethinking, and troubleshooting again and again until results are achieved or a project is abandoned. Success requires perseverance, hope, and an indefatigable resilience to frustration. Consequently, chemistry provides opportunities for God to foster Christ-like diligence, industry, patience, and courage. Chemistry, pursued in this manner, can indeed be a tool of Christian discipleship.

Within the church chemists have an opportunity to encourage the church to become more open to God's wisdom in creation. A case in point is Christianity's historic engagement with atomic theory, which has been characterized more by a theologically informed optimism than simplistic notions that science and religion are incompatible. Even though the atomic picture of matter has been associated with a purposeless view of the cosmos throughout most of the church's history, the Church Fathers distinguished the concept of atoms from simplistic materialism. Christian thinkers like John Wycliffe, Pierre Gassendi, and John Dalton even advanced atomic ideas. Remarkably, Christian reflection on Dalton's chemically grounded atomic theory helped motivate the research that culminated in America's first Chemistry Nobel Prize.[27] A lesson of this history is that science and religion can have fruitful dialogue, particularly when characterized by mutual respect for the legitimate roles both science and religion have in discerning the wisdom of God resident in creation.

Acknowledgements

The author would like to thank Professors Michael Everest and Kristi Cantrell for helpful suggestions.

Bibliography

Atkins, P. W. *On Being: A Scientist's Exploration of the Great Questions of Existence.* Oxford: Oxford University Press, 2011.
Barrow, John D., and Frank J. Tipler. *The Anthropic Cosmological Principle.* Oxford: Oxford University Press, 1986.
Behe, Michael J. *Darwin's Black Box: The Biochemical Challenge to Evolution.* New York: Free Press, 1996.

---

27. Henry, "Atomism," 123; Contakes and Kyle, "Josiah Parsons Cooke Jr.," 14–17.

Brooke, John Hedley. "Chemistry." In *The History of Science and Religion in the Western Tradition: An Encyclopedia*, edited by G. B. Ferngren, E. J. Larson, and D. W. Amundsen, 378–83. New York: Garland, 2000.

Brouwer, Darren. "Better Living through Chemistry? Why Chemists Need to Be Humanists." *Comment*, June 23, 2016. https://www.cardus.ca/comment/article/4895/better-living-through-chemistry/.

Charles, Daniel. "The Idol of Progress." *Sojourners Magazine* 35.8 (August 2006) 24–27.

Collins, Francis S. *The Language of God: A Scientist Presents Evidence for Belief*. New York: Free Press, 2007.

Contakes, Stephen M., and Christopher Kyle. "Josiah Parsons Cooke Jr.: Epistemology in the Service of Science, Pedagogy, and Natural Theology." *Hyle—International Journal for the Philosophy of Chemistry* 17.1 (2011) 1–23.

Contakes, Stephen M., and Taylor Jashinsky. "Ethical Responsibilities in Military-Related Work: The Case of Napalm." *HYLE—International Journal for the Philosophy of Chemistry* 22.1 (2016) 31–53.

Coulson, C. A. *Science and Christian Belief*. The John Calvin McNair Lectures. Chapel Hill: University of North Carolina Press, 1955.

Crouch, Andy. *Culture Making: Recovering Our Creative Calling*. Downers Grove: InterVarsity, 2008.

Fabbrizzi, Luigi. *Beauty in Chemistry: Artistry in the Creation of New Molecules*. Berlin: Springer, 2012.

Francis, Pope. *Laudato Si': On Care for Our Common Home*. http://w2.vatican.va/content/francesco/en/encyclicals/documents/papa-francesco_20150524_enciclica-laudato-si.html.

Glazer, Myron, and Penina Migdal Glazer. *The Whistleblowers: Exposing Corruption in Government and Industry*. New York: Basic Books, 1989.

Hakfoort, C. "Science Deified: Wilhelm Ostwald's Energeticist World-View and the History of Scientism." *Annals of Science* 49.6 (1992) 525–44.

Hefner, Philip J. *The Human Factor: Evolution, Culture, and Religion*. Minneapolis: Fortress, 1993.

Henry, John. "Atomism." In *The History of Science and Religion in the Western Tradition: An Encyclopedia*, edited by G. B. Ferngren et al., 139–45. New York: Garland, 2000.

Hoffmann, Roald. "Fritz Haber." In *The Same and Not the Same*, 167–76. New York: Columbia University Press, 1995.

Jeffreys, Diarmuid. *Hell's Cartel: IG Farben and the Making of Hitler's War Machine*. New York: Metropolitan, 2008.

Leegwater, Arie. "Loving the Kingdom and Responsible Technology." *Perspectives on Science and Christian Faith* 62.4 (2010) 233–34.

LIFE. "Throwaway Living." *LIFE Magazine*, August 1, 1955, 43–44.

McGrayne, Sharon Bertsch. *Prometheans in the Lab: Chemistry and the Making of the Modern World*. New York: McGraw-Hill, 2001.

McLeish, Tom. *Faith and Wisdom in Science*. Oxford: Oxford University Press, 2014.

Monsma, Stephen V., ed. *Responsible Technology: A Christian Perspective*. Grand Rapids: Eerdmans, 1986.

Morrison, Abraham Cressy. *Man in a Chemical World: The Service of Chemical Industry*. New York: Scribner's, 1937.

Polkinghorne, John. "Cross Traffic between Science and Theology." *Perspectives on Science and Christian Faith* 43 (1991) 144–51.

Power, Amanda. *Roger Bacon and the Defence of Christendom*. Cambridge: Cambridge University Press, 2013.
Rodricks, Joseph V. *Calculated Risks: The Toxicity and Human Health Risks of Chemicals in Our Environment*. 2nd ed. Cambridge: Cambridge University Press, 2007.
Rouwet, D., G. Tanyileke, and A. Costa. "Cameroon's Lake Nyos Gas Burst: 30 Years Later." *Eos*, July 12, 2016. https://doi.org/10.1029/2016EO055627.
Stenger, Victor J. *God and the Atom*. New York: Prometheus, 2013.
Stoltzenberg, Dietrich. *Fritz Haber: Chemist, Nobel Laureate, German, Jew*. Philadelphia: Chemical Heritage, 2004.
Theisen, Wilfred. "The Attraction of Alchemy for Monks and Friars in the 13th–14th Centuries." *The American Benedictine Review* 46.3 (1995) 239–53.
Wigner, Eugene P. "The Unreasonable Effectiveness of Mathematics in the Natural Sciences." *Communications on Pure and Applied Mathematics* 13.1 (1960) 1–14.

16

Wisdom in Physics

Arnold E. Sikkema

One of my colleagues reports an incident pivotal to his development as a scientist. He had come running inside during recess, excitedly reporting to his grade-school teacher that he had seen the moon even though it was daytime, only to be told, "Johnny, the moon only shines at night. Now, go back outside and play." Wisdom knows when to trust our senses and when to accept authority, and how to proceed in the face of such a conflict. In this case, I suppose it's remotely possible that the teacher had a twinkle in her eye, suspecting that little Johnny might be moved along in his career path by this incident. This episode indeed led to his realization that this teacher was not an authority on matters of astronomy.

My Journey into Physics

One of God's greatest gifts to humanity is our curiosity. We are deeply driven by a desire to inquire. We want to know how things work, why things happen the way they do, where we come from, what our destiny is, how to thrive, and how to be accepted. Curiosity is a cornerstone of the academic enterprise; teaching has the capacity to nurture or stifle it. The event which nucleated my desire to study physics was a tenth grade science teacher's inability to answer my question, "How does a car continue to move along the road when there is no net force acting upon it?" He had transmitted the received knowledge of Newton's first law of motion, but was unable to satiate my desire to understand this more deeply.

At the beginning of one of my graduate courses, the professor wrote in all-caps at the top of the blackboard, "Question Authority!" I ironically, and perhaps somewhat impertinently, objected, "What gives you the authority to tell us to question authority?" It is indeed essential in physics (and in all science and scholarship generally) to critically discern new and old ideas regardless of the real or perceived academic stature of the one expressing it, but wisdom is required in terms of how such questioning is best undertaken.

My path through the completion of high school, university, and graduate school has seen my attitudes about physics change. To me, likely driven by my joy and success in calculating parabolic trajectories of baseballs, physics was an exact science by which all motion could be perfectly described and explained at any level. Pride accompanied my mathematical prowess, both on a personal level and on a "professional" level. I saw physics as the discipline of disciplines, the foundation of all knowledge, the basis upon which all science rests. Even the Bible should be supportable from the results of physics and cosmology, according to my naïve pseudo-fundamentalist approach. After a few undergraduate projects in the Einsteinian theory of gravity (general relativity) and its cosmological models (specifically big bang theory), I departed the field fearing its challenge to my assumed Biblical young-earth thinking and simplistically and arrogantly proclaiming (though inwardly doubting) the solution of an only apparent history.[1]

Turning my interest toward condensed matter theory, in particular magnetism and superconductivity (attempting to explain the 1986 surprise of ceramic materials having no electrical resistance, a phenomenon remaining unexplained to this day), I delved deeply into quantum theory. Impressed by its beauty, depth, and universality, I was further confirmed in my belief of the fundamental character of physics: Surely all else depends upon physics, and physics can in principle resolve any problem in its omni-competence. While there remain many, including some prominent physicists, who make such grand claims, I grew to recognize this as foolish reductionism.

This recognition was due in large part by mentorship and guidance from wise men and women in my local church. They opened up for me a world where physics could play its proper place among the disciplines rather than, as I had viewed it, as the top of the stack or its cornerstone. This is the world of Christian philosophical reflection, in particular the thinking of some in my own Reformed heritage, particularly the early twentieth century

---

1. Sikkema, "A Phoenix Universe?" This view I have replaced with a recognition (in fact the Christian confession) that God creates realities, and not appearances. *All quotations of the Bible in this chapter are from the NIV.

writings of Abraham Kuyper,[2] Herman Dooyeweerd,[3] Klaas Schilder,[4] and the late twentieth-century work of Al Wolters.[5] The kernel of wisdom in this strand of thought, for my purposes in physics, is its identification of reductionism and its problems. Reformational philosophy acknowledges the utter dependence of all things upon the Creator who establishes their meaning, purpose, and relationships. Human descriptions of created things range across the disciplinary spectrum. Physics is the science of the physical aspect, namely that of *interaction*; as such, our laws of physics describe and explain interactions (for example, via concepts such as force and energy) and in so doing physics relies upon the numerical, spatial, and kinematic aspects and allows for biotic, psychic, and higher aspects.

The Joy of Physics

Telling people that I am a physicist has pretty predictable results. The most common response is "You must be smart!" This fits a popular stereotype that scientists, especially theoretical physicists, have a level of thinking not typically reached by others, often coupled by personal experiences of inability in or avoidance of science generally or physics in particular. It unfortunately ignores the fact that there are many types of intelligence, as well as many other fields in which significant skill and expertise are involved. The second most frequent response I appreciate more: "I loved physics in high school!" This is often followed by stories of how much fun physics was, with an entertaining and enthusiastic teacher who used riveting demonstrations and exciting projects.

Physics *is* fun! There are very many everyday experiences and objects that can be used to demonstrate important principles of physics, how things interact and move (or remain static). Many of us are familiar with striking displays such as the surprising wine-bottle balancer or "magic" (magnetic) suspended weights. They draw us in and can conceptually illustrate basic ideas in satisfying ways. Some effort, requiring mathematics, is needed to reach deeper levels of appreciation for the beauty and consistency of physics.

Besides the exciting demos which can be done in introductory physics, such as the bowling ball pendulum swinging back until almost hitting the professor in the nose, there is the joy of success in solving problems. This is unfortunately not achieved by everyone in a physics course (not even

2. Kuyper, "Calvinism and Science."
3. Dooyeweerd, *New Critique*.
4. Schilder, *Christ and Culture*.
5. Wolters, *Creation Regained*.

those who study diligently), but it certainly is a goal of the subject. Calculating something from first principles, confirming the same using a different method altogether, and especially seeing it work in real life can all bring a significant sense of accomplishment and appreciation.

Experiments in neuroscience have demonstrated that mathematicians, when viewing equations, exhibit measurable brain responses similar to those of others experiencing great artworks.[6] This gives further confirmation to what mathematicians and physicists (for whom mathematics serves effectively as a language) have often thought. In fact, since the beauty of a theory in physics is so well correlated with its success, it is one criterion used in judging theories.

I consider the consistency and beauty of physics as a suggestive, if not convincing, signpost to the goodness of the Creator. He has made a world of beauty not only at the level of universal visual appeal, but at levels and scales which can be experienced uniquely in multiple different perspectives. We can receive such a gift with thankfulness, praise, and worship.

Humility, Wisdom, and Peer Review

It is not widely recognized that academic work in general has humility at its core. A popular perception, also in the Christian church, is that those holding academic degrees are arrogant. Having the letters "PhD" behind our names has puffed us up and we carry an air of superiority, claiming an elite status due to our knowledge and skills, looking down our noses from our ivory towers at the uneducated masses. To be sure, such caricatures are not entirely unfounded; still, certain features of academic work can be seen as intrinsically humble. Ringenberg notes humility as one necessary characteristic of the Christian academic.[7] We can see this most clearly in the way in which we put forward our contributions to the academic community in submission to peer evaluation. When we have arrived at what we believe is a valuable contribution to the scholarly community, we submit our work to the rigorous analysis and thorough critique of others in the field. In doing so, we recognize our descriptions and explanations are tentative and stand ready to have our observations, methods, and conclusions variously rejected, returned for further work, significantly or moderately refined, or possibly even accepted.

It is wise (and necessary) to humbly submit ourselves to the process of peer evaluation because we recognize that our perspectives and approaches

6. Zeki et al., "Experience of Mathematical Beauty."
7. Ringenberg, *Christian College*, 15–17.

might very well be misguided or incorrect. Being subjected to criticism can be terrifying and humiliating, but having one's work pass peer review is gratifying and an encouragement that our contributions have value. We also humbly accept the results of peer evaluation, realizing that it is the community of scholars, and not we ourselves, which defines our field of study.

In this way, we recognize our role as academics to not only experience the joy of discovery or synthesis ourselves but to also share this with others. For scientific knowledge is something to be shared for the common good of humankind. Publishing our academic work is one way in which we love God (by sharing our discoveries about the world he has made) and love our neighbor (by providing opportunities for others to benefit from our work in various ways).

When called upon to be a peer evaluator, we must exercise wisdom as well. We abide by the ethical standards of our academic community by providing fair and honest reviews and not illegitimately taking the ideas for ourselves.[8] Academia is littered with stories of reviewers calling for the rejection of papers but then doing minor changes and dishonestly submitting someone else's work to another venue as if it were their own.[9] Wisdom calls for integrity and humility in scientific work and publishing.

Physics and God's Covenant Faithfulness

Most of us who daily report for work or school set our alarm clocks in order to ensure we wake up in time. It is interesting to reflect on elements of the worldview embedded in this habit. One is articulated by David in both Psalms 3 and 4, where we read, "I lie down and sleep; I wake again, because the LORD sustains me" (3:5) and "In peace I will lie down and sleep, for you alone, LORD, make me dwell in safety" (4:8). The Psalmist identifies the trust we exhibit in submitting ourselves into the care of our covenantally faithful God and Father ("LORD"). We cannot sustain ourselves but cast ourselves in utter dependence upon God to ensure our safety.

The second worldview element seen in setting alarm clocks is the explicit acknowledgement that we are expecting there to be a future, a new day, a time when the sun will rise again for us to go about our work or studies. This expectation we consider well founded on the basis of experience, or perhaps of science. We are confident that the earth will keep turning and the sun will keep shining. Science can indeed be used to predict events well into the future; for example, NASA has published a listing of long solar eclipses

8. Graf et al., "Publication Ethics."
9. Laine, "Scientific Misconduct Hurts."

for the next four thousand years (and the previous six thousand years).[10] But such predictions, including our expectation of tomorrow, cannot be seen as founded upon science. Instead, they depend on the continued regularity of the world. This regularity is taken for granted in science, and can be described and explained in terms of conservation laws and our mathematical analyses of realities such as stable orbits and operation of forces. But it is only the Christian worldview which has a solid foundation for this regularity.[11] Wisdom acknowledges that the world exhibits regularity only because its creator remains faithful to the covenant he has made with the world as he sustains it by his word.[12]

God's covenant with creation is expressed at various points in Scripture. In Genesis 8:22, accompanied by the post-flood rainbow, God promises, "As long as the earth endures, / seedtime and harvest, / cold and heat, / summer and winter, / day and night / will never cease." Connecting his covenant with Israel to his covenant with creation, "The word of the LORD came to Jeremiah: 'This is what the LORD says: "If you can break my covenant with the day and my covenant with the night, so that day and night no longer come at their appointed time, then my covenant with David my servant . . . can be broken and David will no longer have a descendant to reign on his throne . . . If I have not made my covenant with day and night and established the laws of heaven and earth, then I will reject the descendants of Jacob and David my servant" (Jer 33:19–21, 25–26).

God's sustaining of all things is likewise articulated in a few passages. Consider Hebrews 1:3: "The Son is the radiance of God's glory and the exact representation of his being, sustaining all things by his powerful word" and Paul's writing in Colossians 1:15–17: "The Son is the image of the invisible God, the firstborn over all creation. For in him all things were created: things in heaven and on earth, visible and invisible, whether thrones or powers or rulers or authorities; all things have been created through him and for him. He is before all things, and in him all things hold together."

Thus the Christian worldview acknowledges God as the source of the regularities within created reality, and it is wise to accept this as the foundation upon which science is able to function insofar as it uncovers, describes, and explains regularities.

Wisdom does not consider the universe to be a machine. While indeed the mechanical universe model was able to arise because of the advances in

10. NASA, "Ten Millennium Catalog."

11. Judaism and Islam would share with Christianity the Old-Testament aspect of this foundation, but (as noted below) Christianity deepens this with its Trinitarian perspective and Christ's sustaining word.

12. Morris and Petcher, *Science and Grace*, 99.

Newtonian physics, it is important to realize that behind the functioning of the cosmos is not a machine but a person. Poythress writes, "The Bible shows us a personalistic world, not impersonal law. What we call scientific law is an approximate human description of just how faithfully and consistently God acts in ruling the world by speaking. There is no mathematical, physical, or theoretical 'cosmic machinery' behind what we see and know, holding everything in place. Rather, God rules, and rules consistently."[13]

In fact, one can go further and acknowledge that the One over, under, behind, around, in creation is in fact Three: a tri-personal God. Psalm 33:6 proclaims, "By the word of the Lord the heavens were made, their starry host by the breath of his mouth." Herein, "Lord," "word," and "breath" have been widely suggested as pointing to the three persons of the Trinity, and Hebrews 1:3 given above speaks of "word" as "sustaining all things." Deism supposes a creator setting up the show at the outset and from that point forward no longer being involved, theism acknowledges a personal God interacting with the world, but Trinitarian Christianity celebrates the tri-personal involvement of God even in the physics of the world.[14]

Wisdom, while acknowledging a covenant-keeping tri-personal God as the source of regularity and predictability, does not pretend that all things are absolutely regular. Even in the physical features of the universe, by which I mean those explored within the discipline of physics, we have the subatomic realm with its quantum uncertainty principle and probabilities as well as nonlinear systems with their chaotic patterns of behavior (such as the atmosphere's "butterfly effect" in which tiny causes have vast results). Expecting only predictability and periodicity does not match with reality, and wisdom accepts that even in physics we will be presented with unexpected and challenging realities. Furthermore, when we move on into the biological and human realms, regularity becomes even less ubiquitous; this can be seen, for example, in the reality of true agency as well as in the difficulties encountered upon trying to develop quantitative theories in these fields. More is always at play.

Two Kinds of Laws

Physics is often seen as a discipline which describes and explains the natural world in terms of "laws." We have, for example, Kepler's laws of planetary motion, Newton's law of gravity and his three laws of motion and force, the zeroth to third laws of thermodynamics (including the law of conservation

---

13. Poythress, *Symphonic Theology*, 107.
14. Polkinghorne, *Science and the Trinity*.

of energy). Wisdom recognizes that such "laws of nature" are our human articulations of patterns of regularity and relationships we can explore, and are not at the same level as the means by which God as creator and sustainer governs the creation. That is, while our laws of physics are mathematical, descriptive, human-formulated, subject to revision, increasingly verisimilitudinous, and apparently generally applicable, God's word for the physical aspect of creation is covenantal, prescriptive, partially revealed, substantially unknowable, and reveals his faithfulness, omnipotence, omniscience, wisdom, love, and goodness.[15]

Order as Gift, Idol, and Task

Natural science, especially physics, works with order in creation. Morris and Petcher describe order as both a given and a task.[16] It is a gift of the Creator that there is (physical) order within the creation, and humanity has received the task of discerning and developing this order in what Wolters[17] suggests should be called the "creation mandate" of Genesis 1:28 (more often called the "cultural mandate"): "God blessed [mankind] and said to them, 'Be fruitful and increase in number; fill the earth and subdue it. Rule over the fish in the sea and the birds in the sky and over every living creature that moves on the ground.' " Wolters notes, "There is, as it were, a growing up (though not in a biological sense), an unfolding of creation. This takes place through the task that people have been given of bringing to fruition the possibilities of development implicit in the work of God's hands."[18] Thus order in creation is both gift and task: God made the world with order, and we are called to bring further order. Physics participates in this task through the recognition of certain kinds of order, structure, relationships, and interactions at the physical level.

Taking a cue from a presentation by Iwan & Amanda Russell-Jones subtitled "Reflections on Home as Gift, Idol, and Task,"[19] we would be wise to recognize that especially in physics it is possible to make an idol out of the good gift and task of cosmic order. We could grow to believe that all things depend not on God but upon the absolutely autonomous functioning of the world. One might suppose that the laws of physics are inviolable even

---

15. For more on this, see Sikkema, "Laws of Nature."
16. Morris and Petcher, *Science and Grace*, 216, 224, 241.
17. Wolters, *Creation Regained*, 42.
18. Wolters, *Creation Regained*, 44.
19. Russell-Jones, "Dwelling Place."

by God, as noted by Olson,[20] or that miracles cannot and did not happen, or that God cannot in a meaningful way interact personally with the world. One might suppose physics can, at least in principle, exhaustively explain everything at all levels of reality, being the ultimate and final cause for each event. We should eschew all such forms of idolatry and instead nurture wise approaches to accepting order as gift and task.

Within physics there is talk of a theory of everything. This is actually only a putative theory *of fundamental physics* by which we seek to explain all types of interactions between subatomic particles like electrons and quarks. Claims that physics can in principle explain literally everything are contrary to a basic Christian worldview perspective in which God is sovereign and personally engaged with the cosmos instead of leaving it alone to function solely according to principles of physics. These "theory of everything" ideas are also opposed by the reality of emergence both in physics[21] and beyond,[22] where the fact is that in many cases complete knowledge of the parts of a system still leaves one utterly incapable of predicting the behavior of the system. Wisdom shuns the idolatrous ideal of physics explaining all things and sees physics instead in its proper place among the various disciplines and ways of knowing.

Modern Physics and Christianity

Much of the popular view of physics is based on classical (Newtonian) physics, characterised by its continuity, certainty, predictability, determinism, objectivity, reductionism, naïve realism, and a dualism between particles and waves. With a worldview built on this pre-1900 perspective, it could be possible to consider the universe as an unflinchingly rigid clockwork mechanism. Modern theories of physics, largely unknown or considered mysterious (even mystical) to the general public, have brought a significant change to this picture. Especially the world of quantum physics did so, ushering in a world of uncertainty, probability, indeterminism, subjectivity, holism, critical realism, and wave-particle duality. Some of these advances are rightly seen as being more amenable to certain ideas within a Christian perspective such as human free will and responsibility, as well as personal divine activity, and so can be more fruitfully integrated within an overall world picture.[23]

20. Olson, *Essentials*, 250.
21. Laughlin, *A Different Universe*.
22. Morowitz, *Emergence of Everything*.
23. See, for example, Barr, *Modern Physics and Ancient Faith* and Polkinghorne, *Faith of a Physicist*.

Another discovery of the early twentieth century was the realization that galaxies are moving away from us in a way which can be naturally explained as beginning from a common point a finite time ago. Perhaps surprising to many Christians are two historical facts: first, that this idea was due in the first instance to a Catholic priest and physicist Georges Lemaître, and second, that big bang theory was opposed by atheist physicists (who preferred a universe which had always existed) for sounding too much like Genesis.[24]

Wisdom notes, however, that we should not overemphasize what we might consider to be the coherence, concordance, or consistency of current theories of physics with a Christian perspective. Theories in physics, as in all of science, are subject to change and often say less than we might think. For example, stating that because of big bang theory we now have scientific proof of or evidential support for the truth of the Bible's doctrine of creation, in particular that the world had a beginning, is too strong a claim. For big bang theory does not describe the *origin* of the universe, but only its *history* as far back as we can see, which is understood by current physics to be about 10^{-43} seconds, *not 0 seconds*, after the singularity. So we must avoid overstating the evidence of an absolute beginning. We also should be careful of dismissing ideas such as big bang and multiverse theories[25] simply because of concerns that they may be contradictory to what we or others might take to be the Biblical narrative.[26]

Conclusion

The natural sciences, especially physics, are the modern incarnations of what had been, until the nineteenth century, called "natural philosophy." Biophysicist Tom McLeish aptly describes science as "the love of wisdom to do with natural things."[27] Each scientific discipline does this in its own way. Over two decades of teaching, it has been my great joy to share the delight, challenge, insight, depth, aesthetic, and awe of physics. Inherent to physics is indeed a "love of wisdom to do with natural things."

Physics is the systematic study of how things interact. Being dependent upon experimentation and observation, it is an empirical discipline. What a blessing it is to study and work in a field which is so dependent upon our senses! The apostle John gives a rousing endorsement to the value

24. For more details, see Barr, *Modern Physics*.
25. Page, "Does God So Love the Multiverse?"
26. Haarsma and Haarsma, *Origins*.
27. McLeish, *Faith and Wisdom*, 248, 269.

of our senses in his affirmations of the reality of Jesus when he wrote, "That which was from the beginning, which we have *heard*, which we have *seen* with our *eyes*, which we have *looked at* and our *hands have touched*—this we proclaim concerning the Word of life. The life *appeared*; we have *seen* it and testify to it, and we proclaim to you the eternal life, which was with the Father and has *appeared* to us. We proclaim to you what we have *seen* and *heard*, so that you also may have fellowship with us" (1 John 1:1–3).

The apostle Paul notes, "For since the creation of the world God's invisible qualities—his eternal power and divine nature—have been clearly seen, being understood from what has been made" (Rom 1:8). It is wonderful when doing our work in physics to reflect upon the fact that our creator has made a universe which reflects not only his power and divinity, but also his faithfulness, patience, creativity, beauty, love, mercy, glory, goodness, and *wisdom*![28]

Bibliography

Barr, Stephen M. *Modern Physics and Ancient Faith*. Notre Dame: University of Notre Dame Press, 2003.

Dooyeweerd, Herman. *A New Critique of Theoretical Thought*. Translated by David H. Freeman and William S. Young. Philadelphia: Presbyterian and Reformed, 1969.

Graf, Chris, et al. "Best Practice Guidelines on Publication Ethics: a Publisher's Perspective." *International Journal of Clinical Practice* 61.152 (2007) 1–26.

Haarsma, Deborah B., and Loren D. Haarsma. *Origins: Christian Perspectives on Creation, Evolution, and Intelligent Design*. Rev. ed. Grand Rapids: Faith Alive, 2011.

Kuyper, Abraham. "Calvinism and Science." In *Lectures on Calvinism: The 1898 Stone Lectures*. Grand Rapids: Eerdmans, 1931.

Laine, Christine. "Scientific Misconduct Hurts." *Annals of Internal Medicine* 166 (2017) 148–49.

Laughlin, Robert B. *A Different Universe: Reinventing Physics from the Bottom Down*. New York: Basic Books, 2005.

McLeish, Tom. *Faith and Wisdom in Science*. Oxford: Oxford University Press, 2014.

Morowitz, Harold J. *The Emergence of Everything: How the World Became Complex*. Oxford: Oxford University Press, 2002.

Morris, Tim, and Don Petcher. *Science and Grace: God's Reign in the Natural Sciences*. Wheaton: Crossway, 2004.

Olson, Roger E. *The Essentials of Christian Thought: Seeing Reality through the Biblical Story*. Grand Rapids: Zondervan, 2017.

Page, Don N. "Does God So Love the Multiverse?" In *Science and Religion in Dialogue*, edited by M. Y. Stewart, 380–95. Oxford: Wiley-Blackwell, 2010.

Polkinghorne, John. *Science and the Trinity: The Christian Encounter with Reality*. New Haven: Yale University Press, 2004.

---

28. Wiseman, "Science as an Instrument of Worship."

Poythress, Vern. *Symphonic Theology: The Validity of Multiple Perspectives in Theology.* Grand Rapids: Zondervan, 1987.

Ringenberg, William C. *The Christian College and the Meaning of Academic Freedom: Truth-Seeking in Community.* New York: Palgrave Macmillan, 2016.

Russell-Jones, Iwan, and Amanda Russell-Jones. "Dwelling Place: Reflections on Home as Gift, Idol, and Task." Paper presented at Regent College, September 22–24, 2017.

Schilder, Klaas. *Christ and Culture.* Translated by G. van Rongen and William Helder. Winnipeg, Manitoba: Premier, 1977.

Sikkema, Arnold E. "Laws of Nature and God's Word for Creation." *Fideles* 2 (2007) 27–43.

———. "A Phoenix Universe? Discussions on Cosmogony." In *Proceedings of the 4th Canadian Conference on General Relativity and Relativistic Astrophysics*, edited by Gabor Kunstatter et al., 90–93. Singapore: World Scientific, 1992.

Wiseman, Jennifer. "Science as an Instrument of Worship." https://biologos.org/articles/science-as-an-instrument-of-worship.

Wolters, Albert M. *Creation Regained: Biblical Basics for a Reformational Worldview.* 2nd ed. Grand Rapids, Eerdmans, 2005.

Zeki, Semir, et al. "The Experience of Mathematical Beauty and Its Neural Correlates." *Frontiers in Human Neuroscience* 8.68 (February 2014). https://www.frontiersin.org/articles/10.3389/fnhum.2014.00068/full.

17

Seeking Wisdom in Engineering and Computer Science

Derek C. Schuurman

Although I now teach computer science, memories of my initial fascination with technology are with radio. Radio may be dismissed by some as an antiquated technology from a bygone era, but it captured my imagination as a young boy. I can still picture myself as a young teen hunched over what was, already then, an old-fashioned shortwave radio. It had a large wooden cabinet, which glowed from the inside from an array of vacuum tubes hidden behind a wide front panel. A tall needle would whiz back and forth in response to rotating a large tuning dial used to select the frequency. I was amazed to hear distant shortwave radio stations broadcasting from exotic locations around the world. How could such a thing be possible? How do radio signals encode sounds and travel around the globe? My technical curiosity led to years of tinkering with crystal radios, ham radios, and assorted electronics.[1]

The curiosity initially sparked by radio quickly migrated to early personal computers. The flashing green cursor that greeted me on those early computer screens seemed to beckon me to type. I was captivated by the notion that I could fashion computer code to create worlds formed in my own imagination. In the words of the respected computer scientist, Fred Brooks, "The programmer, like the poet, works only slightly removed from pure thought-stuff. He builds his castles in the air, from air, creating by exertion

---

1. The recollections in this opening paragraph are part of a longer article on the topic: Schuurman, "Ham Radio," 15.

of the imagination."[2] This delight in creating new technology is not unique to programmers. The civil engineer, Samuel Florman, writes that "at the heart of engineering lies existential joy," which he describes as "the deep-down satisfactions that stem from engaging in the technological work that human beings instinctively want to do."[3]

After high school, my delight in tinkering with technology led to studying electrical engineering at a large public university. It was here that I developed and deepened my knowledge of computers and electronics. When I completed my studies, I went to work in industry as an engineer. My delight in technology continued to fuel enthusiasm for my work, but gradually I began to wonder about my career. As time passed, I found myself sitting in a cubicle farm increasingly wondering what my faith had to do with my technical work. What do bytes have to do with beliefs? On occasion I would contemplate full-time ministry, a job that might feel more like "kingdom work" than engineering. I even took part-time courses in theology while I continued working as an engineer.

It became clear to me that my exquisite technical education failed to equip me with a framework for seeing my job in a Christian context. In the years that followed, I gradually began to connect the dots between my faith and my vocation in technology (an ongoing process that continues to this day). I gradually began to see how technology can, in principle, be directed in God-honoring ways and contribute to human flourishing. I have found that the best place to start for the Christian in computer science or engineering is to situate their discipline within the wider biblical story. The biblical narrative presents a distinct worldview providing us with "spectacles" which help us to see more clearly.[4] Just as a gear-box mediates between an engine and the tires, a biblical worldview "mediates between the power of the gospel and human life where that gospel must be brought to bear."[5] This worldview is shaped by the biblical themes of creation, fall, redemption, and restoration.

Technology as Part of Creation

The fact that we are excited by the creative possibilities in technology should come as no surprise. The creation story tells us that God created us in his

---

2. Brooks, *Mythical Man-Month*, 7.
3. Florman, *Existential Pleasures of Engineering*, 101, 184.
4. Calvin, *Genesis*, 1:62.
5. Wolters, *Creation Regained*, 142.

own image (Gen 1:27), and part of how we reflect that is in our creative culture-making activities. This idea was further articulated by Fred Brooks:

> Why is programming fun? What delights may its practitioner expect as his reward? First is the sheer joy of making things. As the child delights in his mud pie, so the adult enjoys building things, especially things of his own design. I think this delight must be an image of God's delight in making things, a delight shown in the distinctness and newness of each leaf and each snowflake.[6]

In the creation story, we read about the cultural mandate in which God calls humans to care for and unfold the possibilities in creation (Gen 1:28). Creation is full of latent potential, in art, music, culture and also technology. Already in Genesis 2:12 we read "The gold of that land is good; aromatic resin and onyx are also there." God provides a land full of raw materials and with a host of culture-making possibilities. Early in Genesis we read of people uncovering these possibilities: Jubal, the "father of all who play stringed instruments and pipes" and Tubal-Cain who "forged all kinds of tools out of bronze and iron" (Gen 4:21–22). In the field of computing, Charles Babbage is often recognized as the "father of computers" and Ada Lovelace is credited with being the first programmer. It is important to recognize that creation does not just consist of seas, stars, birds and trees–it includes all the things that God has ordained to exist, and that includes both the materials and the possibilities for technology.

As a young hobbyist, I gradually learned of the technical possibilities in creation. It began by following directions in books and magazines to build simple electronic circuits. Later, I continued by writing simple computer programs as I explored the world of computing.[7] Eventually I went on to study engineering and my technical toolbox continued to grow. I learned the deep mathematical principles that describe the operation of computers and electronic circuits. I learned various laws which describe how electrical circuits behave and some of the principles of computing. The regularity and order of creation is not a coincidence, but brings to mind the providential hand of Christ in whom all things continue to "hold together" (Col 1:17). It became clear to me that the creation was both wonderfully complex and intricately ordered.

The mathematical basis of my engineering education served to underscore the notion that the physical creation has a "numerical" aspect. Numbers capture one part of created reality which can be counted, measured,

---

6. Brooks, *Mythical Man-Month*, 7.
7. My first computer was a Sinclair ZX81.

and simulated. Even this book has numeric aspects: page numbers, word counts, size and dimensions, an ISBN number, and a price. Computers are well suited for capturing and analyzing the numeric aspects in creation, which can be found virtually everywhere. In fact, even the cells in our body possess DNA which stores biological information.

The ability of computers to perform vast amounts of computations has opened new vistas. While the seeds of fractal geometry were planted centuries ago, it was not until the advent of the computer that people like Benoit Mandelbrot were able to explore deeply the beauty and wonder of fractals.[8] More recently, data science and "big data" harness computers to peer further into a fascinating world of patterns. Many scientists rely on data to gain further insights into creation. The Large Hadron Collider, the world's largest particle accelerator, will eventually generate about 15 petabytes of data per year.[9] Bankers, factories, social networking websites, health care providers, and retailers all generate a deluge of data each day. Within this data are patterns and information that can be sifted to gain insights into virtually all aspects of creation. Even researchers in the humanities have embraced data mining and analysis techniques as part of a new field called the "digital humanities." We live in an "information age," a time of "big data" that has provided new insights into societal and human patterns that were heretofore never imagined.

Technology also helps us to observe creation in ways we could not do otherwise. The Mars Rover taking images on the surface of Mars, the Hubble telescope peering into distant galaxies, electron microscopes observing molecular structures, and remote sensing satellites are all examples of technological instruments, which have increased our awe and wonder. Even in our technical work, the elegance of a computer algorithm[10] or a clever digital circuit can be a source of aesthetic delight. Indeed, modern technology can help us join with the Psalmist who declared, "Great are the works of the Lord; they are pondered by all who delight in them" (Ps 111:2).

The Fall: Technology Pitfalls and Distortions

Technology, like many good things, can also be misdirected and used to fashion golden calves. I studied electrical engineering at a time of immense growth in electronics and personal computing. I must confess, being

---

8. Mandelbrot, *Fractal Geometry of Nature*.

9. A petabyte is equivalent to a million gigabytes. See McFedries, "Coming Data Deluge," 19.

10. An "algorithm" is a step-by-step method to solve a problem.

immersed in that world, I became susceptible to the notion that many problems had potential technical solutions. Tucked beneath the seemingly neutral content in my engineering education was the implicit notion that the world was like a machine that could be controlled and optimized. As a young teen standing at the threshold of the personal computer revolution, it was hard not to be swept away by the possibilities that were now opening.

Decades ago, the philosopher of technology, Jacques Ellul, warned about *technique*, which he defined as "the totality of methods, rationally arrived at and having absolute efficiency (for a given stage of development) in every field of human activity."[11] The book *Algorithms to Live By* describes how efficient algorithms can assist in making decisions as mundane as finding a parking spot and as passionate as finding a spouse. The authors, Christian and Griffiths, suggest that while "computer science can't offer you a life with no regret," it can help optimize decisions to offer "a life with minimal regret."[12] A more light-hearted book, *Geek Logik*, offers "foolproof equations for everyday life" covering topics from dating and romance to finance and health.[13] Such thinking elevates the mathematical aspect of reality and does not adequately recognize the complexity and diversity in creation. These books illustrate a type of *reductionism*, one that suggests everything can be boiled down to an equation or an algorithm. However, in the words of the computer scientist and virtual reality pioneer Jaron Lanier, "information underrepresents reality."[14]

The disciplines of computer science and engineering do offer wisdom, which provides one type of knowing about the world, one that can be incredibly powerful. But this wisdom becomes folly when it is used to explain and control all of reality. Eventually this can lead to a "tower-of-Babel" culture where people replace their need for God with a reliance on the possibilities of modern technology. This results in *technicism,* a trust in technology as savior of the human condition.[15] This is essentially idolatry: exchanging the creator for something in creation. But idols do not deliver on their promises. Marshall McLuhan, the famous media theorist, suggested that as we push technologies to an extreme they often reverse and yield the *opposite* of what they promise. For example, social media promises to enhance our social

11. Ellul, *Technological Society*, xxv.
12. Christian and Griffiths, *Algorithms to Live By.*
13. Sundem, *Geek Logik.*
14. Lanier, *You Are Not a Gadget*, 69.
15. Schuurman, *Faith and Hope in Technology,* 69.

connections, but if it is pushed to an extreme we are left "alone together," isolated in front of a glowing rectangle.[16]

Some even look to technology to solve the problem of death. Ray Kurzweil, an accomplished inventor and engineer, has suggested that eventually we will be able to scan the state of the human brain and upload it into a computer to escape our mortality.[17] This idea (which has been referred to as the "rapture of the geeks"[18]) relies on a materialist view of what it means to be human that reduces humans to the laws of physics and chemistry.[19] In his book, *Playing God*, Andy Crouch observes that "Every idol makes two simple and extravagant promises. 'You shall not surely die.' 'You shall be like God.'"[20] Psalm 115:8 states that all who make and trust in idols will become like them, and in the case of the rapture of the geeks, the end goal is to literally become like a computer.[21]

Technology has the pitfall of leading to pride, much like the builders of the tower of Babel who sought to "make a name for themselves" (Gen 11:4). God speaks to his people about how he will bring them to "a land where the rocks are iron and you can dig copper out of the hills" (Deut 8:9), a source for raw materials for tools and other technology. But this verse is closely followed with a caution not to become proud but to remember that these things come from the LORD (Deut 8:11, 14, 18). The story of King Uzziah describes his technical accomplishments in building towers and cisterns and inventing clever devices to defend walls and towers (2 Chr 26:10, 15). But we read that "after Uzziah became powerful, his pride led to his downfall" (2 Chr 26:16). Wisdom ought to lead to epistemological humility, understanding our limits and finiteness, also in our technological pursuits. "The fear of the LORD is the beginning of wisdom" (Prov 9:10a).

Redemption and Responsible Technology

Despite the possibility for sinful distortions, technology can, in principle, be directed in God-honoring ways. The question about whether technology is good or bad is a false dichotomy. Rather, the relevant question is: to what end is our technology directed? Technology is not neutral since it can nudge

---

16. The phrase "alone together" is taken from the title of the book by Sherry Turkle, *Alone Together*.
17. Kurweil, *Singularity is Near*, 324.
18. Zorpette, "Waiting For the Rapture," 32–35.
19. Dickerson, *Mind and the Machine*, xxvi–xxvii.
20. Crouch, *Playing God*, 64.
21. For a further discussion of this topic, see Schuurman, "Rapture of the Geeks."

users in either more obedient or less obedient directions. If this is the case, we need to design technology wisely so that it brings honor to God. But how can technology be directed towards kingdom goals?

One obvious way to be a Christian in technology is to look for opportunities to share the gospel. I have found that as I have rubbed elbows and interacted with others in my technical work that our conversations often eventually drift to bigger philosophical questions. In particular, technologies such as artificial intelligence and robotics open up fundamental questions about consciousness and what it means to be human. Already at the dawn of computer science, pioneers such as Alan Turing asked questions about whether computers could "think."[22] Books such as *Gödel, Escher, Bach*, written by the cognitive science and computer science professor Douglas Hofstadter, explore the beauty and wonder of recursion and self-reference, concepts frequently used in computer science.[23] Donald Knuth, a highly respected computer scientist, gave a series of lectures at MIT that were later published in a book entitled *Things a Computer Scientist Rarely Talks About* in which he explores topics such as aesthetics, infinity, computational complexity, and free will.[24] There are many deep philosophical questions that emerge in computer science. Can a computer be creative? What is information? Such questions quickly uncover our presuppositions and are at their root religious questions, which provide a springboard for meaningful dialogue with others.

Another obvious way to direct technology to kingdom goals is to use electronic media and social networking to share the gospel. Indeed, digital technology has provided numerous opportunities to assist in Bible translation and transmitting the gospel. But being faithful in the field of technology goes beyond using it as a tool for evangelism. To begin, we need to capture the big picture of the gospel, one which includes personal salvation but extends to God's redemption plan for the entire cosmos.[25] In the words of Abraham Kuyper, "There is not a square inch in the whole domain of our human existence over which Christ, who is sovereign over all, does not cry: 'Mine!'"[26] In Colossians 1 we read about how God is reconciling "all things" to himself. What's more, he calls us to be agents of reconciliation (2 Cor 5:18–19) and to participate in his kingdom work. God's call and work of redemption extend to all areas of life, including technology.

22. Turing, "Computing Machinery and Intelligence," 433–60.
23. Hofstadter, *Gödel, Escher, Bach*.
24. Knuth, *Things a Computer Scientist Rarely Talks About*.
25. Wolters, *Creation Regained*, 72.
26. Mouw, *Abraham Kuyper*, 4.

The book *Responsible Technology* defines technology as "a distinct cultural activity in which human beings exercise freedom and responsibility in response to God by forming and transforming the natural creation, with the aid of tools and procedures, for practical ends or purposes."[27] This definition reminds us that technology is not just about devices and gadgets, it's a human cultural activity and "culture is what we make of the world."[28] Furthermore, technology is not an autonomous force beyond our control, it is an area where we must exercise both freedom and responsibility. These concepts are important to remember since technology is not neutral, it has profound implications for "what we make of the world."

A book by Cathy O'Neil entitled, *Weapons of Math Destruction*, describes how computer programs are not neutral. She describes the consequences of allowing algorithms and mathematical models to perform tasks such as college rankings, teacher evaluations, employment screening, policing, and credit checks. She writes that "Models, despite their reputation for impartiality, reflect goals and ideology," and "Models are opinions embedded in mathematics."[29] The truth is that technology always has a bias and it is value-laden. In the words of Neil Postman, "Embedded in every tool is an ideological bias, a predisposition to construct the world as one thing rather than another, to value one thing over another, to amplify one sense or skill or attitude more loudly than another."[30] Technologies like the automobile, smartphone, and the internet are not neutral, but have had profound impacts on our world. The computer scientist and engineer who seeks wisdom will begin by recognizing that technology is value-laden. "We shape our tools, and thereafter our tools shape us."[31]

Engineering and computer science are sources of wisdom, but the wisdom available from these disciplines alone is incomplete. Technology and computing professionals ought to partner with other disciplines in the design of products and services. Technology, like other human cultural activities, is not neutral but has significant social, economic, environmental, aesthetic, political, and justice aspects.[32] This has implications for how engineering and computer science ought to be taught. Samuel Florman has observed that in many engineering schools "the least bit of imagination, social concern or cultural interest is snuffed out under a crushing load of

27. Monsma, *Responsible Technology*, 19.
28. Crouch, *Culture Making*, 23.
29. O'Neil, *Weapons of Math Destruction*, 21.
30. Postman, *Technopoly*, 13.
31. Culkin, "Schoolman's Guide to Marshall McLuhan," 70.
32. Schuurman, "Technology Has a Message," 4–7.

purely technical subjects."[33] In fact, a liberal arts education is invaluable for engineers and computer scientists to help develop an awareness of the wider context for their work and to prevent tunnel vision. In order to best serve the end user, an engineer or computer scientist should seek input and help from users and experts in the application area. A digital device may have a technical construction, but it also has an intended cultural context. Consequently, a medical application should be constructed in consultation with health experts, just as educational applications should be designed with input from educators.

In my early work as an engineer, I did not think much about the wider context of the products I was helping to design. In fact, the electronic projects of my youth were sometimes directed towards playing pranks. But over time I gradually began to think more about what responsible technology ought to look like. My doctoral work was in the field of computer vision where I observed the normative directions this research could take. Computer vision can be misused to invade privacy, but it can also be applied to automate dull, dirty and dangerous tasks. Over time I was drawn to applying computer vision to the problem of automating the sorting of recyclable goods.[34] This work grew out of a desire to find normative applications for technology, in this case motivated by improved sustainability and better environmental stewardship. Another project explored introducing a small computer platform along with open source software to serve Christian schools in the majority world.[35] While these projects have been modest in their contributions, they are an attempt to use technology in ways that show love to our neighbor and to care for the earth. Fred Brooks writes that there is the "pleasure of making things that are useful to other people. Deep within, we want others to use our work and find it helpful."[36] Besides being attentive to technical considerations, Christian engineers need to discern opportunities to shape technology in normative ways.

Churches also need to engage the topic of technology. The third Lausanne Congress on World Evangelization that took place in 2010 in Cape Town recognized the importance of "taking the whole gospel to the whole world," including the area of technology. *The Cape Town Commitment* that came out of the Lausanne congress includes a call for authentically Christian responses to technology to ensure it is "used not to manipulate, distort and destroy, but to preserve and better fulfill our humanness." It includes

---

33. Florman, *Existential Pleasures of Engineering*, 92.
34. House et al., "Towards Real-Time Sorting."
35. Schuurman, "Introducing Open Source," 50–53.
36. Brooks, *Mythical Man-Month*, 7.

a call to church leaders to encourage and support church members who are "professionally engaged" in technology and for seminaries to engage this field. It also calls Christians in "government, business, academia and technical fields to form national or regional 'think tanks' or partnerships to engage with new technologies . . . with a voice that is biblical and relevant."[37] Wisdom is often best sought within the wider Christian community.[38]

We must seek guidance from God, also in our technical work. Author and Christian scholar Albert Wolters writes that as we seek guidance we must also recognize the "indispensability of Scripture as well as the exercise of 'sanctified common sense.'"[39] In Romans 12:2 we are reminded, "Do not be conformed to this world but be transformed by the renewal of your mind, that you may prove what is the will of God, what is good and acceptable and perfect." In *Every Good Endeavor*, Tim Keller suggests that the Spirit can help us become wise by making "Jesus Christ a living, bright reality, transforming our character," which "leads to increasing wisdom as the years go by, and to better and better professional and personal decisions."[40]

What we design is not just something we do, but comes out of who we are. In the words of Fred Brooks, "If we would have our creations be true, beautiful, and good, we have to attend to our hearts."[41] The Christian philosopher Jamie Smith writes, "Being a disciple of Jesus is not primarily a matter of getting the right ideas and doctrines into your head . . . rather, it's a matter of being the kind of person who loves rightly."[42] Developing responsible technology requires more than knowledge and know-how, it requires a heart that is aligned with what God desires.

Technology and Eschatology

Many see technology as the eventual solution to all of life's problems. Some have even suggested that through technical progress "the future will be without ignorance, disease, hunger, poverty, and war."[43] This utopian narrative suggests that eventually we will be able to solve all of life's problems.

---

37. Cameron, *Cape Town Commitment*, 38.

38. Examples of communities exploring faith and technology include the Association of Christians in the Mathematical Sciences (https://acmsonline.org) and the Christian Engineering Society (http://www.christianengineering.org).

39. Wolters, *Creation Regained*, 36.

40. Keller, *Every Good Endeavor*, 218.

41. Brooks, "Computer Scientist as Toolsmith," 68.

42. Smith, *Desiring the Kingdom*, 32–33.

43. Reese, *Infinite Progress*, 1.

This view of technology exemplifies technicism and is based on a trust in the promises of technology. By contrast, others view technology with despair, predicting that technology will one day destroy us, as portrayed in science fiction movies like *The Matrix*, *Terminator*, and *Blade Runner*. Variations of the Frankenstein narrative, stories like these depict the horrors of misdirected technology.

By contrast, a Christian view of the future ought to be shaped by the biblical narrative. The healing of the nations will come with Christ's return. Technology will not usher in the new heavens and the new earth. That accomplishment will belong to God—heaven's exclusive "architect and builder" (Heb 11:10). What's more, the new heavens and earth will not be a "disembodied existence in an ethereal realm," but rather "inhabiting a Heavenly City."[44] Tim Keller writes, "The Bible teaches that the future is not an immaterial 'paradise' but a new heaven and a new earth." Keller continues, "In Revelation 21, we do not see human beings being taken out of this world into heaven, but rather heaven coming down and cleansing, renewing, and perfecting this material world."[45] Wolters suggests that "There is no reason to doubt that computer technology and jazz music will survive, largely intact, in the future restored earth."[46] This view ought to encourage us in our cultural work, including technology. Until Christ returns we are called to go out and "make some imperfect models of the good world to come."[47]

Conclusion

The Bible tells us that God has chosen the "time and place" in which we live (Acts 17:26). The memories of my own journey in technology begin with spinning a tuning needle in an antiquated vacuum tube radio around the dawn of the personal computer era. This journey continued with a growing hobby in electronics and computing that propelled me into engineering school and eventually to a career as an engineer. But my passion and technical training did not equip me with the wisdom to faithfully navigate my discipline. Indeed, in the words of Wolters, "Academic brilliance is something quite different from wisdom and common sense."[48] Over the years I felt a call to teaching, which eventually led to a position in computer science at a Christian College. It was here where I grew as a Christian scholar. Through

44. Mouw, *When the Kings Come Marching In*, 19.
45. Keller, *Reason for God*, 32.
46. Wolters, "Living the Future Now," 17.
47. Smedes, *My God and I*, 59.
48. Wolters, *Creation Regained*, 10.

interactions with wise colleagues and reading helpful books, I began to find answers to the questions about faith and technology that first began to percolate while working as an engineer in my office cubicle.

While knowledge is required in computer science and engineering, wisdom is also required to work faithfully and responsibly in these areas. As a teacher, I try to equip my students with a technical toolbox distinguished by competence and professionalism. At the same time, I strive to help them form a more sturdy and comprehensive toolbox that includes a robust Christian vision for the ultimate purpose of their work. Besides our technical skills, engineers and computer scientists need to cultivate hearts of wisdom as we seek to serve Jesus Christ in the fascinating field of technology.

Bibliography

Brooks, Frederick P. *The Mythical Man-Month: Essays on Software Engineering.* Boston: Addison-Wesley, 1995.
———. "The Computer Scientist as Toolsmith II." *Communications of the ACM* 39.3 (March 1996) 61–68.
Calvin, John. *Commentaries on the First Book of Moses, called Genesis, Vol. 1.* Translated by John King. Grand Rapids: Eerdman, 1948.
Cameron, Julia, ed. *The Cape Town Commitment: A Confession of Faith and a Call to Action.* Peabody: Hendrickson, 2011.
Christian, Brian, and Tom Griffiths. *Algorithms to Live By: The Computer Science of Human Decisions.* London: Allen Lane, 2016.
Crouch, Andy. *Culture Making: Rediscovering Our Creative Calling.* Downers Grove: InterVarsity, 2008.
———. *Playing God: Redeeming the Gift of Power.* Downers Grove: InterVarsity, 2013.
Culkin, John M. "A Schoolman's Guide to Marshall McLuhan." *Saturday Review*, March 18, 1967.
Dickerson, Matthew. *The Mind and the Machine.* Eugene, OR: Cascade, 2016.
Ellul, Jacque. *The Technological Society.* New York: Vintage, 1964.
Florman, Samuel C. *The Existential Pleasures of Engineering.* 2nd ed. New York: St. Martin's Griffin, 1994.
Hofstadter, Douglas. *Gödel, Escher, Bach: An Eternal Golden Braid.* New York: Basic Books, 1999.
House, Bryan W., et al. "Towards Real-Time Sorting of Recyclable Goods Using Support Vector Machines." *Proceedings of the IEEE International Symposium on Sustainable Systems and Technology*, Chicago, IL, May 2011.
Keller, Timothy. *Every Good Endeavor.* New York: Riverhead, 2012.
———. *The Reason for God: Belief in an Age of Skepticism.* New York: Riverhead, 2008.
Knuth, Donald E. *Things a Computer Scientist Rarely Talks About.* Stanford: CSLI Publications, 2001.
Kurzweil, Ray. *The Singularity is Near.* London: Penguin, 2005.
Lanier, Jaron. *You Are Not a Gadget.* New York: Vintage, 2011.
Mandelbrot, Benoit. *The Fractal Geometry of Nature.* London: Freeman, 1983.
McFedries, Paul. "The Coming Data Deluge." *IEEE Spectrum* 48.2 (February 2011) 19.

Monsma, Stephen V., ed. *Responsible Technology: A Christian Perspective*. Grand Rapids: Eerdmans, 1986.

Mouw, Richard J. *Abraham Kuyper: A Short and Personal Introduction*. Grand Rapids: Eerdmans, 2011.

———. *When the Kings Come Marching In*. Grand Rapids: Eerdmans, 2002.

O'Neil, Cathy. *Weapons of Math Destruction: How Big Data Increases Inequality and Threatens Democracy*. New York: Crown, 2016.

Postman, Neil. *Technopoly: The Surrender of Culture to Technology*. New York: Vintage, 1993.

Reese, Byron. *Infinite Progress: How the Internet and Technology Will End Ignorance, Disease, Poverty, Hunger, and War*. Austin: Greenleaf, 2013.

Schuurman, Derek C. "Ham Radio—From a Hobby to a Vocation." *Christian Courier*, June 9, 2014. http://www.christiancourier.ca/columns-op-ed/entry/ham-radio-from-a-hobby-to-a-vocation.

———. "Introducing Open Source and the Raspberry Pi to Schools in Developing Nations." *Perspectives on Science and Christian Faith* 67.1 (March 2015) 50–53.

———. "The Rapture of the Geeks." *In All Things*, November 5, 2015. http://inallthings.org/the-rapture-of-the-geeks/.

———. "Technology Has a Message." *Christian Educators Journal* 51.3 (February 2012) 4–7.

Schuurman, Egbert. *Faith and Hope in Technology*. Translated by John Vriend. Toronto: Clements, 2003.

Smedes, Lewis B. *My God and I: A Spiritual Memoir*. Grand Rapids: Eerdmans, 2003.

Smith, James K. A. *Desiring the Kingdom: Worship, Worldview and Cultural Formation*. Grand Rapids: Baker Academic, 2009.

Sundem, Garth. *Geek Logik: 50 Foolproof Equations for Everyday Life*. New York: Workman, 2006.

Turing, Alan. "Computing Machinery and Intelligence." *Mind* 59 (October, 1950) 433–60.

Turkle, Sherry. *Alone Together: Why We Expect More from Technology and Less from Each Other*. New York: Basic Books, 2011.

Wolters, Albert M. *Creation Regained: Biblical Basics for a Reformational Worldview*. 2nd ed. Grand Rapids, Eerdmans, 2005.

———. "Living the Future Now (2)." *Christian Educators Journal* 39.2 (December 1999) 17.

Zorpette, Glenn. "Waiting for the Rapture." *IEEE Spectrum* 45.6 (June 2008) 32–35.

18

Geology

Wise Stewardship of the Earth

MICHAEL GUEBERT

All the earth is mine.

EXOD 19:5

*How many are your works, L*ORD*!*
In wisdom you made them all;
the earth is full of your creatures.

PS 104:24

THREE DECADES AGO, AS an undergraduate geology major and recent convert to Christianity, I realized that if God created the Earth, then he must care for it; and if God cares for it, then, as a Christian, I should care for it too. I then began reconciling science with Scriptures that informed my vocation as an earth scientist. Today I still ponder how best to study God's word and God's world to succeed most effectively in environmental science.

Stewardship of nature that aligns with the findings of science and the counsel of Scripture is one dimension of God-ordained wisdom. That conclusion builds on a basic understanding of the following questions: What is Earth science? What is inherently good about the Earth? What is God's call to Earth stewardship? How well are we stewarding God's air, land, water, and life? How does stewardship of the Earth advance the holistic gospel?

What Is Earth Science?

As geologists, many people assume we love rocks and fossils. We do, but we study so much more, investigating how earth properties and processes interrelate with all other inorganic and organic systems. Earth science studies the form, function, and flow of energy and matter through the air, land, water, and lifeforms on Earth.

Earth science is essential for global development. We study the location, extraction, and restoration of land for metals, minerals, and energy necessary for human development. Earth science informs environmental engineering and public safety in urban settings by locating and protecting air and water resources from environmental threats.[1] We investigate natural processes like floods, landslides, earthquakes, and volcanic eruptions and study how to reduce these hazards by planning, prediction, preparation, and mitigation.[2]

To manage earth resources wisely and to protect humans from natural disasters is one way Christians can more effectively minister God's eternal love and truth to a world in need. As believers in Christ, our study of the Earth alongside Scripture reveals the goodness and witness of God's creation, increases our thanksgiving for his provisions, and defines our responsibility.[3]

God's Call to Steward the Earth

God created humankind in his likeness to represent him and to govern the Earth intelligently (Gen 1:26–27). The command was specific when God told Adam to *tend* and *keep* the garden on his behalf (Gen 2:15). His call to stewardship presupposed the necessity of fertile land for the flourishing of all plants and animals (including humans). As stewards of the land today, it's our responsibility to manage God's earth the very best we can. We honor this call by endeavoring to sustain the health and vitality of all creation.

---

1. See Wessel and Greenberg, *Geoscience for the Public Good*.

2. See Moshier, "What Is God's Purpose," 141–47 for a brief survey of the role of natural disasters in nature, humanity, and theology.

3. Stearley, "Why Should Christians Be Interested," 155–56, and Van Dragt and Clark, "Environmental Stewardship," 158–73.

The Effects of the Fall on Creation

The Bible foresees the Earth's corruption as a consequence of sin:

> The Earth dries up and withers, the world languishes and withers, the heavens languish with the earth. The Earth is defiled by its people; they have disobeyed the laws, violated the statutes and broken the everlasting covenant. Therefore a curse consumes the earth. (Isa 24:4–6)

> How long will the land lie parched and the grass in every field be withered? Because those who live in it are wicked, the animals and birds have perished. It will be made a wasteland, parched and desolate before me; the whole land will be laid waste because there is no one who cares. (Jer 12:4, 11)

> There is no faithfulness, no love, no acknowledgment of God in the land. . . . Because of this the land mourns, and all who live in it waste away; the beasts of the field and the birds of the air and the fish of the sea are dying. (Hos 4:1–3)

These passages reflect the close association of the natural world to the attitudes and actions of humanity; what God intended to flourish through our wise stewardship has become degraded through our folly. Richard Bauckham explains further: "Creation's mourning is for what we might call ecological death, the kind of devastation of land, through severe drought or desertification that leaves its vegetation withering and its animal life failing. . . . What the land mourns is the effect human wrongdoing has had on all its non-human inhabitants, both flora and fauna."[4]

Artificial modifications of air, land, water, and life occur globally in the following forms: intensification of weather and climate, deterioration of land, diminishment of water supplies, degradation of biodiversity, and land pollution. Our necessary response requires careful science, measured godly wisdom, and competent visionary action. As we evaluate these misfortunes, we can be encouraged by faithful Christians who are integrating science and faith in practical Christian ministry for the welfare of future generations as well as our own.

Intensification of Weather and Climate

This problem forces us to address the controversial "greenhouse effect," in which atmospheric greenhouse gases absorb long-wavelength energy and

---

4. Bauckham, *Bible and Ecology*, 92.

convert it to heat energy, warming the atmosphere. One major greenhouse gas is carbon dioxide. Based on historic and geologic records, including a 650,000 year record of atmospheric carbon dioxide trapped in air bubbles in ice cores from Greenland and Antarctica, we see that atmospheric carbon dioxide has increased significantly since the dawn of the industrial revolution in the mid-18th century. By strong consensus, earth scientists now say it is "extremely likely" (greater than 95 percent probability) that human impact, primarily from burning fossil fuels such as coal and oil, is the predominant cause of 20 °F (10 °C) warming since 1900, making this the warmest century in the history of modern civilization.

A primary impact of rising atmospheric greenhouse gases and associated global temperature increases is a rise in sea levels of 7–8 inches since 1900. This is due partly to melting glaciers and polar sea ice but predominantly from expansion of warmer ocean water. If global temperatures increase as expected, the sea level will rise 1–4 feet by 2100. Already, increases in daily tidal flooding are occurring in over twenty-five US coastal cities, putting their low-lying coastal communities at risk.

Destruction of the Land

Through agricultural intensification, we prioritize short-term production without weighing the long-term harmful consequences of excessive tilling, fertilizing, grazing, and irrigating. These practices, along with the relentless expansion of farmland, can lead to the environmental ills of soil erosion, water contamination, and biodiversity loss. These practices can also release greenhouse gases, making our food system a key contributor to climate change.

Wiser practice based on scientific understanding of the land can yield optimal production while also reaping environmental benefits. Watershed-scale management of soil and water is one example of this kind of best practice. Further agricultural conservation practices such as tillage reduction, stream buffers, cover crops, pest management, fertilizer optimization, and irrigation efficiency can also do much to sustain soil health and productivity.[5]

The recent emphases on soil health and sustainable agriculture are helping us better understand and manage the natural soil and agriculture systems. However, sustainable agriculture is about more than the environment; it is also about economics and social equity. With this in mind, scientists are advancing our management of agricultural landscapes for

---

5. Schnepf and Cox, *Environmental Benefits of Conservation*.

environmental quality by integrating social sciences and effective economic tools.[6]

These three broader concepts of sustainable agriculture—environment, economics, and societal wellbeing—are consistent with major features of biblical wisdom: our care for the Earth (environment), our stewardship of provisions from the land (economics), and the great commandment to love others (society), while adding the Christian themes of redemption and restoration.[7] Our objective in partnering good science with orthodox biblical theology is to conceive of ways to live with the land that are restorative, reconciling, and faithful to God's call to optimal stewardship.[8]

Along these lines, more Christians today are applying biblical principles to farming practices for the purpose of bringing glory to God by providing for the hungry without harming the environment in the process.[9] Several Christian development organizations are carefully integrating scientific and biblical principles of sustainable agriculture into effective international ministry.[10] Specifically, *Plant with Purpose* combines methods of environmental restoration with economic empowerment and social development of the poor to create hope for people in need. Colleges and universities are developing campus gardens for student training in interdisciplinary sustainable food systems and local community engagement.[11] Seminaries are incorporating agricultural education into their curricula with the conviction that environmental science is essential to the act of truly loving our world's communities.[12] And in the United States, more churches and ministries are engaging in sustainable agriculture at the grassroots level. Local *Community Supported Agriculture* (CSA) initiatives and urban farming ministries have tremendous potential for serving Christ in word and deed.

Diminishment of the Global Water Supply

Unfortunately, the human demand for water is rising as the global supply is diminishing, thereby putting at risk both present and future generations.

---

6. Schnepf and Cox, *Managing Agricultural Landscapes*.
7. Hall, "Toward a Theology," 103–7.
8. See Harker and Johnson, *Rooted and Grounded*.
9. See Sorley, *Farming that Brings Glory to God*.
10. Examples include: ECHO, Care of Creation-Kenya, Plant with Purpose, World Vision, Food for the Hungry, Mennonite Central Committee, World Renew, and World Relief.
11. See Sayere and Clark, *Fields of Learning*.
12. See Vanderslice, "Farminaries."

Water consumption for power, industry, agriculture, and domestic use has outpaced human population growth since 1950.[13] The amount of irrigated land is currently five times that of a century ago, dramatically increasing crop yields while water supplies plummet. Such unsustainable rates place additional strain on irrigation and food production.[14]

Beyond decreasing water quantity, we are diminishing water *quality* by sediment from excessive erosion, biological pathogens from animal and human wastes, and toxic chemicals from agriculture, landfills, and industry. Declines in water quality, especially in surface waters, have negative environmental impacts on habitats, biodiversity, and extinctions. Since 1970, the United States has advanced better science and instituted new policies to improve the state of our natural waters. However, for much of the world, especially developing countries, many people still lack adequate access to clean drinking water.

While we have recently improved water access through increased emphasis on global development, we still have a long way to go, especially in sanitation access. We need significant collaboration from multi-national organizations and NGOs. To this end, *Accord Network*, a community of Christ-centered organizations, seeks to leverage the best in relief and development to assist the world's poor. These Christian organizations, especially those within the *WASH Alliance*, are exemplary in their integration of practical ministry with spiritual encouragement.[15]

Diminishing Biodiversity

Biodiversity characterizes the full array of life at all levels from ecosystems to the species that inhabit them. Today, biologists estimate species extinction at alarming rates (100 to 1,000 times greater than recorded in the fossil record). Human factors affecting biodiversity include pollution, climate change, introduction of invasive species, and over-exploitation (excessive hunting and fishing). The greatest human impact on loss of biodiversity, however, is the degradation of land and aquatic habitats. Such intrusive human activities include reckless land development, careless agricultural

---

13. Shiklolmanov, "World Freshwater Resources," 13–24.
14. Rosegrant et al., *Global Water Outlook to 2025*, 2.
15. Examples include: East African Ministries, Engineering Ministries International, Lifewater, Living Water, Map International, Samaritan's Purse, Water 4, Water Mission, World Vision.

practices, mining, road building, and major alterations to streams, lakes, wetlands, and coastal marine systems.[16]

Our most catastrophic alteration, however, results from deforestation, which is responsible for a net removal of 17 million acres each year, including 10 million acres in South America alone.[17] Cleared of vegetation for wood, mining, or alternate land uses, organic soil becomes prone to erosion, which leads to infertile land that will take a long time to recover.

While the loss of biodiversity is important to Christians simply because it curtails creation's witness to the fullness of God, all Christians should be concerned by the extinction of species that are essential to balanced ecosystems. At the same time, what right do we have to knowingly prevent future generations from seeing these spectacular species with their own eyes?

What More Must We Do?

It will take more than science to reverse environmental decline. Optimal stewardship of the environment will require a sacrificial change in human behavior based on an understanding that environmental stewardship is an expression of love for future generations and ultimately of God, Earth's creator.

In his 2015 Encyclical, *Laudato Si'—On Care for Our Common Home*, Pope Francis released scientific and ethical statements on climate change, water degradation, biodiversity loss, and social degradation. Commenting on this degradation, he insists that we understand our stewardship as a "culture of care"—for all that exists: creation, the environment, all creatures, our neighbors, the vulnerable, and much more.[18] This return to a biblical ethic of Earth stewardship, aware of our participation with God in the redemption of all things (Col 1:19–20), could propel us toward more effective evangelism and discipleship.[19]

Beyond Stewardship: The Redemption of All Things

Christians recognize God as both creator, revealing his glory in what he has made, and as covenant partner, inviting us to join him as his stewards

---

16. Van Dyke, "Diversity of Life."
17. Mongabay, "Global Deforestation Rates."
18. See DeWitt, "Earth Stewardship and *Laudato Si*," 273.
19. For a concise summary of Christian environmental ethics, see Gushee, "Environmental Ethics," 245–65.

in caring for the Earth. We also, of course, celebrate God as redeemer, not only of human beings but also "all things." Biblical eschatology envisions God's people eventually regaining the *imago Dei* in conjunction with the restoration of the Earth:

> The creation waits in eager expectation for the sons of God to be revealed. For the creation was subjected to frustration, not by its own choice, but by the will of the one who subjected it, in hope that the creation itself will be liberated from its bondage to decay and brought into the glorious freedom of the children of God. We know that the whole creation has been groaning as in the pains of childbirth right up to the present time. (Rom 8:19–22)

Jürgen Moltmann is joined by a rapidly increasing number of theologians in this vision of Christian ecological eschatology: "The embodiment of the messianic promises to the poor and the quintessence of the hopes of the alienated is that the world should be 'home.' This means being at home in existence—that the relationships between God, human beings and nature lose their tension and are resolved into peace and repose."[20]

Biblical theology thus envisions God's people recommitting to their God-commissioned stewardship of nature in an eschatological context of hope—the vision of what the book of Revelation describes as "the new heavens and the new earth" (Rev 21:1). This eschatological salvation envisions a comprehensive resurrection that includes all of creation.[21]

God's solution to both the fall of humankind and the disruption of the cosmos is found in his re-creative power in the triumph of Jesus' death and resurrection. In the same way that Adam's sin affected all of creation (Gen 3:17–19), so too does Christ's sacrifice promise redemption to all of creation.

> For Christ is the image of the invisible God, the firstborn over all creation. For by him *all things* were created, things in heaven and on earth, visible and invisible . . . all things were created by him and for him. . . . For God was pleased to have all his fullness dwell in him, and through him to reconcile all things to himself, whether things on earth or things in heaven, by making peace through his blood, shed on the cross." (Col 1:15–16, 19–20)

---

20. Moltmann, *God in Creation*, 5.

21. A helpful book-length development of ecological eschatology is found in Moo and White, *Let Creation Rejoice*.

As Van Dyke clarifies, the *"all things"* that God created, "things in heaven and on earth" are the same *"all things"* that God is reconciling to himself. The redemption here is not merely personal, or even merely human; it extends to all creation in the same way the covenant following the flood was not merely with Noah, but with "all living creatures of every kind on the earth" (Gen 9:12–17).[22]

The church is responsible for proclaiming and implementing the redemption and restoration that creation is eagerly anticipating. N. T. Wright's exegesis of Romans 8:19–22 affirms this very message: "The answer, if the creator is to be true to the original purpose, is for humans to be redeemed, to take their place at last as God's image bearers, the wise steward they were always intended to be."[23] In so doing, we participate in what theologians call *realized eschatology*—the unfolding now of what will consummate in the end-times. Our acts of ecological stewardship and restoration foreshadow God's ultimate recreation of the heavens and the earth (Rev 21:1).

Conservation and the Gospel

Wise stewardship of the Earth evidences the power of the gospel to restore "all things," while honoring the LORDship of Christ over his creation. In taking this form, stewardship of the Earth is an essential complement to Christian discipleship.

Earth stewardship "is an integral part of our mission and an expression of our worship of God."[24] As Stott and Wright explain, "Integral mission means discerning, proclaiming, and living out the biblical truth that the gospel is for individual persons, *and* for society, *and* for creation. All three are broken and suffering because of sin; all three are included in the redeeming love and mission of God; all three must be part of the comprehensive mission of God's people."[25] In this view of "environmental missions," our proclamation of how Christ's resurrection brings peace and reconciliation to all that is marred by sin includes our demonstration of holistically "caring for the environment and making disciples among all peoples."[26]

---

22. Van Dyke, *Redeeming Creation*, 86–87.

23. Wright, *Romans*, 596.

24. The Lausanne Movement most recently recognized this in *The Cape Town Commitment* in 2010, and subsequently in the "Call to Action" at the Global Consultation on Creation Care and the Gospel in 2012.

25. Stott and Wright, *Christian Mission in the Modern World*, 54

26. Bliss, *Environmental Missions*, 17. See also Bell and White, *Creation Care and the Gospel*.

Bibliography

Bauckham, Richard. *The Bible and Ecology: Rediscovering the Community of Creation.* Waco: Baylor University Press, 2010.

Bell, Colin, and Robert S. White. *Creation Care and the Gospel: Reconsidering the Mission of the Church.* Peabody: Hendrickson, 2016.

Bliss, Lowell. *Environmental Missions: Planting Churches and Trees.* Pasadena: William Carey Library, 2013.

DeWitt, Calvin B. "Earth Stewardship and *Laudato Si'*." *The Quarterly Review of Biology* 91.3 (Sept 2016) 271–84.

Gushee, David. "Environmental Ethics: Bringing Creation Care Down to Earth." In *Keeping God's Earth: The Global Environment in Biblical Perspective*, edited by Noah J. Toly and Daniel I. Block, 245–65. Downers Grove: InterVarsity, 2010.

Hall, Steven. "Toward a Theology of Sustainable Agriculture." *Perspectives on Science and Christian Faith* 54 (2002) 103–7.

Harker, Ryan D., and Janeen Bertwsch Johnson, eds. *Rooted and Grounded: Essays on Land and Christian Discipleship.* Eugene, OR: Pickwick, 2016.

Moltmann, Jürgen. *God in Creation: A New Theology of Creation and the Spirit of God.* Philadelphia: Fortress, 1993.

Mongabay. "Global Deforestation Rates." https://rainforests.mongabay.com/deforestation.html.

Moo, Jonathan A., and Robert S. White. *Let Creation Rejoice: Biblical Hope and Ecological Crisis.* Downers Grove: InterVarsity, 2014.

Moshier, Stephen, O. "What is God's Purpose for Natural Disasters?" In *Not Just Science: Questions Where Christian Faith and Natural Science Intersect*, edited by Dorothy F. Chappell and E. David Cook, 141–48. Grand Rapids: Zondervan, 2005.

Rosegrant, Mark W., et al. *Global Water Outlook to 2025, Averting an Impending Crises.* Washington, DC: International Food Policy Research Institute, 2002.

Sayere, Laura, and Sean Clark. *Fields of Learning: The Student Farm Movement in North America.* Lexington: University of Kentucky Press, 2011.

Schnepf, Max, and Craig Cox, eds. *Environmental Benefits of Conservation on Cropland: The Status of Our Knowledge.* Ankeny, IA: Soil and Water Conservation Society, 2006.

———. *Managing Agricultural Landscapes for Environmental Quality: Strengthening the Science Base.* Ankeny, IA: Soil and Water Conservation Society, 2007.

Shiklolmanov, Igor A. "World Freshwater Resources." In *Water in Crises: A Guide to the World's Freshwater Resources*, edited by Peter H. Gleick, 13–24. New York: Oxford University Press, 1993.

Sorley, Craig. *Farming that Brings Glory to God and Hope to the Hungry: A Set of Biblical Principles to Transform the Practice or Agriculture.* South Hadley, MA: Doorlight, 2009.

Stearley, Ralph, "Why Should Christians Be Interested in Geology?" In *Not Just Science: Questions Where Christian Faith and Natural Science Intersect*, edited by Dorothy F. Chappell and E. David Cook, 148–58. Grand Rapids: Zondervan, 2005.

Stott, John, and Christopher J. H. Wright. *Christian Mission in the Modern World.* 2nd ed. Downers Grove: InterVarsity, 2008.

Vanderslice, Kendall. "Farminaries: From Souls to Stomachs, Seminaries are Looking to Expand their Reach." *Christianity Today*, January 25, 2018. https://www.christianitytoday.com/ct/2018/january-february/farminaries.html.

Van Dragt, Randy, and James A. Clark. "Environmental Stewardship: What Are the Roles for Science and Faith?" In *Not Just Science: Questions Where Christian Faith and Natural Science Intersect*, edited by Dorothy F. Chappell and E. David Cook, 158–73. Grand Rapids: Zondervan, 2005.

Van Dyke, Fred. "The Diversity of Life: Its Loss and Conservation." In *Keeping God's Earth: The Global Environment in Biblical Perspective*, edited by Noah J. Toly and Daniel I. Block, 93–115. Downers Grove: InterVarsity, 2010.

Van Dyke, Fred, ed. *Redeeming Creation: The Biblical Basis for Environmental Stewardship*. Downers Grove: InterVarsity, 1996.

Wessel, R. Gregory, and Jeffrey K. Greenberg. *Geoscience for the Public Good and Global Development: Toward a Sustainable Future*. Paper presented at The Geological Society of America in Boulder, Colorado, 2016.

Wright, N. T. *Romans*. Vol. 9 of *The New Interpreter's Commentary on the Bible*. Edited by Leander E. Keck. Nashville: Abingdon, 2015.

19

The Wisdom of Ethical Sustainability
Brian R. Brock

CHRISTIAN TALK ABOUT WISDOM today typically gurgles happily along in the regions of beauty, craftsmanship, wholeness, integration and virtue that are wonderfully warm, fuzzy—and reassuring. In this chapter I want to propose that we have a lesson still to learn from the biblical wisdom tradition, its insistence that it is not easy to stay on the path of wisdom (Prov 1:20–33). We fallen humans avoid the costs that come with being seekers of truth and living integrated lives fundamentally oriented by the fear of the LORD, the font of human wisdom.

Even more troublingly, when we are not living in wisdom we travel alternative paths on which we can lose sight of it entirely (Prov 4:19). The good news of the wisdom tradition, however, is that God has not left humans alone in this state of wandering indefinitely down their self-destructive paths. Instead wisdom seeks us out, *calls* to us from a distance, reaching into the most intimate spaces of our daily lives with the offer of salvation (Prov 1:20; 8:1).

The divine call that comes to us through creatures draws us into a delight in the works of the Creator of heaven and earth that empowers new ways of living. Provoked by this critical edge in the biblical wisdom traditions, in this chapter I would like to pursue an investigation into the paths along which our delight is currently leading us in the modern developed world. What does the way we live our material lives tell us about what really delights us? The stream of clothes, energy and food that passes into and out of our homes and bodies might well tell us something about our true delights, so exposing the paths on which our lives are in fact travelling.

Life on the Sustainability Low Road

Consider the utterance that has become all too familiar in churches today: "Christians should be stewards of creation and leaders in thinking about sustainability." Before we start nodding in agreement, let's pause for a moment to ask how such talk coheres with the lives we lead as inhabitants of the developed west. It seems safe to assume that when we say we want to live "simply and sustainably" we mean that we want to leave a world for future generations that is at least not much worse than the one we were born into. We are participants in a beautiful and rich creation, and we don't want to spoil it.

Here's the problem: we Americans have contributed to altering this world in ways that are much more far-reaching than any generation of humans who have ever lived on this planet. If there was going to be a contest in world history for the title of "least sustainable lifestyle," we come dangerously close to the top of the list. If every person alive was suddenly to be elevated to the consumption patterns of Americans (a hope that we often stoke by way of our vision of the "American dream"), it would take the resources of four earths to sustain it. Only Kuwait, Australia, United Arab Emirates and Qatar consume more of the world's resources per capita.

It is realities like these that make me suspect that any faithful investigation of wisdom in relation to our living on this planet will need to ask some more unsettling questions about what we're actually doing when we claim that we'd like to live more sustainably. If we are going to get anywhere serious on this topic we are going to at least be prepared to admit that we might well ask such questions from an already compromised position. We need to admit that we are tempted to slap a "greenest SUV" badge on our current lifestyles. It's true that some SUVs are less wasteful than the next gas guzzler, but we should at least admit the absurdity of wanting to have the biggest car on the road *and at the same time* that it be sustainable.

Like Christians in general, only rarely will you catch contemporary theologians offering general, and typically vague, exhortations for more sustainable development. One exception is the French theologian Jacques Ellul, who devoted a whole chapter in *The Technological Bluff* to the theme, though his real concern in doing so was to highlight the wastefulness of modern consumer society. While I will agree with him that modern technological societies produce unbelievable waste as a matter of course, we can probably say more than he does in concluding that Christians respond to sustainability questions by insisting that elected officials deal with the problem. The treatment by the American theologian Norman Wirzba's *Renewing*

Religion in an Ecological Age is theologically richer, but still only two pages long.

My point is that there has been remarkably little willingness among modern Christians to ask what our espousal of sustainability actually commits us to doing in our daily lives—which is why we find ourselves in such a conflicted position. Most of us want for good, Christian reasons to take the sustainability high road, believing that Christians really ought to be on that high road, while having no idea what that could possibly mean in our day to day lives. The wisdom traditions offer us a first clue here that something is amiss, because wisdom is something that is precisely located in your practical knowledge of how to *do* things. We know how to *say*, but not really how to *do* sustainability.

The Underworld of Waste

What would it look like to face this dilemma honestly? Leland Ryken's contribution to this volume highlights the capacity of literature to tempt us to look more closely at our own lives. Good literature offers us critical purchase on our own lives by helping us to better perceive the path we are travelling.

The American novelist Don Delillo's longstanding and wide-ranging interest in the sustainability of the American lifestyle usefully advances the Christian quest to hear the call of an environmental wisdom. His breakthrough novel *White Noise* follows a suburban family evacuated from their home in the wake of an "airborne toxic event." As they flee in the family station wagon, their worried discussions surface many of our often subconscious fears about the toxicity of the modern built environment, saturated as it is with airborne pollutants, synthetic materials, and artificial foodstuffs.

I want here, though, to draw out some of his reflections from a later novel, *Underworld*. I don't think it is accidental that the cover photo shows a tiny church with a cross on top sitting beneath the looming and dark twin towers in New York, nor that the central character is a waste engineer struggling with his faith and his fear of death.

Already with the title, DeLillo is signaling that he is updating the ancient assumption that how you live is directly connected to what you think happens to the dead. The Egyptians believed Osiris was the god of the underworld, while the Greeks thought that Charon the boatman ferried the dead across the river Styx to deliver them into the hands of the god Hades and his menacing three-headed dog Cerberus. It was in this context that eleven times in the Gospels Jesus makes reference to the afterlife as a threatening place by calling the alternative to the kingdom he inaugurates "Gehenna."

Here is where it gets interesting. "Gehenna" is another name for the valley of Hinnom on the southwestern side of the old city of Jerusalem. Archeologists have shown that there have been graves in this valley for centuries, and Judas is thought to have been buried there. There is also a Christian tradition that during Roman times the valley had become a dump where fires continually burned the city's trash and where the dead bodies of criminals and animal carcasses were discarded.

In offering us a bridge from our modern world back to Jesus' talk about Gehenna, DeLillo's work thus gives us a way to think more deeply into the connections between death, perdition, and garbage to which Jesus is drawing our attention.

The waste engineer who is one of the main characters in *Underworld* is named Nick Shay. His job has made him think much more deeply about how contemporary living demands a certain relationship to garbage.

> My firm was involved in waste. We were waste handlers, waste traders, cosmologists of waste. . . . We built pyramids of waste above and below the earth. The more hazardous the waste, the deeper we tried to sink it. The word plutonium comes from Pluto, the god of the dead and ruler of the underworld. They took him out to the marshes and wasted him as we say today, or used to say until it got changed into something else. . . . I travelled to the coastal lowlands of Texas and watched men in moon suits bury drums of dangerous waste in subterranean salt beds many millions of years old, dried-out remnants of a Mesozoic ocean. It was a religious conviction in our business that these deposits of rock salt would not leak radiation. Waste is a religious thing. We entomb contaminated waste with a sense of reverence and dread. It is necessary to respect what we discard. . . . Waste has a solemn aura now, an aspect of untouchability. White containers of plutonium waste with yellow caution tags. Handle carefully. Even the lowest household trash is closely observed. People look at their garbage differently now, seeing every bottle and crushed carton in a planetary context."[1]

To be a waste engineer means spending one's life in the places where our stuff goes when the rest of us throw it "away." Though not really a believer, Nick finds himself in such places facing the almost religious force of the no-man's-land that is the modern landfill.

1. DeLillo, *Underworld*, 88, 106.

> In Holland I went to VAM, a waste treatment plant that handles a million tons of garbage a year. I sat in a white Fiat and swept past windrows of refuse heaped many stories high. Down one towering row and around another, waves of steam rising from the tapered heaps, and there was a stink in the air that filled my mouth, that felt deep enough to singe my clothes. Why did I think I was born with this experience in my brain? Why was it personal? I thought, Why do bad smells seem to tell us something about ourselves? The company manager drove me up and down the steaming rows and I thought, Every bad smell is about us. We make our way through the world and come upon a scene that is medieval-modern, a city of high-rise garbage, the hell reek of every perishable object ever thrown together, and it seems like something we've been carrying all our lives.[2]

Realizations of this sort led Nick and his wife first to recycling, and then beyond it, to a much deeper transformative vision of their everyday lives.

> Marian and I saw products as garbage even when they sat gleaming on store shelves, yet unbought. We didn't say, What kind of casserole will that make? We said, What kind of garbage will that make? Safe, clean, neat, easily disposed of? Can the package be recycled and come back as a tawny envelope that is difficult to lick closed? First we saw the garbage, then we saw the product as food or lightbulbs or dandruff shampoo. How does it measure up as waste, we asked. We asked whether it was responsible to eat a certain item if the package the item comes in will live a million years.[3]

Nick and Marian had discovered something crucial about modern waste production. The contents of the contemporary landfill are born in our *perceiving* the material world in a specific way.

From Commodities to Trash

Let's think for a minute about that most familiar of modern inventions, the Styrofoam cup. It is designed to be thrown away as soon as it is used. What makes it attractive is its offering itself to us as an object for which we will not have to care. It will serve us only once. The thought that we might clean dirt or lipstick off of it and use it again revolts us. If we pause to examine these feelings about a lowly Styrofoam cup we can begin to come to terms with

---

2. DeLillo, *Underworld*, 104.
3. DeLillo, *Underworld*, 121.

how deeply we have been trained in one of the core objectives of modern capitalism: to break down the tendency of human beings to care for the material things of this world.

The technical term for this process is commodification, and the commodity was one of the defining conceptual innovations of modern capitalism. The commodity is an object designed to be discarded and replaced in order to keep the waterwheels of commerce turning. It comes with an aesthetic too: like the modern hotel room, the whiteness and promise of sterility held out to us by the Styrofoam cup also offers the guilty pleasure of claiming something that has been touched by no one else by "dirtying" it with our physical presence before discarding it.

Consider how an apple is transformed into a commodity. From time immemorial humans have picked and eaten this fruit, throwing away the leftovers and expelling the waste products of digestion. Where population densities were high these waste products might have pooled to become smelly, threaten groundwater supplies, or attract various creatures who live off these wastes. But by the working of these living beings these wastes would have soon been reclaimed by the earth. In short, you don't need a landfill for these types of waste, and that's why we can legitimately call them sustainable. These are processes, however, that we can try to circumvent. Commodification is one of those attempts.

To transform an apple into a commodity we need to put several very uniform and visually stereotypical apples on a Styrofoam undertray and wrap everything up in transparent plastic. While this new object, the apple-as-commodity, can be handled differently than the old box of apples, sorted by machines, for instance, or thrown into a bag for home delivery after having been purchased on line, it also commits us to something new beyond the wastes which have always attended apple eating. We will call this something new "trash," in this case, whatever is left over from the apple mixed with several kinds of plastic which were always destined, *from the very beginning*, to be discarded. This is why modern garbage has a very different constitution than simple waste, and is much less sustainable as a result.

Like the Styrofoam cup, what ultimately makes the apple-as-commodity a marketable item is the promise it holds out of having been removed from the nexus of life. The imperatives of the commodity—to be uniform, visually attractive and interchangeable—also signal its having been extracted from the cycles of the rest of the organic world. It is the *image*, then, of an apple that we are actually buying when we buy them in the commoditized form. Remember that the plastic wrapping means we can no longer smell or taste the food that we are about to eat. The philosopher Greg Kennedy calls this the paradox of commodification.

> By emptying the [lived] world of physical things and filling it with seemingly immaterial concepts, commodification creates trash, that is, beings whose disposal supposedly leaves no physical consequence or remainder. But the cost and woes resulting from unchecked consumption of disposables have forced the consumer society to acknowledge the paradox that plagues it: the greater the number of rationalized commodities it deals with, the more massive the material debris it leaves behind. For now, the following statistic suggests the hidden reality of rationalization: "The United States devotes about 4 percent of its energy to packaging food, almost as much as American agriculture uses to grow the food."[4]

Theologically speaking, every time we use the word "food" we are admitting that we are living organisms destined to die, who must ingest other living things in order to go on living. This cycle is sustainable. We *can*, however, attempt to resist acknowledging this reality in the ways we eat, by, for instance, packaging things to make them look more like "product," or by creating ever more elaborate and energy intensive ways to slow spoilage. The cost of such measures, however, is easily measurable in terms of fossil fuel use and garbage production. Just as importantly, when we eat commoditized food that we can't taste or feel before we buy it, what results looks much less like an integrated life in which eating plays a central part and more like a fragmented life that must sometimes be put on pause to "fuel up."

As inhabitants of a world that trains us as consumers, what we can't see is any practical alternatives. The call of wisdom thus appears in the guise of a question: Are there more caring and attentive ways to proceed as mortal beings who must eat?

Does Recycling Equal Sustainability?

Perhaps the solution is to recycle more? The genesis of recycling is important here. It was manufacturers who invented and spread the modern concept of recycling and did so because they wanted to *increase* consumption rather than reduce it: "The Container Corporation of America commissioned the design a few months after the first Earth Day [in 1970] to advertise its reprocessed products and left the logo in the public domain for others to adopt."[5] The success of this public relations campaign is indicated by how

---

4. Kennedy, *Ontology of Trash*, 75.
5. O'Lear, *Environmental Politics*, 122.

infrequently we consider what happens once we have put materials into the recycling bin. Even in the mid-1990's:

> Recycling did not minimize the creation of discards. Instead, this back-end refuse management strategy left wasteful mass production and consumption unaltered and even encouraged it. People started believing that their trash was now benign. Today it's likely that more Americans recycle than vote—yet greater amounts of rubbish are going to landfills and incinerators than ever before. . . . Just because materials are hauled away in a recycling truck doesn't mean that they actually get reprocessed. Almost half of discarded newspapers and office paper is buried or burned, while two-thirds of glass containers and plastic soda and milk bottles are trashed instead of recycled.[6]

The disturbing reality is that mass recycling as we know it today could only get started when people begin to think of garbage as a commodity or resource. Remember that we started picking up litter because we could sell the aluminium cans for cash? Garbage brokers make no bones about it: their interests are first in profit and only secondarily in reducing the volume of garbage going into landfills.

> It is quite misleading to see today's passion for recycling as a return to the lifestyle of a century or so ago. Recycling co-exists with an intensive, high-volume disposable lifestyle that has kept waste levels at a plateau reached in the 1970s-'80s and far exceeds anything seen in earlier periods; recycling bins even encouraged the triumph of the disposable bottle over the returnable version. Today's Americans discard as much packaging waste as their grandparents—and that is after recycling bottles and newspapers.[7]

The inventors of the cultural habit of recycling have achieved exactly what they intended: an increasing rate of turnover, especially of paper and plastic. The idea of recycling, which was never intended to reduce overall waste or consumption, has thus successfully been harnessed to generate higher profits by way of increased consumption.

Perhaps we should admit that industrialized recycling regimes as we know them are really delay tactics that stop us asking the most important theological questions. For instance, when we *sort* recycling, are we in this process learning to *value* creatures, to be *reconnected* with creation? Such a

---

6. Rogers, *Gone Tomorrow*, 176–77. Cited in O'Lear, *Environmental Politics*, 122.
7. Trentmann, *Empire of Things*, 642.

practice can certainly never teach us to *care* for things. Recycling might be able to teach us to see what we once considered worthless to be *financially* valuable, *tradable*—but this is very different from drawing us into *care* for any creaturely entity.

Caring for Creation

To face such questions about the things we throw away is to unleash a deluge of further questions about the things we keep, because while we are consuming and recycling more we are simultaneously wasting and hoarding more. Experts tell us, to take one example, that in the western world today fully a quarter of the food people buy ends up uneaten in the garbage—a level of organic waste that contributes substantially to CO_2 emissions. This is exacerbated by developments in management and logistics techniques over the last two decades. Whereas bulk waste was once generated by companies disposing of overproduced commodities during periods of economic crisis, consumers have now become used to routinely throwing away excessive goods they have purchased during periods of normal economic stability and prosperity.[8]

Other cultural developments continue to exacerbate these developments. In the developed world the number of people living alone has doubled in the last two decades. Individuals living on their own consume proportionally much more energy and material than people living together—in the way that a family buying a gallon of milk consumes less than four people individually buying their own milk and storing it in their own refrigerators. While individual appliances have also become more efficient during this period, operational waste and resource extraction has continued to climb as people have larger houses, mechanically heat and cool more rooms of their houses, take more showers, put more electrical appliances in each room, and furnish each room with more things than ever before in human history.

And off site storage continues to mushroom. There are currently more than 50,000 self-storage facilities in the United States, cumulatively offering space three times the size of Manhattan. This growth is happening at the same time that American homes are getting bigger and their attics more overstuffed. For every three to four TVs and computers being used in an American home today there is an average of one old one in the attic. Consumerism apparently not only trains us today to be happy to dispose and consume more things but to hoard at the same time.

8. Trentmann, *Empire of Things*, 649–51.

Wisdom reaches into such a lifestyle by calling us to move beyond narrower questions of pollution and waste and toward broader questions about metabolic circulation. Even as we citizens of the modern west are recycling more and are becoming increasingly concerned to emit less waste, the reality is that at this very moment we are simultaneously drawing an exponentially expanding stream of raw resources out of mines and wells and damming up more of what comes out of these extraction processes in storage units, homes and attics.

The time has come to stop and ask ourselves: To what do we commit ourselves when we confess with the Nicene Creed that God is our Father, "Creator of heaven and earth?" Here again DeLillo's instincts draw very near to the gospel message: "What we are reluctant to touch often seems the very fabric of our salvation."[9]

The Creaturely Wisdom of Bad Stewards

Neither lady wisdom nor Jesus Christ come to us to rescue us from this world, but to make us more *part of it*, to make us more *attentive* to how we are engaging with it. Confessing the Father of Jesus Christ as Creator brings us face to face with the reality that, though reusing glass bottles and sorting our recycling may be salutary, it is the energy hungry and thing-filled lives we lead that most loudly announces the path we are travelling through our Creator's world.

As we travel down this path the call of created wisdom asks us to consider whether, at the root of our rampant consumption, might lie a rampant acquisitiveness. In the New Testament James succinctly sums up the early Christian embrace of this aspect of Old Testament wisdom:

> Who is wise and understanding among you? Show by your good life that your works are done with gentleness born of wisdom. . . . For where there is envy and selfish ambition, there will also be disorder and wickedness of every kind. (Jas 3:13, 16; cf. Rom 1:21–22)

Covetousness here appears as being more concerned with acquiring things for myself than acquiring that true wisdom whose value is greater than any gold (Prov 8:11; 16:16). Such covetousness is a road to Gehenna, a path the wisdom writers depict as a living death that terminates in a wasteland.

The alternative to covetousness, insists James, is wisdom and understanding, literally "intelligence." He is intentionally taking up the Old

---

9. DeLillo, *White Noise*, 31.

Testament definition of wisdom as practical intelligence—to be distinguished from knowledge of theories or universal truth claims. For James wisdom is existential intelligence, a practical know-how for living in the world which alone counts as a true confession that we fear the LORD.

To those of us living in the western world, it is now all too clear that the call of wisdom can only come to us as a confrontation, a killing and resurrection. It is a call for repentance and the transforming of our minds amidst the stuff that we array around ourselves like fig leaves. In the creaturely call of wisdom, Jesus offers us his new kingdom in order to rescue us from a Gehenna of our own making. The fear of *this* LORD is the beginning of wise living as creatures, which is why Jesus himself encourages us to think *first* of ourselves as bad stewards in need of mustering all the creativity and faith we can in order to receive the salvation on offer from the situation we sinners have created for ourselves (Luke 16:1–14).

Caring for creation is not an optional part of Christian discipleship. Though not of it, we remain in this world. The path for which we have been created is that of the One who was mistaken for the gardener after his resurrection. Our salvation is not one that removes us from a world we've trashed but is a learning in the most practical of ways what it might mean that we were created to be gardeners.

Bibliography

DeLillo, Don. *Underworld*. London: Picador, 1999.

———. *White Noise*. New York: Penguin, 2016.

Kennedy, Greg. *An Ontology of Trash: The Disposable and Its Problematic Nature*. Albany: State University of New York Press, 2007.

O'Lear, Shannon. *Environmental Politics: Scale and Power*. Cambridge: Cambridge University Press, 2010.

Rogers, Heather. *Gone Tomorrow: The Hidden Life of Garbage*. New York: The New Press, 2005.

Trentmann, Frank. *Empire of Things: How We Became a World of Consumers, from the Fifteenth Century to the Twenty-First*. New York: Harper, 2016.

20

Psychology and Christian Wisdom
David N. Entwistle

My fascination with psychology began in high school, when an introductory course opened my eyes to psychology's interconnections with biology, human development, emotion, memory, cognition, social influence, personality, learning, psychological disorders, and psychotherapy. Not long thereafter, I spent a summer working at a psychiatric hospital, which confirmed my sense of calling and vocation.

After three decades of teaching, research, and writing about psychology and Christianity, I have come to appreciate its essential role as a source of knowledge, wisdom, and healing. This does not, however, mean that every psychological theory, perspective, or technique is fully consonant with a Christian outlook on life. In fact, modern psychology is often characterized by individualism and reductionism that run counter to Christian views of human personhood. Such points of divergence are not inherently rooted in the discipline of psychology, but are in part consequences of Western, Modernist, Enlightenment thinking that has led to an aggrandized view of the "autonomous self" within the broader culture. Studies demonstrate, for instance, that the migration from rural to urban environments from 1800–2000 was accompanied by a decreased sense of social obligation and social belonging and an increase in individualistic and materialistic values.[1]

While some aspects of modern psychology diverge from Christian orthodoxy, differences are not the rule. In this chapter, I will survey ways modern psychology helps us to see the wonder and complexity of human beings, as well as ways a Christian worldview can serve as a useful

---

1. Greenfield, "Changing Psychology of Culture."

corrective to Modernist assumptions, which shape alternative psychological perspectives.

What Is Psychology?

Psychology is the *science of behavior and mental processes*.[2] Psychology is a science because one of its central methodologies is the scientific method. The scientific method in turn is shaped by reason, tradition, and philosophical assumptions. So, to say that psychology is a science is not to say that it is only about established empirical facts. Psychologists create theories and hypotheses that are informed and shaped by their philosophical assumptions and worldviews. However, while not every theory or hypothesis is amenable to the scientific method, empirical methods are among the major means by which psychologists pose questions and evaluate evidence.

Psychology does not confine itself to *human* behavior and mental processes, however. Psychologists study rats and chimps and dolphins, too, and we often learn much about human behavior by studying our fellow creatures. The scope of what we explore is far-ranging; we study anatomy and physiology, neurotransmitters and brains, and many physical substrates of behavior. We study thinking, attitudes, emotions, intelligence, motivation, social influences, personality, and a host of things that are not directly observable. My own subfield, clinical psychology, which includes psychopathology and psychotherapy, is arguably the most influential part of the discipline. Not only is the territory vast, but the subject matter is complex. We utilize many viewpoints in recognizing the complexity of behavioral causation: biological, psychological, and social perspectives. While some of our methods are new (e.g., brain imaging techniques), many subjects have ancient roots (Hippocrates, for instance, classified causes of mental disturbance, and Aristotle pondered the workings of consciousness).

While we grapple with age-old questions, psychology as a science is a very young field. Herman Ebbinghaus, a pioneer of psychology, claimed that psychology has a short history, but a long past.[3] By this he meant that only recently has the scientific method been applied to the study of human beings. Long before Wilhelm Wundt started his psychological laboratory in 1879, psychology had been a focus of philosophy, particularly within metaphysics and ethics. The physical and medical sciences, too, had begun to investigate human behavior and mental processes from a biological perspective. World religions provided contexts for understanding human purpose

---

2. Myers, *Psychology*.
3. Cited in Boring, *History of Experimental Psychology*, ix.

and obligations. Artists, poets, writers, physicians, scientists, philosophers, theologians and many others explored the contours of the human mind and body long before psychology defined itself as a science, often with insights that are still meaningful and relevant today. Yet none of these other ways of thinking about human beings was completely displaced by psychology. One cannot "do" the science of psychology without first having made numerous assumptions about human beings that are based not on science, but on one's philosophical and religious assumptions about what it means to be human.[4] These assumptions can have far-reaching effects.

If the human being is seen as a complex animal only, behavior inevitably will be explained strictly in terms of biology and reinforcement history. In this case, free will is either seen as an illusion or is held without philosophical grounding. Alternatively, if the stating premise is that human beings are basically good and prone to self-actualization, human evil becomes a practical and philosophical puzzle.

In keeping with the theme of this book, it is not surprising that psychology overlaps with literature, history, theology, philosophy, sociology, and biblical studies. Psychology's unique methods and its influence on modern society, however, affirms psychology's essential place in Christian higher education. In the Christian liberal arts, we recognize that all the academic disciplines work together to give us a more complete picture of God and creation.

A Christian View of Persons

Christian theology lacks an empirical framework for understanding humanity, which psychology and the other sciences can provide. Theology, however, does share with psychology an interest in the nature and functioning of human beings. Reformed theologians often contextualize biblical thinking about the grand narrative of God's interaction with human beings under the headings of creation, fall, redemption, and consummation. Each of these elements is crucial if we are to understand human beings rightly. In what ways are human beings best understood as creatures? In what ways are we best understood as fallen? In what ways do the incarnational, salvific, and restorative elements of the biblical story help us to understand humanity? And how does the teleological framework of humankind's future shape how we ought to live in and understand the present? Clearly, all of these questions are relevant to a Christian understanding of human behavior and mental processes. Given the constraints of the current volume, we will

---

4. Koch, *Psychology in Human Context*.

narrow our focus to consider how psychology and theology jointly help us understand human personhood; namely, what it means to be a fallen human being created in the image of a holy God.

In Genesis 1–2, God looks upon his handiwork and proclaims it *good*. Even without having been made in the image of God, human beings as creatures would still be *good*, not in the sense of *virtuous*, but in the sense of having been *valued* by their creator. When we identify things that are laudable in human beings, sometimes what we see is attributable to the general goodness of creation. When we consider that humans are uniquely created in the image of God, however, we see new potentials, abilities, and roles that complete the creation; "God saw all that He had made, and it was *very good*" (Gen 1:31, NIV). In unique ways that are not directly expressed in the text of Scripture, humanity completes and embellishes the creation that was already good. This goodness is a gift from God:

> We are situated within relationships to our Creator, to each other, and to the rest of creation. While this view highlights the goodness of creation, it also acknowledges that we are limited creatures. It professes that our lives are contingent upon God's care and by right ought to be dedicated to His ends. Christian theology asserts that humans are finite rather than infinite, derivative rather than original, dependent rather than autonomous.[5]

It may not always be possible to discern between goodness that is creational and goodness that expresses the *imago Dei*, but in either case, that goodness comes from God as Psalm 100:3 declares, "It is He who has made us, and not we ourselves." This premise, of course, is the wedge that separates Christian views from secular ones, which presuppose autonomous views of the self as an individual's construction.[6] The latter comes at the price of natural law, relational identity, supernatural reality, biblical authority, and the wholesale dismissal of tradition.

While Christians affirm the value of human beings as creatures and image bearers, the complicating truth is that currently we are only able to study *fallen* humanity. Created perfect, we now suffer the dysfunctions of sin.[7] Hence, to disregard either our genesis as creations of God or the systemic effects of sin will lead inevitably to inaccurate assessments of

---

5. Entwistle, *Integrative Approaches*, 72.

6. It should also be noted that secular Western ideas about autonomy also conflict with Eastern views that emphasize collective responsibility.

7. Interestingly, however, Scripture never explicitly portrays the *imago Dei* as having been damaged or marred, though it certainly does affirm that we are bent and disordered: Kilner, "Humanity in God's Image."

human psychology. To paraphrase C. S. Lewis, *the devil sends errors in pairs*.[8] We can overemphasize human good and human potential, just as we can overemphasize human limitations, human disorder, or human evil. Early rabbinic writers kept this tension (perhaps mirrored by Paul in Rom 7:19) by affirming that within every human being is a continuum between *yetzer hara* (inclination toward evil) and *yetzer hatov* (inclination towards good).[9] Thus, our first insight is cautionary: as we explore the *imago Dei*, we dare not forget other influences on human psychology.

The Imago Dei in Psychology and Christianity Integration

In the past forty years, evangelicals have tried to think carefully about the integration of psychology and the Christian faith, though often focusing more on human limitations than on human potential.[10] Perhaps this imbalance reflects psychology's preoccupation with abnormal human behavior,[11] while neglecting the resilient *good* that survives even in fractured human beings. While humans are uniquely created in the image of God, we are part of the created realm. This means that we can learn about human psychology by studying animals, which share much of our physiological architecture.[12]

We are also created with limitations. Normal human limitations such as the finite capacity of short term memory, the inability to perceive visual and auditory stimuli outside of a tightly bounded range, and the egocentrism of young children are not necessarily the result of the fall. Humans have finite capacities because God intentionally designed us to be limited creatures. On the other hand, people have the capacity to be and do good because we were created by a good God.[13]

The Christian concept of creation in the image of God is important for a Christian understanding of psychology in at least three ways. First, it explains the eternal value of human beings. Second, it affirms humankind's responsibility to steward the earth as God's representatives (Gen 1:27–28). Third, it affirms humankind's uniqueness as creative, relational, thinking beings. We will explore each of these in order, beginning with the value of human beings.

---

8. Lewis, *Mere Christianity*, 160.
9. Amsel, *Jewish Encyclopedia*; Davies, *Paul and Rabbinic Judaism*.
10. Entwistle and Moroney, "Integrative Perspectives."
11. Seligman and Csikszentmihalyi, "Positive Psychology."
12. See Erickson, *Christian Theology*, 512.
13. Phelps, "Imago Dei and Limited Creature," 362–63.

Human Value

While some psychologists see human beings as merely complex animals, most psychologists acknowledge some degree of human uniqueness.[14] The American Psychological Association's *Code of Ethics* affirms the unique value of human persons, stating that psychologists must "respect and protect civil and human rights and the central importance of freedom of inquiry and expression" (Preamble). "Psychologists respect the dignity and worth of all people" (Principle E). From a Christian perspective, that humans are created in the image of God affirms their eternal value. Humanistic psychologists—notwithstanding their often overly optimistic views of human goodness—have been right to defend the inherent dignity of human beings. Existential therapists also have been right to draw attention to the uniqueness of humans as distinctively aware of their finitude and their ability to be self-reflective.

Human Capacities

The structural view of the *imago Dei* focuses on how human beings reflect certain capacities of God such as reason, faithfulness, sacrificial love, creative aptitude, and moral conscience. One can scarcely imagine contemporary psychology without acknowledging the vast research on human capacities such as intelligence, moral reasoning, memory, emotion, character development, and compassion.

Understanding these functions requires comprehension of the complex biochemical processes that allow a sensory neuron to be affected by light, sound, touch, or some other external stimuli, as neurons pass this information on from one to another, processed by the interneurons of the brain and spinal cord. That these processes actually work as they do in the array of dimensions that they do complements the premise of *imago Dei* anthropology—that in many mysterious and remarkable ways, we are, indeed, like God.

---

14. Radical behaviorists, such as B. F. Skinner, insist that human beings are completely determined by genes and reinforcement; in their view, human beings have no freedom. Skinner further argues in his classic treatise, *Beyond Freedom and Dignity*, that human beings have no unique dignity—they are just complex animals. Similarly, some contemporary psychologists believe that all behavior can be explained by neurophysiological mechanisms. Such denials of human freedom, however, run into a cul de sac, which C. S. Lewis pointed out long ago in his classic work, *Miracles*: The only way one can trust the validity of reason is if reasoning is not wholly determined by natural processes.

Human Relationality

The relational view of the *imago Dei* focuses on how humans mirror the triune nature of God—individual, yet in relationship. Many of psychology's subfields focus on relationality—dating, marriage, friendship, parenting, love, and so forth. Since we are dealing with fallen humanity, psychology also studies human brokenness in its myriad forms—domestic violence, grudges, family discord, combative work relationships, hatred, terrorism, and even sadism. Fortunately, psychology holds out hope for the restoration of relationships, exploring such topics as forgiveness and reconciliation, which are at the heart of the Christian message. Psychology can be one means through which we participate in this salvific work. Indeed, the Greek cognate *therapuein* is a frequent descriptor of Jesus' healing ministry in the Gospels (e.g., Matt 8:16).

Psychology can contribute to the healing mission exemplified by Christ, working towards goals such as restored relationships, effective communication, and appropriate boundaries—markers of what Christians identify as essential components of authentic covenant relationships.

The Scientific Method as One Way of Understanding Human Behavior

The scientific method is essential to the study of behavior. Consider, for example, psychology's earliest experiments on reaction time. There is a gap between when we perceive a stimulus and when we respond to that stimulus. Psychology allows us to study what goes on in the gap between stimulus and response as the nervous system processes and responds to the world around us. The scientific method can also help us evaluate the efficacy of therapeutic interventions. Few things illustrate the impact of psychology in the modern world more than the psychotherapies and medicines that can reduce suffering and improve mental health outcomes. Thanks to the scientific method, psychopharmacology revolutionized the treatment of schizophrenia in the 1940's and has been immensely helpful in creating drugs which can help people suffering from many psychological disorders. "Talking cures," too, have demonstrated efficacy in treating a wide range of human problems. We can assess intelligence and diagnose learning disabilities through the application of the scientific method to psychometric evaluation. Because of well-designed experiments, we have a better understanding of the dangers of prejudice and groupthink,[15] as well as factors that promote or inhibit these phenomena. We understand how phobias are

---

15. Groupthink is a corporate mentality that discourages creativity and individual responsibility.

conditioned and how traumatic responses can be extinguished because of carefully constructed empirical studies.

Because the scientific method is a powerful tool with which we can investigate observable phenomena, it is important that students know how this method works, as well as the limited kinds of questions to which it can be applied. A Christian liberal arts education should allow students to appreciate and employ multiple epistemic strategies and to exercise critical thinking skills as they evaluate knowledge claims. In light of this observation, we now turn our attention to explore the complexity of human behavior.

The Recognition That Behavior Is Multi-Determined

To understand behavior and mental processes, we have to look at a huge array of factors: mind, body, emotions, family, culture, religion, cognition, unconscious mental processes, and learning history. Psychology's biopsychosocial perspective recognizes that we are incredibly complex beings. While many psychologists study discrete aspects of behavior, we recognize that none of these aspects operate in isolation from the others, and that a holistic approach which acknowledges the multi-determined nature of behavior is warranted when trying to understand behavior and mental processes. As one surveys the chapters of an introductory psychology textbook, the complexity of behavior is replete, encompassing neurotransmitters at the micro level to complex social forces at the macro level, with a host of other factors in between.

Brokenness is complex. When someone struggles with depression, a learning disability, dementia, a broken relationship, or any other problem, it is important to recognize that many factors can contribute to these difficulties. As Christians, it is important that we appreciate the many causes of behavior and resist oversimplification. Doing so may prevent us from an overly simplistic view of causation and should help us to humbly restrain our impulses to be naively overconfident.

Human Brokenness

Brokenness—from Alzheimer's disease to zoophobia—reminds us that the world is not as it should be. Psychology provides insight into many causes and forms of mental disease. It can excite our desire to discover ways of bringing relief to those who suffer. Research can help us discover factors that contribute to distress and dysfunction, and it can help us identify factors that make people more resilient and less likely to experience adverse outcomes. Psychology—with a firm research base wedded to human compassion—can promote wellness and restoration. It can also remind us of the incredible capacity we have towards evil.

In social psychology, we confront prejudice, discrimination, conformity, authoritarianism, chauvinism, and bullying. Classic studies warn us that we have a propensity for rationalizing, overlooking, condoning, and committing evil. Indeed, as the theologian Richard Niebuhr (1965) famously remarked, "The doctrine of original sin is the only empirically verifiable doctrine of the Christian faith."[16] Yet even faced with evil and suffering, we also see inclinations towards compassion and justice that speak to the moral duality of our nature. Such is the complexity of the human being.

Concluding Thoughts

As a clinical psychologist, I believe the opportunities I have to contribute to the healing and relief of suffering is part of God's redemptive work in the world, even in instances when I do not mention faith issues with clients. As a professor, I cherish the privilege of helping students to learn and to think carefully about my discipline. I love the fact that my profession allows me to interact intimately with people, whether clients or students, as they navigate their lives and as some of them seek to understand how God may use them in furthering his saving work on earth. Being a psychologist has been, for me, a holy calling.

As a psychologist, I cannot help but stand in awe of my creator as I study human complexity and proclaim with the psalmist, "I am fearfully and wonderfully made!" (Ps 139:14). Likewise, I cannot help but observe the effects of the fall in human brokenness and human sinfulness (which, it must be pointed out, are not synonymous). I also observe areas where secular views in my profession sometimes stand in sharp contrast to Christian views, especially in terms of individualism and reductionism.

Western psychology sometimes overemphasizes individualism, independence, autonomy, and personal happiness. Christianity, by contrast, insists that the chief end of humankind is to love God and neighbor (Matt 22:66–40). Biblical wisdom thus defines identity as inextricably bound to our atoning relationship with God, who breathed life into our bodies, offers grace and redemption through the life, death, and resurrection of Jesus Christ, and who longs to redeem all of creation. Our unity in Christ through baptism, according to Paul, transcends divisions of ethnicity and

---

16. Niebuhr, *Man's Nature*, 24.

social position (Rom 6:1-13; Gal 3:27-28). Indeed, Paul's metaphor of the church envisions a body of mutually dependent parts of which we are all indispensable members (1 Cor 12:12-14).

As a Christian, I am humbled to see how psychology can help bring about a more complete understanding of human beings who are created in the image of God, and, though fallen, are so loved by God that he took on human flesh and suffered and died that we might be reconciled to him.

Bibliography

Amsel, Nachum. *The Jewish Encyclopedia of Moral and Ethical Issues*. Northvale, NJ: Aronson, 1996.

Boring, Edwin G. *A History of Experimental Psychology*. New York: Appleton-Century-Crofts, 1929.

Davies, William David. *Paul and Rabbinic Judaism: Some Rabbinic Elements in Pauline Theology*. 4th ed. Philadelphia: Fortress, 1980.

Entwistle, David N. *Integrative Approaches to Psychology and Christianity: An Introduction to Worldview Issues, Philosophical Foundations, and Models of Integration*. 3rd ed. Eugene, OR: Wipf & Stock, 2015.

Entwistle, David N., and Stephen K. Moroney. "Integrative Perspectives on Human Flourishing: The *Imago Dei* and Positive Psychology." *Journal of Psychology and Theology* 39.4 (2011) 295–303.

Erickson, Millard J. *Christian Theology*. Grand Rapids: Baker, 1996.

Greenfield, Patricia M. "The Changing Psychology of Culture from 1800 through 2000." *Psychological Science* 24 (2013) 1722–31.

Kilner, John F. "Humanity in God's Image: Is the Image Really Damaged?" *Journal of the Evangelical Theological Society* 53.3 (2010) 601–17.

Koch, Sigmund. *Psychology in Human Context: Essays in Dissidence and Reconstruction*. Edited by David Finkelman. Chicago: University of Chicago Press, 1999.

Lewis, C. S. *Mere Christianity*. San Francisco: HarperOne, 1943.

———. *Miracles*. San Francisco: HarperOne, 1947.

Myers, David G., and C. Nathan DeWall. *Psychology*. 11th ed. New York: Worth, 2015.

Niebuhr, Reinhold. *Man's Nature and His Communities: Essays on the Dynamics and Enigmas of Man's Personal and Social Existence*. New York: Scribner's, 1965.

Phelps, Matthew P. "Imago Dei and Limited Creature: High and Low Views of Human Beings in Christianity and Cognitive Psychology." *Christian Scholar's Review* 33 (Spring 2004) 345–66.

Seligman, Martin E. P., and Mihaly Csikszentmihalyi. "Positive Psychology: An Introduction." *American Psychologist* 55.1 (2000) 5–14.

Skinner, B. F. *Beyond Freedom and Dignity*. New York: Knopf, 1971.

21

Sociology for People of Faith
... and Anyone
JAMES M. AULT JR.

Beginnings

I CAME TO SOCIOLOGY out of a commitment to help solve the problems in the world I saw around me, from my vantage point in the Northeastern United States in the 1960s. The civil rights movement, encountering violent pushback here and there, was morphing into the black power movement. Our nation's first Catholic president, John F. Kennedy, a symbol of change, was shot dead during a public parade in Dallas, Texas. And the Vietnam War was intensifying, stirring domestic divisions that would inflame the nation.

Entering Harvard College in 1964, I decided to major in Government, an area of study I thought might help prepare me to make a difference. My commitments, looking back, were carried by an ethic of love and service rooted in faith in God's love in Christ, instilled in me by my parents. My father was a Methodist minister, loved into the faith, he would say, by his Sunday school teachers in the Pennsylvania railroad town where he grew up and met my mother, his lifelong partner in ministry. My own faith as a praying youth was nurtured both in our household and in the various loving congregations my parents served during my childhood.

How amazing it was, then, that early on at Harvard I found myself an atheist, if I thought about it at all. And what is so remarkable about this profound transformation is how seamlessly and unnoticeably it took place, without soul-searching or intellectual battles. I just slipped into believing that God didn't exist but was simply a creation of the human imagination. How this profound transformation quietly took place defies simple explanation. Some light can be shed on it, however, by the discipline of sociology that shaped my vocation.

Sociology, or knowledge of the "social"—that is, human beings' relations with one another—overlaps with other social science disciplines, like political science, social psychology, economics, and social anthropology. They all, in different ways, and with different foci, study social relationships among human beings—how they work, their structures, and effects. Despite their substantial overlaps, these disciplines can exist on college campuses as tightly bordered communities paying little attention to one another. And all these disciplines, including sociology, have been wracked historically by at times bitterly contested internal divisions based on differences in outlook, method, and ideology. One prominent division in contemporary sociology, for example, is that between those favoring quantitative research methods using standardized questionnaires and those preferring ethnographic or historical research. My key teachers and I favored the latter.

Academic Journey

I initially became interested in Karl Marx's emphasis on class and class conflict in political life and the importance of the ways in which an economic surplus is appropriated from workers by a ruling class, whether capitalists from wage workers, aristocrats from peasants, chiefs from tribal people, or party chiefs from citizens.[1] This approach to understanding politics was embodied in exemplary ways by my great teacher at Harvard, Barrington Moore Jr. His magnum opus, *The Social Origins of Dictatorship and Democracy: Lord and Peasant in the Making of the Modern World*, sought to understand, through comparative historical analysis of class relations, why democracy emerged in some nations—like England, France, the United States, and India—and why dictatorships emerged in others—like Russia, Germany, Japan, and China.[2]

The Vietnam War gave direction to my studies, as it demonstrated that we Americans did not adequately understand the social bases of politics in what we then called the "underdeveloped" or "developing world." (Our

---

1. I did not embrace Marx's commitment to socialism and took no interest in his limited thinking about religion.

2. Moore, *Social Origins of Dictatorship and Democracy*.

extended military involvements in Iraq and Afghanistan show we still have not come far enough in that area.) I turned, then, to better understanding the "developing world" and ended up applying Moore's methods to understanding different paths of political development in the then-new nations of postcolonial Africa. I chose Africa because I had ended up in London, studying as an occasional student at the University of London's School of Oriental and African Studies, and wanted to spend time that year seeing and experiencing life on the ground in some part of the developing world.

After six months of traveling through East Africa to Zambia, the focus of my research, I returned to Massachusetts to begin doctoral studies in sociology at Brandeis University. Following my coursework, I returned to Zambia for a year of dissertation research, where I learned more lasting sociological lessons through life experience than by the archival research I was engaged in. Among other things, my time in Africa transformed my relationship with African-American life, showing me some of its distinct and valuable cultural roots. And it opened my eyes to the realities of kinship and family networks that helped me see similar realities in the United States at work in the "culture wars" coming to paralyze American politics.

Brandeis' Sociology Department provided the advantage of continued study with Barrington Moore and with one of his protégés, George Ross, who had joined its faculty. There I found among my fellow students tremendous colleagues so important in one's educational journey. They included gifted students of religion like Nancy Jay and Karen Fields, who would go on to retranslate and reinterpret Emile Durkheim's classic, *The Elementary Forms of Religious Life*, and Fatima Mernissi, a pioneering feminist scholar in the Arab world.

Under our brilliant teacher, Egon Bittner, we discovered new and fruitful ways to understand culture and society. Egon was born into a Jewish family in Czechoslovakia in 1921. As a teenager during the Holocaust, he lost his entire family and suffered brutal imprisonment in Auschwitz. After emigrating to the United States and resuming his studies, he became part of an innovative movement in sociology called "ethnomethodology," guided by the school of philosophical thought called phenomenology.[3]

"What is a phenomenon?" I still remember Egon asking us pointedly one day in class. "A phenomenon," he went on to explain, is "an event in the consciousness." And, since certain routine events in the consciousness are shaped by assumptions we humans carry and share with those we live and interact with—our family, neighbors, and our society—phenomena are a

---

3. See the founder of Ethnomethodology, Harold Garfinkel's *Studies in Ethnomethodology*.

place to witness and explore the workings of "culture." And it is the taken-for-grantedness of deeper layers of culture that hold its greatest power. This is evident in the fact that often it is only when we leave our familiar world of shared assumptions, say, to a foreign country, that we notice and discover that we, indeed, have something called "culture." Though we hadn't been aware of it, it was something shaping our very being, our routine interactions with all those around us, our very identity.

Deeper Understandings of Society and Culture

Egon Bittner's teachings brought me to a deeper understanding of culture, its concrete pervasiveness, yet often unnoticeable character, and the ways it is present and rooted in our everyday lives. Other conceptions of culture prevalent in sociology at the time, like that of Talcott Parsons, then at Harvard, characterized culture as a set of abstract social norms (or social rules) shaped by common values, all of which seemed to have a life of their own, functioning systematically together. They were often seen as things unto themselves rather than as an integral part of the agency of ordinary people in their daily lives, where culture is continually reproduced, and, in the process, continually changed in both conscious and unconscious ways. And in Parsons's more abstract conception, the depth of culture's taken-for-grantedness and its concrete presence tended to disappear.[4]

Bittner's teachings also clarified critical differences between the natural and social sciences, particularly the inherent limits on objectivity in the latter, a point made by Max Weber, the classical founder of modern sociology, in his concept of *Verstehen*, or understanding.[5] For example, to see a young woman seated in a group listening to a speaker suddenly raise her arm might prompt us to think that she wants to ask a question. But, if the speaker has just asked the audience about their loyalty to the Nazi party, the young woman's raised arm might take on an altogether different meaning, as a pledge to that cause. On the other hand, in a village meeting in a tribal society, the young woman's raised arm in the midst of a speech by a chief might be unthinkable as a request to ask a question, given the social norms of gender, eldership, and respect in such contexts. It might, then, be more accurately understood as an expression of hearty agreement or praise. And in a Pentecostal church her raised arm might be seen simply as an enthusiastic response to the Holy Spirit!

---

4. Cf. Parsons, *Social System*.
5. Weber, *Economy and Society*, 4.

The point here is that for any observer, or social scientist, to correctly identify the action of a raised arm for what it "objectively" is, they must understand what raising an arm in any of these contexts might mean and actually does mean to the young woman herself and those around her. They must build upon—and, therefore, partake of—the meanings of the young woman and those around her—their individual and collective assumptions—in order to understand the action for what it really is. That is, as Max Weber put it, all knowledge of social reality is inescapably subjective, and value-related, because it is based on the observer's understanding of the meant sense, the intention, of the actor, and, therefore, part and parcel of his or her culture. As the phenomenologist Alfred Schutz explained, "The thought objects constructed by the social scientist in order to grasp this social reality have to be founded upon the thought objects constructed by the common-sense thinking of men living their daily life within their social world."[6]

During my studies I noticed that most discussions among sociological theorists about the importance of Max Weber's concept of *Verstehen* to their discipline did not show an understanding of it in these deeper terms I learned from Egon Bittner and Alfred Schutz. This taught me an important lesson: that many practitioners of the discipline operate at superficial and often inadequate levels of understanding, not only of the classic thinkers they tout, but also the concrete realities they deal with in their research and teaching.

"Family-Value" Conflicts in American Life

In my own work, this deeper understanding of the nature of culture came into play when I discovered that a classic anthropological study of family and marriage, *Family and Social Network* by Elizabeth Bott, held perspectives that helped answer a longstanding question plaguing us sixties radicals: why are we white and middle-class?[7] Why did our sixties feminism, for example, which focused on transforming gender relations in family and personal life, arise among white professionals like us and have little appeal to working-class women or women of color?

I came to see that in an African-American or white working-class or small-business family living within a close-knit network of extended-family ties, women as housewives and mothers are more apt to rely on women relatives for help rather than their husbands, who might spend their weekends

---

6. Schutz, *Collected Papers*, 59.
7. Bott, *Family and Social Network*.

out fishing with their cousins or "the guys." These women would not see the need to join a "consciousness-raising" or "support group," the organizational bedrock of sixties feminism designed to relieve the social isolation white middle-class housewives generally experienced. Furthermore, their bonds of cooperation and mutual support as women kin—a source of their subtle yet substantial collective power—were grounded in traditional definitions of gender that sixties feminism was calling to overthrow.[8]

As I shifted my doctoral dissertation research from African politics to this subject in American politics, I soon realized that understanding why sixties feminism didn't appeal to some women was just a step removed from understanding why some women would militantly defend tradition in the family like those forming the popular base of socially conservative movements then fueling the New Right. In the early 1980s I got a postdoctoral fellowship from a new women's studies center at Brown University to do ethnographic research among New Right groups near my home in Northampton, Massachusetts, where I had come to teach sociology at Smith College. They included right-to-lifers, parents campaigning against sex education in a rustbelt mill town, conservative Catholics running a home school, and a Jerry Falwell-inspired fundamentalist Baptist church in Worcester, Massachusetts, founded by a pastor who was then vice president of the Massachusetts chapter of Falwell's Moral Majority.[9]

The fact that the New Right activists I met were from diverse religious backgrounds—Catholic, Jewish, Protestant, and other—and that in each religious tradition one could find their liberal opponents, suggested that something besides religion was at work in shaping their outlooks. All the social conservatives I met in the course of my research were formed, and most still lived within, a context of strong extended-family ties. Frank Valenti, the founding pastor of the fundamentalist church I studied, for example, was from a family of Italian immigrants who ran a construction business that employed multiple family members. The church grew largely by recruiting members through extended-family ties, like Falwell's own church had.[10]

---

8. For a full interpretation of how class differences in family structure affect support for sixties feminism, see Ault, "Class Differences in Family Structure."

9. For an account of this research and of my making an intimate documentary on this fundamentalist congregation, see Ault, *Spirit and Flesh*.

10. Falwell, *Strength for the Journey*, 182. NB: The name "Frank Valenti" is a pseudonym used in my book, *Spirit and Flesh*.

Sociological Practice in Documentary Filmmaking

As soon as I walked through the doors of Pastor Valenti's church, I saw a social world that helped make sense of new right enthusiasms. For that reason I thought it would be an important subject for a documentary film, given escalating conflicts in American life the Moral Majority and New Right represented at the time. Though I had always been interested in film, I never thought of making one. But, one of my close friends from Brandeis, Nancy Jay, was friends with the family of John Marshall, one of the pioneers of *cinéma vérité* documentary filmmaking in the United States. In *cinéma vérité* film the story is told not by narration, but by scenes of real life and stories told to camera by those involved. John lent his support to the project and introduced me to that genre of filmmaking.

Another challenge I faced was that I had not given much thought to religion. I turned to my close friends and colleagues from Brandeis, Nancy Jay and Karen Fields, by now both award-winning authors on religion, and asked them how best to portray faith in a documentary film.[11] "Show people facing challenges anyone can relate to," Karen and Nancy both wisely advised, "and then show them wrestling with those problems in terms of their faith." That is exactly what we did and it proved to be a beautiful formula for character-driven storytelling, as well as cross-cultural understanding.[12]

But, would the leaders of a Moral Majority church trust a sociologist educated at Harvard and Brandeis—"the churches and synagogues of secular humanism" as Pastor Valenti called such institutions—to make an intimate film about them for national broadcast on PBS? How that happened, and how these experiences ended up impacting my own faith journey can be found in my book, *Spirit and Flesh: Life in a Fundamentalist Baptist Church*.[13] Suffice it to say here, sociologically based understandings were key to persuading church leaders to open themselves up to our filming. It is only when subjects feel you understand what's important to them—what they are all about—that they feel comfortable sharing their intimate life stories on camera.

---

11. For example, Fields, *Revival and Rebellion*, and Jay, *Throughout Your Generations Forever*.

12. One reviewer said our final film, *Born Again*, was like a soap opera, but real, and set in a fundamentalist church. This approach proved effective also in my *African Christianity Rising* documentary film series exploring the sources and directions of Christianity's explosive growth in Africa and bringing viewers into the cultures and worldviews involved.

13. Ault, *Spirit and Flesh*.

Sociological reflections, for example, helped me understand things that continue to perplex liberals: like why conservatives can be Pro-Life while lauding military service. Liberals often think this obvious contradiction—being Pro-Life yet pro-war—simply confirms conservatives' untrustworthy, hypocritical character. However, in a world where people depend on family helping out even when it is inconvenient, or their own resources are wearing thin, opposition to abortion and support for military service go hand in hand, since both represent meeting family obligations of an ultimate kind. For men, this calls them to be willing, as a requirement of male honor, to risk sacrificing their lives for family and country—and, most immediately, for "brothers" in their own unit. For women it involves having and caring for that child even when it isn't convenient and requires personal sacrifice. Right-to-Lifers readily drew the connection between their opposition to abortion and wider duties to family in the maxim they frequently proclaimed: "If life isn't safe in the womb," they would declare, "it isn't safe in the nursing home!"

Deeper insights came later in my research, like understanding how fundamentalist churches can champion the kind of black-and-white moral absolutes liberals dismiss as rigid and unrealistic, yet attract adherents who find such church teachings eminently practical. Understandings came when I noticed that, even though Pastor Valenti vehemently preached "God hates divorce," I would then see him and other church members openly helping this or that woman leave or divorce her husband. Puzzled by these unspoken contradictions, I finally asked one member why they were helping Peggy divorce her husband. He looked at me nonsensically as if I were crazy to ask, and then, in exasperation, spit out the, to him, obvious explanation: "Everybody knows he's been pissing away the family income with his drugs and snowmobiles!"[14]

I soon realized that "everybody knows" was key here. In a family-based church community made up of extended families accustomed to sharing beyond the walls of nuclear family privacy—a community rife with gossip, rumor and talk—moral judgments about any specific situation took place against the background of a firm bed of shared knowledge about the concrete circumstances involved: what "everybody knows." For that reason, general rules, in this case against divorce, did not matter. And there was no need to clarify the rule that "God hates divorce," by adding "except under x, y, or z conditions." "God hates divorce" was less a hard-and-fast rule than a moral exhortation, a watchword, a saying. That is generally true also for how Bible verses came into use at Pastor Valenti's church. It never troubled

---

14. Ault, "What Liberal Delusions About Conservatism Teach," 8.

members that one verse might contradict another, since everybody would know when "turn the other cheek" was called for and when "an eye for an eye."[15] These habits of thought in their largely oral culture also help explain how they could easily pick what biblical verses best suited their preferred teachings in a given situation—and their own traditions—while ignoring others.

Yet, how different moral culture is among professionals living within loose-knit social networks, where, for example, colleagues generally don't know one another's families or one's different sets of friends or acquaintances. In these contexts, social norms cannot rest on a firm bed of common knowledge of specific people and events. Therefore, general rules loom larger in building a moral compass for life. Realistic rules are needed, for example, to clarify when divorce may be acceptable under x, y or z conditions.

Furthermore, in order to shape such realistic rules for life one naturally draws on general knowledge of relevant social realities. Raised with such habits of thought in our day-to-day practices of figuring out how to live rightly, we are primed to absorb the general, abstract world of academic learning about society, unlike those raised in village-like contexts like the members of Pastor Valenti's church. The latter are more at home in the personal and concrete, rather than the abstract and impersonal, in metaphor rather than concept—or like Jesus, perhaps, in parables rather than propositions. Therefore, they don't take as easily to forms of learning dependent on abstract generalizations prevalent in "higher learning." This is one obstacle formal education has yet to recognize and tackle in trying to educate many of the underserved in American life whose worlds and cultures are generally more shaped by such close-knit extended-family ties.

Reflections on Atheism and the Post-Enlightenment Outlook of the West

These reflections also shed light on the question I raised at the outset: how a faithful young person like myself could slip unnoticeably into atheism during his first year or so in college. Building a framework of sensible, realistic rules for life by drawing on knowledge accumulated in higher learning comes with certain foundational assumptions built into it.

The empirical sciences in the West were created by focusing solely on what one could see, feel, or touch, setting any and all spiritual realities aside for the purposes of their development. Such a methodological assumption remains simply that: an assumption, and something not proved—or even

15. For more examples and further discussion, see Ault, *Spirit and Flesh*, 186–200.

provable—by empirical science. However, when its findings become built into a framework for living, into a broader outlook or worldview, it naturally becomes a worldview that has no place for the workings of spirit or of God. In fact, any consideration of the work of God, or any spiritual entities, may be felt to hurt the integrity of a person's reasoned outlook. As the outspoken atheist Stephen Hawking once put it, "A physicist can't allow his calculations to be muddled by belief in a supernatural creator."[16] I believe this is a major reason why I, as a believing young person, in the process of building an outlook for life with resources from the empirical sciences of higher learning around me, unnoticeably slipped into atheism during my college years. And it represents, perhaps, an inexorable force drawing geographically mobile professionals toward an atheistic worldview, a worldview made up of propositions created with the assumption that spiritual realities are irrelevant or nonexistent.

What can be called this broader post-Enlightenment outlook of the West was embodied in how Christianity was delivered by western educated missionaries to much of the developing world. This became clear to me in an extensive documentary film project I undertook to explore the sources and directions of Christianity's explosive growth in Africa. According to Andrew Walls, a key consultant in the project and the world's leading scholar of Christianity's spread across cultures, while the post-Enlightenment outlook of the West allowed for certain crossings of the boundary between the spiritual and material worlds—like Jesus' virgin birth, for example—it excluded most effects of the spiritual world on the material one.[17]

"Why didn't the missionaries from Europe tell us that Jesus heals?" asked groups of early Ghanaian converts to Christianity after World War I upon reading a newsletter sent out by steamship from a faith-healing church in the United States. These conversations led to their creating new independent congregations which would eventually grow, through various splits, into what is now Ghana's largest church, the Church of Pentecost Ghana.[18] I came to see that healing and deliverance ministries, including exorcisms, were critical in unleashing Christianity's explosive growth in Africa across denominations, including Presbyterians, Anglicans, Catholics, etc.[19] I came to see also, at a deeper level, that certain spiritual forces felt to be at work in daily life in many African contexts—like curses, witchcraft, or the work of

16. From Stephen Hawking quoted in the film, *Theory of Everything*. Quoted by Robert Barron in his review "The Theory of Everything."

17. Andrew Walls interviewed by James Ault: Ault, "Andrew Walls."

18. Ault, *In the Feet of African Christians*, 16–17, citing Mohr.

19. See my *African Christianity Rising* films and Ault, *In the Feet of African Christians*.

evil spirits—could be better understood through sociological reflections on the subliminal forces at work in extended-family relationships critical for peoples' well-being and security.[20] On a recent production trip to Ghana I noticed that in driving all around its sprawling capitol city of Accra and its surroundings I never saw a single homeless person as they now are to be seen on the streets of cities all over the United States. And, another telling feature of Ghanaian society: nursing homes and senior living centers are virtually nonexistent. Extended family members care for their own and are expected to—and, hence, peoples' interest in having a good number of children.

The Homosexual Issue in Church and Society

My documentary film project on Christian growth in Africa also made me increasingly aware of how social realities shared by Africans and social conservatives in the United States would help us understand difficult conflicts over the issue of homosexuality arising in the world church and beyond. Where extended families are the building blocks of life, marriage generally involves less sharing and less intimacy than in the "companionate marriages" associated with isolated nuclear families. Instead, family life is typically divided into women's and men's worlds. At Pastor Valenti's church, for example, at men's gatherings, like Saturday morning prayer breakfast, one would typically hear men say things like "Women! Go figure!" about this or that puzzling thing "the other" gender might do. I remember one church member telling me that her attitude as a young woman contemplating marriage with a husband was "Go get one and see what you can get from him!"

In such contexts sex is not typically embraced as an important vehicle for cultivating emotional intimacy or romantic love in marriage. In fact, the growth of new models of marriage involving romantic love in the United States, points out historian Helen Horowitz, doesn't take place until the mid-19th century, and then among urban professionals in New York City.[21] Outside such narrow contexts sex as a vehicle for emotional intimacy wasn't generally seen as an important part of marriage. Rather than being part of your very identity, sex could be seen as just fun, as recreation done on the side. AIDS spread to East Tennessee and West Virginia, for example, by truck drivers having sex with gay prostitutes at truck stops and then returning to their families without any sense, in the main, that this was part of

---

20. Ault, *In the Feet of African Christians*.
21. Horowitz, *Rereading Sex*.

their identity.[22] Similar patterns can be found among aristocrats in Europe or the propertied upper class in the United States, where extended families congeal around family fortunes and are lived out on family estates and in upper-class men's and women's clubs. I remember, for example, a friend from such an upper-class family in New York City explaining to me that her father's mistress had signing privileges at their country club. And in much of sub-Saharan Africa, husbands and wives, while maintaining steadfast loyalties to one another and to their progeny and wider families, may live apart from one another for years. A Kenyan friend adept at noticing differences between culture "at home" and in the United States, where she now lives, pointed out that in Kenya you never see husbands and wives hugging each other in public.

If sex as a vehicle for emotional intimacy in marriage is not seen as important in such contexts, then, why does the issue of homosexuality raise such opposition? And why is something like gay marriage seen by some as a threat to the family? It is important to note that homosexual acts themselves—especially, but not only, if discrete—often do not raise objection; but publicly declared homosexual identity and the public right to marry can. In such contexts where women's and men's worlds prevail, same-sex ties often trump couple relationships. In a teenage gang of African-American women in one inner city neighborhood near me in western Massachusetts, for example, to become a member of the gang a girl must have sex with several guys among a list of neighborhood "studs" her "sisters" recognize. Notice, rather than being a vehicle to build emotional intimacy with the man involved, sex is used here to create bonds of mutual dependence among girl gangers. In such cultural contexts, how might making homosexual marriage legitimate be seen by these girl gangers, by their parents or by their community?

Or, to take a different example, in much of sub-Saharan Africa men and women usually sit separately at church or public meetings, not with their spouses. Men often walk hand-in-hand with one another freely on the streets, sharing physical affections of a purely fraternal kind. Now, imagine how the idea of homosexual marriage might be seen in any of these contexts of same-sex solidarities, where the opposite sex is seen as "other" and sex is not seen as a vehicle of emotional intimacy at the heart of marriage. In such contexts could not campaigns for homosexual rights and homosexual marriage be felt to threaten the kinds of family lives they know, families whose patterns of heterosexual procreation are felt to create security for their own future? Rather than seeing these people as hopeless homophobes,

---

22. Verghese, *My Own Country*.

more liberally minded Americans need to realize they are living in a different context, bearing in mind the seismic changes in gender and sexuality we in the United States experienced through the *tsunami* of the "sexual revolution," feminism, and so on, in the 1960's and 1970's. Such forces transformed many Americans' taken-for-granted assumptions about gender and sexuality. To cite one telling example, in just one decade centered on the 1970s we saw most of our colleges suddenly convert from being same-sex to co-educational institutions. We should also bear in mind that it was during this period that the divorce rate in the United States skyrocketed and that, even after it subsided, the United States still leads the world in divorce by far, pointing, perhaps, to some of the challenges modern marriage based on romantic love fueled by sexual intimacy holds.

Sociological reflections on changes in the nature of marriage engendered by dramatic differences in the wider fabric of family life should help us understand those who differ from us on issues of gay rights or gay marriage. Rather than dismissing one another as either hopeless homophobes, on the one hand, or intractable purveyors of sin, on the other, we can and should understand why others see these issues differently, given the social contexts of family life and marriage they live in and take for granted.

Conclusion

I hope these reflections help readers see the value of sociology in helping us think wisely about important problems we face: like family-value conflicts paralyzing our nation's politics, or different views of the spiritual world in global contexts, or conflicts over homosexual rights around the world. These are simply a few of the infinite number of important problems that cry out for better understanding and can benefit from insightful sociological reflection. But, a few caveats are in order before I close.

As I mentioned above, useful and profound insights in sociology are likely to come from deeper understandings of the nature of culture and society that only a minority of practitioners achieve. Operating at a more superficial level, many social scientists are swept up by fashionable waves in their disciplines marked often by novel terminology that soon becomes *de rigueur* to mark one as a *bona fide* member of a fashionable movement—for example, in "post-modernist" thought, terms like "discourse," "narrative," or "hybridity," come to mind.

Moreover, many social scientists, I've observed, are unaware of some of the most taken-for-granted elements of their own culture that differ from those of people outside their particular world, or "bubble," as some observers call it—for instance, their more individualistic nuclear family patterns versus the close-knit extended family ties commonly found among working-class, small-business and even upper-class folks described above, as well as being more widely found in Africa and other parts of the "two-thirds" world. Consequently academics generally hold decidedly more liberal views on the family-value issues dividing our nation, and are often puzzled by, and routinely misread, those not sharing those views. This is evident, among other things, in their repeated failures to predict, and take account of, the popular appeal of social conservatism in American politics.[23] Granted, such persistent blindness can perhaps be understood by recognizing that family life, where we typically end and begin each day, constitutes perhaps some of the most deeply taken-for-granted and, therefore, unnoticeable, elements of culture shaping our lives.

Furthermore, when social scientists frame and interpret standardized questionnaires, their ignorance of realities many of their subjects take for granted lead to errors in understanding subjects' responses and, therefore, in measurements they tabulate as "proof" of this or that generalization. While some realities are easier to measure than others, too many fall under the assessment Egon Bittner shared about quantitative research in class at Brandeis. "I'd like to be able to measure my results, like anyone," Egon admitted to us, but added tellingly, "I just don't think they often know what they're measuring."[24]

In addition, as heavy bearers of the post-Enlightenment culture of higher learning in the West, social scientists generally have no place for spiritual realities or God in their intellectual frameworks or personal worldviews. They are often puzzled by, and not infrequently look down upon, people of faith. And, perhaps given historic and ongoing battles they've experienced with those defending tradition in the United States, often from Christian standpoints, not a few have distinct prejudices against Christians

---

23. For an exploration of liberal academics' repeated misunderstandings of social conservatives, see Ault, "What Liberal Delusions About Conservatism Teach."

24. And there are times when both authors and their critics miss problems in what's being measured. Take just one example from a much-praised and otherwise insightful study on American politics based on quantitative research, Robert Putnam's *Bowling Alone*. Putnam seeks to measure the degree of "social connectedness" of people, versus their "social isolation" or "individualism," by how many voluntary associations they join. But the people I met at Pastor Valenti's church were so busy with their extended-family relationships, and with their "church family," that they had little time for becoming involved in any other voluntary associations, and generally did not. Were they more socially isolated or individualistic than the upper-middle-class housewife who gets involved in voluntary associations to free herself from the social isolation of home? No, on the contrary (Ault, *Spirit and Flesh*, 112n27).

per se. In my own journey as both an academic sociologist and documentary filmmaker, I've encountered such prejudices: from being pilloried by feminist colleagues for exploring reasons why some women were not into sixties feminism—and were even antifeminist—to seeing my documentary work on African Christianity brushed aside with a grimace by public broadcasters in the West uncomfortable with its matter-of-fact, non-dismissive portrayals of African Christians' spiritualties (even while some were championing documentaries featuring wildly distorted and purely negative portrayals of African Christians).[25]

I remember returning to attend the American Sociological Association's annual meeting to show my film *Born Again* on Pastor Valenti's church, and noticing there was a meeting of the Christian Sociological Association at the same time as my screening. I was curious to see what it represented. So, once I got my film running, I ran to their meeting and found 30-some young academics, mostly white but some of color, in intense conversation, mainly sharing "war stories" about the disapproving and even hostile reactions colleagues had when learning of their Christian faith. This was over a generation ago, but I continue to encounter and hear of such prejudices and intolerance in academic communities, leading me to continue to identify with, and find comfort in, Bob Dylan's song recounting similar prejudices he experienced, being booed offstage again and again because of his newfound faith in Christ in the 1970s. Dylan sings:

> And they, they look at me and frown,
> They'd like to drive me from this town,
> They don't want me around,
> 'Cause I believe in you.
>
> They show me to the door,
> They say, "Don't come back no more,"
> 'Cause I don't be like they'd like me to.
>
> And I walk out on my own,
> A thousand miles from home,
> But I don't feel alone,
> 'Cause I believe in you.[26]

---

25. Cf. the current head of the BBC for Religion championing *Saving Africa's Witch Children*, and several films following its example, including *Britain's Witch Children*.

26. Portions from Bob Dylan's song "I Believe in You" on his album *Slow Train Coming*, 1979. Written by Bob Dylan. Copyright ©1979 by Special Rider Music. All rights reserved. International copyright secured. Reprinted by permission.

So, the message from my journey, like Bob Dylan's, is: have faith; God is with you. Find those teachers and practitioners of social thought—whether sociologists, anthropologists, political scientists, philosophers or economists—who can help you understand its most profound and useful truths. And embrace colleagues with whom you can grow. And, above all perhaps, remember that your journey is not something you can predict or control. It remains in God's hands. When I think about my own journey—choosing to study African politics and carrying lessons from that experience (especially about extended-family life) to the Valenti's church, and eventually finding in documentary filmmaking satisfying work drawing not only on my sociology, but also on artistic sides of me set aside in higher learning, as well as on pastoral gifts inherited from my father—I find myself simply saying, "Thank you, God!"[27]

Bibliography

Ault, James M., Jr. "Andrew Walls—Effects of the Enlightenment on Christianity." www.vimeo.com/10825114.

———. "Class Differences in Family Structure and the Social Bases of Modern Feminism." PhD diss., Brandeis University, 1981.

———. *In the Feet of African Christians*. https://jamesault.wordpress.com/2010/12/03/in-the-feet-of-african-christians-exploring-christianitys-explosive-growth-in-africa-introduction-2/.

———. *Spirit and Flesh: Life in a Fundamentalist Baptist Church*. New York: Knopf, 2004.

———. "What Liberal Delusions about Conservatism Teach." *Society* 46.6 (2009). http://jamesault.com/wp-content/uploads/2013/03/liberal-delusions-10.1007_s12115-011-9500-1.pdf.

Barron, Robert. "The Theory of Everything: A God-Haunted Film." *Strange Notions* (blog), n.d. http://strangenotions.com/a-theory-of-everything-a-god-haunted-film/.

Bott, Elizabeth. *Family and Social Network*. 2nd ed. New York: Free Press, 1971.

Dylan, Bob. "I Believe in You." *Slow Train Coming*. Special Rider Music. New York: Colombia Records, 1979.

Falwell, Jerry. *Strength for the Journey: An Autobiography*. New York: Simon & Schuster, 1987.

Fields, Karen E. *Rivival and Rebellion in Colonial Central Africa*. Princeton: Princeton University Press, 1985.

Garfinkel, Harold. *Studies in Ethnomethodology*. Englewood Cliffs: Prentice Hall, 1967.

Horrowitz, Helen. *Rereading Sex: Battles over Sexual Knowledge and Suppression in Nineteenth-Century America*. New York: Knopf, 2002.

---

27. For an account of my return to faith in the wake of the release of our film *Born Again*, see Ault, *Spirit and Flesh*, 332–49.

Jay, Nancy. *Throughout Your Generations Forever: Sacrifice, Religion, and Paternity.* Chicago: University of Chicago Press, 1992.

Mohr, Adam. "Capitalism, Chaos, and Christian Healing: Faith Tabernacle Congregation in Southern Colonial Ghana, 1918–26." *Journal of African History* 52.1 (2011) 63–83.

Moore, Barrington, Jr. *Social Origins of Dictatorship and Democracy: Lord and Peasant in the Making of the Modern World.* Boston: Beacon, 1966.

Parsons, Talcott. *The Social System.* England: Routledge & Paul, 1951.

Schutz, Alfred. *Collected Papers, Vol. 1: The Problem of Social Reality.* The Hague: Nijhoff, 1967.

Verghese, Abraham. *My Own Country: A Doctor's Story.* New York: Random House, 1994.

Weber, Max. *Economy and Society: An Outline of Interpretive Sociology, Volume 1.* Edited by Guenther Roth and Claus Wittich. New York: Bedminster, 1968.

22

Anthropology's Contribution to Integrated Christian Wisdom

KERSTEN BAYT PRIEST

ANTHROPOLOGY IS THE ONLY academic discipline historically that endeavored to develop a science of the human based on a systematic focus on all of humankind, not just its Western variants. Indeed, anthropology invites us to study the lifeways of other societies in comparison with our own that we might grasp self-reflexively the richness of our humanity in the context of all humanity. As Christian educational institutions increasingly see themselves as preparing students for global engagement, one might naturally expect anthropology to be a core part of the curriculum. But this is seldom the case.

Indeed, there is often ambivalence, if not outright suspicion, of anthropology—and of sociology.[1] As a professor with advanced degrees in both anthropology (MA, University of South Carolina) and sociology (PhD, Loyola University), and who has taught anthropology and sociology over many years in a variety of institutions, I have often reflected on this ambivalence.

As a public-school-educated Californian, it was in my undergraduate major in Bible and theology at Columbia International University—and especially through the teaching of two favorite professors—that I gained the foundation that would shape my understanding of the issues. Professor "Buck" Hatch had studied anthropology and sociology at the University of Chicago in the 1940's, and President Robertson McQuilkin had read extensively in anthropology while a missionary in Japan. In my memory, both

---

1. Priest, "Value of Anthropology for Missiological Engagements," 27–42.

used similar approaches, although only McQuilkin's approach to Christian integration was articulated in print.[2]

Hatch, like fellow North Carolinian Billy Graham,[3] credited anthropology with helping him understand just how wrong his racial assumptions had been. And McQuilkin, like countless other missionaries,[4] was deeply and intuitively convinced of the profound value of anthropology for missionaries.[5] Unlike some theologians who've treated theology and anthropology purely as competing alternatives that Christians must choose between,[6] Hatch and McQuilkin celebrated the value of anthropology for helping Christians understand our humanity—both personal and communal. And yet McQuilkin also stressed the "noetic effects" of sin. That is, he taught that human sinfulness is present not only in our embodied activities, but in our intellectual endeavors. Thus, while highly valuing the social sciences, he stressed that we must never read the writings of social scientists as if those writings contain fully validated and completely reliable truth. In his view, Christians should begin all inquiry with the assumption that God is "the fundamental fact, the central equation, the integrating factor" for understanding the universe, including the human universe. Therefore, it follows that any intellectual enterprise which proceeds on the alternative assumption that there is no God will inevitably involve some degree of reality distortion.

As he explained, some arenas of knowledge have minimal overlap with the subject matter of Scripture, and thus pose less likelihood of conflict (e.g. mathematics). But Scripture extensively addresses human realities (greed, envy, anger, pride, violence, forgiveness, love, family, hospitality), which means there is extensive overlap in subject matter with the human sciences. And since the human sciences are less than purely objective, and since as sinners we are hardly neutral when we consider our own human condition, it should not surprise if we encounter social scientists making claims and assumptions that are less than fully congruent with biblical teaching. That is, the Christian engagement with the human sciences, McQuilkin insightfully suggested, would likely encounter both high levels of overlap in content and high potential for conflict.

---

2. McQuilkin, "Behavioral Sciences," 31–43.
3. Greer, "Change Will Come," 4–6.
4. Priest, "Anthropology and Missiology."
5. Priest and Barber, "Culture and the Missional Engagement."
6. Such as Milbank, *Theology and Social Theory* or McGrath, *Scientific Theology: Nature*, 15–18.

Importantly, McQuilkin and Hatch taught and modeled an approach to ethics, hermeneutics, and the human sciences—by way of a vital relationship with Jesus and with the Scriptures—as a core starting point for intellectual integration. Their claim: "What the Bible teaches should be trusted as true!"

But how exactly should the Christian appropriately engage anthropology? First, we must recognize that Christian ambivalence towards anthropology is not purely irrational.

Reasons for Ambivalence toward Anthropology

The following commonly articulated criticisms of anthropology illustrate the sort of issues involved.

Anthropology as Hostile to Christian Faith

If God is the starting point for knowledge, then any discipline that seems to repudiate God might naturally rouse ambivalence in Christians. And it is not hard to find evidence within early anthropology of anti-God or anti-religious sentiments.[7] When E. B. Tylor, often thought of as the "father" of modern anthropology, explained the value of studying primitive peoples, it was in terms of its value for discrediting theologians: "Theologians all to expose, 'tis the mission of primitive man."[8] When Sir James Frazer jettisoned his Scotch-Presbyterian roots and developed theories about magic being replaced by religion, which in turn would be replaced by modern science, this was hardly a neutral, objective paradigm of historical progression from the standpoint of evangelical Christian faith.[9] In his article "Religion and the Anthropologists," E. E. Evans-Pritchard indicated that most anthropologists were "bleakly hostile" toward the Christian faith. He says that, while a few British anthropologists (including himself) were Christians, "I do not know of a single person among the prominent . . . anthropologists of America at the present time who adheres to any faith."[10]

In short, any discipline is created and sustained through the activities of a social community with its own gate-keeping mechanisms, reward structures, and criteria of judgment. And that community may exercise,

---

7. Milbank, *Theology and Social Theory*.
8. Quoted in Taylor, *Beyond Explanation*, 17.
9. Larsen, *Slain God*, 37–79.
10. Evans-Pritchard, "Religion and the Anthropologists," 45.

transmit, and be characterized by values and commitments that are not purely rational and objective.[11] For anthropology in particular, this may well create challenges and tensions for Christians who wish to engage. In his recent comparison of academic disciplines, George Yancey finds high levels of prejudice against evangelical Christians in departments of anthropology, followed closely by departments of English.[12]

But human finitude and the noetic effects of sin have potential to affect scholarship in any discipline far beyond contexts where religious topics are in view, such that disciplines sometimes have unfortunate histories that permanently taint the discipline in the minds of many, making it difficult for them to appreciate all that the discipline truly has to offer.

Anthropology in Service of Colonial and Racial Projects

Consider, for example, one common objection to anthropology based on the historical role of anthropology in serving colonial and racial projects. When E. B. Tylor and others articulated paradigms for understanding cultural differences in developmental terms, with each society categorized and placed along a spectrum in terms of their supposed stage as savage, barbaric, or civilized, this rather conveniently served to justify colonial projects. "Civilized" societies could justify their interventions as helping less developed ethnic groups more quickly "evolve" toward civilization. Later functionalist approaches similarly proved remarkably convenient to colonial administrators. In both cases, early anthropological analyses obscured the dynamics of economic domination and oppression.

Similarly, when early anthropologists meticulously measured human bodies, bones, and skulls as part of evolutionary science, this contributed to "racial science"—racial ideologies justifying racial hierarchies, eugenics, and oppression, including at Harvard University and the Smithsonian.[13] Indeed, such anthropological writings and typologies directly and perniciously influenced biblical scholars into "reading modern racial ideologies back" into their "biblical interpretation."[14] For many who learn of this part of anthropology's history, it is the entire discipline they reject.

---

11. Smith, *Sacred Project of American Sociology*.
12. Yancey, *Compromising Scholarship*, 117.
13. Gould, *Mismeasure of Man*.
14. Priest and Nieves, "Conclusion," 324–27.

Assessing and Responding to This Ambivalence

So, if we grant that there are legitimate grounds for people to have ambivalence towards the discipline as it has functioned, then what are the implications?

Anthropology and Race

How should the historical role of anthropology in constructing and justifying racial and colonial hierarchies inform our engagement with the discipline? This should, at a minimum, provide a salutary reminder that even academics at elite institutions with a high degree of consensus are motivated beings whose finitude and sinfulness sometimes result in sustained bias and error. But there is no reason to think this is truer of anthropology than of any of the other human sciences or humanities. Whether the topic is race, gender, marriage or socialization, Christians should never assume that any of the human sciences are providing purely objective truth that should be exempted from searching critique.[15] The Christian doctrine of creation (including the idea of common human ancestry), for instance, should have immediately alerted Christian scholars of an earlier era to the problematic dimensions of eugenicist racial science.

But an adequate solution to bad anthropology must not rest exclusively on an appeal to theology (as John Milbank would seem to have it). Instead, it must also involve correctives carried out by anthropologists within the discipline of anthropology—and with methods and data suitable to the discipline. And indeed, it is precisely because of the research and writings of later anthropologists that we now know so much about the flaws of an earlier racial anthropology. A little-known story of collaboration between two towering figures in the human sciences, who resisted the racist, segregationist status quo of America's citizens, is worth recounting in order to illustrate the power of good anthropology to correct flawed understandings of the human.

As already mentioned, one lineage of early anthropologists gathered skulls and bones from around the world and argued that brain size and cranial shape varied by racial group and was correlated with intelligence, the less evolved having smaller round heads and the most advanced having larger elongated heads. They developed a racial "science" that located "Negroes" at the bottom and Caucasians at the top,[16] thus providing "scientific"

---

15. Smith, *Sacred Project of American Sociology*.
16. Gould, *Mismeasure of Man*; Meneses, "No Other Foundation," 535–45.

justification for the political and legal subjugation of African peoples in America. Native Americans, Chinese, Irish, and Eastern European Jewish immigrants, among others, suffered similar stigmatism within a constantly shifting derogatory racial classificatory system.[17]

But Franz Boas, a German Jewish anthropologist who came to be known as the "father of American anthropology," demonstrated the fallacious assumptions and flawed methods of earlier anthropologists. By measuring the heads of hundreds of immigrants from across Euro-American "racial" groups in a longitudinal inter-generational study, he demonstrated, for example, that environmental factors associated with better diet dramatically increased the body height and cranial size of those raised in America. That is, he showed that earlier anthropologists had been misconstruing variations impacted by environmental and dietary factors as if they were static race-based cranial attributes—cranial attributes which in turn were interpreted as measures of racial intelligence. Indeed, Boas, along with countless other anthropologists, insisted that physical features and measurements did not meaningfully explain cross-cultural differences.[18]

The Rebel of American Sociology Appeals to the Father of American Anthropology

So, when the preeminent Harvard-trained black sociologist W. E. B. Du Bois, with righteous academic indignation, sought help in counteracting racial "science" propagated by anthropologists and others, it was to anthropology—a better version of anthropology—that he turned. In 1905, he approached Boas about the possibility of collaborative research on African Americans similar to what Boas had carried out with other immigrant groups. Boas was interested and sought support for the project from Washington, DC funders. But those controlling research funds had little interest in a critique of racialized science.[19] Instead, the funds were channeled toward research on Native American peoples—funding that coincided with a national fascination at the time with the exotic.

Nevertheless, Du Bois was undeterred in his quest to interrogate the faulty racial assumptions upon which segregation as a social policy was based. Convinced of the potential value of anthropology, he continued to pursue Boas. Indeed, the convergence of Du Bois's and Boas's politically driven efforts to fight racism is worth recounting because it interrogates the

17. Gould, *Mismeasure of Man*; Paris, "Race," 22–24.
18. Zumwalt and Willis, *Franz Boas and W.E.B. Du Bois*, 52.
19. Zumwalt and Willis, *Franz Boas and W.E.B. Du Bois*, 44–48.

notion that anthropology, by definition, was a discipline solely in service of Empire.

On October 11, 1905, W. E. B. Du Bois invited Dr. Franz Boas of Columbia University to attend the eleventh Atlanta Conference for the Study of Negro Problems (May 29–30, 1906) to both present research and act as secretary. Du Bois was a professor at Atlanta University. He proposed that Boas also give the college's commencement address the following day and Boas agreed. The correspondence between these two brilliant morally motivated scholars is retold by African American anthropologist, William Shedrick Willis.[20] Their interdisciplinary vision of social science in service of humanity's suppressed people would be sparked during those days together.

Atlanta University was a unique institution in the deeply entrenched segregationist South, a South where lynchings were frequent. In fact, on September 22, 1906, thousands of white Atlanta residents rioted and beat any black person they encountered, killing more than twenty.[21] In stark contrast, Atlanta University had an interracial faculty and student body. Their resistance to prejudice and discrimination put them at odds with stalwart proponents of segregation in the state government, so that their efforts to receive state funding received minimal attention.[22] Yet, in their unique collegial space, black students and academics found supportive white collaborators.

When Boas arrived, he discovered a financially beleaguered but highly motivated group of African American academics doing serious research on subjects ranging from education to public health and pathology. Boas's conference paper received a lukewarm reception. However, graduation day went differently. Despite his accent and hour-long reading of historical and cultural facts, it was an electrifying success. Willis explains why:

> The commencement address was a remarkable attack on the doctrine of white supremacy, which held that black people were biologically inferior and were incapable of making contributions to white civilization. It was also a challenge to the prevailing belief in much of anthropology and in white-dominated science that racial identity determined cultural behavior. Boas attacked the racist notion of African savagery, another assumption called forth to deny black capacity to contribute to white civilization. He did this by describing the achievements of

---

20. Zumwalt and Willis, *Franz Boas and W.E.B. Du Bois*, 44–48.
21. Blum, *W.E.B. Du Bois: American Prophet*, 39.
22. Zumwalt and Willis, *Franz Boas and W.E.B. Du Bois*, 43.

blacks in pre-colonial Africa, achievements that were an "early and energetic" development in world culture.[23]

While Boas's suggestions regarding practical action for black enfranchisement were disappointing, and in the vein of Booker T. Washington's accommodationist approach, it was the detailed cultural knowledge that gave Du Bois and the large assembled audience a sense of pride and hope, grounded in ethnographic detail.

Boas's revised address was published in *The Bulletin*, a monthly publication of Atlanta University. It was not read or reviewed in white circles. However, the impact of Boas's anthropological knowledge, with its respectful, detail-rich, cross-cultural approach, countered common racial ideas propagated both popularly and in scholarly circles at the time, inspiring Du Bois to investigate thoroughly the cultural connection between Africa and America. He did just that in *The Negro* (1915) and in the data-rich detail of *Black Folk Then and Now* (1939). Du Bois credited the anthropologist Franz Boas for his "enlightenment" in the books he wrote and in his public addresses, such as the 1911 First Universal Races Congress in London.[24]

Unfortunately, without funding, Du Bois could not research on the scale that Boas had been able to. Although he soon left his university post, Du Bois took the tools of anthropology and applied them to his emerging concern with political engagement for social change both in the United States and Africa. He co-founded the National Association for the Advancement of Colored People (NAACP) and worked alongside other black intellectuals and activists to dismantle America's Jim Crow segregation. As editor of *The Crisis*, he systematically reported data on the almost weekly lynchings across America. African Americans became familiar with the wisdom of anthropology through Du Bois. And well-read white Christian leaders, even in the South, became aware of scientifically accurate anthropological understandings about African Americans.[25] However, the majority of white America would cling to quasi-scientific race ideology and racialized theology far into the twentieth century. It took the concerted effort of the NAACP and the Civil Rights movement to dismantle Jim Crow laws in the effort to erase the color line.

23. Zumwalt and Willis, *Franz Boas and W.E.B. Du Bois*, 57.

24. Zumwalt and Willis, *Franz Boas and W.E.B. Du Bois*, 67; Zuckerman, *Social Theory*, 26–29.

25. See, for example, Priest, "Sharing the Gospel," 129–30.

Human Science Wisdom and Christian Integration

In summary, although early anthropologists sometimes deployed their scholarship in service of racial and colonial projects, later scholars used the tools and strengths of anthropology to resist and dismantle pseudo-scientific racial projects. Some of these scholars were Christians. Most were not. And yet, as McQuilkin taught me, both Christians and non-Christians are able to arrive at solid understandings of many things through careful observation and logic. Like Abraham Kuyper before him, but with a different language, McQuilkin affirmed the notion of "common grace" as relevant to scholarship.

John Wesley, another whose writings have influenced me, argued that "Good men [even if they are not Christians] avoid sin from the love of virtue."[26] I suggest Boas, the secular anthropologist, and Du Bois, who was known to entwine Scripture throughout his morally engaged scholarship, *both demonstrated a virtuous* prophetic call to the American conscience, even though many of their contemporaries (both Christian and non-Christian) were blind to the structural injustice of American segregation.

Just as tools of anthropology, used by virtuous scholars, helped dismantle Jim Crow, tools of anthropology have been wisely wielded in the hands of deeply committed Christians. Historically, it was Christian missionaries who often came to deeply appreciate the value of anthropology for understanding the people with whom they served. Many such missionaries became anthropologists themselves. Missiology departments in places like Fuller Theological Seminary, Asbury Theological Seminary, and Trinity Evangelical Divinity School have often had professional anthropologists on their faculty, helping prepare career missionaries for cultural understandings that should inform their lives and ministry. But anthropology in service of career missions is only one of a number of possible directions that anthropology can take us. And the relationship of anthropology to career missions is a story others have told.[27]

Christian Anthropology at Work Today

But the anthropologically informed scholarship of most contemporary Christian anthropologists is not focused on educationally preparing missionaries for career service in distant places. In the remaining portion of this chapter, I will briefly point out a few fields in which Christian

---

26. Wesley, "Almost Christian," 2.
27. See Priest, "Anthropology and Missiology."

anthropologists are currently at work. I will illustrate how I have used anthropology in my own work, and will suggest some implications for Christian Higher Education.

The "anthropology of Christianity" is a growing subfield of scholars that includes Jewish, Catholic, secular, and evangelical Christians and that focuses on researching contemporary Christianities all over the world. Christian anthropologists that have been central participants in this emerging field of study include, for example, Brian Howell at Wheaton College, Naomi Haynes at the University of Edinburgh, Edwin Zehner at Walailak University (Thailand), and Marla Frederick of Harvard University.[28]

One emerging pattern of global Christian involvement has involved groups of Christians using brief vacation slots of time to travel around the world in various acts of service on short-term mission trips. A variety of Christian anthropologists have researched and written on this topic, including Robert Priest, Brian Howell, Edwin Zehner, Kevin Birth, and myself.

But in addition to ethnographic study of Christianity, Christian anthropologists have also worked to foster a discussion between theology and anthropology. For example, Derrick Lemons (University of Georgia), with funding from the John Templeton Foundation, has organized a working group of anthropologists and theologians to engage conversations on the value of theology to anthropologists and the value of anthropology for theologians, with a forthcoming edited book with Oxford University Press. Also with Templeton funding, Eloise Hiebert Meneses has led in the development of a Master's program in theological and cultural anthropology at Eastern University. This program provides summer scholarships for graduate anthropology students to carry out "ethnography through eyes of faith," and regularly holds colloquia with visiting anthropologists. It sponsors an online journal (*On Knowing Humanity Journal*)—and brings together anthropology and theology scholars for joint publications.[29]

Other Christian anthropologists study illness and health, human sexualities, poverty and poverty alleviation, global music, human trafficking, or race and ethnicity. Rather than attempt to summarize the full range of topics studied by Christian anthropologists, and what integration might look like for them, I will illustrate selectively from my own scholarship what integration has involved. My own anthropologically informed research has focused on the intersections of gender and religion, including women's involvement in short-term mission, in exercising leadership in religious contexts, and in addressing human trafficking. I have also focused repeatedly on realities

28. Frederick, *Between Sundays*.
29. Meneses and Bronkema, *On Knowing Humanity*.

related to the church and race. Since this paper gives a glimpse of earlier anthropological treatment of race, I will briefly summarize my own more recent involvements on this topic, embedded as they are in a community of Christian anthropologists with convergent concerns and research interests.

In South Carolina when I was pursuing a graduate degree in anthropology in the mid-1990's, racially motivated church burnings were regularly occurring, and controversy over the Confederate flag flying over the State capital building was intense. Local churches were, with few exceptions, either completely black or completely white. That is, 11 AM Sunday morning was truly the most segregated hour in Columbia! Like many Christians, my husband, anthropologist Robert (Bob) Priest, and I were concerned with the church's witness and influence in such a racially charged environment and decided as a family to join a welcoming Afro-Baptist church, where we learned new embodied forms of worship. Soon afterward, our pastor announced that our church would merge with a white Baptist church as a testimonial example to the wider Columbia community that unity in Christ was possible. Initial enthusiasm for the merger was high, and both pastors enthusiastically endorsed my request to be able to study the merger for my thesis research, which I carried out under the supervision of an African American anthropology mentor and professor. At that point, all of us optimistically thought we would have a positive story to tell. But over the next months, I observed that each community had differing worship practices (stepping and clapping, call and response, testifying) and differing criteria of judgment related to such practices and that these "out-of-awareness" differences contributed to profound misunderstandings, hurt feelings, and loss of trust—with the merger effort dissolving painfully. Worship practices defaulted to the white church's patterns. My MA thesis in anthropology at the University of South Carolina (1998) carefully analyzed the way in which these cultural practices and judgments contributed to the merger failure.

In the meantime, Bob was carrying out parallel research on another Columbia religious institution and the history of its engagement with segregation. Over the next couple of years, we discovered that all across the country there were other Christian anthropologists, as well as sociologists and historians, bringing the strengths of anthropology to bear on helping Christians think about how to engage racial divides and injustices. Bob submitted an initial proposal to Oxford University Press, which featured my master's research on this merger attempt as a sample chapter and proposed an edited volume that would help Christians and churches positively engage across racial lines. With a positive response from an Oxford editor, we were soon able to gather an ethnically diverse team of scholars, including theologians, biblical scholars, historians, psychologists, and sociologists, but with the largest number of contributors being anthropologists—Marla Frederick, Brian Howell, Jenell Paris, Robert Priest, Eloise Meneses, Michael Jindra, and myself (by this time I'd become a hybrid anthropologist/sociologist). We repeatedly met over three years to plan, read, comment on each other's chapters, and build our relationships. The book, *This Side of Heaven: Race, Ethnicity, and Christian Faith* was intended as an explicitly integrative volume that would feature anthropology prominently, but in positive relationship to biblical and theological studies, and to the other disciplines. I still use this book in courses I teach on diversity and inequality.

Indeed, scholars who recognize and use the power of qualitative/ethnographic research are fostering a growing research-based conversation—a nascent community that does reputable integration across Christian and secular academies *and* conforms to socially related commands of Scripture: "The LORD has told us what is good. What is required is this: to do what is just, to show constant love, and to live in humble fellowship with our God" (Mic 6:8).

Along the way, I have had the unique privilege to make my intellectual journey alongside a deeply committed husband and Christian anthropologist. Bob's publications have been an education.[30] I watched Bob sort his way through secular minefields to select research topics relevant to the questions a Christian would ask. His example encouraged me to do the same, especially while at the University of South Carolina. I learned courage—that it is worth choosing topics central to concerns of Christ and his kingdom. Together we spent almost two years in the Amazon during Bob's PhD field research and have since traveled to Peru, the Dominican Republic, and Kenya—collaborating with national Christian scholars in those locations—researching issues relevant to the global church. As a couple, we proofread and critique each other's writing, working strategically to integrate our knowledge in the human sciences.

An important insight I've also realized as a Christian anthropologist/sociologist is that the Christian community (and I include myself) can be quite blind to its socio-cultural position as "knower." Often our Biblical/theological knowledge is assumed to be "objective" without the recognition that even theology is shaped by the socio-cultural context from which theology is done. Good theology ought to approach the task of "knowing" with humility as much as any discipline, recognizing its own particular frames, emergent from particular historic socio-cultural contexts that can potentially distort the message of Scripture.[31] While specific claims of sociologists

---

30. Priest, "Missionary Elenctics," 291–315; Priest, "Missionary Positions," 29–68.
31. Tienou, "Samaritans."

or anthropologists need to be carefully considered and sometimes critiqued, framing theology and Biblical Studies as in principle opposed to anthropology/sociology is unproductive. It is precisely because Scripture is about *people,* situated in sociocultural contexts, and about God's work *within* those frames to bring redemption through his socio-historically located Son, that both explicit social teaching and profound human concepts are available to the Christian. Indeed, it is social and behavioral sciences, which can relevantly extend these teachings and concepts into our world today, providing invaluable knowledge for the church to further God's purposes on earth.

So, as Christian Higher Education administrators enthusiastically recruit more minority and international students, their strategy for "diversity" needs to be coupled with not only theological knowledge but also intentional commitment to clear cultural understandings. While good intentions can accomplish much, Scripture also warns: "It is not good to have zeal without knowledge, nor to be hasty and miss the way" (Prov 19:2). Life's journey alongside diverse people requires love *informed by* sophisticated cross-cultural understanding. In truth, cross-cultural misunderstandings and clashes will inevitably occur. And, when they do, anthropology, more than any other discipline, can provide helpful discipline-specific tools to identify culture shock and locate the natural ethnocentrism that so easily shades perceptions. This sort of wisdom goes beyond Human Resource approaches based on "compliance models" that teach tolerance in order to keep institutions in good legal standing. Proactive Christian anthropology seeks to create *intentionally diverse counter-cultural community.* Nurturing a campus where rich diversity can flourish requires proactive steps such as recruitment of diverse administration and faculty, expanded curriculum and course offerings, and respectful collaboration with social scientists and stakeholders of diversity. It can be done—recall the case of Atlanta University and Du Bois's collaborative work with the anthropologist, Franz Boas!

While anthropology's theoretical and methodological tools may be less familiar, they are nevertheless invaluable for personnel and professors in Christian Higher Education who also want to develop and expand excellent "global" academic and ministry programs. Research shows that semester abroad education and short-term mission trips are more wisely undertaken with anthropological preparation (c.f. *Effective Engagement in Short-term Missions: Doing it Right*).[32]

In conclusion, anthropology has much wisdom to contribute to authentic Christian discipleship. It provides a broad, holistic approach to understanding cultural variability within humanity across space and time.

---

32. Priest, *Effective Engagement in Short-term Missions.*

Its discipline-specific methodologies promote self-reflexivity, appreciation of other lifeways, and also recognition of humanity's brokenness. Finally, good anthropology commends thoughtful Christians to be empathetic and engaged *world* citizens—a prerequisite for authentic participation in our LORD's Great Commission (Matt 28:18–20).

Bibliography

Blum, Edward J. *W.E.B. Du Bois: American Prophet*. Philadelphia: University of Pennsylvania Press, 2007.
Evans-Pritchard, Edward. "Religion and the Anthropologists." In *Essays in Social Anthropology*, 29–45. New York: Free Press, 1963.
Frederick, Marla. *Between Sundays: Black Women and Everyday Struggles of Faith*. Berkeley: University of California Press, 2003.
Gould, Stephen J. *The Mismeasure of Man*. New York: Norton, 1981.
Greer, C. "Change Will Come When Our Hearts Change: An Interview with the Rev. Billy Graham." *Parade*, October 20, 1996.
Larsen, Timothy. *The Slain God: Anthropologists & the Christian Faith*. Oxford: Oxford University Press, 2014.
McGrath, Alister E. *Nature*. Vol. 1 of *Scientific Theology*. New York: T. & T. Clark, 2002.
McQuilkin, Robertson. "The Behavioral Sciences under the Authority of Scripture." *Journal of the Evangelical Theological Society* 20 (1977) 31–43.
Meneses, Eloise. "No Other Foundation: Establishing a Christian Anthropology." *Christian Scholar's Review* 29 (2000) 535–45.
Meneses, Eloise, and David Bronkema, eds. *On Knowing Humanity: Insights from Theology for Anthropology*. New York: Routledge, 2017.
Milbank, John. *Theology and Social Theory: Beyond Secular Reason*. Oxford: Blackwell, 1990.
Priest, Robert J. "Anthropology and Missiology: Reflections on the Relationship." In *Paradigm Shifts in Christian Witness: Insights from Anthropology, Communication, and Spiritual Power*, edited by Charles Van Engen, 23–32. Maryknoll: Orbis, 2008.
———. "Missionary Elentics: Conscience & Culture." *Missiology: An International Review* 22.3 (1994) 291–315.
———. "The Missionary Positions: Christian, Modernist, Post-modernist." *Current Anthropology* 42.1 (2001) 29–68.
———. "Sharing the Gospel in a Racially Segregated Society: The Case of Columbia Bible College, 1923–1963." In *This Side of Heaven: Race, Ethnicity and Christian Faith*, edited by Robert J. Priest and Alvaro L. Nieves, 129–39. Cambridge: Oxford University Press, 2007.
———. "The Value of Anthropology for Missiological Engagements with Context." *Missiology: An International Review* 43 (2015) 27–42.
Priest, Robert J., ed. *Effective Engagement in Short-Term Missions: Doing It Right*. Pasadena: William Carey Library, 2008.
Priest, Robert J., and Alvaro L. Nieves. "Conclusion." In *This Side of Heaven: Race, Ethnicity and Christian Faith*, edited by Robert J. Priest and Alvaro L. Nieves, 323–34. Cambridge: Oxford University Press, 2007.

Priest, Robert J., and Ron Barber Jr. "Culture and the Missional Engagement with Good and Evil: What We Learned About Contextualization from J. Robertson McQuilkin." In *Transformed from Glory to Glory: Celebrating the Legacy of J. Robertson McQuilkin*, edited by Christopher R. Little, 183–200. Fort Washington: CLC Publications, 2015.

Smith, Christian. *The Sacred Project of American Sociology*. New York: Oxford University Press, 2014.

Taylor, Mark Kline. *Beyond Explanation: Religious Dimensions in Cultural Anthropology*. Macon: Mercer University Press, 1986.

Tienou, Tite. "The Samaritans: A Biblical-Theological Mirror for Understanding Racial, Ethnic, and Religious Identity?" In *This Side of Heaven: Race, Ethnicity, and Christian Faith*, edited by Robert J. Priest and Alvaro L. Nieves, 211–22. Oxford: Oxford University Press, 2007.

Wesley, John. "The Almost Christian." http://www.pinpointevangelism.com/CheckYourself/Articles/JohnWesley-AlmostChristian.pdf.

Yancey, George. *Compromising Scholarship: Religious and Political Bias in American Higher Education*. Waco: Baylor University Press, 2011.

Zuckerman, Phil, ed. *The Social Theory of W.E.B. Du Bois*. Thousand Oaks: Pine Forage, 2004.

Zumwalt, Rosemary Levy, and William Shedrick Willis. *Franz Boas and W.E.B. Du Bois at Atlanta University, 1906*. Philadelphia: American Philosophical Society, 2008.

23

To Us and Through Us

A Theology of Business

KENMAN L. WONG

SEVERAL YEARS AGO, I posed the following question during the initial meeting of a graduate level class at Seattle Pacific University: What does faith have to do with business? One student scanned the room, then nervously raised his hand and averred, "To be honest, nothing that I can see. Christianity is about attaining heavenly riches while business is about the pursuit of earthly ones." Initially, the stark contrast he painted made me step back, but then I realized he was giving voice to thoughts that others in the class likely shared and that he was providing a near perfect setup to begin the term.

What indeed does the Christian faith (as defined by its *telos*, core convictions, and values) have to do with the world of commerce? Our prevailing cultural wisdom seems to suggest there is very little overlap. *USA Today* reduces business to "Money," the title of its middle section.[1] Frequent headlines (i.e., Wall Street scandals, VW's emissions cheating, Uber's high-tech efforts to skirt local laws) reinforce suspicions that despite lots of recent talk about "corporate citizenship," business is really about the unabated quest for wealth. Sadly, many Christians (like my former student), aside from a nod toward being a nicer, more honest person, have difficulty coming up with a more theologically satisfying answer.[2]

---

1. I am indebted to Scott Waalkes for pointing out this reductionistic title. See Waalkes. "Money or Business," 15–40.

2. For a more thorough discussion of the consequences of an erroneous theology of

The purpose of this essay is to establish the integral relationship between faith and business; that the latter is a venue of service to God and a great source of *spiritual* wealth and wisdom.[3] I will argue that truly "Christian" business calls for reimagining our entrepreneurial visions and objectives to create places where God's work can happen through us *and* to us.

I'd like to begin by examining my former student's beliefs about the relationship between faith and business. As I became acquainted with him during the term, it became clear that his church upbringing was like mine. He was raised in a tradition that was an unwitting carrier of Medieval Christianity's bifurcated view of work: clergy had noble "callings"/"vocations," while everyone else had mere "jobs."[4] This historical distinction has likely contributed to the unspoken belief that "secular" professions are only useful as platforms to share the gospel and/or to earn money to support the work of churches and missionaries. Although important, exclusively emphasizing these instrumental purposes of work communicates to those employed in "secular" professions that the actual work they do is devoid of intrinsic value to the kingdom and is outside of God's care and concern.

Congregants often receive these messages about work, subtly. For example, when someone leaves "secular" work to follow a call into "the ministry," celebrations ensue, whereas a pastor moving to another line of work raises concerns about scandal or burnout. Likewise, students leaving on summer missions trips are "commissioned," yet hands are rarely ceremonially laid upon those about to commence internships in architecture, technology, law, the arts, and engineering.

The perceived distance between a legitimate calling and *business* is even greater. Faith communities (especially churches and schools) that sanctify "secular" professions still frequently convey an unspoken assumption that if someone isn't called to work in the church ("full-time ministry"), he or she should go into a "helping" profession like health care, teaching, or counseling. Recently, my own university's career center sent out an invitation to an event where students could "find work that had *purpose*." Predictably, it was a job fair where only *non-profit* organizations were represented. Business seems to sit at the bottom of the vocational hierarchy and carries the status of "necessary evil." It is rarely seen as a legitimate expression of faith, a tool to advance God's work, or as an arena for spiritual formation.

The effects of these types of messages are far from negligible. A young executive I recently interviewed for a documentary film project shared

---

work/business, see Van Duzer, *Why Business Matters To God*.

3. I am indebted to Steve Garber for emphasizing use of the word integral as opposed to integration when discussing vocation. See Garber, *Visions of Vocation*.

4. For a more comprehensive discussion of the history of vocation, see Hardy, *Fabric of this World*.

that for most of her life she carried the burden of thinking that the only way she could please God was to serve as a missionary in remote locations with dangerous living conditions. Following college, she worked as a nurse. Over time, she discovered she was blessed with managerial talents and took positions in administration, landing as a Senior Executive in a health care organization that serves thousands of patients in a rural community. Even though she helped in the direct healing of patients as a nurse and now directs initiatives to improve patient outcomes and increase service to poor members of the community, until recently she was deeply burdened with the sense that she was only playing in the consolation bracket. It wasn't until she stumbled across a church that was offering a course on vocational theology that she came to see her daily work (innovating, planning, leading, creating efficiencies) as a mission for the kingdom.[5]

Her story is one that is familiar to many Christians who believe that only volunteer activities matter to God, leaving them with a bifurcated (Sunday vs. Monday) approach to their lives. Although my student couldn't see it at first, faith and business are already integral. Since business involves matters God cares deeply about, namely people, natural resources, and money (all frequently mentioned in the Bible), every business decision really is an expression of one's theology, well-formed or not.[6] For example, the way we treat customers and employees reflect our beliefs (or assumptions) about the extent to which our faith and our work are connected and about how much God values people.

The key issue then is intentionality. How do we make sure that our decisions align with good theology so that our work advances God's work in the world? A good place to start is with a correct understanding of the mission of God (*Missio Dei*). The overarching creation, fall, and redemption narrative and many passages of Scripture indicate that God's ongoing work involves more than just "saving souls." Rather, his mission is about *Shalom*, or the restoration of all that is broken. In fact, the word "world" in John 3:16 comes from the Greek word "*kosmos*" which means the entirety of creation. God desires for us to flourish by being in relationship with him (Deut 6:4–6; Matt 22:34–46; John 15:4), to have physical abundance (Exod 3:8; Eccl 2:24; 3:12; Joel 3:18; 1 Tim 6:17), and to live in right relationship with others and with nature (John 13:35; Rom 12:18; Col 3:12–15). Jesus' life exemplified this mission as he bridged the spiritual rift between God and humans, while also healing the sick and restoring relationships.

---

5. Personal interview with Emily Padula. May 29, 2017.

6. For a thoughtful discussion of how business decisions are reflections of theology, see Sherman, "Every Business Decision."

In light of this holistic understanding of mission, distinctions diminish between sacred and secular work. As the Protestant Reformers and many subsequent theologians have argued, all work, apart from the sinful, represent avenues to glorify God and advance his purposes. In our earthly work, we are called to serve as God's representatives on earth. We are conduits of common grace, or as Luther put it, we are the "masks" he hides behind to care for those he loves. Work is not just a platform for evangelism or to earn money to fund ministries, but a venue by which we can directly "seek the welfare of the city" (Jer 29:7).

When business people and organizations create, innovate, design, and efficiently distribute the goods and services we use, they play indispensable roles as "cocreators" in cultivating *Shalom* on earth.

Business also generates lots of employment. Work is not just essential for household incomes, but provides purpose in the lives of workers and enables their growth and development. Business also has the unique ability to build economic capital necessary to sustain governments, schools, and non-profits. Indeed, business generates forms of capital with social, political, and aesthetic benefits.[7] As Mark Meehan puts it, "It [business] is not a means to the end of ministry; when understood in a biblical framework, business is itself a redemptive process of ministry."[8] In other words, conceiving of business *as* mission is insufficient. Business *is* mission.

While all work has nobility and can meaningfully serve God's eternal purposes, we lament that business does not always positively affect society and its motives are not always altruistic. The cosmos, including the business sector, bears the staining effects of the fall with the result that our work reflects that brokenness. An honest look reveals that business is often not as it should be. Some businesses function with principles that disregard love of God and love of neighbor, so we can't advocate business without carefully clarifying what business should look like when conducted for the advancement of the kingdom of God.

For example, investors often demand short-term (quarterly) profitability over the well-being of key stakeholders. This leads to situations like we have with our current airline travel. Airlines used to compensate executives primarily on the basis of customer satisfaction ratings. Now their pay is driven almost exclusively by revenue[9] with the result that travelers suffer

---

7. For a more comprehensive discussion of the ways business serves God's purposes, see Van Duzer, *Why Business Matters to God* and Kenman Wong and Scott B. Rae, *Business for the Common Good*.

8. Meehan, "Business Is Mission," para. 4.

9. Schwartz, "Behind Discomforts in the Air."

profit-based cancellations, delayed flights, crammed seats, and added baggage fees.

Moreover, some business methods and outputs harm other forms of capital. For instance, goods and services that promote selfish consumerism and irresponsible materialism can divide people, erode social capital, put our environment at risk, and threaten our spiritual well-being. In other cases, businesses disregard health risks to the work force in order to offer consumers convenience and low prices. In worst case scenarios, businesses reduce employees to economic tools whose work is devoid of human agency and purpose, motivated by techniques that solely emphasize financial advancement.

In biblical theological terms, we are living "between the times," so that businesses often have to make decisions that seem less than perfect and yet still have to be made—greater of goods or lesser of evils kinds of decisions. Consider the situation faced by Hans and April Hess, the founders of Elevation Burger. The Hesses founded the chain with locations in the United States and the Middle East with the redemptive purposes of improving health and the environment and to help change the fast food industry by serving hamburgers made from organic beef and french fries cooked in olive oil. However, the Hesses faced a quandary when they contemplated a perfect alternative to sodas made with unhealthy high fructose corn syrup. After much deliberation, they made the difficult decision to continue serving the popular soda brands, because the profit helped subsidize the costs of the food, allowing the restaurant to remain price competitive:[10] Hans Hess explains:

> If you want to have a business that can sustain itself, then you have to make some of these compromises and choices. You can't let perfect be the enemy of the good. . . . So we still have soda fountains because that's how we, in some ways, make it financially. But at the same time, I would rather have somebody coming in and having an organic burger with that Coke rather than [going to] the other guys, where they're going to have the Coke and the factory burger.[11]

Despite tradeoffs, our present work can be animated (as is the Hesses) by a hopeful vision of a future time when all will be made whole (consummation). In addition to co-creation, we are partners with God in his work of renewal/redemption by reimagining business in the places where the fall is felt most. Starting with a different purpose, we are to reimagine business

---

10. Personal interviews with Hans Hess on March 10, 2017 and May 15, 2017.
11. Hess, "Elevation Burger," para. 7.

models and activities so that they more closely align with the kingdom, where the *primary* aim of business is no longer profit, but redemption and renewal. Profit is necessary to keep an organization afloat, finance growth and innovation, and reward investors; however, it's not the only goal or even the most important goal of business.

Instead, a significant aim should be life enhancing products and services that uphold other forms of capital (social, spiritual, and relational). As Lee Hardy puts it,[12]

> Simply having the right attitude . . . is not enough. One must take into the consideration the social content of one's work: Am I, in my job, making a positive contribution to community, am I helping to meet legitimate needs, am I somehow enhancing what is true, what is noble, and what is worthy in human life?

Customers are no longer to be viewed as sources of revenue, but as neighbors with whom true relationships should be built and whose best interests should be protected and prioritized. Employment is no longer only about a contractual agreement, but is a venue where people can fully live out their vocations and grow into their God intended fullness.

One organization that actively engages in re-imagining business as creative and redemptive work is San Francisco based Dayspring Technologies. Inspired by a talk at an Intervarsity Urbana Conference, Dayspring was founded by two recent college graduates with backgrounds in engineering (Chi-Ming Chien from Stanford) and computer science (Danny Fong from Berkeley). Dayspring sees itself as bearing witness to God's redeeming work in the marketplace. The company sees maximizing right relationships with the community, employees, and clients as key objectives. Initial funding came in the form of unsecured loans from members of the local church the two founders attended. Dayspring is small (just over twenty employees), but has done technology consulting for organizations like The North Face, Home Depot, The Golden State Warriors, and Mercy Corps. The company also developed a highly popular budgeting app.

On the surface, none of this is that unusual for a technology company. However, Dayspring is located in the Bayview neighborhood of San Francisco, a low-income, high crime neighborhood. So, it's not a place where tourists wander nor where image conscious tech firms locate their offices. For the founders and employees of Dayspring, however, moving to Bayview from a more traditional business district was intentional. The aim was to join the work God is already doing in renewing a poverty-stricken

---

12. Hardy, *Fabric of This World*, 95.

neighborhood. Dayspring shares a building with Redeemer Church where co-founder Danny Fong is now the pastor. Dayspring and Redeemer partner in multiple initiatives in the neighborhood including a loan fund (Neighbor Fund) to help other local businesses secure working capital and the launch of a prep school (Rise Academy). The company also supports other community initiatives like an entrepreneurship academy and a legal clinic.

In addition to the company's community investments, Dayspring seeks to offer products and services that work toward reconciliation and renewal. For example, its popular Goodbudget app (based upon the envelope system) seeks to help families be more fiscally and relationally whole through features that promote transparency. Even though it took a long period for the app to be financially self-sustaining, a freemium model is used because executives believe it's a better way to earn revenue than selling sensitive user data to advertisers.

Dayspring leadership is also committed to the well-being of employees. Chien strongly believes that the default should be that regular rhythms of rest (Sabbath) are built into the employment relationship. Rather than over-promising to acquire work, as is typical to do in consulting, Dayspring will make realistic bids (and risk losing them) on delivery dates to avoid overworking and overtaxing employees. The company is also committed to pay equity and boosting the ability of the lowest paid employees to afford to live in a very expensive area by maintaining a compressed pay ratio. Despite being in the technology business, Dayspring executives are also keenly aware of the alienating effect computers can have. To build community, employees are encouraged to get most of their work done together, physically present, in the office. Dayspring is an outstanding example of an organization that is reimagining business activities in light of God's restorative work.[13]

Wisdom Formation

In addition to being a means of participating in God's renewing work, business is also a venue that God uses for our spiritual formation. In other words, God's transforming work also happens to us. It may be especially welcoming news for those who feel stuck in their jobs and can't see any greater purpose beyond earning money to pay bills that one of the most important products of our work turns out to be us. Brother Lawrence gained much wisdom doing mundane and humble work (peeling potatoes) in the kitchen of a monastery, so one can easily imagine the possibilities in the challenging and

---

13. Personal interview with Chi-Ming Chien on February 13, 2017.

complex world of business.[14] Hans Hess (Elevation Burger) states: "What I found was that the business presented many, many, many opportunities to be conformed to the image of Christ in a suffering sense ... if that's the meaning of my business then I'll receive it. I don't want that (riches) to be the endpoint of the meaning of my business."[15]

To better our chances that formation (vs. malformation) occurs, however, the proceeding arguments matter greatly. It's important to first establish that God is present in and cares about our daily work. Then we can make work integral to our spiritual life and we can trust that he will use it for his purposes. Furthermore, the ends (purpose) of our work matters. Our loves become ordered (Augustine) in large part by what we spend our time pursuing.[16] In our daily work, we encounter and live into larger narratives about purpose, pursue objectives and engage with people, numbers and technology. These activities comprise what James K. A. Smith calls "cultural liturgies":[17]

> Liturgies—whether sacred or secular ... shape and constitute our identities by forming our most fundamental desires and our most basic attunement to the world. In short, liturgies make us certain kinds of people, and what defines us is what we love ... Liturgies aim our love to different ends precisely by training our hearts through our bodies. They prime us to approach the world in certain ways, to value certain things, to aim for certain goals, to pursue certain dreams, to work together on certain projects. In short, every liturgy constitutes a pedagogy that teach us in all sorts of precognitive ways, to be a certain kind of person.

If we see the purpose of our work as pursuing profit alone, for example, it is more likely that we will treat people as objects to be used rather than as neighbors to be loved. In so doing, we will be formed (or more accurately, malformed) into being a certain kind of person. Thus, a renewed understanding of business and how it fits into God's redemptive work is essential as our souls will be shaped accordingly.[18]

---

14. Brother Lawrence, *Practice of the Presence of God*.

15. Personal interview with Hans Hess on March 10, 2017.

16. Augustine thought of ethics as "rightly ordered love." See Augustine, *City of God*, 15.23.

17. Smith, *Desiring the Kingdom*, 25.

18. For a more comprehensive discussion on how business is a formational/ malformational activity see: Wong, Baker, and Franz, "Reimagining Business Education as Character Formation," 5–24.

How might God use our work in business to form us? While by no means exhaustive, the following represent a few ways. First, business often functions as a crucible to test, deepen, and refine our faith (defined here as "belief in things unseen" as opposed to a set of doctrines or moral convictions). Working in business often involves lots of uncertainty and risk taking. Whether launching a venture, hiring someone new, taking a product to market (or improving an old one) or accepting (or electing to pass up) a promotion or new opportunity, the outcome is unknowable. Risk taking can be an act of faith that forces us to trust God. To be certain, financial success is by no means promised. Rather, trusting that God will use any outcome for his purposes helps to strengthen our faith. In fact, it's often through failure that we are most vulnerable and thereby open to instruction and formation. Our worldly idols and sources of identity are stripped away and we can learn to surrender and grow most in our dependency on God.

Business also helps us develop forbearance and humility. In our work with others, whether peers, supervisors, subordinates, customers, or suppliers, conflicts will invariably arise because of differences in personality, management style, or competition. For example, a successor may falsely criticize your work to make his or her changes appear to be greater improvements than what they really are. These types of situations present us with opportunities to develop our capacities for forbearance, patience, and grace. The point here isn't to promote getting stepped on by colleagues but to encourage faithfulness and intentionality in our response. We can "fight fire with fire" or act in a way that enables God to shape us and that prioritizes right relationships.

Business can also help develop empathy and care for others. Developing and marketing products or services that help people truly flourish requires a great deal of careful attentiveness to what people need. For example, sales can be more than a mere transaction when salespersons show genuine empathy and care by asking questions, authentically listening, and then providing information to help the customer determine if a product or service will meet his or her needs. Acting more like a trusted advisor who looks out for the best interests of the customer, the salesperson truthfully represents the product or service, even if the eventual verdict is a "no sale."

Flow Automotive Companies (30+ dealerships in North Carolina and Virginia) is an example of a business in the negatively reputed world of automobile dealerships that practices a faith informed sales approach. Recognizing the expense cars represent to households (averaging about $33k in 2017) and the disastrous financial consequences of a mistake, CEO Don Flow is adamant that using leverage based on information inequities to sell cars is wrong. At his dealerships profit isn't earned based on what customers don't know, but upon superior service and value. Discovering that poor customers often pay more for a car, Flow dealerships moved to a fixed price model to insure justice. Sales people sign a covenant with strong ethical commitments and the entire operation is customer centric. Flow has similar practices while purchasing trade-ins, offering financing and repairing cars. The model seems to work well as customer reviews are very high.[19] Conducting business in this fashion (as opposed to high pressure sales) forms us into people who care for and honor others.

When approached with theological lenses, business is about something other than the focused pursuit of earthly riches. Spiritual treasures are moved to the center of the frame. Business is a means to participate in God's redemptive activity, as it transpires both in the world and in our own lives. God's work happens through us and to us. We are both conduits and recipients of common grace. Seen in this light, faith has everything to do with business.

Bibliography

Augustine. *The City of God against the Pagans*. Translated by W. W. Dyson. Cambridge: Cambridge University Press, 1998.

Erisman, Albert. "Don Flow: Ethics at Flow Automotive." http://ethix.org/2004/04/01/ethics-at-flow-automotive.

Garber, Steven. *Visions of Vocation: Common Grace for the Common Good*. Downers Grove: InterVarsity, 2014.

Hardy, Lee. *The Fabric of This World: Inquiries into Calling, Career Choice and the Design of Human Work*. Grand Rapids: Eerdmans, 1990.

Hess, Hans. "Elevation Burger, How Do You Change a Flawed Institution?" *Faith & Leadership* (blog), July 16, 2012. https://www.faithandleadership.com/elevation-burger-how-do-you-change-flawed-institution?page=full.

Lawrence, Brother. *The Practice of the Presence of God*. In *The Treasury of Christian Spiritual Classics: Complete and Unabridged with Contemporary Introductions*, 563–84. Nashville: Nelson, 1994.

Meehan, Mark. "Business Is Mission." https://www.cardus.ca/comment/article/2053/business-is-mission/.

Schwartz, Nelson. "Behind Discomforts in the Air: Wall Street's Pressure for Profit." *New York Times*, May 28, 2017.

Sherman, Amy L. "'Every Business Decision is a Theological Decision:' An Interview with CEO Eric Stumberg." *Flourish San Diego*, February 21, 2017. https://www.madetoflourish.org/resources/every-business-decision-theological-decision-interview-ceo-eric-stumberg/.

Smith, James K. A. *Desiring the Kingdom: Worship, Worldview and Cultural Formation*. Baker Academic, 2009.

19. Personal interview with Don Flow on May 9th, 2017. Also see Erisman, "Don Flow: Ethics at Flow Automotive."

Van Duzer, Jeff. *Why Business Matters To God*. Downers Grove: InterVarsity, 2010.

Waalkes, Scott. "Money or Business? A Case Study of Christian Virtue Ethics in Corporate Work." *Christian Scholars Review* 38.1 (Fall 2008) 15–40.

Wong, Kenman, and Scott B. Rae. *Business for the Common Good*. Grand Rapids: InterVarsity, 2011.

Wong, Kenman, et al. "Reimagining Business Education as Character Formation." *Christian Scholars Review* 45.1 (Fall 2015) 5–24.

24

Finding Wisdom in Economics
Hadley T. Mitchell

The origin of economic activity, like work itself, is prelapsarian. That is to say, even before the fall, Adam was given the responsibility "to work and keep the Garden of Eden" (Gen 2:15, ESV). Adam was put in charge of creation and thus was to be occupied with its well-being. Thus, from its inception, economics entails the notion of stewardship, the optimal utilization of one's resources. Only with the fall, and the consequent curse, would scarcity exist, as the ground was cursed to bring forth "thorns and thistles" and work itself became arduous, requiring "the sweat of your face in order to eat bread" (Gen 3:17).

The Blessing of Work

The divine sanction of work is found in the fourth commandment, properly called by John Murray[1] "the work commandment"—"Six days you shall labor and do all your work" (Exod 20:8), but the seventh day is to be a day of rest—both rest from our secular vocation and rest within our relationship with God, anticipating our future eternal rest.[2] The fourth commandment both sanctions and gives dignity to work, while it places our secular vocation within the context of our relationship with God and our duty to honor and glorify him. While the way we work can either be doxological or

---

1. Murray, *Principles of Conduct*, 82.
2. The first six days of Creation, God worked. In Genesis 2, on the 7th day, God rested. This paradigm from Genesis 3 is recalled in Exodus 20:5 to justify the divinely ordained weekly work/rest cycle.

self-focused, the fourth commandment is to remind us of the doxological use of work, as well as the need for rest in our lives. Even within our secular vocation, we should strive to use those gifts and abilities he has given us to his glory, rather than focus on our self-aggrandizement. The importance of this idea is that all Christians, not just the clergy, have a divine calling to their vocation, by which all Christians are to serve and honor God through their vocation, whatever it may be.

From the second generation of mankind onwards, the idea of specialization of work became manifest. The specialization of labor entails trade, the interaction of other producers within the community. This, in turn, entails economics. Both local commerce and international trade existed from the earliest of times, whether we consider the Mideanite Ishmaelites who sold Joseph as a slave to Potiphar in Egypt (Gen 37:25–26), or Solomon's Jerusalem, to which the "ships of Tarshish" brought "apes and peacocks" (1 Kgs 10:22). Apes and peacocks bespeak world trade; apes from East Africa, peacocks from India. Solomon's Jerusalem was thus involved in international trade. Furthermore, Solomon facilitated trade between Egypt and the Hittites, dwellers of what is now Turkey. Through these economic changes Israel prospered.

Commerce, in turn, leads to money. Money originally consisted of precious metals. With the death of Sarah (Gen 23), Abraham wanted to acquire the cave of Machpelah for a burial site. What occurs there is an interesting form of exchange, known as potlatching. With potlatching, each party wants to appear to out-give the other, potentially shaming the other if he fails to be adequately generous. Abraham went to the gate of the city, where commercial and legal transactions would occur, there meeting the owner, Ephron, in order to buy the cave. Ephron, having stated that it was worth four hundred shekels of silver, offered to give it to Abraham. Abraham weighed out the aforementioned price, "according to the weights current among the merchants" (Gen 23:16). Because this was 1200 years prior to the invention of coined money, he weighed out the appropriate amount of silver nuggets.

Adam's prelapsarian duty to work is consonant with the biblical teaching that God works. Indeed, the Judeo-Christian tradition teaches that God's work is threefold: the work of creation, providence (or sustaining the universe and governing all things), and redemption (providing salvation for his people). Engagement in work is an important aspect of being created in God's image. Work is thus a component of our human responsibility as stewards over creation and a potentially exhilarating and joyous way of serving and glorifying God. Work is inherently good. Unemployment, by contrast, is detrimental to both society and the welfare of individuals created in God's image.

Definition and History

The term "economics" comes from two Greek words: *oikos* (house) and *nomos* (law). In ancient Greece, economics was concerned with the proper stewardship of one's possessions, or the proper management of the household. While there were earlier contributions to the discipline of economics, most scholars date the 1776 publication of Adam Smith's *Wealth of Nations* as essentially being the beginning of economics as an academic discipline. Because this deist had been influenced in Newton's laws of mechanics, and thereby held to the idea of Natural Law, he sought to set forth the natural laws of commerce and economics. He taught that it was self-interest, and not the general notion of benevolence or the love of fellow man, that causes the market to function well.

> It is not from the benevolence of the butcher, the brewer, or the baker, that we expect our dinner, but their regard to their own interest. We address ourselves, not to their humanity, but to their self-love, and never talk to them of our own necessities but of their advantages. Nobody but a beggar [chooses] to depend chiefly upon the benevolence of his fellow citizens.[3]

Hence, the competition among butchers, using Smith's example, means for a butcher to retain a given customer's business, rather than losing that customer to the competition, he must give the best possible cut of meat at a lower price than his competitors. Thus, individual self-interest benefits society as a whole. The author of this principle of human self-interest was already a respected professor of moral philosophy, who had authored the highly acclaimed *Theory of Moral Sentiments* (1759).

Economics thus deals with the problem of having unlimited wants while facing a limited ability to satisfy those desires. Thus, having to make choices in a finite world leads to a fundamental notion in economics: *opportunity costs*—what we must give up in order to have something else. Opportunity costs apply to every area of one's life: time spent doing something as well as the monetary resources expended. To take one course at the university means that any different course offered at the same time can't be taken. To work for one firm entails not being available to work at another. Even the

---

3. Smith, *Inquiry into the Nature and Causes*, 27.

wedding vow of "forsaking all others" implies there's an opportunity cost in marrying your chosen spouse!

Economics conjures up images of greed, exploitation, and cutthroat capitalism. But that generalization is simplistic. Pure economics is a noble venture of faith and obedience (see Matt 25:14–30). Economics is the discipline of wise stewardship resources: time, money, talents and God-given abilities. Thus, even within a fallen world, wise economics can improve lives and raise standards of living for entire societies, while mitigating the suffering that comes with life in a fallen world–Joseph's wise economic counsel of Pharaoh prior to seven years of famine in Egypt is a classic biblical example (Gen 41).

Nearly two hundred fifty years after Adam Smith, technological changes, the free market system, and advanced legal structures have in fact elevated the standard of living within many regions in the world. Joseph Schumpeter has commented that the genius of capitalism is not making more silk stockings for the queen, but making them cheaply enough to be available to every factory girl.

Economics and Legal Integrity

Free-market economics requires legal protection in the form of property rights and secure contracts.[4] For individuals to be free to buy and sell, legal systems must protect economic freedom. Developments within jurisprudence, such as the law of contracts or the protection of property rights (starting with real property, conceptually being extended first to tangible property, and subsequently intangible property),[5] have facilitated the improvement in market systems. Technological innovations have facilitated better transportation and communication links. These technological improvements, leading initially to the Industrial Revolution, have led to a massive increase in the production of consumer and industrial goods thereby raising living standards significantly. Economics, together with appropriate developments in jurisprudence facilitating and protecting market systems gives us an explanation for this significant rise in standards of living.

Meanwhile, Alexander Gerschenkron's concept of "the advantage of backwardness"[6] explains how backward countries can catch up with the cutting-edge technology of the West. China, for example, has, in a couple

---

4. For example Oman, *Dignity of Commerce*.

5. Intangible property rights include such notions as patents or copyrights, rewarding inventors, authors, and composers or performers of music.

6. Gerschenkron, *Economic Backwardness in Historical Perspective*, 7.

of decades, achieved the economic status that took the United States and Europe a couple of centuries. This occurred because China didn't have to invent, for example, the automobile or the computer, but could start with existing technology. For example, not needing to renovate existing railways, China could start with cutting-edge technology to build the levitron train, capable of speeds up to 200 miles an hour.

Recently, the "hockey stick" model has emerged to explain the growth of world income over the centuries. Agnus Maddison,[7] calculating global standards of living since the time of Christ, found that from AD 0 to 1800 the annual incomes oscillated around $200—$300 per capita[8] in terms of the 1990 buying power of the US dollar. This was true regardless of context—whether ancient Rome, Middle Kingdom China, or medieval Muslim Babylon. Then, starting around 1800 AD, standards of living took off in the West, particularly as a consequence of the Industrial Revolution. Today, in Norway, for example, the per capita Gross Domestic Product[9] (GDP) is around $38 *per day*! This nearly horizontal per capita output persistent for centuries, which started to increase significantly around 1800 in the developed world, is known as the "hockey stick model." Thus, the big question is not "Why is the Third World so poor?" The more baffling question is "Why has much of the West become so prosperous compared to earlier stages of human history?"

AD 1800 corresponds with the advent of economics emerging as a discipline, starting with the writings of the Physiocrats[10] in late 18th-century France and the later publication of Adam Smith's 1776 *Wealth of Nations*. Gains in scientific knowledge, technological improvements, better defined property rights, and enforcement of the laws of contracts all contributed to economic advance. Maddison emphasizes the use of technology in the industrial revolution, resulting from progress in education and knowledge, starting in Britain in the early 19th century, spreading to the United States, France and other parts of Western Europe as factors significantly increasing per capita incomes and higher standards of living.

7. Maddison, *Contours of the World Economy*.

8. This includes consumption of self-produced goods and services, included in the calculation of economic output and consumption within the economy. Output was measured in terms of 1990 dollar prices.

9. The Gross Domestic Product is the total dollar value of all final goods and services produced within a country during the year, at current market values. To see what that means for the average person, we divide the GDP by the size of the population to get the average income, or the per capita GDP.

10. The Physiocrats was a short-lived school of economics which developed in France during the 1750s, towards the end of the *ancien* régime in France. The resistance to this school sealed the fate of the French monarchy.

Hernando de Soto's *The Mystery of Capital*[11] contends that one of the main reasons why the United States and Canada have a much more prosperous economy is due to our legal system inherited from Britain, which allows banks to make loans based upon collateral owned by borrowers. With collateral, there is less risk to the lender, so that they are more willing to lend. This means that a person can leverage earlier labor, invested in property to secure additional property, or to make new investments to expand business. Without such loans, businesses would have a hard time expanding. Thus, the notion of property rights, already emphasized in the Pentateuch,[12] is vital for our economic prosperity.

The concept of "possessions," or having property rights itself is a biblical one, implicit in and protected by the 8th commandment—"Thou shalt not steal" (Exod 20:15). Private property, then, is divinely sanctioned, further motivating one to work to enjoy the fruits of one's labor, thus enabling one to provide for one's family, as well as to be generous towards those in need.[13] Property rights are important, both as a motive to work to provide for their family, and as the consequent reward for having worked.[14]

With property rights, charity entails a person's willingly giving what that person has in order to help another. Although divinely ordained, property rights must also be defined by human civil law in order to be defended and maintained by courts or civil magistrates. *Those countries that have sound legal codes protecting property rights are generally those having the greatest prosperity*. In The United States, property rights are protected by the Fifth Amendment to the US Constitution, which provides for eminent domain.

This follows from the principle that people respond to rewards. Hard earned rewards stimulate productivity.[15] Human beings by nature do

---

11. de Soto, *Mystery of Capital*.

12. As Israel conquered the Promised Land under Joshua, the land was distributed by tribe, then by clans within those tribes, and finally by families within each clan. Land could not be sold "in perpetuity," but could either be redeemed by the family that sold it, or would revert, without cost, to the original owners or their heirs in the Year of Jubilee. This was to prevent the perpetual impoverishment of individuals and their descendants. Having land, in that agrarian society, was the means by which one could provide for their families.

13. The law of gleanings provided that the poor could go through the fields to harvest what was left behind after the harvesters had gathered the crops (see Ruth 2).

14. These truths explain the failure of socialism. Wherever socialism or communism has existed, it has led to lower living standards. Seventy years of communism in the Soviet Union failed to change this aspect of human nature.

15. Excessive taxation either reduces property rights or creates a disincentive to work. With a highly progressive income tax, individuals are less likely to work, seeking

not work for the good of the state the way they do for the interests that are front and center in their own lives; namely, their families, their local communities, and themselves. The Pilgrims, for example, pursued the ideals of Plato's *Republic* during their first year in New England by sharing land communally. They quickly discovered, however, that it didn't work. And they nearly starved as a consequence. The next year they divided the land and allowed each person to work for the well-being of their family. The change stimulated productivity resulting in the abundance we still commemorate at Thanksgiving.

Economics and a Healthy Society

Only work, only the actual production of goods and services, creates wealth. This means that private property rights are necessary to provide a sufficient reward for the hard work and innovative minds producing those goods or services. Thus the implications of the 8th commandment—"Thou shalt not steal"—entail that property rights, as being divinely authorized, must be respected and defended by legal means within the laws of a country for the general prosperity of that country to persist. Hence, countries whose laws respect private property prosper considerably more than those whose laws allow the redistribution of property at governmental hands.[16] This takes us back to the notion of self-interest, so central to Adam Smith's views.

There is a paradox here. Human nature requires a mechanism to restrain evil. We need government. Yet, over time, even the best governments suffer corruption. Paul, writing during the reign of Nero, enjoins us to "be subject to the governing authorities" (Rom 13:1, ESV) because God has given officials authority to rule. God therefore has sanctioned human government.

Going a step further, Paul warns: "Whoever resists the authorities, resists God." Thus, we as citizens must respect and honor those whom God has put into authority (Rom 13:7). So, the paradox is that we need governments

---

leisure instead. Likewise, those investing in businesses are less likely to expand their businesses, thereby not creating jobs for others. Yet, as privately owned businesses are generally much more efficient than state-owned businesses, taxing prosperous entrepreneurs at too high a rate discourages further investments. Fewer businesses means fewer jobs for those not able to create jobs for themselves.

16. This is why the Soviet Union ultimately collapsed. Gorbychev eventually recognized that people are not sufficiently motivated to work for the good of society. Human nature manifests itself in work for personal advancement. Adam Smith wisely understood the universal truth that markets enable people acting in their own self-interest to be simultaneously working for the well-being of society as a whole.

to limit sinful action; but human governments are themselves comprised of sinful human beings.

The United States has a noble Constitution. But the Constitution is useful only to the extent that it is respected and followed by those in power. The Constitutional Fathers, in general, recognized the tendency of those in government to become corrupt; that is why they provided for ammednments to the Constitution. Thus, the principle emerging from the Reformation applies to civil matters too—*semper Reformanda*. Just as the great reformers of the Reformation taught that the church ever needs to be reformed, so, too, must we be mindful to prevent corruption and excessive increases in governmental power. "Eternal vigilance is the price of liberty."

For these reasons a Christian discussion of economics must include conversation about government and political science.[17] Federalist Paper #51 said it well: "If we were angels, we would not need a government; if our politicians were angels, we would not need a constitution."

One of the great sources of progress, oddly enough, is failure. But it is precisely these failures that lead the determined inventor or innovator to try again and again until success is achieved. The commercial cleanser "409" has its name because it took 409 changes of ingredients to arrive at the right formula. Success often comes through learning what does *not* work. How many filaments did Thomas Edison try before he invented the light bulb?

Envious critics of entrepreneurial wealth fail to calculate the social benefits of economic advancement. Better products make for higher standards of living, more efficient work, and better infrastructures—imagine society without electric light or bathroom cleansers!

Originally, God blessed Adam and Eve with dominion and stewardship over creation. Relative to their needs, they had an abundance. But with disobedience and the fall, work became arduous and production declined.[18] Abundance gave way to scarcity due to moral corruption and God's curse upon the land.

Conclusion

How does economics aid in cultivating Christian wisdom necessary for discipleship? First, repentance should alter the believer's economic motives. Coveting, self-motivated consumerism, should give way to faithful,

---

17. This concern was addressed initially from a secular perspective by the so-called Virginia School of Economics, including the work of James Buchanan and Gordon Tullock. See Buchanan, *Economics and Ethics*.

18. Gen 3:17.

obedient, productive stewardship, as Jesus encourages in his parables on money usage (Matt 25:14–30). Second, God's love poured forth into the believer's heart (Rom 5:5) should evidence itself in generous sharing with those in need (see Eph 4:28; 2 Cor 8–9). Third, this spiritual transformation encourages productive work as an expression of worship. Properly understood and responsibly stewarded, robust economic activity can generate a benevolent prosperity for the advancement of God's work in the forms of evangelism and dicipleship. Fourth, wise economics can aid in mitigating some of the consequences of the fall. Robust economies produce better hospitals, advancements in medical technology, advancements in agricultural production, and as we have argued, increased opportunities and qualities of life for the poor.

Yet, increased wealth also has its dangers. Discipleship brings with it the awareness that followers of Jesus cannot worship God and mammon (Matt 6:24). As an act of discipleship, economics is subservient to the Lordship of Christ and is always careful to attribute ultimate worth to God alone—"to love the Lord our God with all our heart, soul, and strength" (Deut 6:5) and to honor God with the first fruits of our wealth (Prov 3:9–10). Deterring self-confidence and pride should always be a spirit of thanksgiving that honors God as the provider of all the resources necessary for our economic wellbeing. Without God's provision, there would be nothing to economize.

If "eternal vigilance is the price of liberty," so much the more for God's people as we maintain our spiritual priorities. We are to "seek first the Kingdom of God, and all these things will be added" in God's time as we progress toward eternal life in the new heavens and the new earth. To work hard and to be productive, even taking calculated risks, is eternally wise. Stewardship of time, effort, and material resources is the responsibility of every follower of Jesus, as we seek to give back to God thirty, sixty, and one hundredfold. Economics thus is an essential tool that Christians can and must employ as we endeavor with the Westminster Shorter Catechism "to glorify God and to enjoy him forever."

Bibliography

Buchanan, James M. *The Economics and Ethics of Constitutional Order*. Ann Arbor: University of Michigan Press, 1991.

de Soto, Hernando. *The Mystery of Capital: Why Capitalism Triumphs in the West and Fails Everywhere Else*. New York: Basic Books, 2000.

Gerschenkron, Alexander. *Economic Backwardness in Historical Perspective: A Book of Essays*. Cambridge: Belknap, 1962.

Maddison, Agnus. *Contours of the World Economy, 1–2030 AD: Essays in Macro-Economic History*. New York: Oxford University Press, 2007.

Murray, John. *Principles of Conduct*. Grand Rapids: Eerdmans, 1971.

Oman, Nathan B. *The Dignity of Commerce: Markets and the Moral Foundations of Contract Law*. Chicago: University of Chicago Press, 2016.

Smith, Adam. *An Inquiry into the Nature and Causes of the Wealth of Nations*. Vol. 2 of *The R. H. Campbell, R. H. and A. S. Skinner, Glasgow Edition of the Works and Correspondence of Adam Smith*. Edited by W. B. Todd. Oxford: Clarendon, 1776.

25

Transformation and Restoration through Athletics and Kinesiology
Dave Wolf

OF THIS I WAS sure: I will *never* coach. Yet here I am beginning my twenty-seventh year as the Head Men's Soccer Coach and Associate Professor of Kinesiology at Westmont College (Santa Barbara, CA). How in the world did this happen? One thing is certain; the road has been unconventional, if not completely backwards. Typical vocational journeys begin with a period of preparation followed by résumé distributions, job searches, interviews, and candidate visitations. In my case, it was the exact opposite: the opportunities presented themselves first, and then I went about the business of trying to understand what in the world I was actually charged to do in the very fields I had once adamantly foreclosed.

The more important question is what have I learned along the way? Deeper still could be the question of what wisdom reveals within these reluctantly assumed disciplines. Furthermore, are they in fact two distinct disciplines (coaching an intercollegiate athletic team and teaching Kinesiology), or can they be considered together? I have often heard it said that "coaching is teaching" and to a large degree I believe that statement is true. It is also true that I'm both more comfortable and confident in the coaching role, a place where I experience a deep sense of God's call on my life—*to bring the aroma of Jesus Christ to the sport of soccer (or football, as the world calls it)*.

I have chosen to look at each of these areas separately before showing their commonalities and supportive interrelationships. The context for both will be the Christian Liberal Arts program at Westmont, where I've coached and taught since 1991. Westmont has been a marvelous place to coach and teach. I've been blessed with spectacular departmental colleagues who genuinely care for the student athletes in their charge. Four in particular, Kinesiology Department Chair, Chris Milner; Head Men's Basketball Coach, John Moore; Head Men's Baseball Coach, Robert Ruiz; and Head Men's and Women's Cross Country/Track and Field Coach, Russell Smelley, have each made significant contributions to this chapter. I'm grateful for their insights, encouragement, and friendship.

Athletics and Coaching: The Goals of Character Transformation and Spiritual Growth

Recent history has introduced to college sports the phrase "one and done." If you're unfamiliar, the phrase refers to elite athletes deciding ahead of time to attend college for one year to train under an elite coach as preparation for a professional sports career. For their part, the sponsoring universities compete for the notoriety of national championships by hosting professional caliber athletes for one year of intense competition prior to the professional draft; hence, the phrase "one and done." The advantage of the "one and done" experience is that it puts players on the fast track to lucrative professional contracts, while minimizing the risk of career-ending injuries. College in these cases is a *de facto* minor league system for athletes. Its allure is understandable for economically challenged recruits, whose talents offer the hope of spectacular wealth.

"One and done" is thus a success and wealth strategy that presupposes the dispensability of educational integrity and character growth prior to professional careers.

But is it wise? Is it a wise best practice for the athletes and their families? Is it wise for even the most talented, who, like all of us, will have lives after the decline of their youth and physical vitality? And is "one and done" wise for institutions that purportedly exist for the purpose of *education*—an enterprise accomplished by the virtues of discipline, delayed gratification, sustained hard work, and the compounding benefits of long-term investments? Is "one and done" worth the forfeit of the university's soul and the individual's character?

Economically, perhaps, in the short-term. *But what about in every other way—the ways that make us human and the ways that make us permanently capable?*

A substantive argument can be made that four years of comprehensive, character-cultivating education at a solid university can accomplish more for the long-term best interests of a recruit (and their families) than millions of dollars in instant cash. This is because the acquisition of wisdom is priceless and its value is timeless. As Proverbs attests, wisdom's "profit is better than the profit of silver, and its gain than fine gold. She is more precious than jewels; and nothing you desire compares with her. Long life is in her right hand; in her left hand are riches and honor" (Prov 3:13–16). Indeed, wisdom acquired through character transformation and spiritual growth is essential for a noble life of productive, meaningful long-term success—what the philosophers call "human flourishing." But enduring wisdom isn't acquired instantly. In sports, as in every other dimension of life, wisdom takes its time, always prioritizing best practices for the best eternal outcomes.

Why was I once opposed to the thought of coaching? In many ways, I had already experienced college athletics in its purest and finest form at Wheaton College in Wheaton, Illinois. Wonderful coaches who were a terrific blend of mature role models and demanding leaders made coaching an attractive, commendable career. Talented teammates, who worked extremely hard, took every aspect of their lives seriously, and who became lifelong friends made the environment of athletics a desirable future. And an institution that was beautifully balanced, structurally elite, and deeply committed to authentic faith cultivation and integration made coaching a holistic calling worthy of a life's commitment. To top it off, while none of those qualities and attributes is a guarantee for competitive statistical success, we had that too, winning the 1984 NCAA Division III National Championship and amassing a 39-game unbeaten streak over a two-year period. Winning was routine.

Despite this wonderful experience, I was determined to go a completely different direction . . . or so I thought. To be blunt, the primary reason was sheer arrogance. My mindset was, "What if I ever have to coach someone who doesn't work as hard as I do? No thanks."

At some point early on in my college experience, the notion of trying to play soccer professionally started to gain traction. My appetite for training was insatiable. While I trained morning, noon, and night, I concurrently and somewhat subconsciously began developing a "blind spot" disdain for others who lacked that type of focus and intensity (my sister diagnosed me as "obsessive compulsive"). At the time, I considered my thoughts entirely rational. But now I recognize that I had become, at best, dangerously nearsighted and, at worst, exceedingly condescending. I can't imagine I was much fun to be around during this stage of my life.

Unknowingly, I was about to have a wakeup call to the reality of one of the treasures of wisdom that I've grown to value deeply as I retrace my spiritual growth. Growth is painful. And it's not always physical.

The Wisdom of Exposure: The Truth of One's Identity

Boy did I find this out. Bret Hall was an assistant coach at Wheaton during my playing days and a man that I absolutely idolized. Having also played at Wheaton, Bret went on to have a wonderful professional playing career, most notably with the Chicago Sting of the North American Soccer League (NASL). I wanted to be him, and I took literally everything he encouraged me to do in my training. And train I did. Here I was a student-athlete at a wonderful Christian Liberal Arts College with my own father on the teaching faculty in the Religious Studies department. Yet all I wanted to do was chase around 12 pounds of compressed air on a soccer pitch.

The summer prior to my junior year Bret called, asking to have a chat. I was excited to meet with him, anticipating a pat or two on the back and possibly a ramping up of my training as I continued to pursue my goals and ambitions. The conversation unfolded differently than I could have ever imagined and, within five minutes I was weeping uncontrollably at Bret's kitchen table. Exposed. He had the courage to point out who I really was, and arrogance was at the core. That five-minute conversation changed the course of my life.

I returned to Wheaton that fall a different person. For starters, I was just a better teammate. Secondly, I had a greater awareness of others and saw more than just my own agenda. I was also sensing, possibly for the very first time, that God was "at work," and that my athletic experience would be foundational to that. I signed a professional contract almost immediately after my senior year, and embarked on a very modest six-season professional indoor soccer career (the only form of "professional" soccer that existed at that time in the United States). Morally and ethically, it was a world I was not ready for. However, for good or for ill, I had developed strong convictions about who I was and what I was aiming for. Those convictions undoubtedly helped mitigate the parts of me that were naïve and inexperienced. Subtly, however, I was also adhering to a form of conditional love; i.e., "If I behave, then God will give me what I want." That would prove to be very dangerous for me.

After my first indoor season (1985–86), I received an invitation from my former Wheaton teammate Tom Engstrom, who had just been named Head Men's Soccer Coach at King's College in Briarcliff Manor, New York. I believe at the time Tom was the youngest head coach in college soccer. His request was simple: "Come help me run my first training camp at King's." What I heard was, "Hey, come on out to New York with me and you can train for 10 days in preparation for your next indoor season." This trip turned out to be another pivotal moment in my journey. And, similar to my conversation with Bret, I was about to experience something I was not anticipating and did not see coming.

The Wisdom of Diversity: The Realization that Not Everyone Has to Be Exactly Like Me

Upon my arrival, I very quickly found myself forgetting about my own agenda, my own training protocol, and really locked in on Tom. I watched him, at 22 years of age, interact with this incredibly diverse collection of players, and I began to learn a critical lesson: not everyone has to be exactly like me. Those ten days taught me about the individual journeys that ALL of us are on, and the poignant ways that coaching, athletics, and competition can be as a laboratory for transformational growth.

My nomadic indoor career took me to a few different cities and finally came to earth with a thud in the spring of 1991. The day my final season ended I got engaged to Jill Robin Barber and shortly thereafter received a phone call from the Westmont Soccer Coach, Bob Fortosis, who was in the midst of accepting a new position with the World Cup organizing committee (an event that the United States would host in 1994). Three months later I arrived in Santa Barbara as the new coach of the Westmont Warriors. I was twenty-seven years old, engaged, in California of all places, and embarking on the very career that I once defied. Like professional indoor soccer, I was once again wading into waters way over my head.

Westmont was in many ways a convergence of the two worlds from which I had just come—the immensely meaningful world of college athletics at a Christian Liberal Arts institution, where the claims of Christ were integrated into every facet of campus life, combined with the exceedingly secular world of professional soccer, where the criteria for judgment were clear, singular, and coldly competitive. While many of the student athletes I've had the privilege of coaching over the years were (and are) deeply committed to their faith and the pursuit of a Christ centered worldview, many did not consider themselves "believers" in the evangelical tradition, although most were open and receptive to the conversations that were taking place. Westmont provided the platform to live out my own faith within the context of God's call on my life, while also providing the opportunity to recruit student athletes from a broad diversity of backgrounds and faith journeys. To this day I am encouraged and motivated by this reality; inspired by Westmont legend Ruth Kerr's vision, the current leadership of Westmont continues to cultivate this incredibly dynamic reality.

As I reflect upon these past twenty-six years, much could be said. However, I keep returning to a singular theme.

The Wisdom of Transformation

Let me first say that I don't believe that intercollegiate athletics and the world of coaching is the only place transformation and life change can happen, either at Westmont or the many, many outstanding Christian Liberal Arts colleges and universities across this country. There are amazing coaches, teachers, and educators in every corner of the globe and Christian growth can happen through student maturation in each field. That said, I would still maintain that the athletic venture, when optimally engaged, is unique and worthy of affirmation as an *educational* enterprise.

I believe that there are frequent crossroads in athletics where athletes and coaches have to decide whether to avoid or embrace transformational challenges. These crossroads are unique opportunities for personal growth and character advancement. They are tests every bit as important as final exams. For how students and coaches respond to these challenges largely determines how our characters change, whether positively or negatively. While the soccer pitch might strike outsiders as a shallow or artificial crucible for developing Christ-like character—the restoration of the *imago Dei*—it's important to remember that in the mind of the college athlete the stakes involved are serious, personal, and deeply psychological. They are also corporate, relational, and sociological—performed as they are in a team setting in a social context with corporate goals.

For devoted athletes, intense competition at the college level is a refining fire, a furnace where pretense and selfish ambition are challenged to give way to patience, humility, resolve, endurance, self-control, unselfishness, sensitivity to the welfare of others, community, and eternal perspective. Pedagogically, athletics is unique in that things happen that competitors never forget—in games, in practices, in the training room, at halftime, in celebration, and in defeat. To be sure, the changes are not always positive. As I mentioned above, the athlete or coach always faces the temptation to act or speak rashly—in which cases the character risks a downward spiral. Yet the potential is always there for just the opposite—marked positive refinement. And that's what makes ours a unique and special educational discipline. The hard lessons learned in athletics transfer into every walk of life; hence, the New Testament's inclusion of athletic illustrations (1 Cor 9:24–26; 2 Tim 2:5; Heb 12:1).

Allow me to offer a few more reasons why this is indeed the case. First, athletes often *suffer* physically. Striving towards, reaching, and even choosing to remain at the outer limits of one's physical capacity is grueling. However, the knowledge of what one is capable of achieving is not only priceless but also transferrable to almost every other facet of human existence. Without making comparative claims at the risk of reducing God's atoning work to something trite or secular, it's significant that the incarnate Christ and the Suffering Savior combined in the person of Jesus. He accomplished his ultimate victory through suffering. The observation is a reminder that suffering is the expected lot of those desiring increased conformity to the character of our Lord, who accomplished his ultimate mission with unyielding resolve and an invincible faith that the final victory would prove worthy of the pain he endured. Indeed, Jesus understood both the physicality of human existence, as well as the extreme outer boundaries of physical capacity. I have come to believe, both as a former athlete and coach, that experiencing physical suffering, both individually and collectively, is an experience that we resonate with as ultimately essential for success. To be optimally successful, an athletic program must cultivate a vision of excellence that sustains with enduring faith and uncompromising resolve.

"It Doesn't Matter if you Win or Lose . . . Until you Lose" (Snoopy)

The vision I'm commending isn't naïve to the inevitable realities of failure. Make no mistake about it coaches, eventually you will lose. So be prepared!

In the fall of 2003, I had my first losing season at Westmont. I had cruised along for the first twelve years without giving losing much of a thought and then, similar to my conversation with Bret Hall, I got knocked on the seat of my pants. I found that you don't have to value winning or make it a priority if you are, in fact, winning. However, when you are not winning your philosophy of coaching becomes a matter of intense scrutiny. What am I doing wrong? What could I do better? Am I losing my edge? Am I getting outcoached, out recruited, out financed?

The next twelve seasons brought an unforeseen crossroad upon which I would coach harder than ever before but with inferior statistical results. The frustration challenged me in many ways to conduct my public and private life with a higher degree of self-control and personal resolve—to exercise character when under duress.

Among the many, many different places that losing can take us is the question of identity: "Who am I if I lose?" This is where sports can be especially difficult, because losing implies "loser"—a stigma that intense competitors have to dig deep to overcome. Athletics thus demands not only multiple layers of physical suffering but also mental toughness for weeks on end, or, in my case, for years on end. In soccer, even magnificent performances are known to result in losses. When such seems to become routine, soccer can be utterly cruel, unjust, even unfair. And what storyline does that recall?

Losing also begs the question of credibility. Here my Westmont colleague, coach Smelley, cites the unfortunate consequence of out of context misinterpretation of Paul's admonition "Don't you realize that in a race everyone runs, but only one person gets the prize? So run to win!" (1 Cor 9:24). Unfortunately, even among Christians, misinterpretation of this passage leads to the prevailing notion that "in order to witness I must win." But that, of course, was not Paul's message; nor was it Jesus'. For in *popular* terms, neither was successful—Paul was beheaded and Jesus crucified— both in contexts of utter humiliation. For this reason, Nietzsche famously considered Jesus a loser and all Christians weak. Christians, by contrast, understand the paradox of the divine triumph Jesus accomplished on the cross. We do not define ultimate success in "Superman" terms, as did the famous atheist, not even on the playing field.

Cognizant of our higher goals, losing after exercising our best efforts takes us to a crossroad where our true characters are exposed—as was Jesus' in the Garden of Gethsemane. Ironically, we often voice our most powerful testimonies at rock bottom, crisis moments.

Thirdly, the culmination of work as a coach or athlete unfolds in the public domain. This can be exhilarating (when the performances are good and the results positive) but utterly discouraging when debacles happen and execution inexplicably falters. Part of the mental challenge of coaching is that you are often subjected to the scrutiny of others—often others whom you do not know nor have ever met. It's one thing to receive constructive criticism from coaches and teammates who invest a lot of time in you and have your best interests at heart. It's something completely different to experience that from complete strangers.

It is also important to note that while these experiences emerge from physical contests, the lingering test is often psychological: following defeat, how am I going to act and what am I going to say to my players, assistants, and faculty colleagues—not to mention referees, opposing coaches, and the press? Can I sublimate my frustration and anger into comments that are constructive, edifying, and positive? Do I have it in me to communicate confidence, strength, and optimism, while suffering the throes of disappointment? Coaches frequently encounter this crossroad. And how we choose to act in these situations exposes us for who we really are, who we want to be, and whom we really follow. Romans 12:1–2, I believe, points us in the right direction.

> And so dear brothers and sisters, I plead with you to give your bodies to God because of all He has done for you. Let them be a living and holy sacrifice—the kind He will find acceptable. This is truly the way to worship Him. Don't copy the behavior and customs of this world, but let God transform you into a new person by changing the way you think. Then you will learn to know God's will for you, which is good and pleasing and perfect. (New Living Translation)

The best and worst things that I know about myself have revealed themselves within the contexts of physical suffering, losing, and public scrutiny. As a coach, I've come to appreciate and even relish the moments when an athlete finds themselves in one of these "moments" of exposure. When they occur (and they will), I like to be *present*. Words like perseverance, desire, class, composure, and humility come instantly to mind. How often have I said, "The way you handle this (difficult) moment will say much more about you as a man than if all had gone according to plan." I really do believe these events can be, over the course of time, positively transformational.

I also believe in the transformational power of the journey itself and the daily decisions we have the opportunity to make. James Spiegel, in his excellent chapter on the Philosophy of Wisdom, beautifully describes the Aristotelian concept of "habituation," a journey of "active training." The continuation of 1 Corinthians 9 offers an additional challenge: *"So I run with purpose in every step. I am not just shadowboxing. I discipline my body like an athlete, training it to do what it should. Otherwise, I fear that after preaching to others I myself might be disqualified"* (NLT).

Even as I capture these thoughts, I'm thinking about the start of my training camp and the hope that I will be welcoming a group of athletes to campus who have been "purposeful" this summer, actively training for the upcoming season.

Kinesiology: The Art and Science of Human Movement

Did I mention that I do a little teaching as well? Initially it was little more than an afterthought (i.e. in order to be able to coach you also have to do a little teaching). Early in my career I was reliant upon my undergraduate degree in Communication Studies combined with a natural comfort in front of audiences. I quickly learned that disciplined preparation and meaningful content would enhance the training and education I already possessed.

Our college catalog states, "At Westmont, we have been given the charge to train students to study and celebrate God's greatest creation—the human body." There is great beauty to be experienced within the framework of this creation. The beauty of a body in motion, of developmental capabilities, of testing physical limits, of analyzing the psychological and sociological dimensions.

Kinesiology has exploded in popularity during my time at Westmont. And it's also become more sophisticated. Twenty-five years ago we asked students the simple question "Do you want to teach or coach?" For these were *the* two "tracks" of emphasis, so physical education was limited by something of a two-track mind.

Today, by contrast, our graduates serve in the fields of physical therapy, occupational therapy, physician assistant, athletic training, sport psychology, personal training, corporate fitness, gerontology, cardiac rehabilitation, chiropractic, public and global health, nursing, and even medical school. Indeed much has changed.

The Wisdom of Leadership: Participating in the Restoration of Others

There is, I believe, a common thread that connects each of the aforementioned occupational fields—*leadership*. Defining leadership is, at best, tricky and, at worst, seemingly impossible. It is also, in my opinion, nearly unavoidable within the context of this conversation. These are all vocations of *interaction*. Out of these interactions emerge platforms to teach, collaborate, mentor, disciple, live out our faith, and lead. While each of these avenues is noble and worthy of our consideration and participation, ultimately they should all lead to the outcome of restoration *(the return of something to its former, original, normal, or unimpaired condition)*. This also reaches back and connects to our previous conversation about the kinds of wisdom that coaching and the athletic experience offer, in that oftentimes our clientele is vulnerable and exposed.

Aging, injury, illness, pain, hunger, deprivation, discouragement, lack of self-efficacy, anxiety disorders—these are the challenges we help our clients overcome. Our empathy is contrived, however, if all we know and appreciate is life on cloud nine, where our fleeting good health and personal successes blind us to the sobering realities others suffer. I'm convicted of this phenomenon even as I type. Are my eyes open even now? Am I willingly entering these spaces? Am I interacting with genuine felt compassion? Do I empathize? Do I notice?

My greatest teaching joy has been the developing and teaching of a course entitled the *Psychology and Sociology of Movement*. In many ways this course has allowed me to merge my personal athletic experiences into a pedagogical framework of theory. It's given me the opportunity to look at "who I really am" (psychology) within the context of the "societies and cultures in which I live" (sociology). This integration of psychology with sociology has opened up all kinds of faith insights that have generated personal transformation and restoration. Gaining insight about who I really am and what's really of ultimate importance, I find myself more equipped to participate constructively in the lives of others. This is where I see and experience the intersection of coaching and teaching at Westmont College.

As I think back on my own experience, I'm exceedingly grateful that God saw fit to integrate athletics, coaching, and Kinesiology in constructing my own character and also fitting me out for my vocational work with students and athletes. Confidence still fuels my passion for the wisdom and beauty inherent within my disciplines. Mostly, I'm humbled by what athletics and Kinesiology have taught me after all these years. A former naysayer of coaching, I now approach coaching and teaching with eager enthusiasm, knowing that my work serves importantly in God's refinement and restoration of others.

26

Concluding Sapiential Postscript

"Get Wisdom"

JEFFREY P. GREENMAN

Introduction: Get Wisdom

LISTEN TO THE URGENT plea of Proverbs 4:5-9 (NIV):

> Get wisdom, get understanding; do not forget my words or turn away from them.
>
> Do not forsake wisdom, and she will protect you; love her, and she will watch over you.
>
> The beginning of wisdom is this: Get wisdom. Though it cost all you have, get understanding. Cherish her, and she will exalt you; embrace her, and she will honor you. She will give you a garland to grace your head and present you with a glorious crown.

Upon this rationale of biblical revelation, I conclude our volume by arguing that Christians need greater urgency in seeking wisdom ("Get wisdom"), that true Christianity offers an exclusive, Christ-centred way of wisdom which envisions as optimal the fullness of life found in the gospel, and that the end of Christian scholarship and higher education is wise living that aims for nothing less than full imitation of Christ.

The title of this chapter is a nod in the direction of that great theological provocateur, Søren Kierkegaard, who summoned people in nineteenth-century Denmark toward a genuine New Testament Christianity, while registering a blistering critique of what he saw as the tamed and domesticated "official" Christianity of his context. This allusion is a tip-off that suggests the state of things in North American Christianity might be worse than we may be inclined to think, and points toward a different response than we might think necessary. Reading Kierkegaard in the early twenty-first century is sobering, especially with an eye toward the theological and moral incoherence that besets so much of the American evangelical movement. A Kierkegaard-like effort to "reintroduce Christianity into Christendom"[1] (which was echoed so deeply by Jacques Ellul's prophetic voice in twentieth-century France) remains relevant. Where are today's articulate and passionate champions of what William Wilberforce simply called "real Christianity"? My proposal is that what is urgently needed is champions of New Testament Christianity understood as a Christ-centred way of wisdom.

Wisdom as a Way of Life

Philosophers of all stripes agree that wisdom is about the seamless integration of belief and action in the real world. It expresses moral-spiritual integrity of purpose and conduct. As such, wisdom always suggests a way of life. It is seeking after wholeness as persons who are made in the image of God for fellowship with God and neighbors.

Belief and action, theology and praxis, belong together. As a theologian I want to say quite emphatically that our notion of theological reflection must not be reduced to lining up abstract propositions about Christian beliefs. Indeed there is enormous value in the church's ordered reflection on the substance of the gospel. Faith, when it is true to itself, always seeks understanding. There is no excuse for any kind of lazy anti-intellectualism in the church's witness and proclamation. Bad theology not only is boring, but additionally it always tells lies, thereby de-forming and misdirecting human lives and communities. Good theology matters immensely; there is nothing as practical as a good theory—or we can say, a good theology.[2] We must not acquiesce to our anti-doctrinal times, as if the content of Christian confession is not important.

If godly wisdom as a way of life is our goal, then theology must not be *reduced* to setting out an ordered structure or system. We must not settle for that *only*. Consider this example. It is one thing to pass an exam on the *Westminster Shorter Catechism*. That text has its value, of course, as it offers one possible account of a compact, coherent explication of the core tenets

---

1. Kierkegaard, *Concluding Unscientific Postscript*, 2:142.
2. This is the famous "maxim" of social scientist and educator Kurt Lewin.

of Christian faith. But I challenge the value of such an exercise if the test-taker does not also come to embody in their lived reality the content of the faith that is confessed. God's revealed truth is for the sake of life, in fact, a flourishing life in all its fullness (cf. John 10:10). My point is that, beyond getting one's doctrine (understood as a set of abstract propositions) sorted out, it is quite another thing altogether to enter into and make their own the great and compelling vision of the Catechism: "Man's chief end is to glorify God, and to enjoy him forever." A real life in our real world lived to the glory of God is the point of orthodox Christian doctrine. Doctrine is necessary, but not sufficient, for such a life.

Too much catechesis or Christian "education" in the church remains at the cognitive level without penetrating the heart or the imagination or the emotions, and therefore without engaging the whole person. Deep personal change always is more than cognitive. No wonder we see so few Christ-like transformed lives in our world. In the context of Christian colleges and universities, a required course on "Christian Thought" can be a hugely valuable element in an undergraduate education, as many students have little sense of the ordered coherence of Christian beliefs. Many students find that such a course either saves or re-orients their faith. My point is simply that knowing right doctrine (in our heads) and living it (in our hearts and with our hands and feet) are two different things. The former is for the sake of the latter.

French philosopher Pierre Hadot (d. 2010) has shown that for the ancient Greek and Roman philosophers, attaining wisdom was the highest good of human life. Philosophy offered a way of wisdom, nothing less. Hadot notes that ancient philosophical schools offered rival "therapies" for the soul, intended to overcome life's chief obstacles to wisdom: "remedy for human worries, anguish, and misery brought about for the Cynics, by social constraints and conventions; for the Epicureans, by the quest for false pleasures; for the Stoics, by the pursuit of pleasure and egoistic self-interest; and for the skeptics, by false opinions."[3] Whatever the diagnosis and proposed remedy, Hadot asserts that ancient philosophy was "an invitation for each man to transform himself. Philosophy is conversion, transformation of the way of being and the way of living, the question for wisdom."[4] What Hadot called the "spiritual exercises" of ancient philosophy, "did not attempt only to insure behavior in accordance with a code of good conduct but involved all aspects of one's being—intellect, imagination, sensibility, and will."[5] In the ancient world, Christianity's entrance onto the social landscape

---

3. Hadot, *What Is Ancient Philosophy*, 102 (2002 ed.).
4. Hadot, *Philosophy As a Way of Life*, 275.
5. Davidson, "Spiritual Exercises and Ancient Philosophy," 476.

offered an alternative discourse, challenging the pagan patterns by setting side-by-side what Kavin Rowe has called "rival traditions of true lives," each featuring a distinct *metanoia*.[6]

Hadot made a key distinction between "philosophy discourse" and "philosophy itself." He wrote: "For the Stoics, the parts of philosophy—physics, ethics, and logic—were not, in fact, parts of philosophy itself, but the parts of philosophical discourse. By this they meant that when it comes to teaching philosophy, it is necessary to set forth a theory of logic, a theory of physics, and a theory of ethics. The exigencies of discourse, both logical and pedagogical, require that these distinctions be made. But philosophy itself—that is, the philosophical way of life—is no longer a theory divided into parts, but a unitary act, which consists in *living* logic, physics, and ethics. In this case, we no longer study logical theory—that is, the theory of speaking and thinking well—we simply think and speak well. We no longer engage in theory about the physical world, but we contemplate the cosmos. We no longer theorize about moral action, but we act in a correct and just way."[7]

From Hadot's distinction between "discourse about" and "philosophy itself" we see the value in careful, precise thinking. We should even recognize the value in the technical language used by academic specialists in all fields, although such language is sometimes foisted on unsuspecting, innocent bystanders in congregations by Christian scholars who should know better. But Hadot especially helps us to recall that what we seek is a way of life—not a theory of wisdom in the abstract, but its actual practice. A nominal or notional faith is never an adequate response to the call of the gospel. "Faith by itself, if it does not have works, is dead" (Jas 2:17, ESV). Furthermore, the gospel offers more than a new "worldview." I think that "worldview" can be a helpful category to capture the all-encompassing nature of God's truth, but the historic Christian commitment is that following Christ is a matter of right knowledge put into faithful action.

We can extend Hadot's distinction naturally to differentiate "theological discourse" from "theology itself." For instance, the ultimate point of a robust theology of prayer is to pray, that is, to guide and assist the experience of the actual praying by actual people—not to produce a pleasing "academic discourse" about prayer as an observed religious experience of some people. Rightly considered, theology as "discourse" is the essential companion and servant to support and assist a faithful life and active witness in word and deed which is "lived theology itself."

---

6. See Rowe, *One True Life*.

7. Hadot, *Philosophy As a Way of Life*, 266–67.

What the post-Christendom church in the North Atlantic needs above all else is the presence of Christians who live their faith in every area of life and work—yes, in their ordinary life and mundane work—with thoughtfulness and moral integrity. In other words, the world urgently needs Christians who display godly wisdom. Therefore, I say: above all else, get wisdom—pursue a way of life that features an integrated wholeness that displays the fullness of life made possible by the gospel. Proverbs reminds us that such a pursuit is quite costly, but incomparably valuable.

Wisdom Is Personified in Jesus Christ

Where may wisdom be found? This volume asks a perennial and increasingly pressing question. Wisdom is appealing. It sounds like something that everyone would want, whether they are secular or religious in outlook. Our broken, chaotic world cries out for wisdom, most obviously for wise leaders.

But we need to be clear that the Christian vision of wisdom is utterly divergent from the secular wisdom of the world, even from the best of the ancient pagan philosophers. The New Testament is insistent that true wisdom is found only in Jesus Christ—a shocking and scandalous proclamation. As Karl Barth alerted us, *"the gospel is not a truth among other truths. Rather it sets a question mark against all truths."*[8]

First Corinthians 1–2 offers an incomparable passage on divine wisdom, where Paul refutes the traditional pagan understanding of wisdom associated with power, prestige, and pride, by offering a stark alternative in Christ:

> For the message of the cross is foolishness to those who are perishing, but to us who are being saved it is the power of God. For it is written: "I will destroy the wisdom of the wise; the intelligence of the intelligent I will frustrate." Where is the wise person? Where is the teacher of the law? Where is the philosopher of this age? Has not God made foolish the wisdom of the world? For since in the wisdom of God the world through its wisdom did not know him, God was pleased through the foolishness of what was preached to save those who believe. Jews demand signs and Greeks look for wisdom, but we preach Christ crucified: a stumbling block to Jews and foolishness to Gentiles, but to those whom God has called, both Jews and Greeks, Christ the power of God and the wisdom of God. For the foolishness of God is wiser than human wisdom, and

---

8. Barth, *Epistle to the Romans*, 35.

the weakness of God is stronger than human strength. (1 Cor 1:18–25, NIV)

The scandalous offense is here: the crucified Jesus Christ *is* the wisdom of God. Divine wisdom ultimately is not an idea or a message, but a person. This personified wisdom confounds and overturns the world's wisdom and shows it to be foolishness, overturns the world's commitment to power by showing the wisdom of weakness. This message is all the more compelling and more obviously counter-cultural in a world where political and religious leaders commonly glorify personal strength and then proceed to exploit their positions of power for their own self-advantage—usually their financial and/or sexual benefit.

Paul continues by explaining that those who recognize Jesus as wisdom personified have been chosen by God (1 Cor 1:26); it is not a human decision. Jesus as wisdom personified is end-time truth that has been revealed by God (1 Cor 2:7); it is not a human invention. His apostolic method (weakness) and message (Christ crucified) embody the truth of Jesus as wisdom personified (1 Cor 2:2–5); neither is the product of human intelligence. This wisdom reshapes an entire human life, not merely the mind: God is the source of their life in Christ Jesus, "who has become for us wisdom from God—that is, our righteousness, holiness and redemption" (1 Cor 1:30). This is the ancient wisdom shared by pagans and Christians alike: genuine wisdom causes us not merely to know rightly, but to "be" in a different way. For Christians, wisdom is found in the saving action of Jesus, nowhere else. In Christ, and no one else, are "hidden the treasures of wisdom and knowledge" (Col 2:2). This is the unavoidable scandal of the Gospel—incarnation, cross and resurrection each are offensive to the natural mind.

This radical reframing of wisdom has enormous implications. Harris Bechtol explains, "This emphasis on the crucified Christ provides the basis for a different kind of epistemology that displaces human wisdom and knowledge from the place of prominence in favor of God-become-human-and-savior as the center of knowledge."[9] This way of knowing is about more than the intellect. It is about a lived truth, which encompasses all of life—the triad of "righteousness, holiness and redemption" refers comprehensively to the transformation of this life.

This radical vision caught Kierkegaard's imagination in his quest for the restoration of New Testament Christianity rather than the "official" Christianity of a compromised Christendom. Michael Plekon describes Kierkegaard's insistence upon "the infinite qualitative difference" that Christ makes, explaining: "It is the figure of Christ which sets Christianity apart.

---

9. Bechtol, "Paul and Kierkegaard," 930.

Christ is the teacher, but unlike other enlighteners such as Socrates, he is also the truth striven for, the Savior and Atoner. He speaks with more than human perception and authority. The teacher, the message and the goal are one in Christ."[10]

To return to our previous distinction between "theological discourse" and "theology itself," someone can deploy "discourse" to describe the cross in what Kierkegaard would call "objective" terms: "a series of propositions about an historical event to be studied, argued against, and presented in a rhetorically pleasing and convincing manner."[11] On the other hand, "theology itself" for "those who are being saved" (1 Cor 1:18) means responding with the receptivity of faith, recognizing that it involves "subjective" and personal relationship with the crucified Jesus Christ and nowhere else do we find divine life and wisdom. As a result, "Faith no longer treats Jesus as a piece of cognitive content to be studied and mastered, but as a person to whom others must have a relation."[12] This is the work of God's Spirit, not a human work, as Paul explains in 1 Corinthians 2. Bechtol's summary serves us well: "God's work through the Spirit in revealing God's wisdom, Christ crucified, as the way of salvation allows the believer to put her self and the world into perspective by placing both in relationship to Christ."[13]

The recognition that the wisdom of God is found nowhere else but in Jesus Christ, crucified and risen, reminds us to keep the pursuit of godly wisdom resolutely Christ-centered. This is a genuinely radical vision. We are warned against seeking truth about creation, about our world, about human meaning, or hope, or anything else, anywhere else but in Christ. If wisdom is found only in Christ, to say "get wisdom" means, above all else, "seek Christ." This means Christians are called to pursue the way of wisdom which is discovered only in knowing, loving, following, and serving Jesus Christ who is the wisdom of God.

Wisdom in Scholarship and Learning

Entering into the radically Christ-centered vision of wisdom offered by the New Testament is essential for the church in every age. What are the implications of this account for the task of Christian scholarship and learning? Simply put, the proper *telos* of education is the cultivation of character, the

---

10. Plekon, "Introducing Christianity into Christendom," 336.
11. Bechtol, "Paul and Kierkegaard," 935.
12. Bechtol, "Paul and Kierkegaard," 941.
13. Bechtol, "Paul and Kierkegaard," 936.

development of wisdom. *Therefore all Christian learning that is true to itself is cultivating Christ-centered wisdom.*

This means, first, that it is critical for Christian scholars, in every field of expertise and every disciplinary area of research and teaching, to commit themselves to that *telos*. *If Christian wisdom is found only in Christ, then an appropriate whole-person focus of formation necessarily involves a lifelong journey into the deepest intellectual challenge imaginable: to see the significance of Jesus Christ for all of reality, and every aspect of life.* Quite literally, his significance for everything that exists. This is what professional scholars who are Christians as well as students who are Christians (themselves "scholars" in the less specialized, non-professionalized sense) should consider themselves to be doing. If there is no genuine wisdom outside of Christ, then we should expect that all of reality ultimately bears witness to the wisdom of God's design for the creation and redemption of the cosmos in and through Christ. The result should be an increased sense of confidence in the sufficiency of the gospel for understanding all of life.

Second, embracing Christ-centered wisdom as the *telos* of Christian learning invites teachers and students alike to enter into the gospel's work of transformation. The truths of the Christian proclamation are for living. All Christian scholars and teachers need the reminder that *the point of learning God's truth is doing God's truth.* Kierkegaard criticized Christian scholarship's indifference to obedience. Sarcastically he wrote:

> The matter is quite simple. The Bible is very easy to understand. But we as Christians are a bunch of scheming swindlers. We pretend to be unable to understand it because we know very well that the minute we understand, we are obliged to act accordingly. Take any words in the New Testament and forget everything except pledging yourself to act accordingly. My God, you will say, if I do that my life will be ruined. How would I ever get on in the world? Herein lies the real place of Christian scholarship. Christian scholarship is the Church's prodigious invention to defend itself against the Bible, to ensure that we can continue to be good Christians without the Bible coming too close. Oh, priceless scholarship, what would we do without you? Dreadful it is to fall into the hands of the living God. Yes, it is even dreadful to be alone with the New Testament.[14]

Hadot points out there is a sharp division between the kind of learning valued by the modern university project, focused on objectified, mostly written or externalized forms of knowledge and skill, and the ancient philosophical

---

14. Kierkegaard, *Provocations*, 201.

school, "which addressed individuals in order to transform their entire personality... to train people for their career as human beings."[15] For Christian scholars and students, what matters most is the formation of Christ-centered wisdom in our lives. This suggests to me a need to move beyond the language of teaching students to comprehend a Christian "worldview" (which is a constructed human thing) and moving toward the language of enabling students to know and serve Jesus Christ (who is a person who calls us to himself and into his service). Further, this means that we cannot settle for any binary opposition between "piety" and "learning." The Christian vision of learning is nothing less than "scholarly devotion" offered to God in Christ through the Spirit. Scholarly devotion considers the hard work of the pursuit of truth to be an act of worship, and sees the whole business of scholarly life (both its ends and its means) shaped by the gospel's all-inclusive claim on our lives. This is preferable to a "devotional scholarship" that settles for doing scholarship the way the secular academy does it, with merely the addition of a thin veneer of piety or a few Bible verses tacked onto a project that any secular scholar could have produced.

Third, embracing the centrality of Christ-centred wisdom means accepting the primacy of divine revelation for all scholarly pursuits. The project of "faith-learning integration" championed by Christian colleges and universities is susceptible to the distortion of giving, sometimes unintentionally, an assumed primacy to "learning" as the secular academy defines it, then trying to squeeze some "faith" artificially or superficially into the cracks and crevices of a given topic or field. Seldom are topics reconsidered from the ground up, which is what the quest for Christ-centered wisdom would invite. The primacy of divine revelation remains the uncomfortable truth about our knowledge of reality. As theologian Alan Torrance has suggested regarding the church's engagement with culture, "the direction of the pressure of interpretation must always be from God's self-disclosure to our categories of thought, and not from our prior categories of thought to God's self-disclosure. My fundamental role as a theologian is working as hard as I can to ensure that I serve the church by ensuring that that is the directionality in the process of interpretation."[16]

Finally, Christ-centered wisdom is embraced through contemplation and is discovered in prayer. Wisdom is more than cognitive. It is the transformation of the whole person—heart, mind, soul, imagination, strength. To be formed toward divine wisdom as people of faith means nothing less than making space in our lives to enter into the reality of God's truth in the

---

15. Hadot, *What Is Ancient Philosophy*, 260.
16. "Alan Torrance," para. 41.

person of Jesus Christ. It is living in fellowship with the crucified and risen Jesus, in the power of the Spirit. Amidst our busyness and distractedness and pressures to be productive or impressive, my sense is that God is calling Christians scholars and students to a deeper experience of contemplation. Think of the radically counter-cultural example of Mary who sat at the feet of Jesus, listening attentively to his word, while work needed to be done (Luke 10:38–42). The point is that nothing is more important than attending to Jesus. Listening comes before doing. I wonder if the superficiality of faith-and-learning programs owes mostly to a failure to spend sufficient time and energy simply absorbing the truth that divine wisdom is personified in Jesus Christ.

Conclusion

How does all of this relate to the practice of theology—not merely the practice of professional theologians, or formalized "theological discourse," but about all Christians to the extent that we reflect on God and God's ways in the world? For every Christian who thinks about God or prays or speaks about what faith means is a theologian in the basic sense of the word.

Along these lines theologian John Webster argues that all "ministerial work" is secondary and derivative; the primary work is "receiving and meditating upon divine instruction."[17] He offers an insightful definition: "Theology is contemplative consideration of the gospel and its claims upon thought and conduct." Notice that Webster affirms that "thought and conduct" are inseparable, and that each arises inseparably from the gospel. Such a theology of theology, if we can call it that, challenges the rationalistic and reductive assumptions that ultimately do not foster whole person transformation toward the wisdom of Christ. Such a contemplative posture is central to the pursuit of godly wisdom. The ancient philosophical "spiritual exercises" were attempts at self-conversion through self-dialogue, overcoming the passions, and more determined exercises of the will. Alternatively, the Christian vision is for God-given conversion as a gift offering thorough renewal of life accomplished from outside ourselves, through the atoning grace of Christ's cross brought into our experience through the work of the Holy Spirit at the core of our being, so that we become like Christ, entering into his wisdom and truth. This is something completely different from secular therapies. It is the way of transformation found only in the Gospel.

---

17. Topping, "Webster: Why Study Theology?," para. 2.

If so, and if entering into divine wisdom is only through contemplation and prayer, then the only fitting way to conclude this volume is to offer a closing prayer:

> Almighty God, in you are hidden all the treasures of wisdom and knowledge. Open our eyes that we may see the wonders of your Word; and give us grace that we may clearly understand and freely choose the way of your wisdom through Christ our LORD. Amen.[18]

Bibliography

"Alan Torrance: The Future of Theology Lies with the Body of Christ." *Faith & Leadership* (blog), June 16, 2014. https://www.faithandleadership.com/alan-torrance-future-theology-lies-body-christ.

Barth, Karl. *Epistle to the Romans*. Translated by Edwyn C. Hoskyns. Oxford: Oxford University Press, 1933.

Bechtol, Harris B. "Paul and Kierkegaard: A Christocentric Epistemology." *The Heythrop Journal* 55.5 (2014) 927–43.

Davidson, Arnold I. "Spiritual Exercises and Ancient Philosophy: An Introduction to Pierre Hadot." *Critical Inquiry* 16.3 (Spring 1990) 475–82.

Hadot, Pierre. *Philosophy As a Way of Life: Spiritual Exercises from Socrates to Foucault*. Translated by Michael Chase, and edited by Arnold I. Davidson. Oxford: Blackwell, 1995.

———. *What Is Ancient Philosophy?* Translated by Michael Chase. Cambridge: Belnap, 2002.

Kierkegaard, Søren. *Concluding Unscientific Postscript to Philosophical Fragments*. Translated by Howard V. and Edna H. Hong. 2 vols. Princeton: Princeton University Press, 1992.

———. *Provocations: Spiritual Writings of Kierkegaard*. Edited by Charles E. Moore. Farmington: Plough, 2002.

Plekon, Michael. "'Introducing Christianity into Christendom': Reinterpreting the Late Kierkegaard." *Anglican Theological Review* 64.3 (1982) 327–52.

"Prayers for Illumination." http://www.takomaparkpc.org/prayer4Illumination.html.

Rowe, Kavin C. *One True Life: The Stoics and Early Christians as Rival Traditions*. New Haven: Yale University Press, 2016.

Topping, Richard. "Webster: Why Study Theology." https://vst.edu/webster-why-study-theology.

---

18. "Prayers for Illumination," para. 1.

*"So teach us to number our days,
so that we may present to you a heart of wisdom."*
(PS 90:12)

www.ingramcontent.com/pod-product-compliance
Lightning Source LLC
Chambersburg PA
CBHW070012010526
44117CB00011B/1533